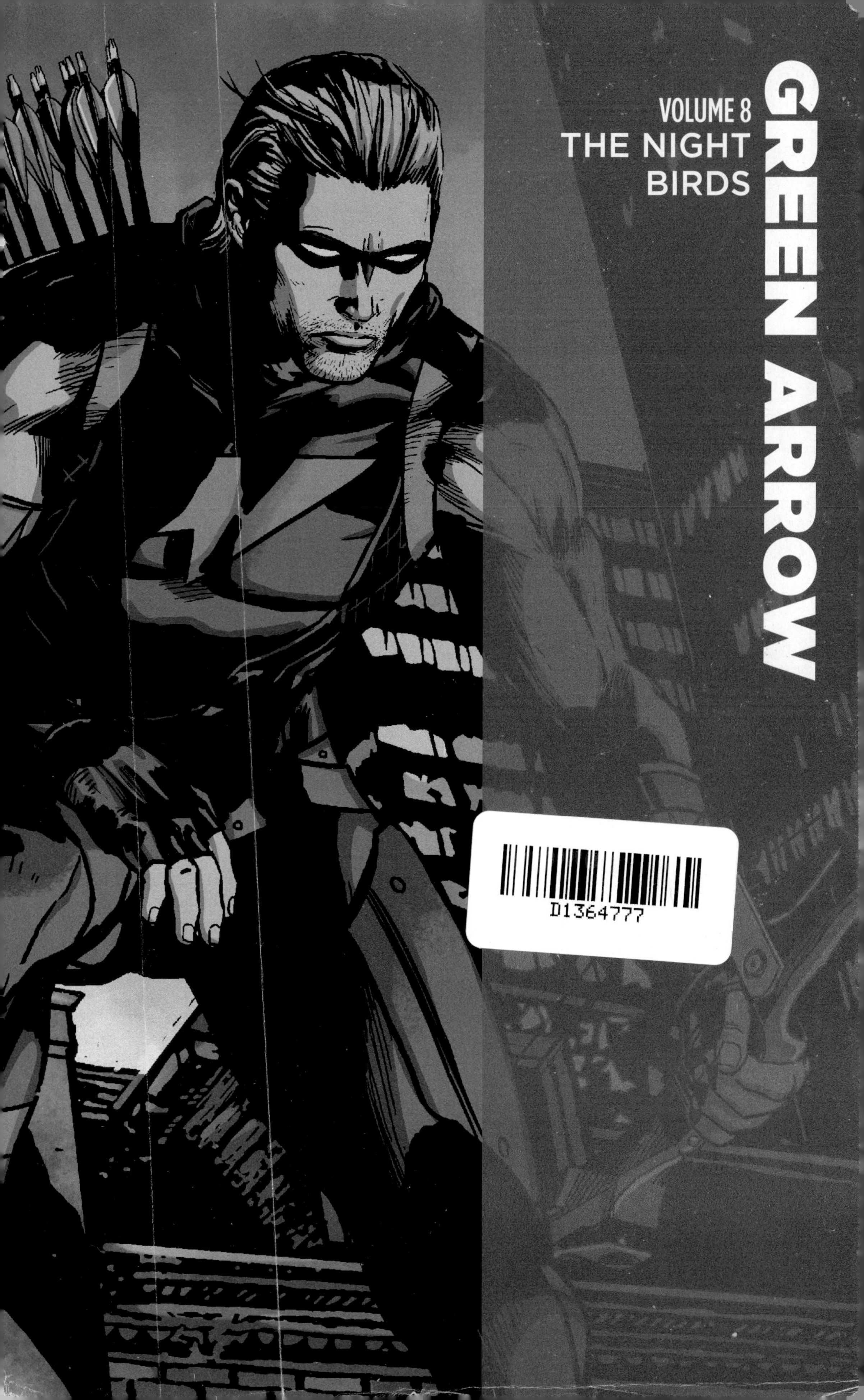
VOLUME 8
THE NIGHT
BIRDS
GREEN ARROW

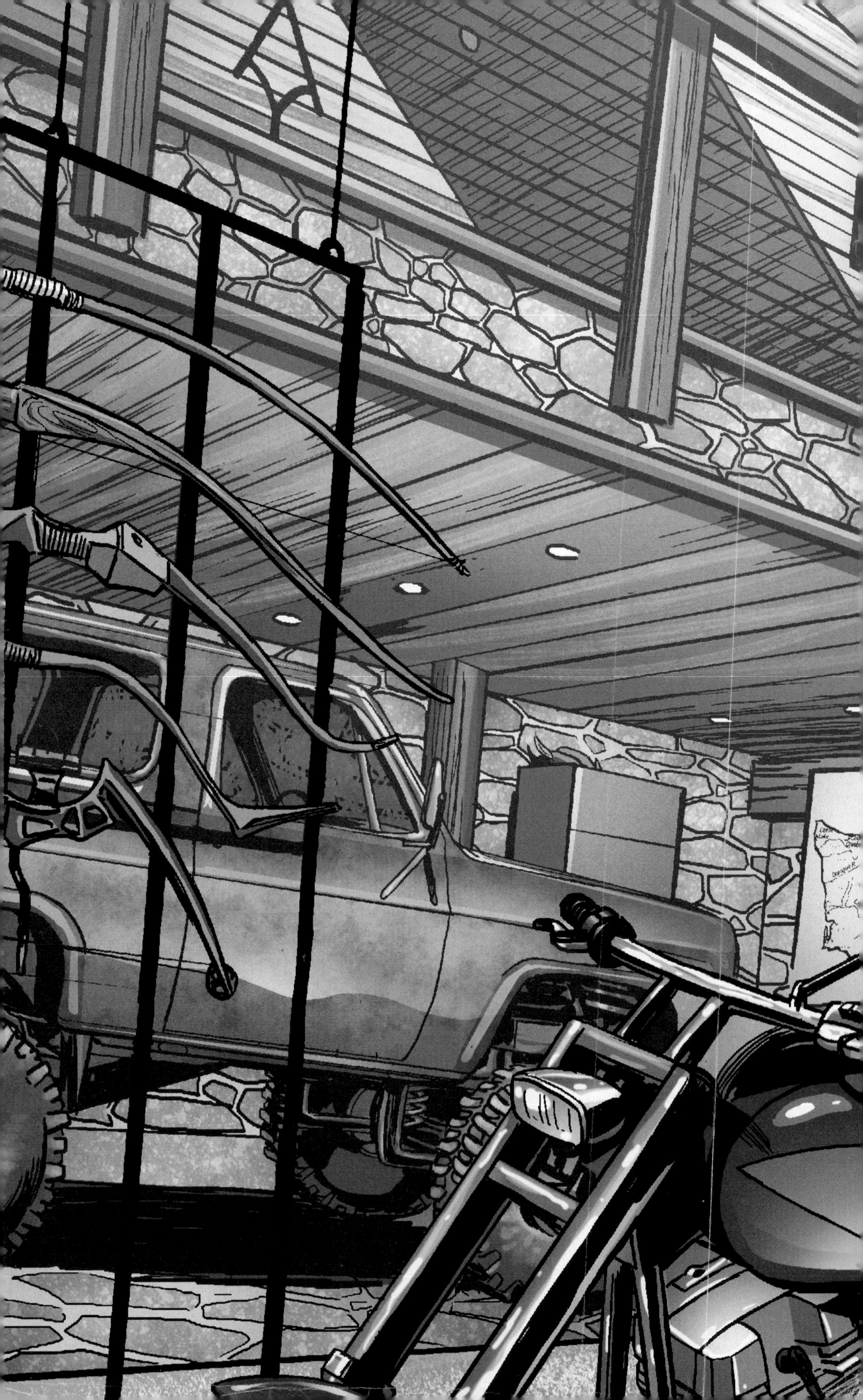

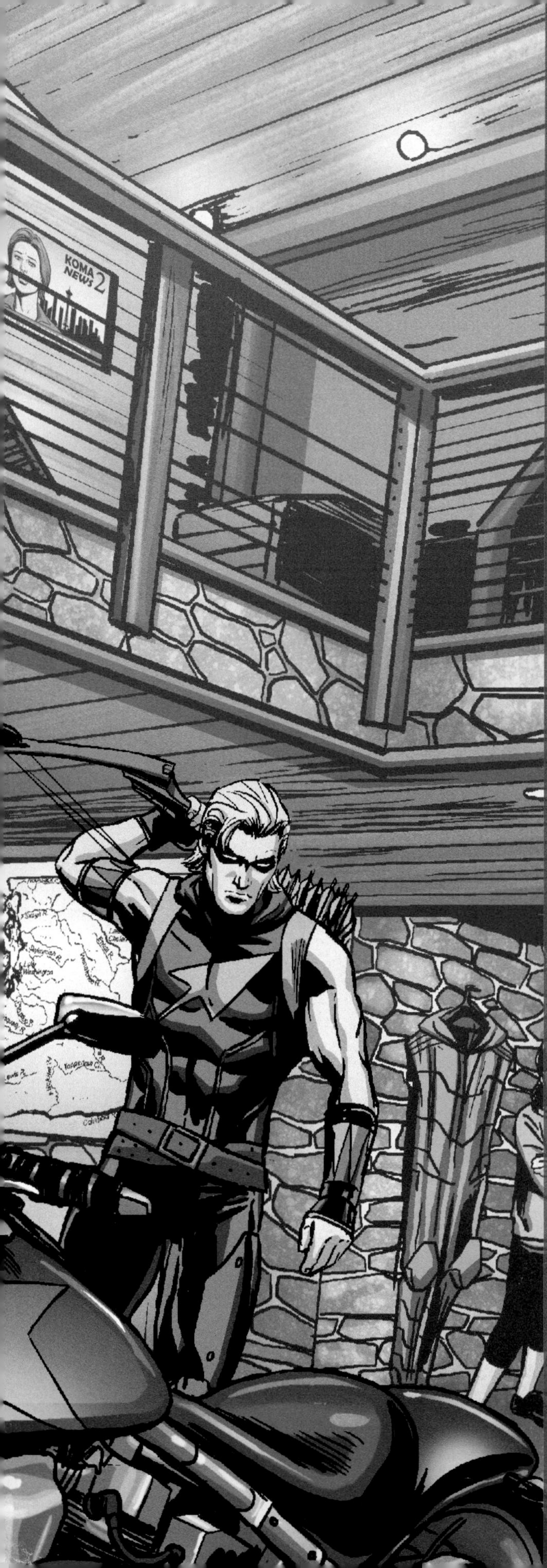
KOMA NEWS 2

GREEN ARROW

VOLUME 8
THE NIGHT BIRDS

WRITTEN BY
BENJAMIN PERCY

ART BY
PATRICK ZIRCHER
FABRIZIO FIORENTINO
FEDERICO DALLOCCHIO

COLOR BY
GABE ELTAEB

LETTERS BY
ROB LEIGH

COLLECTION COVER ART BY
PATRICK ZIRCHER
& GABE ELTAEB

HARVEY RICHARDS BRIAN CUNNINGHAM Editors - Original Series
AMEDEO TURTURRO Assistant Editor - Original Series
JEB WOODARD Group Editor - Collected Editions
ROBIN WILDMAN Editor - Collected Edition
STEVE COOK Design Director - Books
DAMIAN RYLAND Publication Design

BOB HARRAS Senior VP - Editor-in-Chief, DC Comics

DIANE NELSON President
DAN DIDIO and JIM LEE Co-Publishers
GEOFF JOHNS Chief Creative Officer
AMIT DESAI Senior VP - Marketing & Global Franchise Management
NAIRI GARDINER Senior VP - Finance
SAM ADES VP - Digital Marketing
BOBBIE CHASE VP - Talent Development
MARK CHIARELLO Senior VP - Art, Design & Collected Editions
JOHN CUNNINGHAM VP - Content Strategy
ANNE DEPIES VP - Strategy Planning & Reporting
DON FALLETTI VP - Manufacturing Operations
LAWRENCE GANEM VP - Editorial Administration & Talent Relations
ALISON GILL Senior VP - Manufacturing & Operations
HANK KANALZ Senior VP - Editorial Strategy & Administration
JAY KOGAN VP - Legal Affairs
DEREK MADDALENA Senior VP - Sales & Business Development
JACK MAHAN VP - Business Affairs
DAN MIRON VP - Sales Planning & Trade Development
NICK NAPOLITANO VP - Manufacturing Administration
CAROL ROEDER VP - Marketing
EDDIE SCANNELL VP - Mass Account & Digital Sales
COURTNEY SIMMONS Senior VP - Publicity & Communications
JIM (SKI) SOKOLOWSKI VP - Comic Book Specialty & Newsstand Sales
SANDY YI Senior VP - Global Franchise Management

GREEN ARROW VOLUME 8: THE NIGHT BIRDS

DC Comics, 2900 West Alameda Ave., Burbank, CA 91505
Printed by RR Donnelley, Owensville, MO, USA. 6/3/16. First Printing.
ISBN: 978-1-4012-6255-6

Library of Congress Cataloging-in-Publication Data is available.

PEFC Certified
Printed on paper from sustainably managed forests and controlled sources
PEFC
PEFC/29-31-75
www.pefc.org

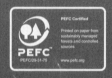

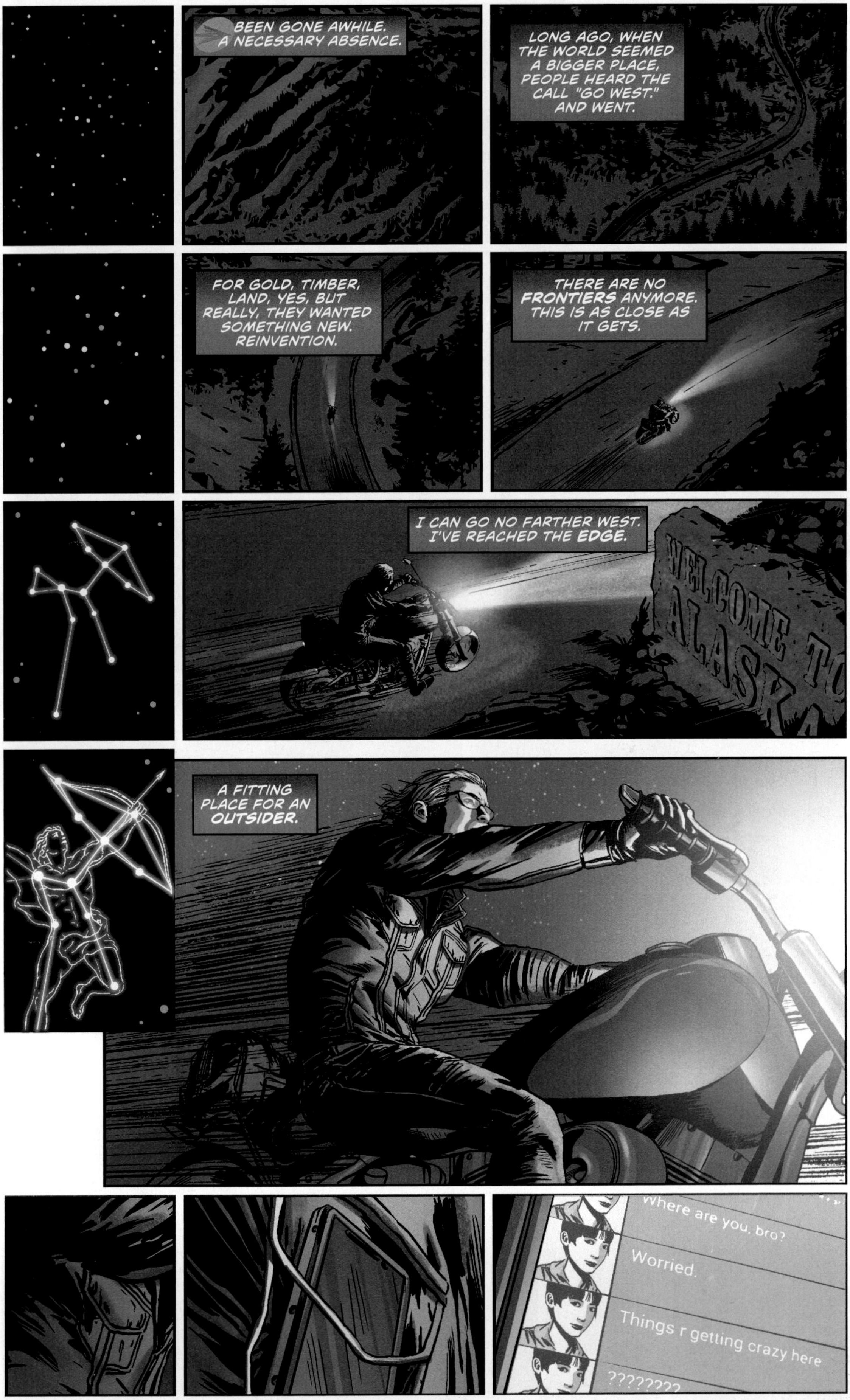
BEEN GONE AWHILE. A NECESSARY ABSENCE.
LONG AGO, WHEN THE WORLD SEEMED A BIGGER PLACE, PEOPLE HEARD THE CALL "GO WEST." AND WENT.
FOR GOLD, TIMBER, LAND, YES, BUT REALLY, THEY WANTED SOMETHING NEW. REINVENTION.
THERE ARE NO FRONTIERS ANYMORE. THIS IS AS CLOSE AS IT GETS.
I CAN GO NO FARTHER WEST. I'VE REACHED THE EDGE.
WELCOME TO ALASKA
A FITTING PLACE FOR AN OUTSIDER.
Where are you, bro?
Worried.
Things r getting crazy here
????????

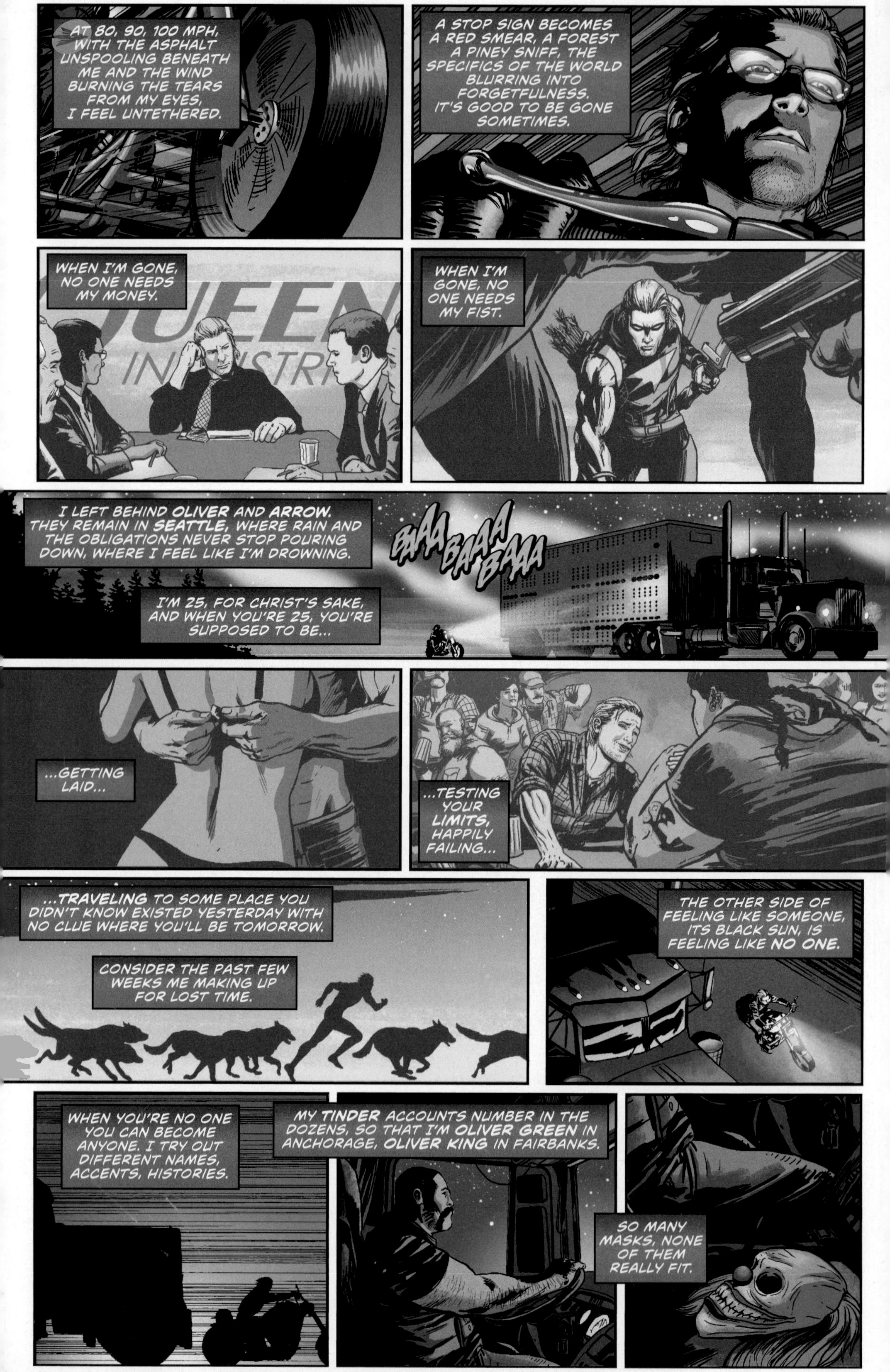
AT 80, 90, 100 MPH, WITH THE ASPHALT UNSPOOLING BENEATH ME AND THE WIND BURNING THE TEARS FROM MY EYES, I FEEL UNTETHERED.
A STOP SIGN BECOMES A RED SMEAR, A FOREST A PINEY SNIFF, THE SPECIFICS OF THE WORLD BLURRING INTO FORGETFULNESS. IT'S GOOD TO BE GONE SOMETIMES.
WHEN I'M GONE, NO ONE NEEDS MY MONEY.
QUEEN INDUSTRI
WHEN I'M GONE, NO ONE NEEDS MY FIST.
I LEFT BEHIND OLIVER AND ARROW. THEY REMAIN IN SEATTLE, WHERE RAIN AND THE OBLIGATIONS NEVER STOP POURING DOWN, WHERE I FEEL LIKE I'M DROWNING.
BAAA BAAA BAAA
I'M 25, FOR CHRIST'S SAKE, AND WHEN YOU'RE 25, YOU'RE SUPPOSED TO BE...
...GETTING LAID...
...TESTING YOUR LIMITS, HAPPILY FAILING...
...TRAVELING TO SOME PLACE YOU DIDN'T KNOW EXISTED YESTERDAY WITH NO CLUE WHERE YOU'LL BE TOMORROW.
CONSIDER THE PAST FEW WEEKS ME MAKING UP FOR LOST TIME.
THE OTHER SIDE OF FEELING LIKE SOMEONE, ITS BLACK SUN, IS FEELING LIKE NO ONE.
WHEN YOU'RE NO ONE YOU CAN BECOME ANYONE. I TRY OUT DIFFERENT NAMES, ACCENTS, HISTORIES.
MY TINDER ACCOUNTS NUMBER IN THE DOZENS, SO THAT I'M OLIVER GREEN IN ANCHORAGE, OLIVER KING IN FAIRBANKS.
SO MANY MASKS, NONE OF THEM REALLY FIT.

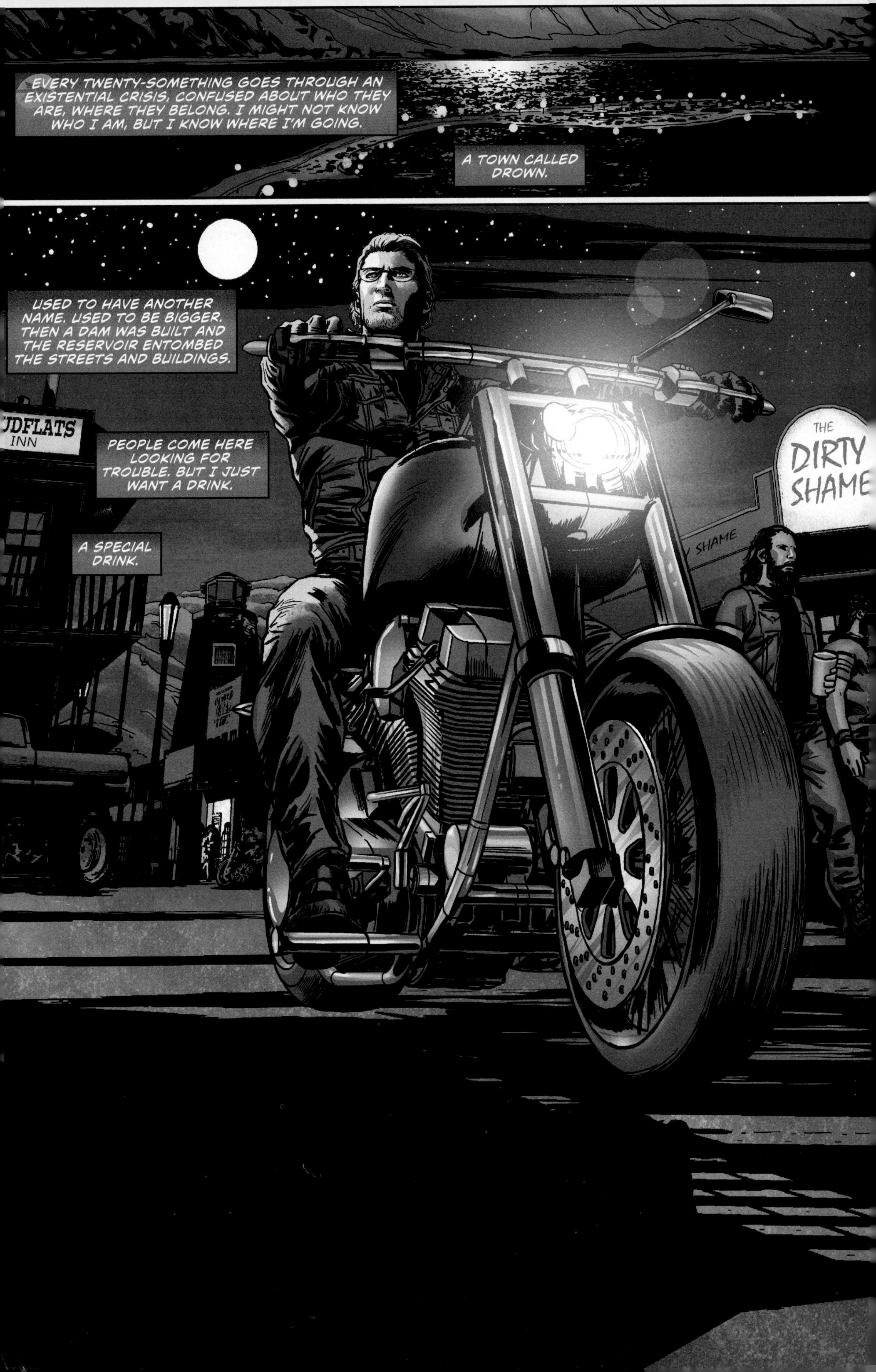
EVERY TWENTY-SOMETHING GOES THROUGH AN EXISTENTIAL CRISIS, CONFUSED ABOUT WHO THEY ARE, WHERE THEY BELONG. I MIGHT NOT KNOW WHO I AM, BUT I KNOW WHERE I'M GOING.
A TOWN CALLED DROWN.
USED TO HAVE ANOTHER NAME. USED TO BE BIGGER. THEN A DAM WAS BUILT AND THE RESERVOIR ENTOMBED THE STREETS AND BUILDINGS.
UDFLATS INN
PEOPLE COME HERE LOOKING FOR TROUBLE. BUT I JUST WANT A DRINK.
A SPECIAL DRINK.
THE DIRTY SHAME

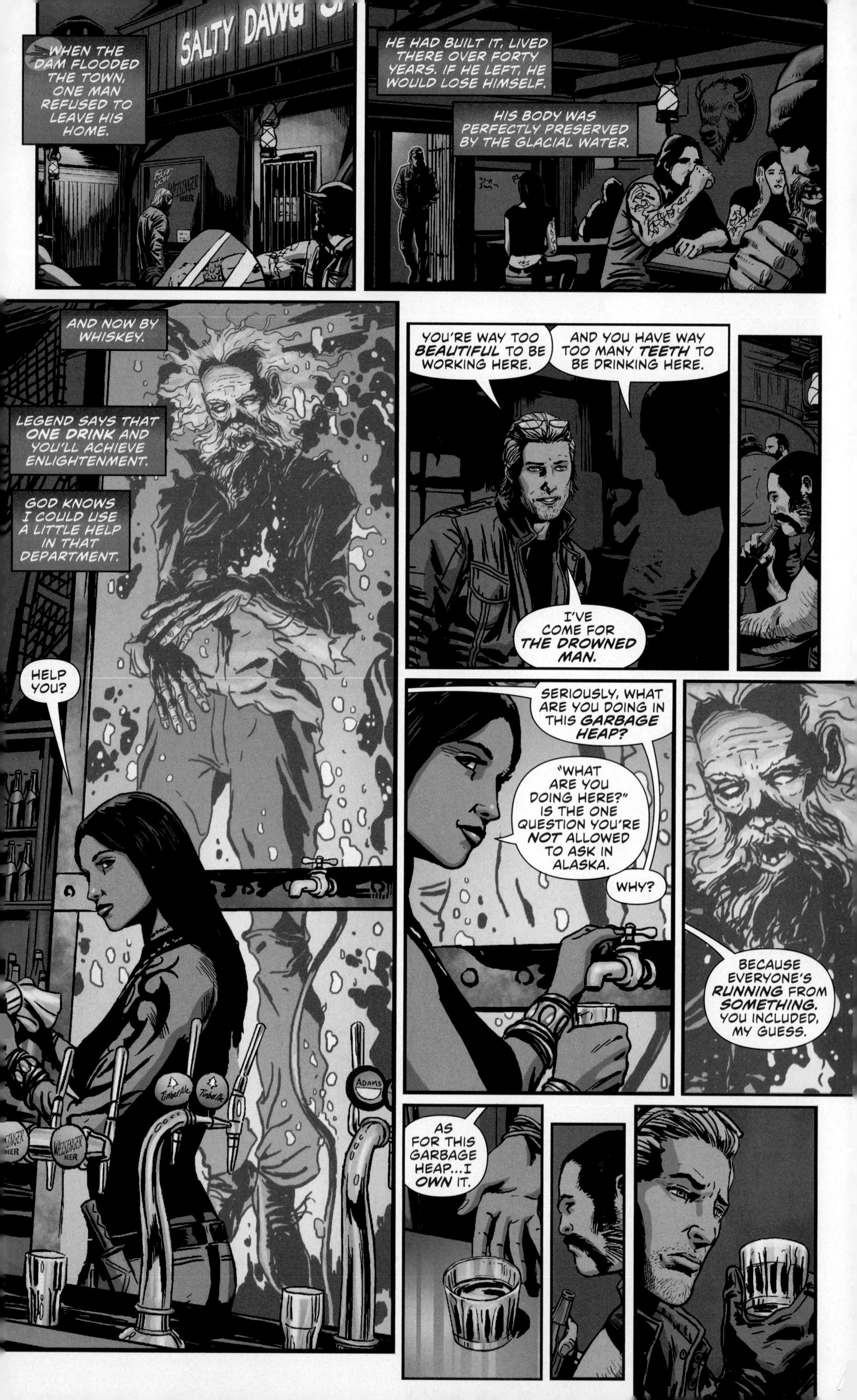
SALTY DAWG
WHEN THE DAM FLOODED THE TOWN, ONE MAN REFUSED TO LEAVE HIS HOME.
WEISINGER BEER
HE HAD BUILT IT, LIVED THERE OVER FORTY YEARS. IF HE LEFT, HE WOULD LOSE HIMSELF.
HIS BODY WAS PERFECTLY PRESERVED BY THE GLACIAL WATER.
AND NOW BY WHISKEY.
LEGEND SAYS THAT ONE DRINK AND YOU'LL ACHIEVE ENLIGHTENMENT.
GOD KNOWS I COULD USE A LITTLE HELP IN THAT DEPARTMENT.
HELP YOU?
TimberAle
TimberAle
ADAMS
WEISINGER BEER
YOU'RE WAY TOO BEAUTIFUL TO BE WORKING HERE.
AND YOU HAVE WAY TOO MANY TEETH TO BE DRINKING HERE.
I'VE COME FOR THE DROWNED MAN.
SERIOUSLY, WHAT ARE YOU DOING IN THIS GARBAGE HEAP?
"WHAT ARE YOU DOING HERE?" IS THE ONE QUESTION YOU'RE NOT ALLOWED TO ASK IN ALASKA.
WHY?
BECAUSE EVERYONE'S RUNNING FROM SOMETHING. YOU INCLUDED, MY GUESS.
AS FOR THIS GARBAGE HEAP...I OWN IT.

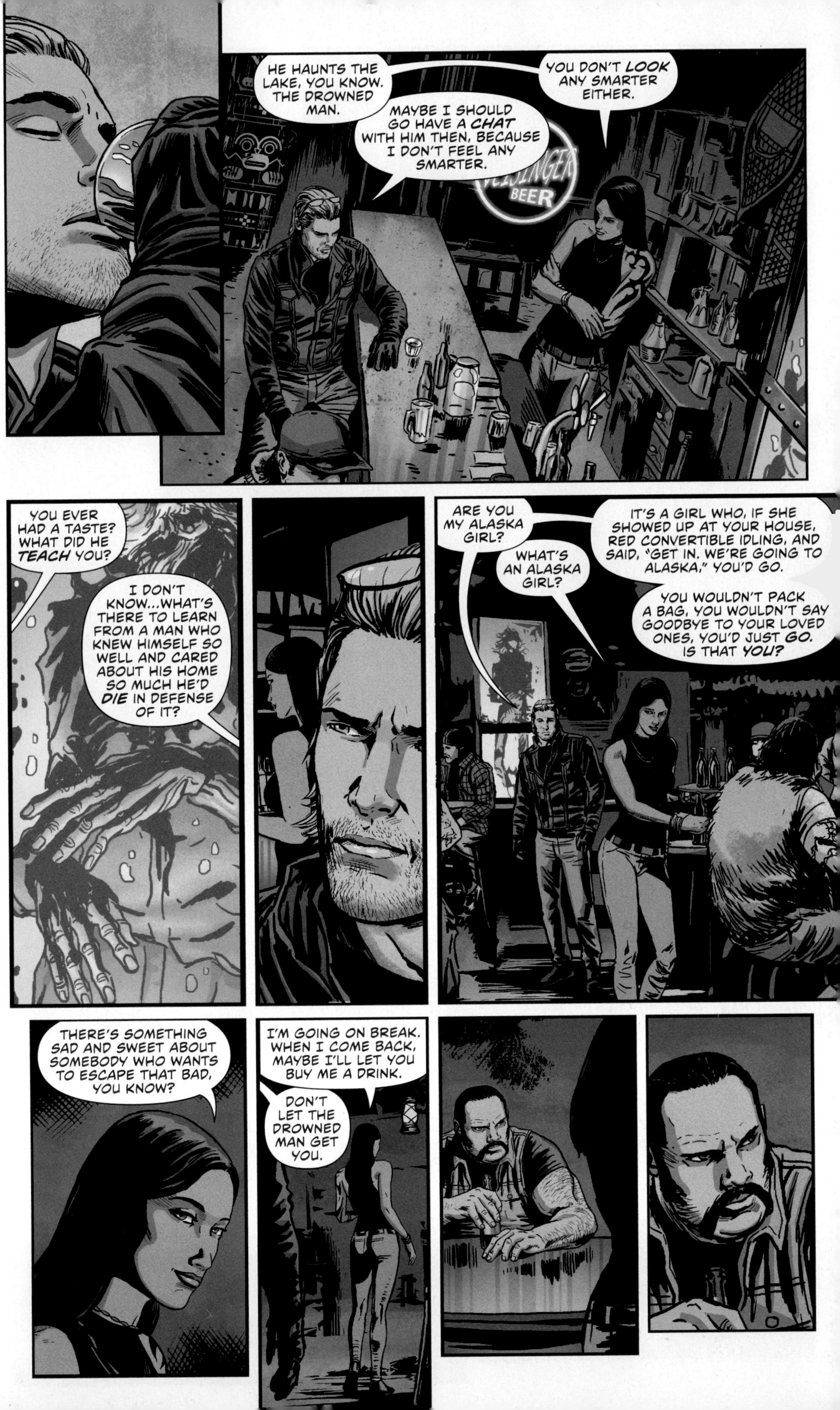
HE HAUNTS THE LAKE, YOU KNOW. THE DROWNED MAN.
YOU DON'T LOOK ANY SMARTER EITHER.
MAYBE I SHOULD GO HAVE A CHAT WITH HIM THEN, BECAUSE I DON'T FEEL ANY SMARTER.
BEER
YOU EVER HAD A TASTE? WHAT DID HE TEACH YOU?
I DON'T KNOW...WHAT'S THERE TO LEARN FROM A MAN WHO KNEW HIMSELF SO WELL AND CARED ABOUT HIS HOME SO MUCH HE'D DIE IN DEFENSE OF IT?
ARE YOU MY ALASKA GIRL?
WHAT'S AN ALASKA GIRL?
IT'S A GIRL WHO, IF SHE SHOWED UP AT YOUR HOUSE, RED CONVERTIBLE IDLING, AND SAID, "GET IN. WE'RE GOING TO ALASKA," YOU'D GO.
YOU WOULDN'T PACK A BAG, YOU WOULDN'T SAY GOODBYE TO YOUR LOVED ONES, YOU'D JUST GO. IS THAT YOU?
THERE'S SOMETHING SAD AND SWEET ABOUT SOMEBODY WHO WANTS TO ESCAPE THAT BAD, YOU KNOW?
I'M GOING ON BREAK. WHEN I COME BACK, MAYBE I'LL LET YOU BUY ME A DRINK.
DON'T LET THE DROWNED MAN GET YOU.

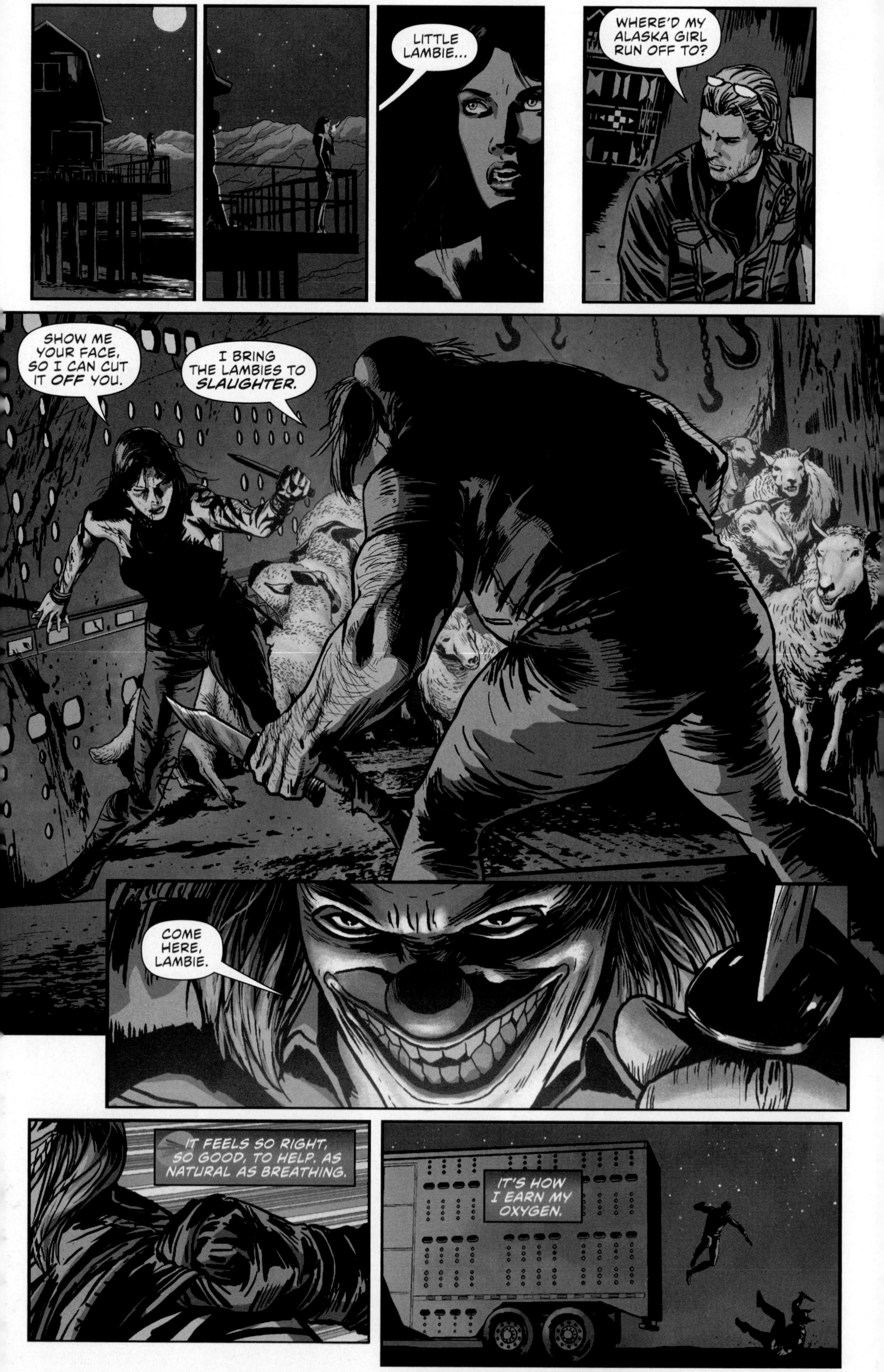
LITTLE LAMBIE...
WHERE'D MY ALASKA GIRL RUN OFF TO?
SHOW ME YOUR FACE, SO I CAN CUT IT OFF YOU.
I BRING THE LAMBIES TO SLAUGHTER.
COME HERE, LAMBIE.
IT FEELS SO RIGHT, SO GOOD, TO HELP. AS NATURAL AS BREATHING.
IT'S HOW I EARN MY OXYGEN.

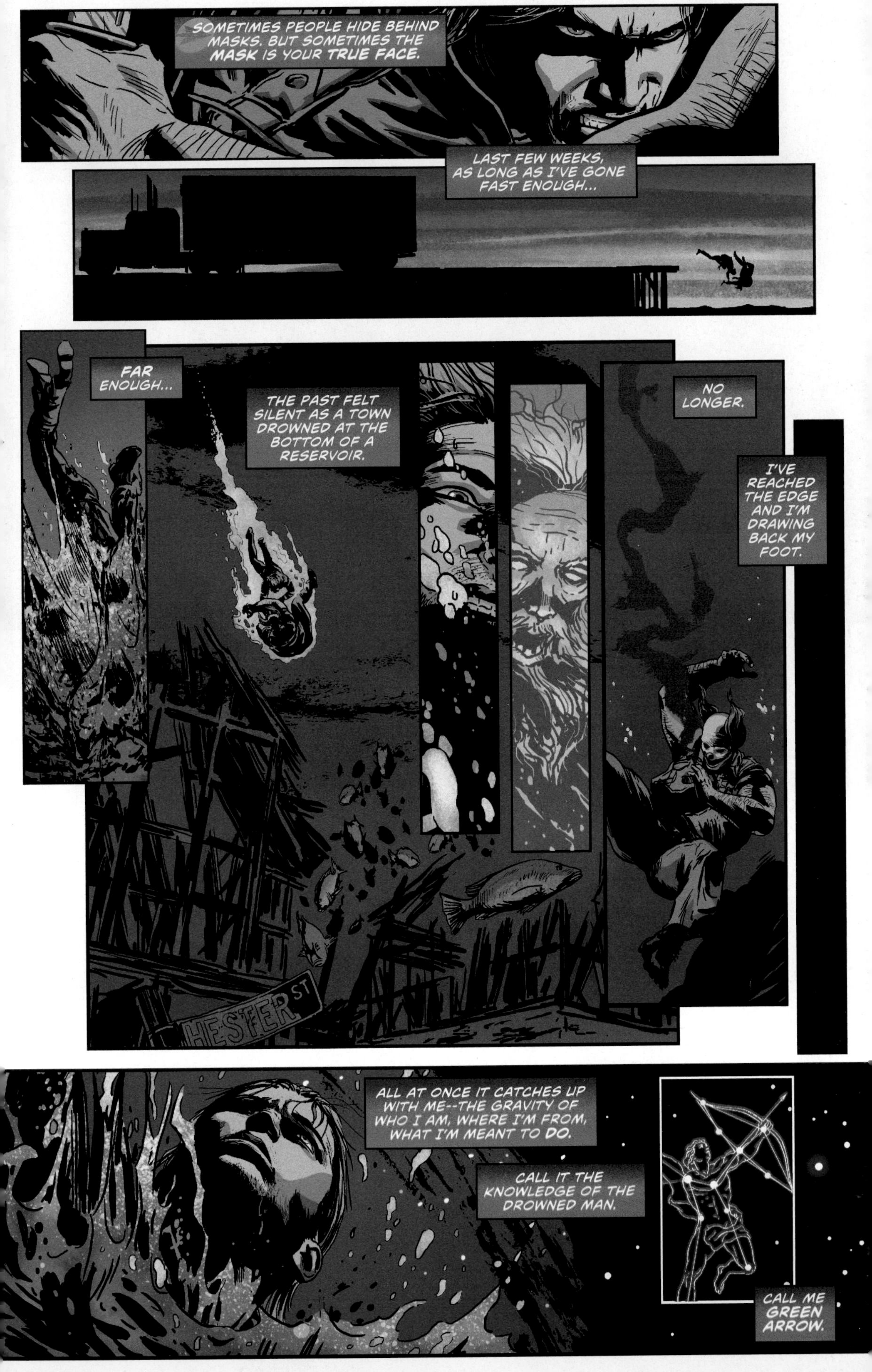
SOMETIMES PEOPLE HIDE BEHIND MASKS. BUT SOMETIMES THE MASK IS YOUR TRUE FACE.
LAST FEW WEEKS, AS LONG AS I'VE GONE FAST ENOUGH...
FAR ENOUGH...
THE PAST FELT SILENT AS A TOWN DROWNED AT THE BOTTOM OF A RESERVOIR.
NO LONGER.
I'VE REACHED THE EDGE AND I'M DRAWING BACK MY FOOT.
HESTER ST
ALL AT ONCE IT CATCHES UP WITH ME--THE GRAVITY OF WHO I AM, WHERE I'M FROM, WHAT I'M MEANT TO DO.
CALL IT THE KNOWLEDGE OF THE DROWNED MAN.
CALL ME GREEN ARROW.

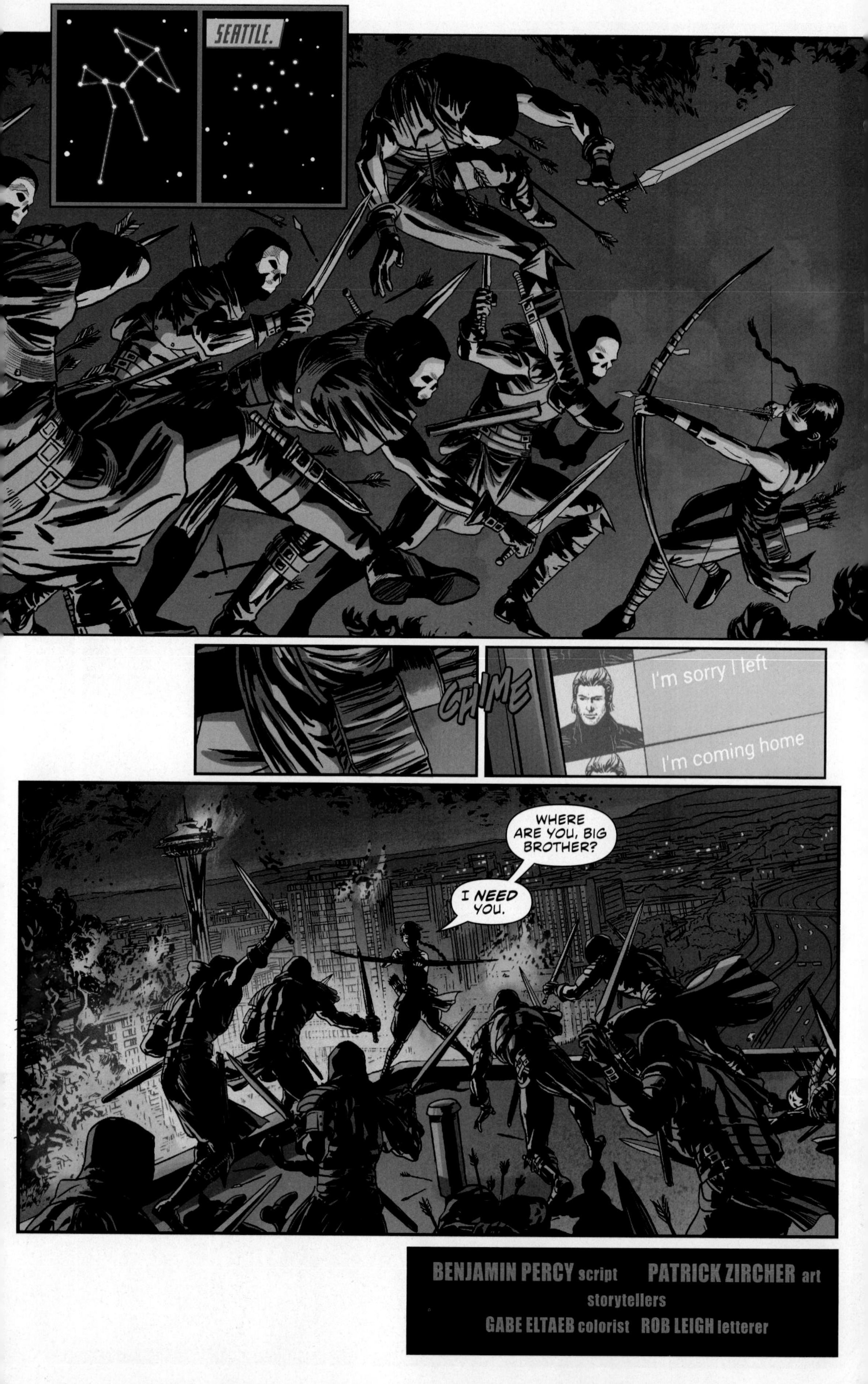

SEATTLE.
CHIME
I'm sorry I left
I'm coming home
WHERE ARE YOU, BIG BROTHER?
I NEED YOU.
BENJAMIN PERCY script PATRICK ZIRCHER art
storytellers
GABE ELTAEB colorist ROB LEIGH letterer

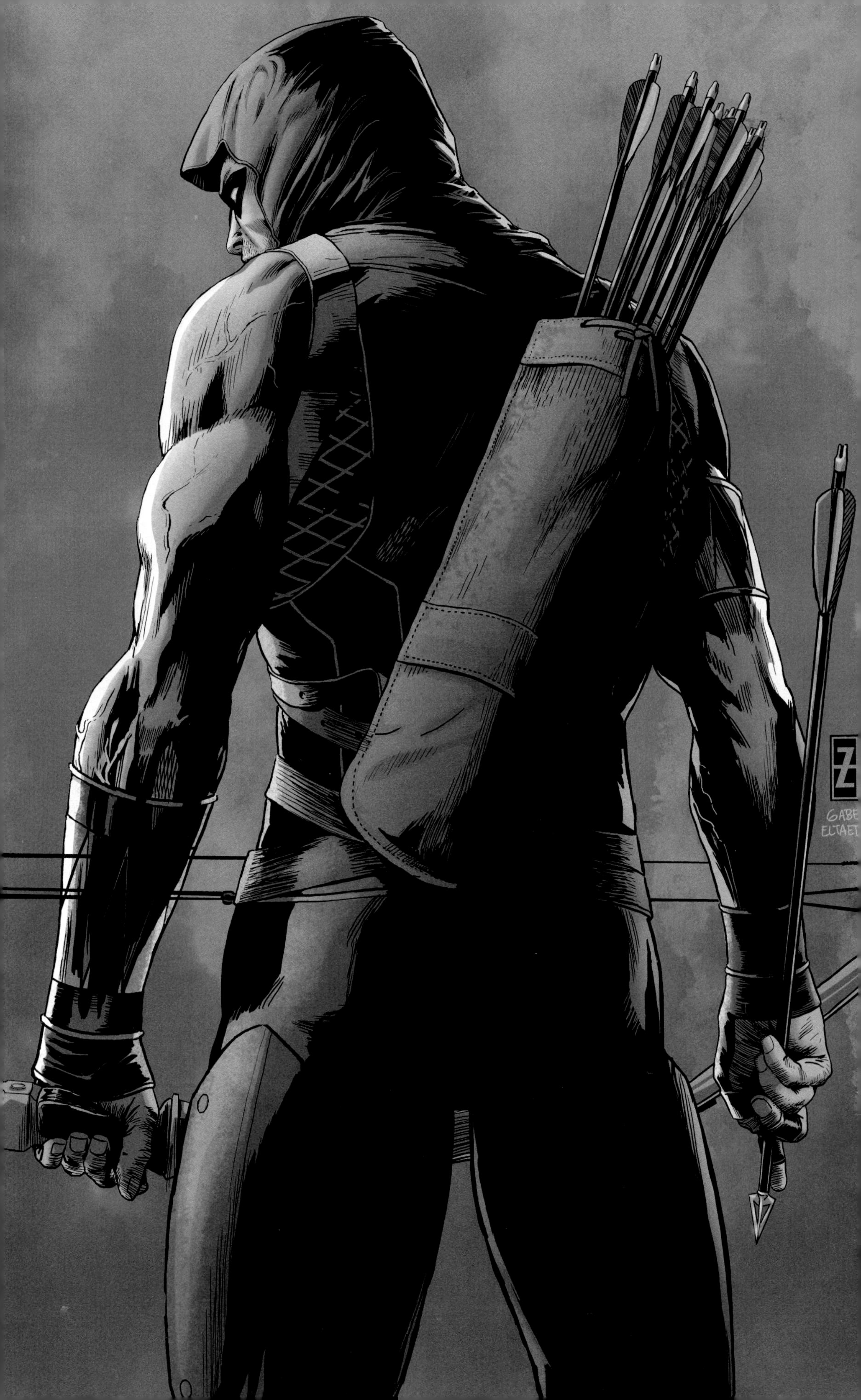
GABE

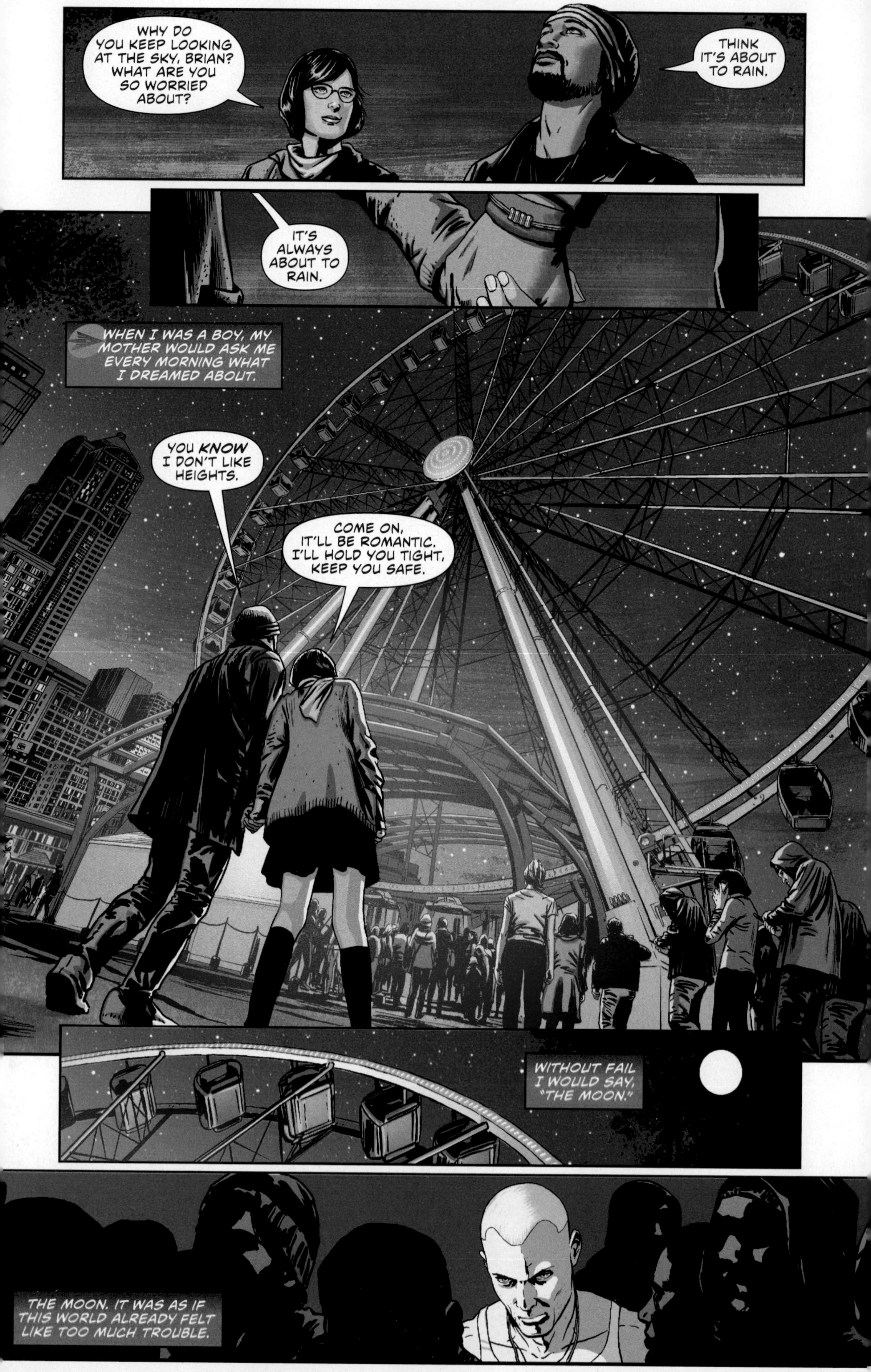
WHY DO YOU KEEP LOOKING AT THE SKY, BRIAN? WHAT ARE YOU SO WORRIED ABOUT?
THINK IT'S ABOUT TO RAIN.
IT'S ALWAYS ABOUT TO RAIN.
WHEN I WAS A BOY, MY MOTHER WOULD ASK ME EVERY MORNING WHAT I DREAMED ABOUT.
YOU KNOW I DON'T LIKE HEIGHTS.
COME ON, IT'LL BE ROMANTIC. I'LL HOLD YOU TIGHT, KEEP YOU SAFE.
WITHOUT FAIL I WOULD SAY, "THE MOON."
THE MOON. IT WAS AS IF THIS WORLD ALREADY FELT LIKE TOO MUCH TROUBLE.

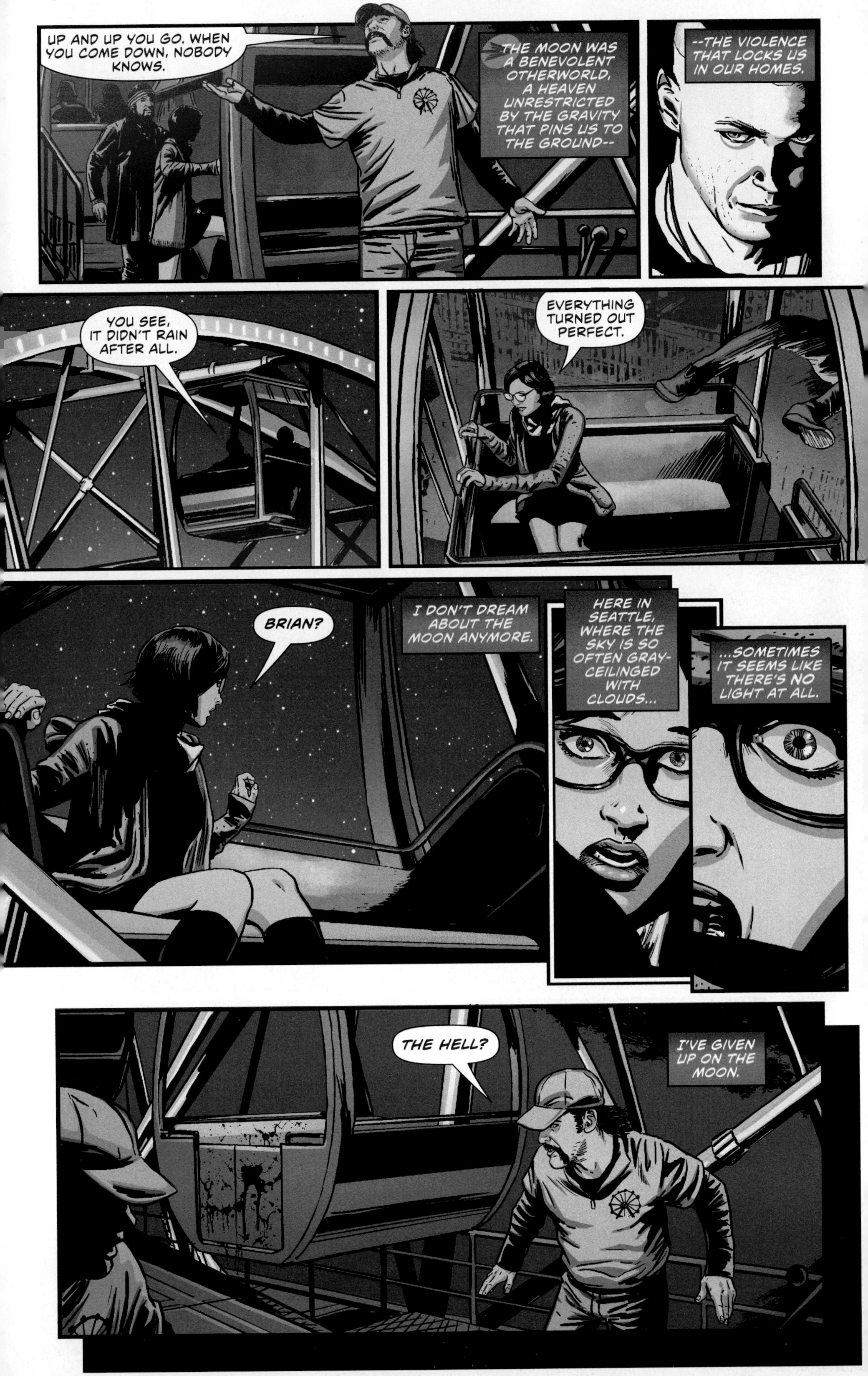
UP AND UP YOU GO. WHEN YOU COME DOWN, NOBODY KNOWS.
THE MOON WAS A BENEVOLENT OTHERWORLD, A HEAVEN UNRESTRICTED BY THE GRAVITY THAT PINS US TO THE GROUND--
--THE VIOLENCE THAT LOCKS US IN OUR HOMES.
YOU SEE, IT DIDN'T RAIN AFTER ALL.
EVERYTHING TURNED OUT PERFECT.
BRIAN?
I DON'T DREAM ABOUT THE MOON ANYMORE.
HERE IN SEATTLE, WHERE THE SKY IS SO OFTEN GRAY-CEILINGED WITH CLOUDS...
...SOMETIMES IT SEEMS LIKE THERE'S NO LIGHT AT ALL.
THE HELL?
I'VE GIVEN UP ON THE MOON.

NO MOON, NO SUN, EVERYTHING'S A SHADOW.

IT'S EASY TO FEEL INVISIBLE IN SEATTLE, A CITY OF STRANGERS.

THIS SENSE OF INVISIBILITY, ANONYMITY, IS MADE WORSE BY THE CONSTANT FOG, WHICH HANGS LIKE A SHROUD--

--MAKES EVERYTHING HALF-GLIMPSED.

IT CAN MAKE PEOPLE THINK THEY CAN GET AWAY WITH ANYTHING...

...EVEN MURDER.

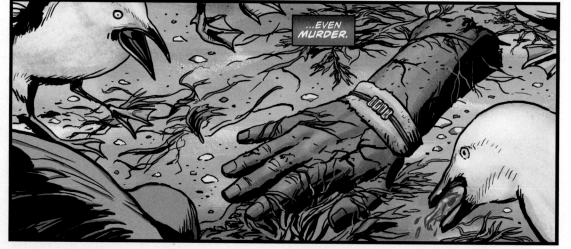

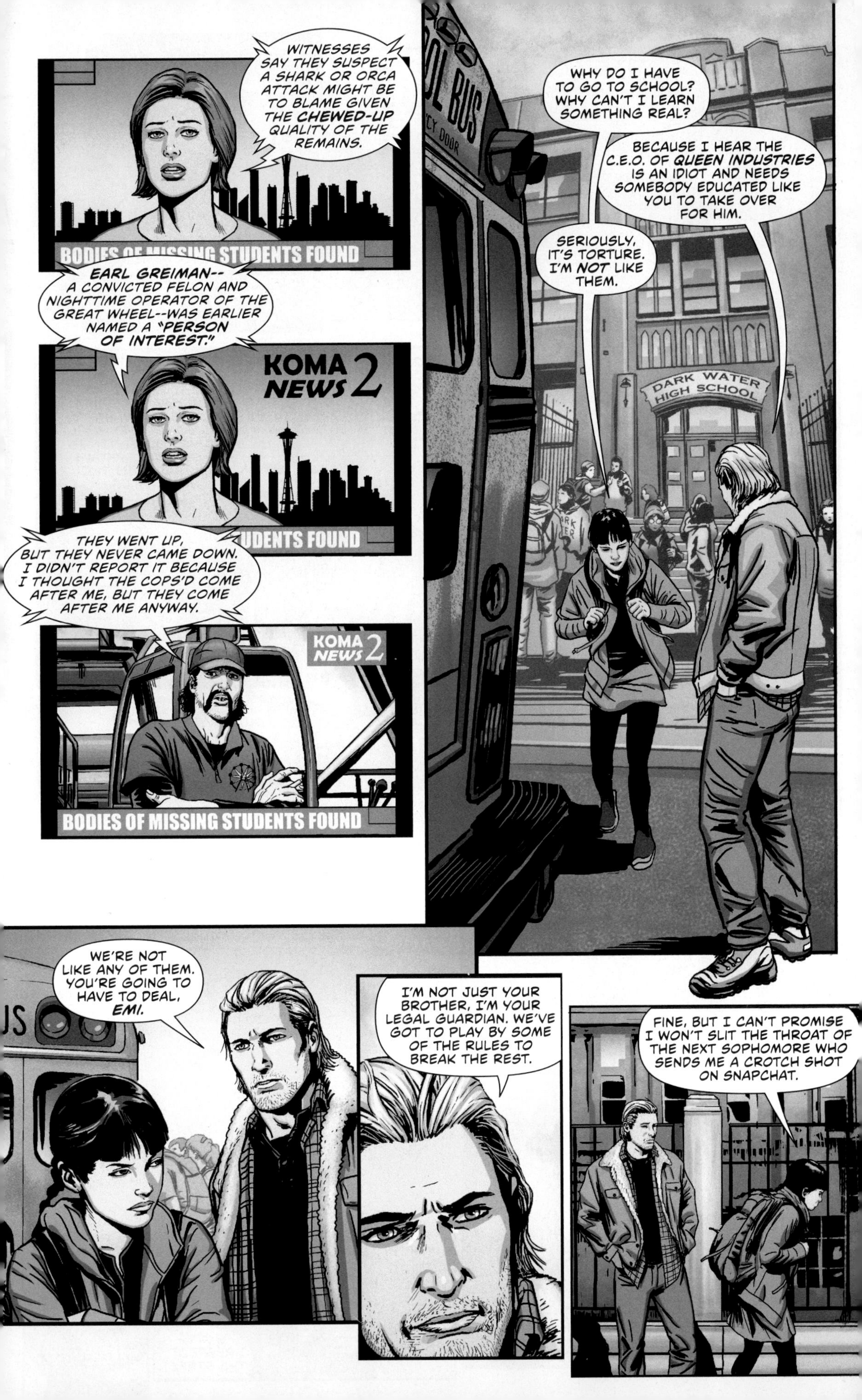
WITNESSES SAY THEY SUSPECT A SHARK OR ORCA ATTACK MIGHT BE TO BLAME GIVEN THE CHEWED-UP QUALITY OF THE REMAINS.
BODIES OF MISSING STUDENTS FOUND
EARL GREIMAN-- A CONVICTED FELON AND NIGHTTIME OPERATOR OF THE GREAT WHEEL--WAS EARLIER NAMED A "PERSON OF INTEREST."
KOMA NEWS 2
THEY WENT UP, BUT THEY NEVER CAME DOWN. I DIDN'T REPORT IT BECAUSE I THOUGHT THE COPS'D COME AFTER ME, BUT THEY COME AFTER ME ANYWAY.
KOMA NEWS 2
BODIES OF MISSING STUDENTS FOUND
DARK WATER HIGH SCHOOL
WHY DO I HAVE TO GO TO SCHOOL? WHY CAN'T I LEARN SOMETHING REAL?
BECAUSE I HEAR THE C.E.O. OF QUEEN INDUSTRIES IS AN IDIOT AND NEEDS SOMEBODY EDUCATED LIKE YOU TO TAKE OVER FOR HIM.
SERIOUSLY, IT'S TORTURE. I'M NOT LIKE THEM.
WE'RE NOT LIKE ANY OF THEM. YOU'RE GOING TO HAVE TO DEAL, EMI.
I'M NOT JUST YOUR BROTHER, I'M YOUR LEGAL GUARDIAN. WE'VE GOT TO PLAY BY SOME OF THE RULES TO BREAK THE REST.
FINE, BUT I CAN'T PROMISE I WON'T SLIT THE THROAT OF THE NEXT SOPHOMORE WHO SENDS ME A CROTCH SHOT ON SNAPCHAT.

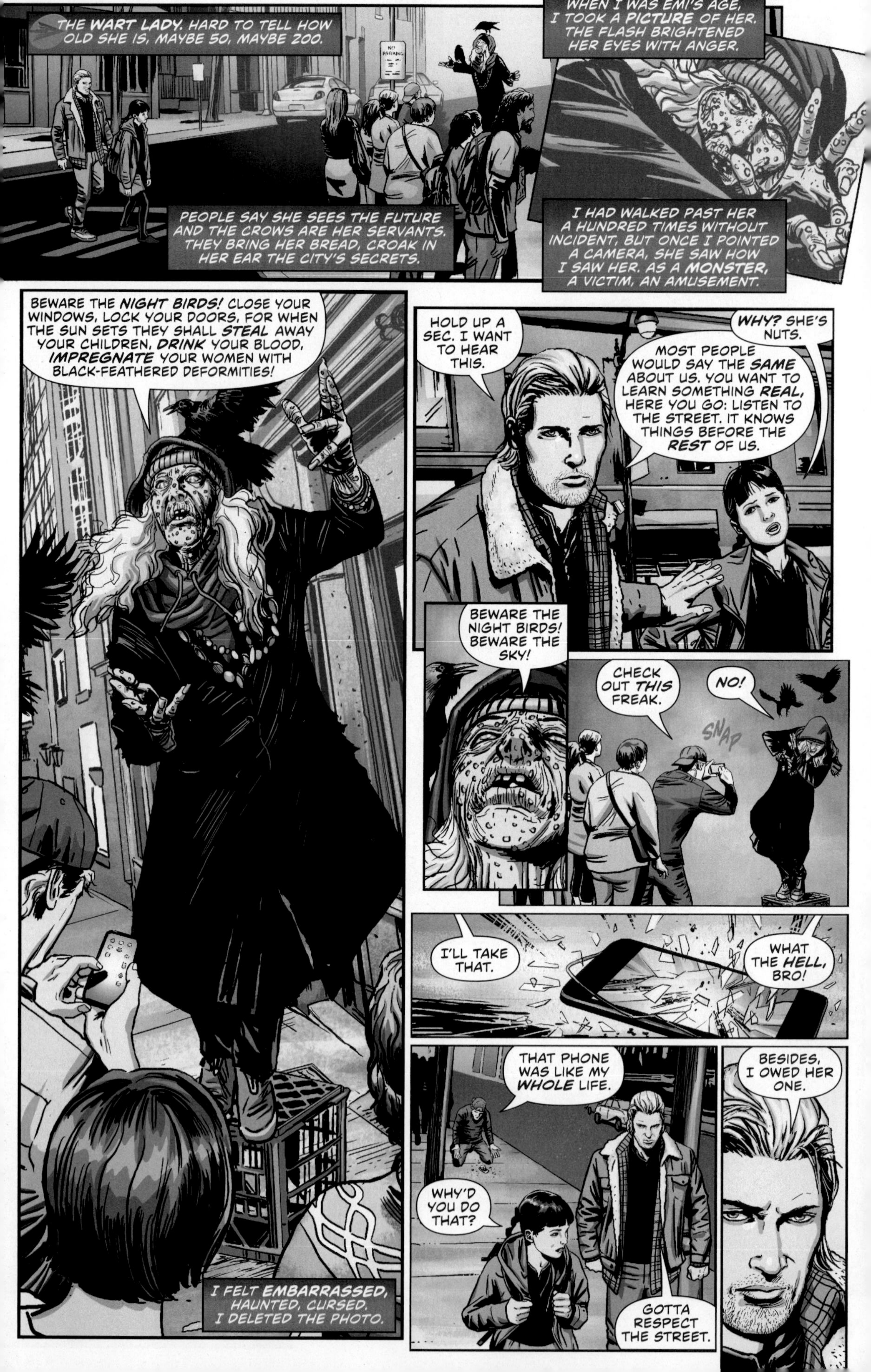
THE WART LADY. HARD TO TELL HOW OLD SHE IS, MAYBE 50, MAYBE 200.
PEOPLE SAY SHE SEES THE FUTURE AND THE CROWS ARE HER SERVANTS. THEY BRING HER BREAD, CROAK IN HER EAR THE CITY'S SECRETS.
WHEN I WAS EMI'S AGE, I TOOK A PICTURE OF HER. THE FLASH BRIGHTENED HER EYES WITH ANGER.
I HAD WALKED PAST HER A HUNDRED TIMES WITHOUT INCIDENT, BUT ONCE I POINTED A CAMERA, SHE SAW HOW I SAW HER. AS A MONSTER, A VICTIM, AN AMUSEMENT.
BEWARE THE NIGHT BIRDS! CLOSE YOUR WINDOWS, LOCK YOUR DOORS, FOR WHEN THE SUN SETS THEY SHALL STEAL AWAY YOUR CHILDREN, DRINK YOUR BLOOD, IMPREGNATE YOUR WOMEN WITH BLACK-FEATHERED DEFORMITIES!
I FELT EMBARRASSED, HAUNTED, CURSED. I DELETED THE PHOTO.
HOLD UP A SEC. I WANT TO HEAR THIS.
WHY? SHE'S NUTS.
MOST PEOPLE WOULD SAY THE SAME ABOUT US. YOU WANT TO LEARN SOMETHING REAL, HERE YOU GO: LISTEN TO THE STREET. IT KNOWS THINGS BEFORE THE REST OF US.
BEWARE THE NIGHT BIRDS! BEWARE THE SKY!
CHECK OUT THIS FREAK.
NO!
SNAP
I'LL TAKE THAT.
WHAT THE HELL, BRO!
THAT PHONE WAS LIKE MY WHOLE LIFE.
WHY'D YOU DO THAT?
GOTTA RESPECT THE STREET.
BESIDES, I OWED HER ONE.

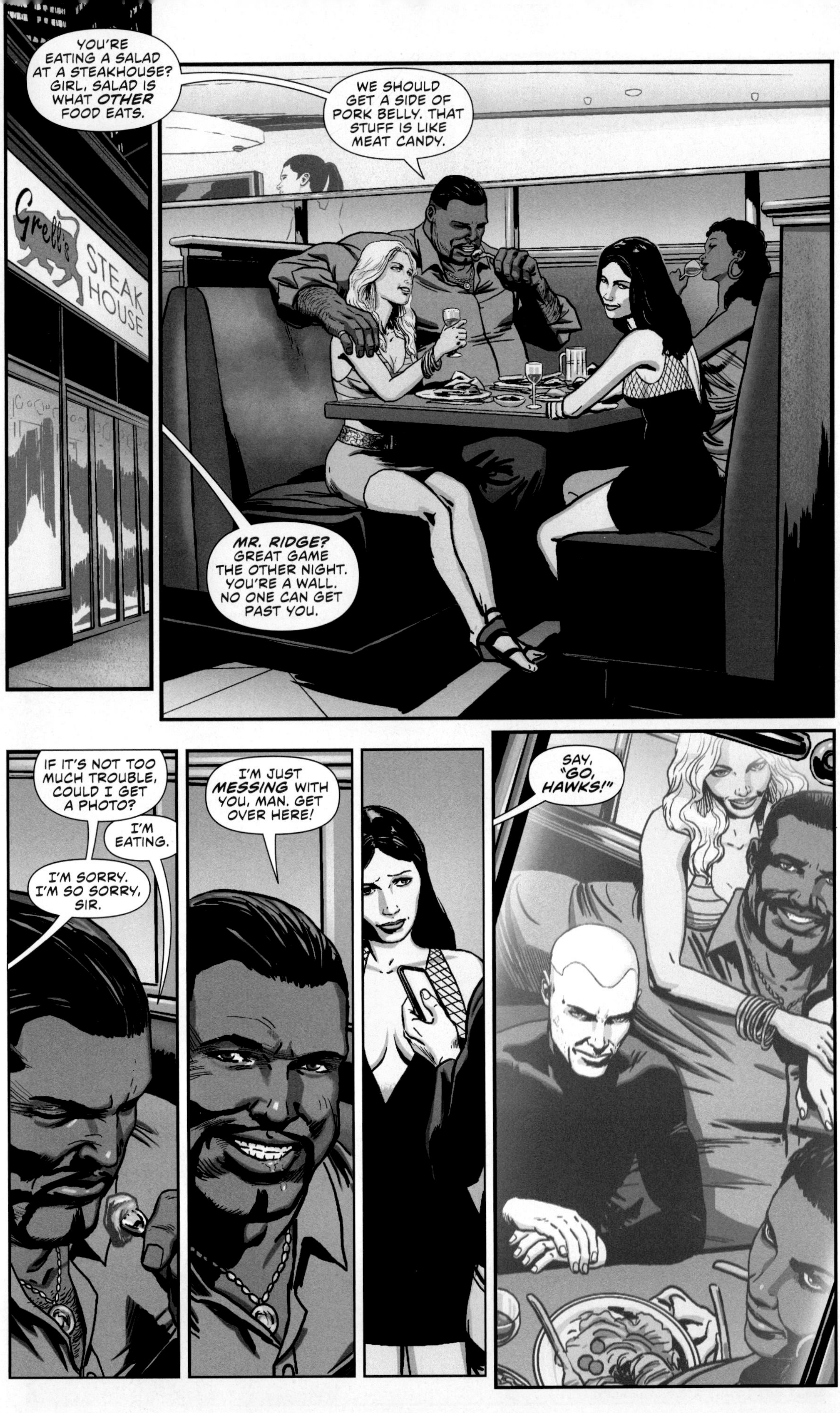
YOU'RE EATING A SALAD AT A STEAKHOUSE? GIRL, SALAD IS WHAT OTHER FOOD EATS.
Grell's STEAK HOUSE
WE SHOULD GET A SIDE OF PORK BELLY. THAT STUFF IS LIKE MEAT CANDY.
MR. RIDGE? GREAT GAME THE OTHER NIGHT. YOU'RE A WALL. NO ONE CAN GET PAST YOU.
IF IT'S NOT TOO MUCH TROUBLE, COULD I GET A PHOTO?
I'M EATING.
I'M SORRY. I'M SO SORRY, SIR.
I'M JUST MESSING WITH YOU, MAN. GET OVER HERE!
SAY, "GO, HAWKS!"

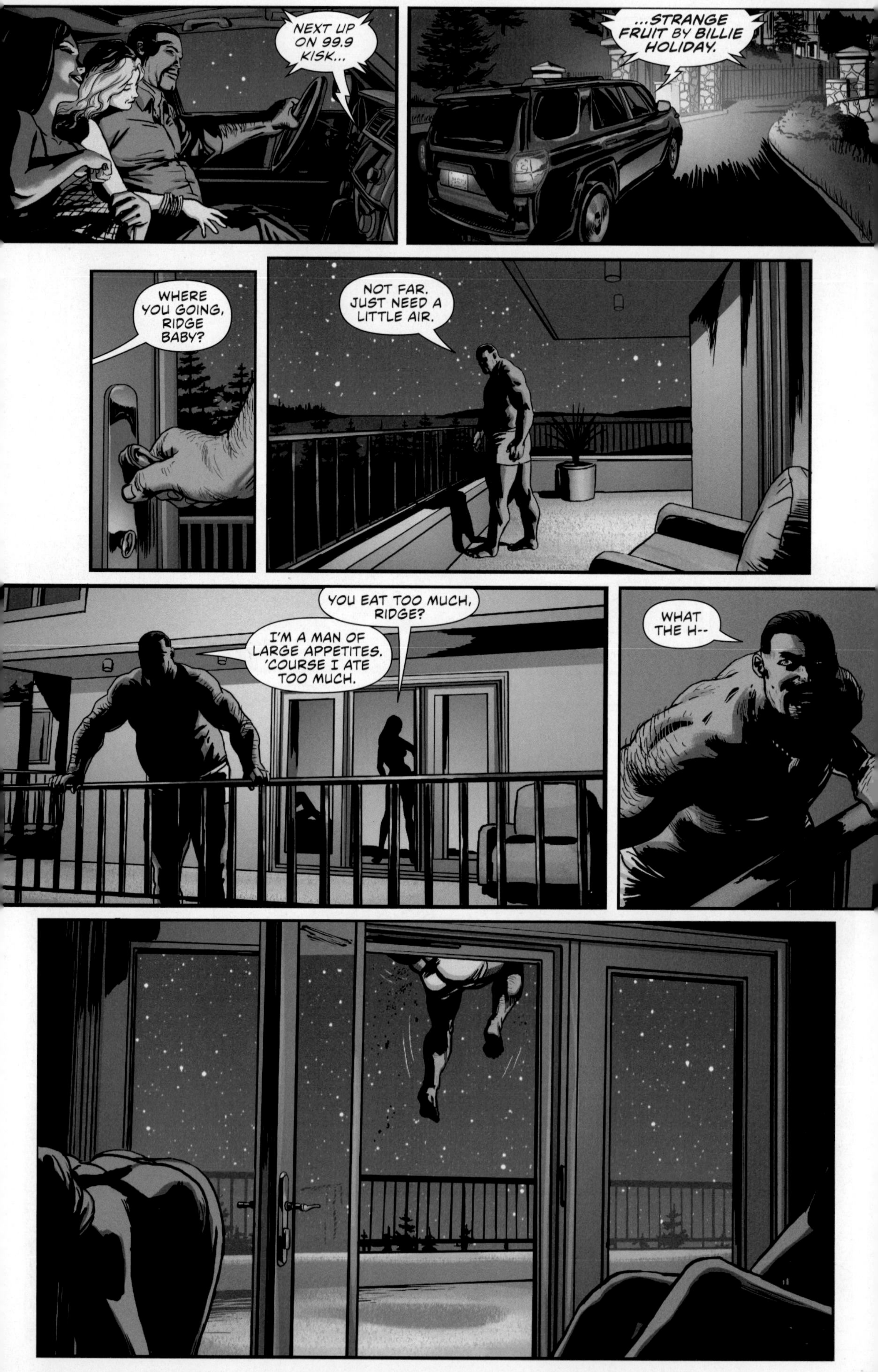
NEXT UP ON 99.9 KISK...
...STRANGE FRUIT BY BILLIE HOLIDAY.
WHERE YOU GOING, RIDGE BABY?
NOT FAR. JUST NEED A LITTLE AIR.
YOU EAT TOO MUCH, RIDGE?
I'M A MAN OF LARGE APPETITES. 'COURSE I ATE TOO MUCH.
WHAT THE H--

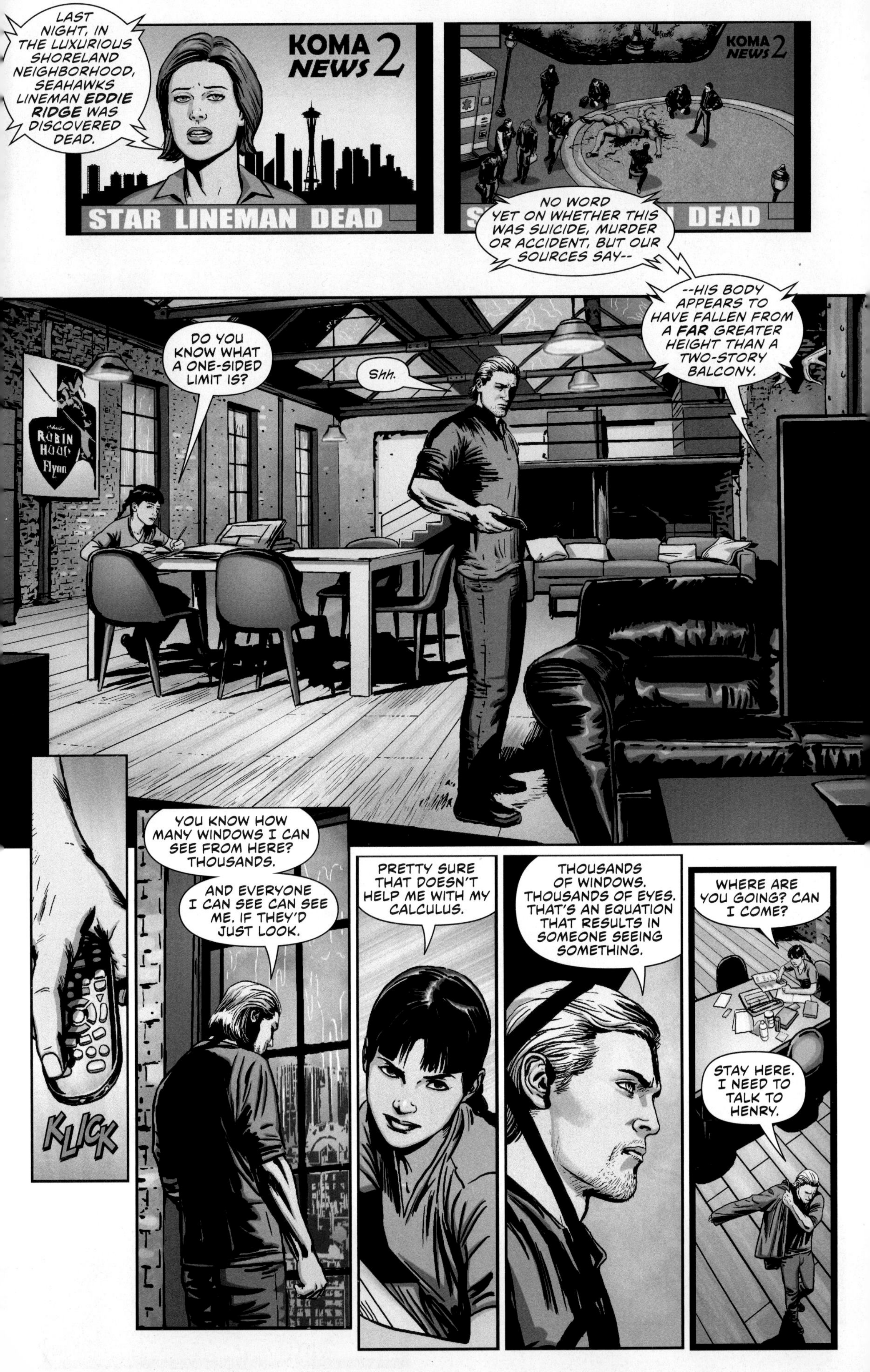
LAST NIGHT, IN THE LUXURIOUS SHORELAND NEIGHBORHOOD, SEAHAWKS LINEMAN **EDDIE RIDGE** WAS DISCOVERED DEAD.
KOMA NEWS 2
STAR LINEMAN DEAD
KOMA NEWS 2
NO WORD YET ON WHETHER THIS WAS SUICIDE, MURDER OR ACCIDENT, BUT OUR SOURCES SAY--
--HIS BODY APPEARS TO HAVE FALLEN FROM A **FAR** GREATER HEIGHT THAN A TWO-STORY BALCONY.
DO YOU KNOW WHAT A ONE-SIDED LIMIT IS?
Shh.
ROBIN HOOD
Flynn
KLICK
YOU KNOW HOW MANY WINDOWS I CAN SEE FROM HERE? THOUSANDS.
AND EVERYONE I CAN SEE CAN SEE ME. IF THEY'D JUST LOOK.
PRETTY SURE THAT DOESN'T HELP ME WITH MY CALCULUS.
THOUSANDS OF WINDOWS. THOUSANDS OF EYES. THAT'S AN EQUATION THAT RESULTS IN SOMEONE SEEING SOMETHING.
WHERE ARE YOU GOING? CAN I COME?
STAY HERE. I NEED TO TALK TO HENRY.

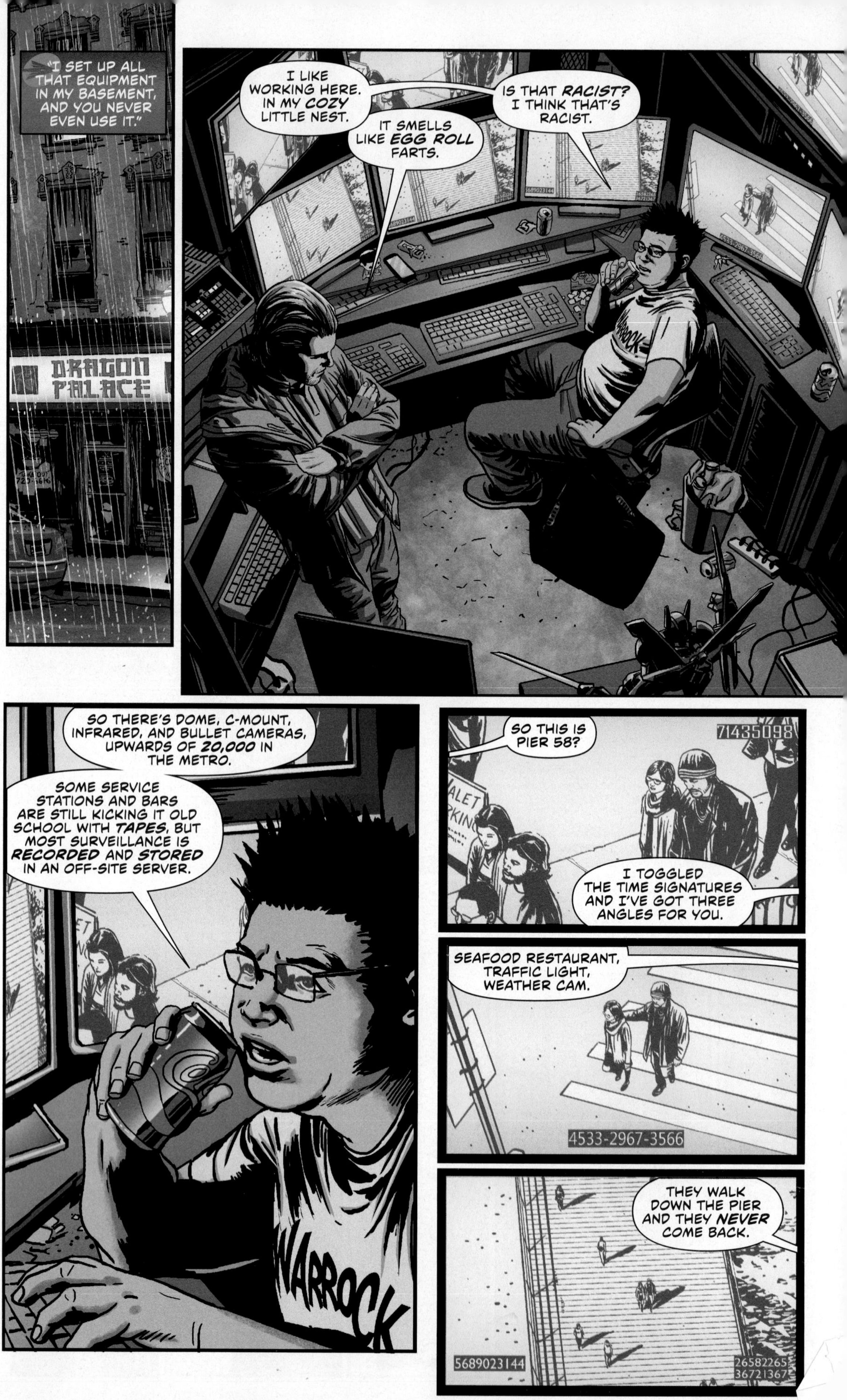
"I SET UP ALL THAT EQUIPMENT IN MY BASEMENT, AND YOU NEVER EVEN USE IT."
DRAGON PALACE
I LIKE WORKING HERE. IN MY COZY LITTLE NEST.
IT SMELLS LIKE EGG ROLL FARTS.
IS THAT RACIST? I THINK THAT'S RACIST.
SO THERE'S DOME, C-MOUNT, INFRARED, AND BULLET CAMERAS, UPWARDS OF 20,000 IN THE METRO.
SOME SERVICE STATIONS AND BARS ARE STILL KICKING IT OLD SCHOOL WITH TAPES, BUT MOST SURVEILLANCE IS RECORDED AND STORED IN AN OFF-SITE SERVER.
WARROCK
71435098
SO THIS IS PIER 58?
I TOGGLED THE TIME SIGNATURES AND I'VE GOT THREE ANGLES FOR YOU.
SEAFOOD RESTAURANT, TRAFFIC LIGHT, WEATHER CAM.
4533-2967-3566
THEY WALK DOWN THE PIER AND THEY NEVER COME BACK.
5689023144
26582265
36721367

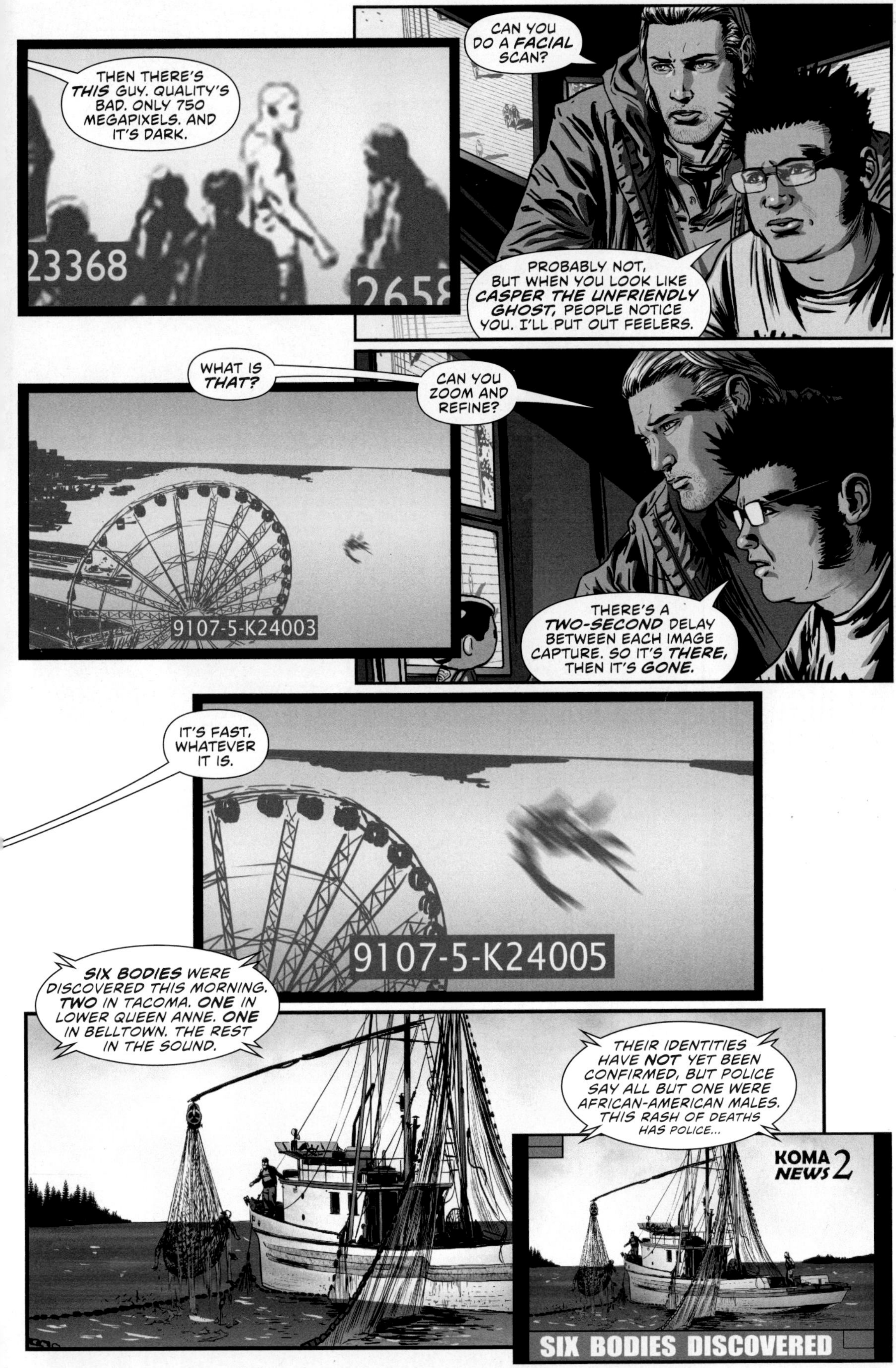
THEN THERE'S THIS GUY. QUALITY'S BAD. ONLY 750 MEGAPIXELS. AND IT'S DARK.
23368
2658
CAN YOU DO A FACIAL SCAN?
PROBABLY NOT, BUT WHEN YOU LOOK LIKE CASPER THE UNFRIENDLY GHOST, PEOPLE NOTICE YOU. I'LL PUT OUT FEELERS.
WHAT IS THAT?
CAN YOU ZOOM AND REFINE?
9107-5-K24003
THERE'S A TWO-SECOND DELAY BETWEEN EACH IMAGE CAPTURE. SO IT'S THERE, THEN IT'S GONE.
IT'S FAST, WHATEVER IT IS.
9107-5-K24005
SIX BODIES WERE DISCOVERED THIS MORNING. TWO IN TACOMA. ONE IN LOWER QUEEN ANNE. ONE IN BELLTOWN. THE REST IN THE SOUND.
THEIR IDENTITIES HAVE NOT YET BEEN CONFIRMED, BUT POLICE SAY ALL BUT ONE WERE AFRICAN-AMERICAN MALES. THIS RASH OF DEATHS HAS POLICE...
KOMA NEWS 2
SIX BODIES DISCOVERED

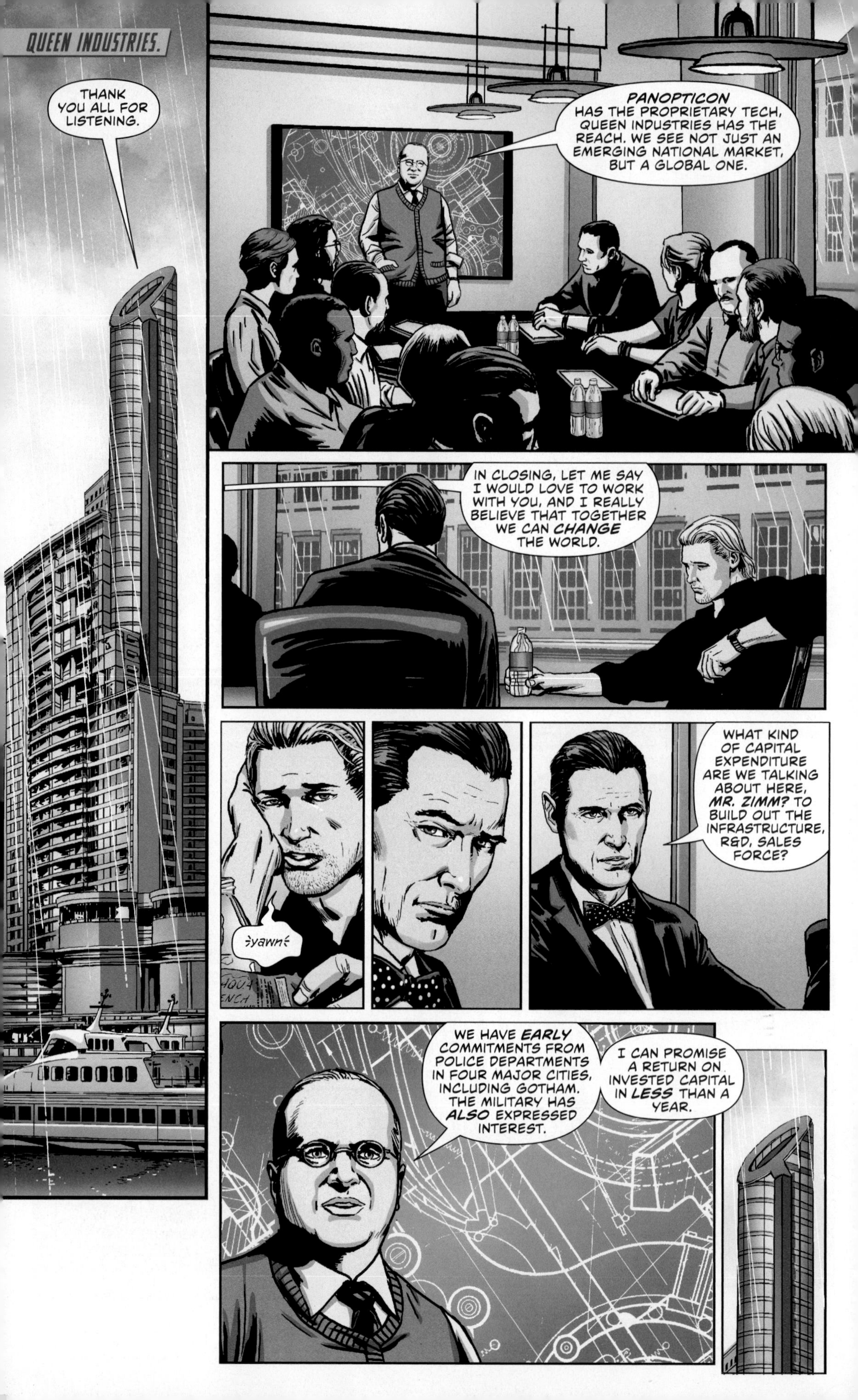
QUEEN INDUSTRIES.
THANK YOU ALL FOR LISTENING.
PANOPTICON HAS THE PROPRIETARY TECH, QUEEN INDUSTRIES HAS THE REACH. WE SEE NOT JUST AN EMERGING NATIONAL MARKET, BUT A GLOBAL ONE.
IN CLOSING, LET ME SAY I WOULD LOVE TO WORK WITH YOU, AND I REALLY BELIEVE THAT TOGETHER WE CAN CHANGE THE WORLD.
yawn
WHAT KIND OF CAPITAL EXPENDITURE ARE WE TALKING ABOUT HERE, MR. ZIMM? TO BUILD OUT THE INFRASTRUCTURE, R&D, SALES FORCE?
WE HAVE EARLY COMMITMENTS FROM POLICE DEPARTMENTS IN FOUR MAJOR CITIES, INCLUDING GOTHAM. THE MILITARY HAS ALSO EXPRESSED INTEREST.
I CAN PROMISE A RETURN ON INVESTED CAPITAL IN LESS THAN A YEAR.

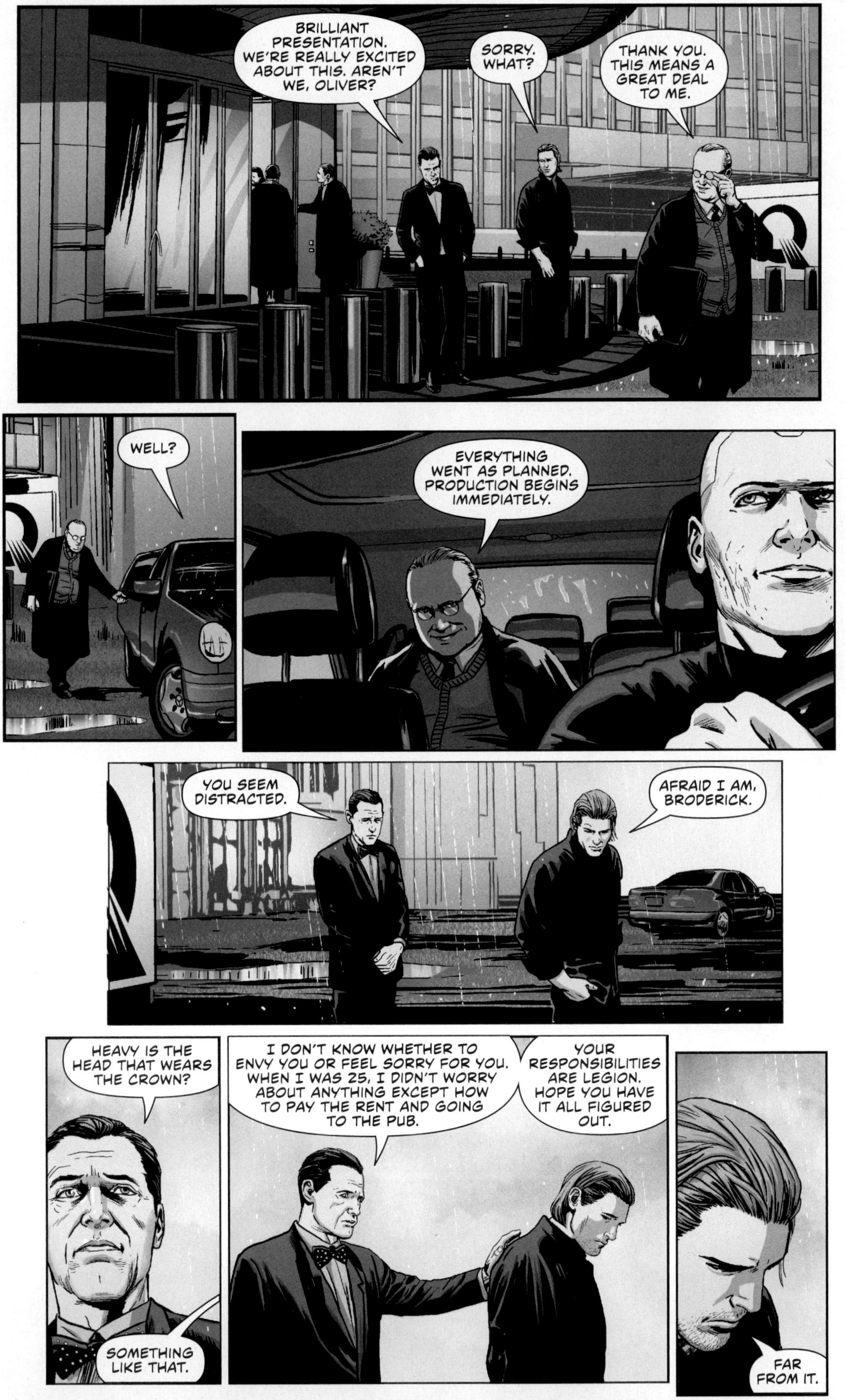
BRILLIANT PRESENTATION. WE'RE REALLY EXCITED ABOUT THIS. AREN'T WE, OLIVER?
SORRY. WHAT?
THANK YOU. THIS MEANS A GREAT DEAL TO ME.
WELL?
EVERYTHING WENT AS PLANNED. PRODUCTION BEGINS IMMEDIATELY.
YOU SEEM DISTRACTED.
AFRAID I AM, BRODERICK.
HEAVY IS THE HEAD THAT WEARS THE CROWN?
SOMETHING LIKE THAT.
I DON'T KNOW WHETHER TO ENVY YOU OR FEEL SORRY FOR YOU. WHEN I WAS 25, I DIDN'T WORRY ABOUT ANYTHING EXCEPT HOW TO PAY THE RENT AND GOING TO THE PUB.
YOUR RESPONSIBILITIES ARE LEGION. HOPE YOU HAVE IT ALL FIGURED OUT.
FAR FROM IT.

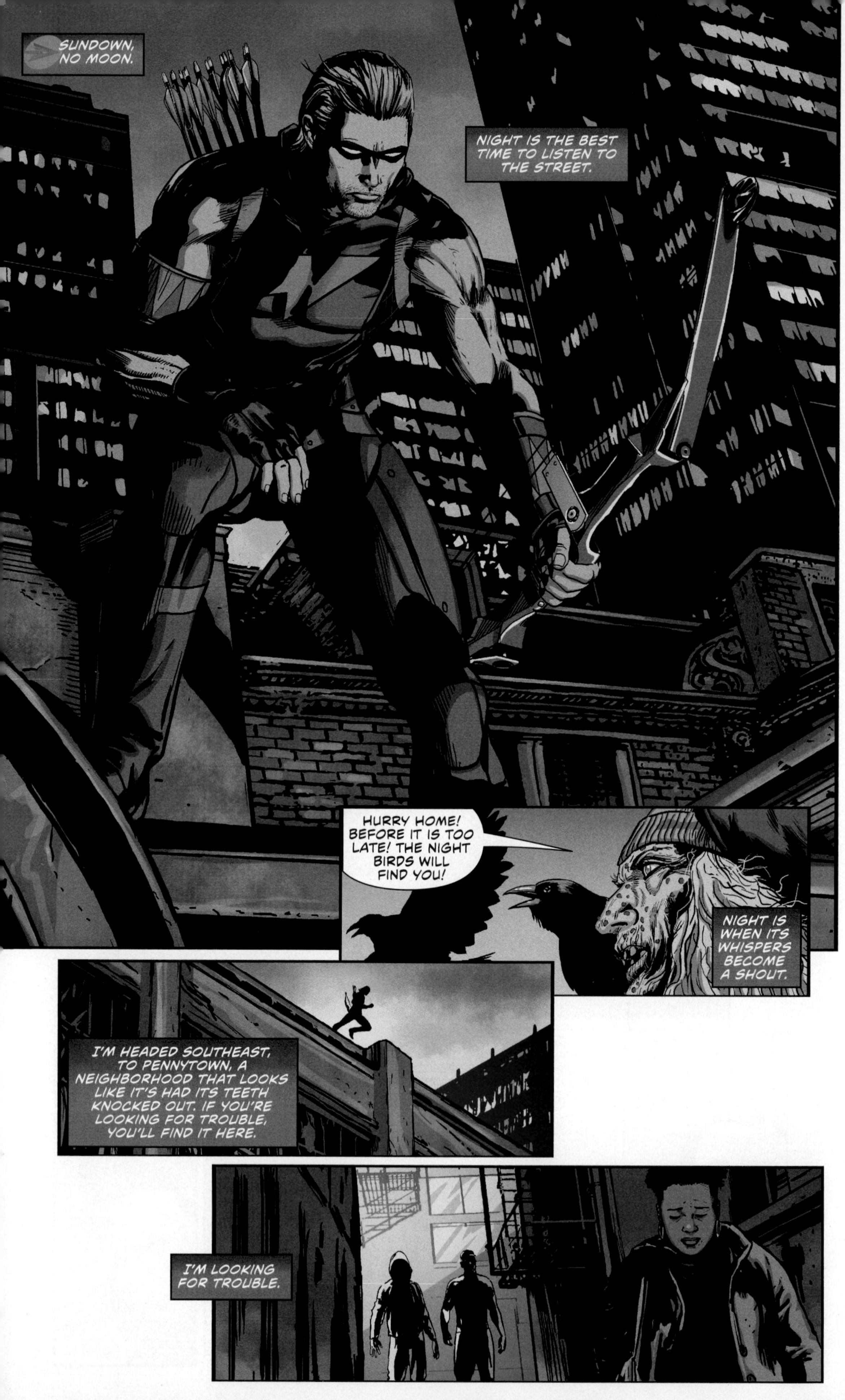
SUNDOWN, NO MOON.
NIGHT IS THE BEST TIME TO LISTEN TO THE STREET.
HURRY HOME! BEFORE IT IS TOO LATE! THE NIGHT BIRDS WILL FIND YOU!
NIGHT IS WHEN ITS WHISPERS BECOME A SHOUT.
I'M HEADED SOUTHEAST, TO PENNYTOWN, A NEIGHBORHOOD THAT LOOKS LIKE IT'S HAD ITS TEETH KNOCKED OUT. IF YOU'RE LOOKING FOR TROUBLE, YOU'LL FIND IT HERE.
I'M LOOKING FOR TROUBLE.

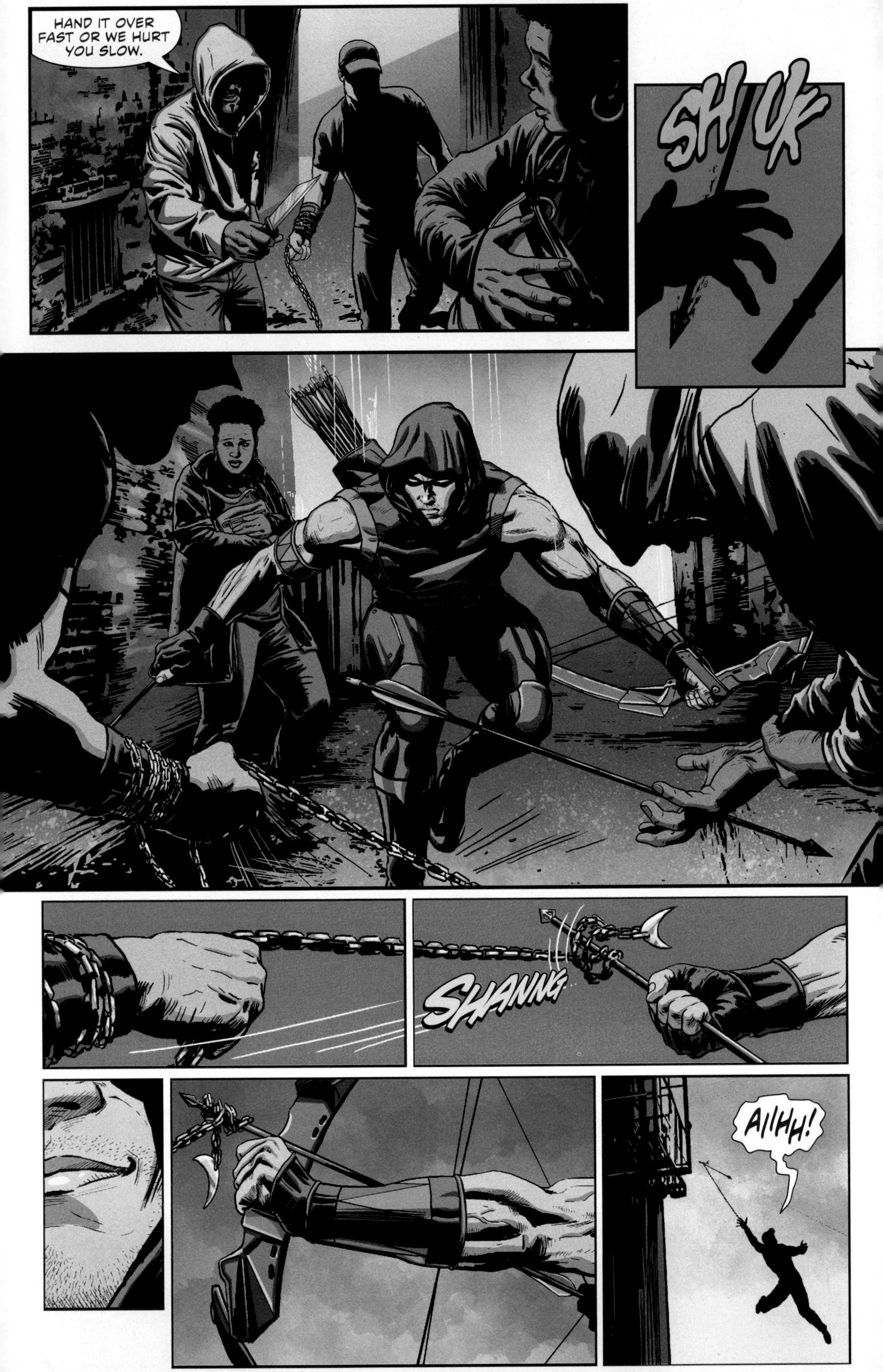
HAND IT OVER FAST OR WE HURT YOU SLOW.
SHUK
SHANNG
AIIHH!

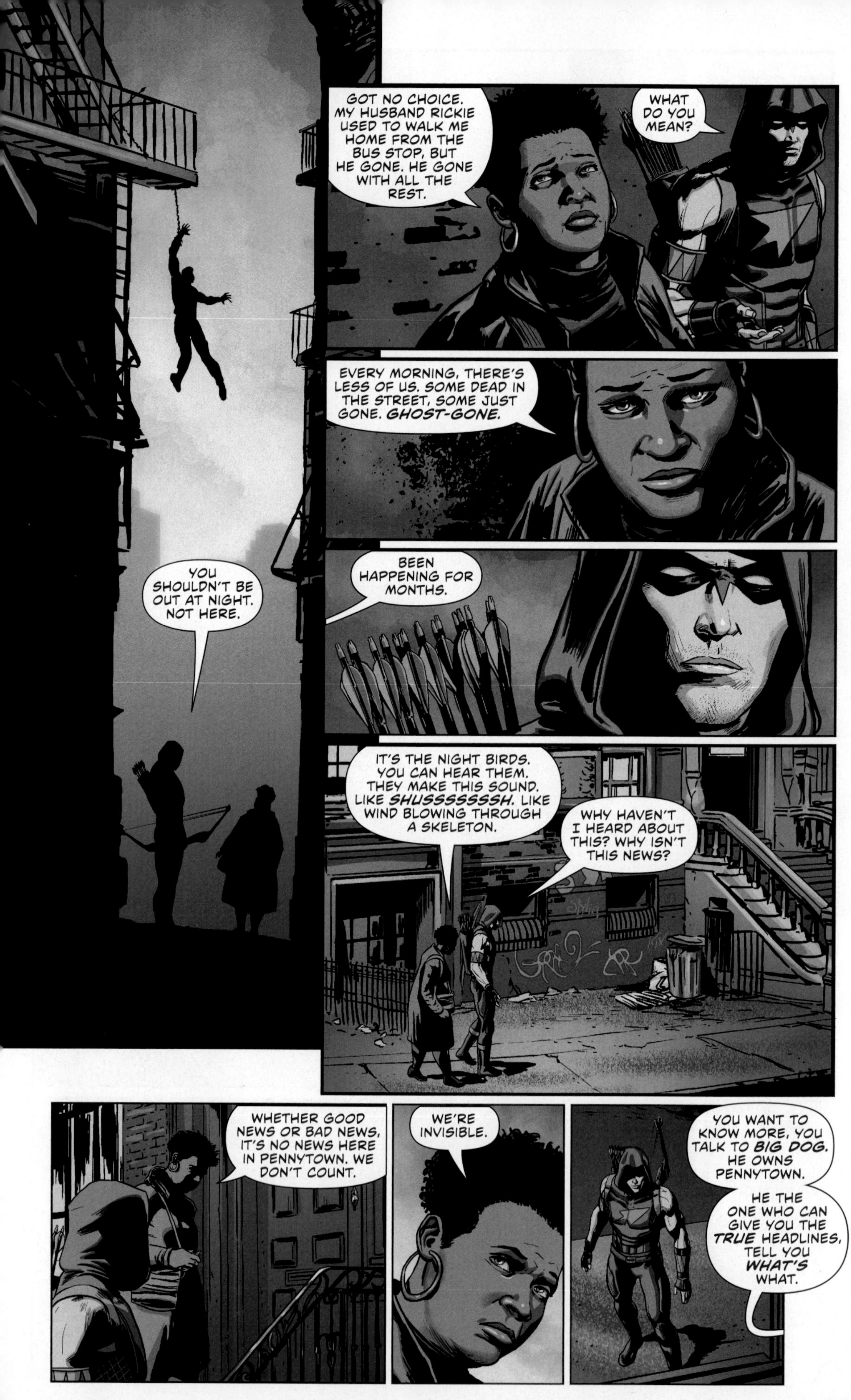
GOT NO CHOICE. MY HUSBAND RICKIE USED TO WALK ME HOME FROM THE BUS STOP, BUT HE GONE. HE GONE WITH ALL THE REST.
WHAT DO YOU MEAN?
EVERY MORNING, THERE'S LESS OF US. SOME DEAD IN THE STREET, SOME JUST GONE. GHOST-GONE.
BEEN HAPPENING FOR MONTHS.
YOU SHOULDN'T BE OUT AT NIGHT. NOT HERE.
IT'S THE NIGHT BIRDS. YOU CAN HEAR THEM. THEY MAKE THIS SOUND. LIKE SHUSSSSSSSH. LIKE WIND BLOWING THROUGH A SKELETON.
WHY HAVEN'T I HEARD ABOUT THIS? WHY ISN'T THIS NEWS?
WHETHER GOOD NEWS OR BAD NEWS, IT'S NO NEWS HERE IN PENNYTOWN. WE DON'T COUNT.
WE'RE INVISIBLE.
YOU WANT TO KNOW MORE, YOU TALK TO BIG DOG. HE OWNS PENNYTOWN.
HE THE ONE WHO CAN GIVE YOU THE TRUE HEADLINES, TELL YOU WHAT'S WHAT.

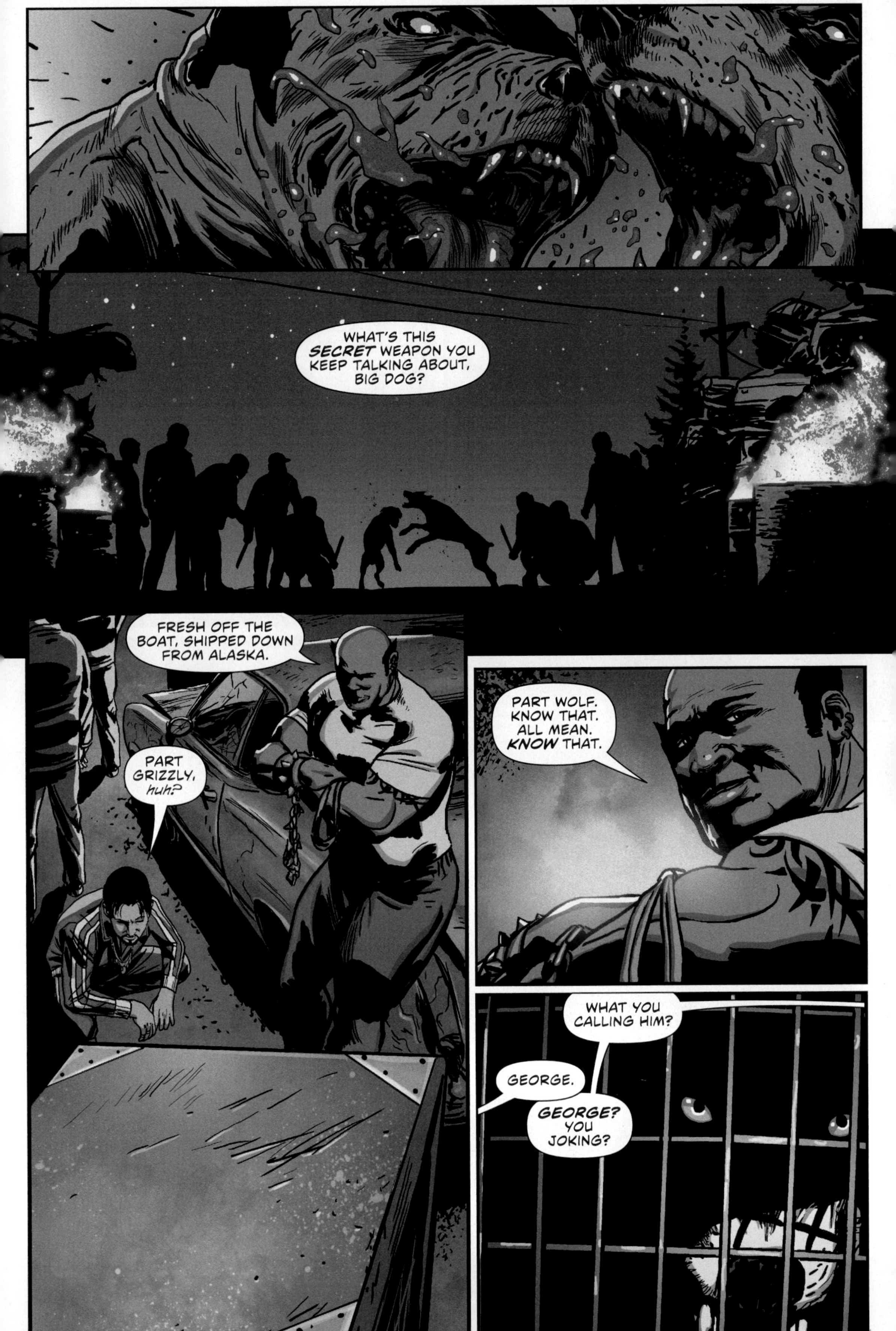
WHAT'S THIS SECRET WEAPON YOU KEEP TALKING ABOUT, BIG DOG?
FRESH OFF THE BOAT, SHIPPED DOWN FROM ALASKA.
PART GRIZZLY, *huh?*
PART WOLF. KNOW THAT. ALL MEAN. **KNOW** THAT.
WHAT YOU CALLING HIM?
GEORGE.
GEORGE? YOU JOKING?

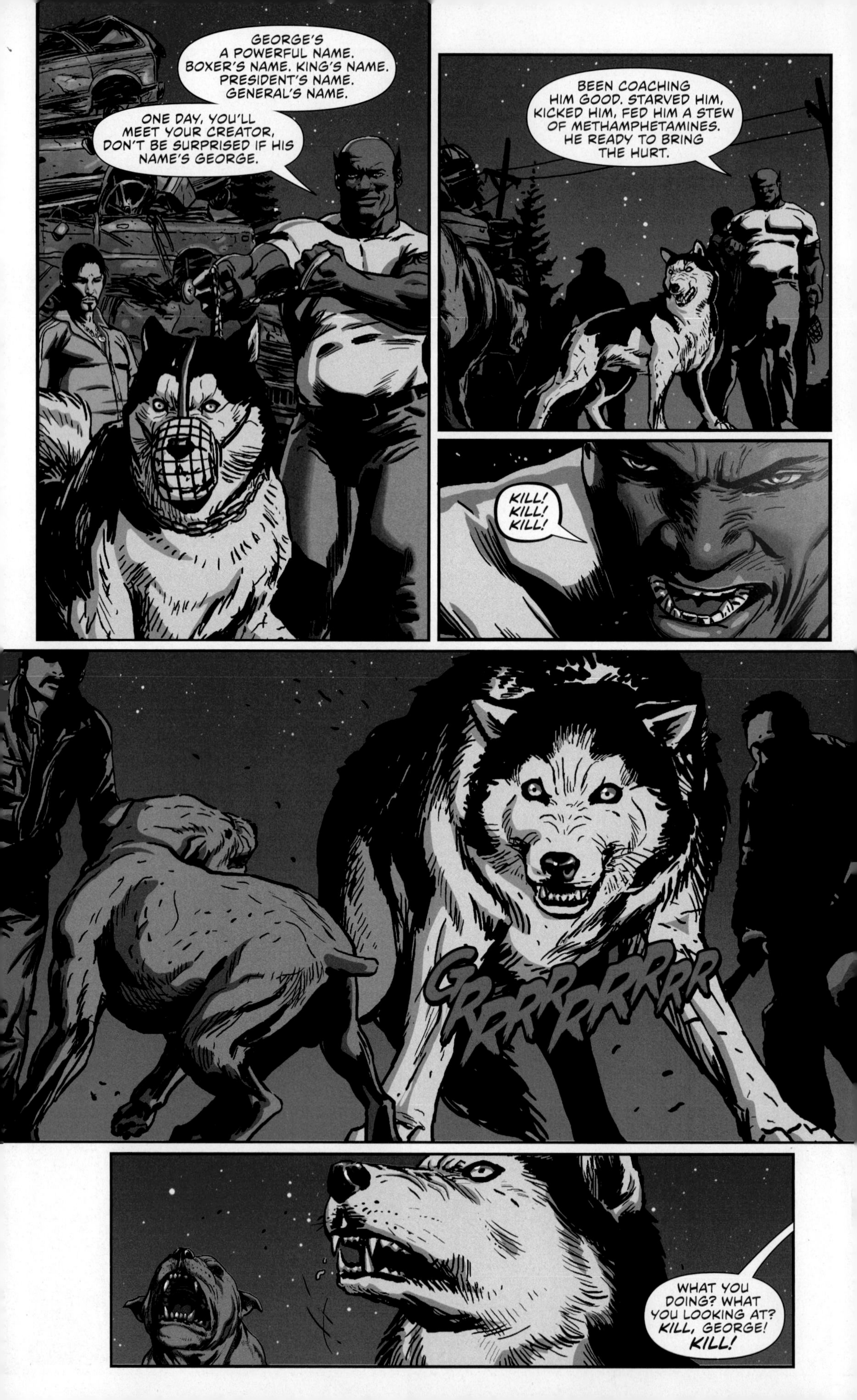
GEORGE'S A POWERFUL NAME. BOXER'S NAME. KING'S NAME. PRESIDENT'S NAME. GENERAL'S NAME.
ONE DAY, YOU'LL MEET YOUR CREATOR, DON'T BE SURPRISED IF HIS NAME'S GEORGE.
BEEN COACHING HIM GOOD. STARVED HIM, KICKED HIM, FED HIM A STEW OF METHAMPHETAMINES. HE READY TO BRING THE HURT.
KILL! KILL! KILL!
GRRRRRRRRR
WHAT YOU DOING? WHAT YOU LOOKING AT? KILL, GEORGE! KILL!

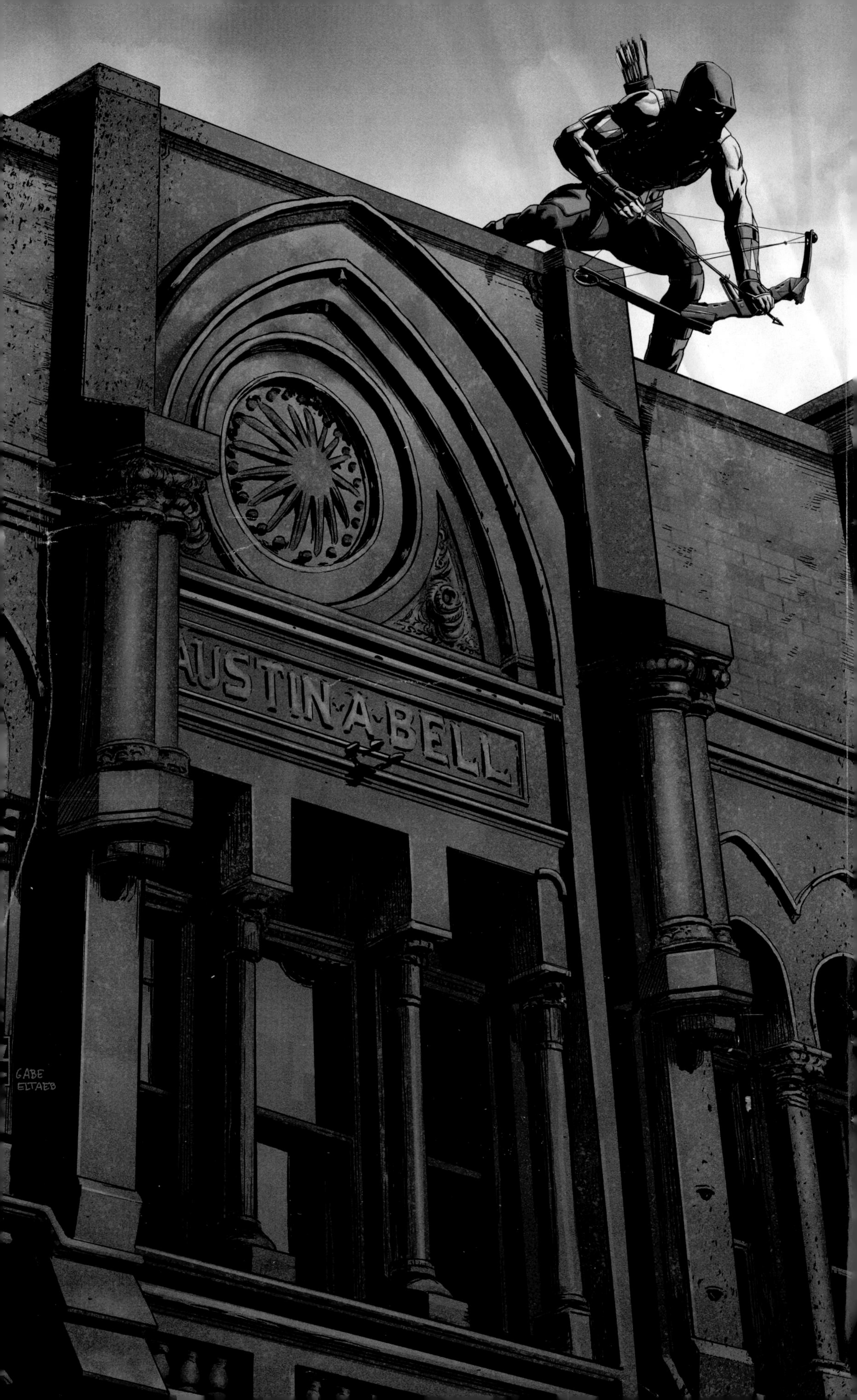
AUSTIN·A·BELL
GABE ELTAEB

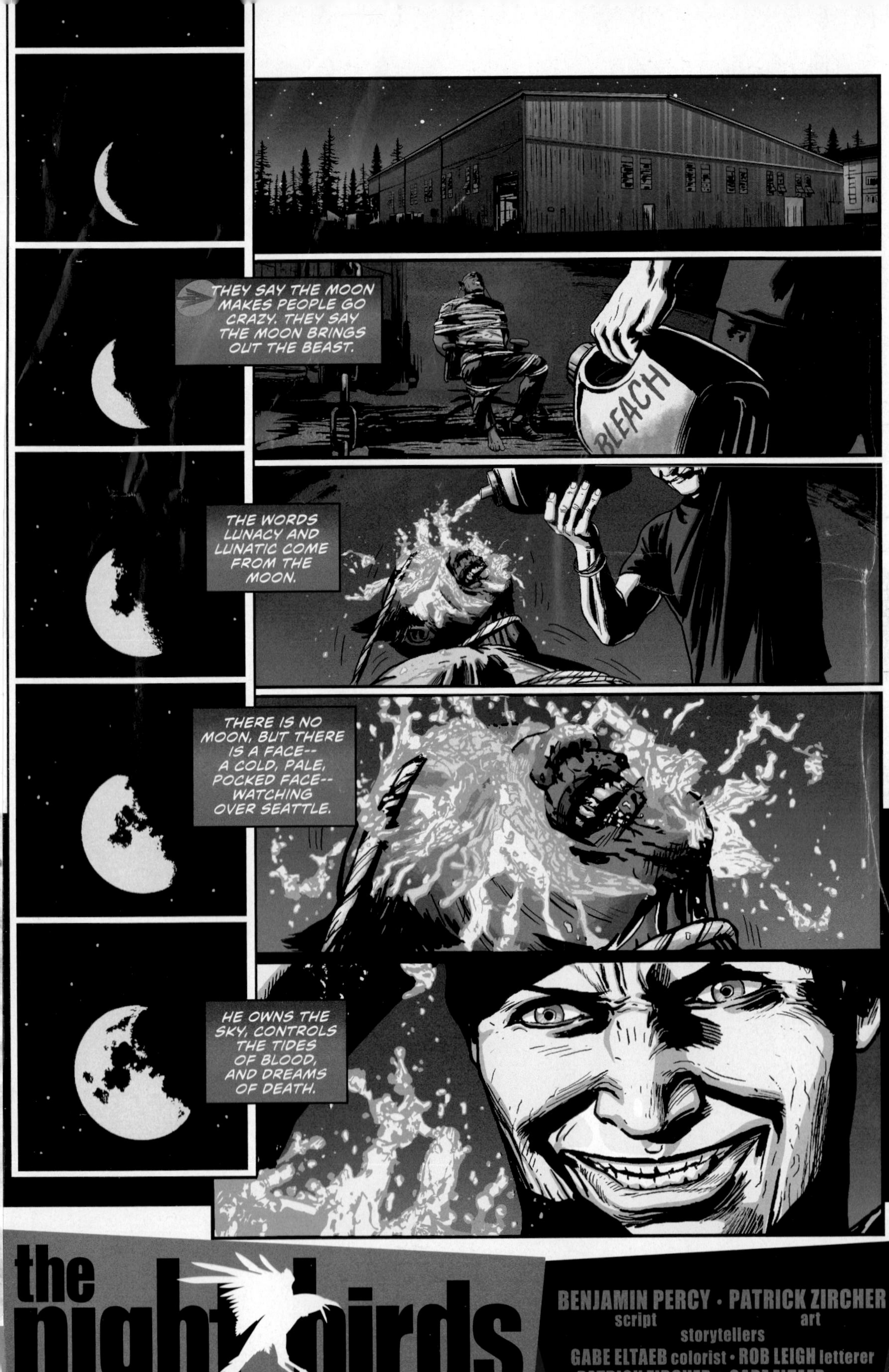

THEY SAY THE MOON MAKES PEOPLE GO CRAZY. THEY SAY THE MOON BRINGS OUT THE BEAST.
BLEACH
THE WORDS LUNACY AND LUNATIC COME FROM THE MOON.
THERE IS NO MOON, BUT THERE IS A FACE-- A COLD, PALE, POCKED FACE-- WATCHING OVER SEATTLE.
HE OWNS THE SKY, CONTROLS THE TIDES OF BLOOD, AND DREAMS OF DEATH.

the night birds

Part 1 of 3

storytellers
BENJAMIN PERCY script · PATRICK ZIRCHER art
GABE ELTAEB colorist · ROB LEIGH letterer
PATRICK ZIRCHER & GABE ELTAEB cover

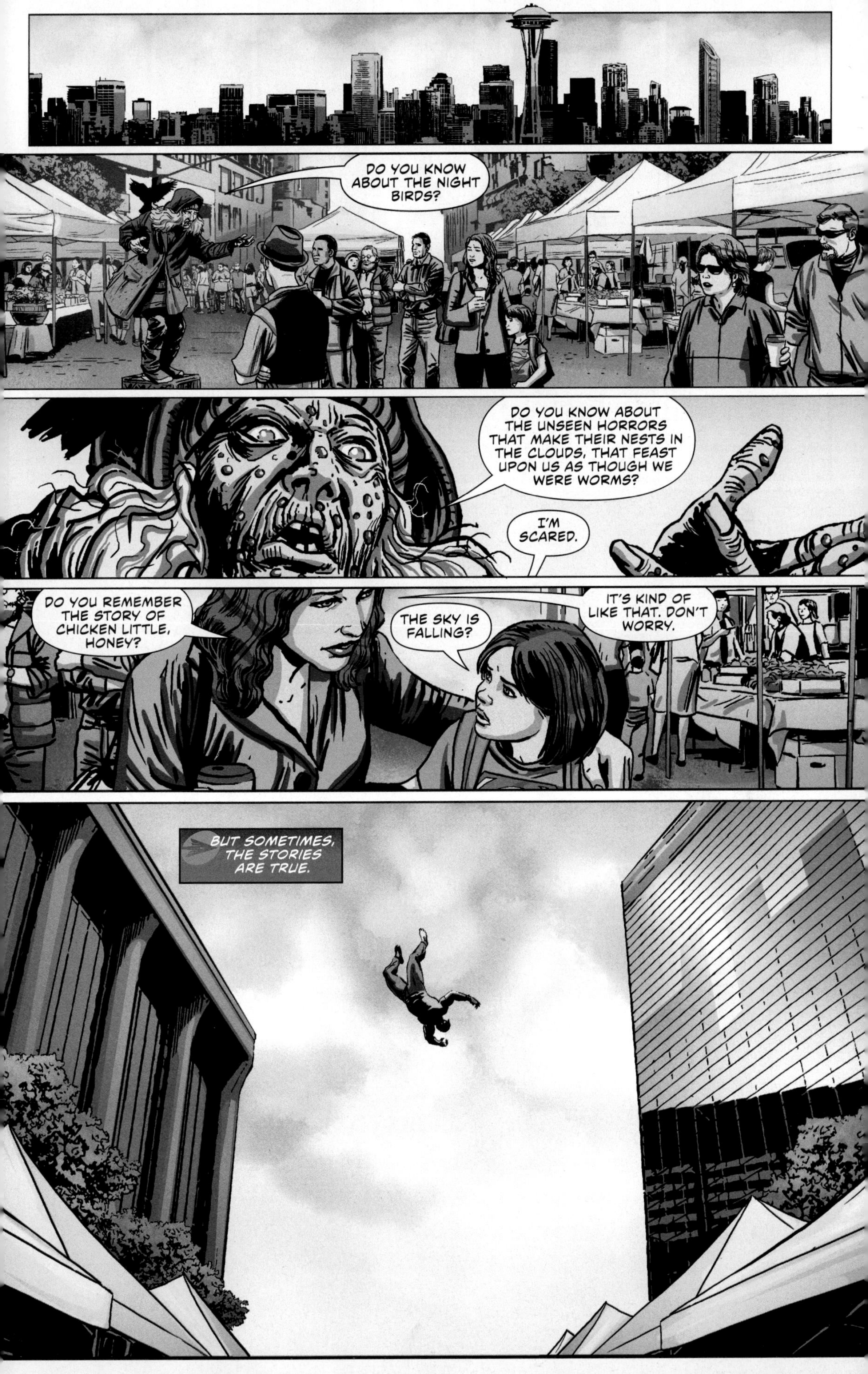
DO YOU KNOW ABOUT THE NIGHT BIRDS?
DO YOU KNOW ABOUT THE UNSEEN HORRORS THAT MAKE THEIR NESTS IN THE CLOUDS, THAT FEAST UPON US AS THOUGH WE WERE WORMS?
I'M SCARED.
DO YOU REMEMBER THE STORY OF CHICKEN LITTLE, HONEY?
THE SKY IS FALLING?
IT'S KIND OF LIKE THAT. DON'T WORRY.
BUT SOMETIMES, THE STORIES ARE TRUE.

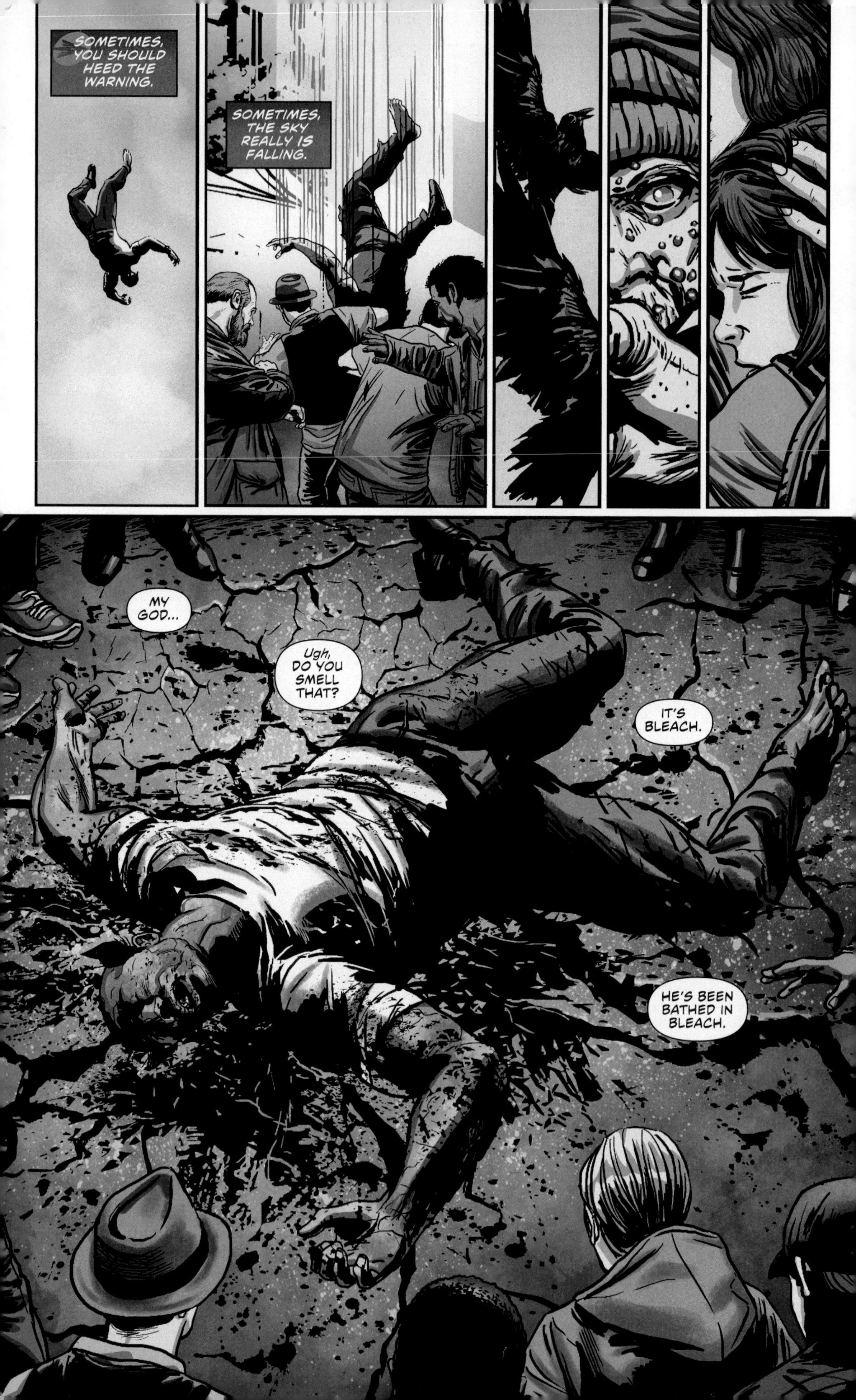
SOMETIMES, YOU SHOULD HEED THE WARNING.
SOMETIMES, THE SKY REALLY IS FALLING.
MY GOD...
Ugh, DO YOU SMELL THAT?
IT'S BLEACH.
HE'S BEEN BATHED IN BLEACH.

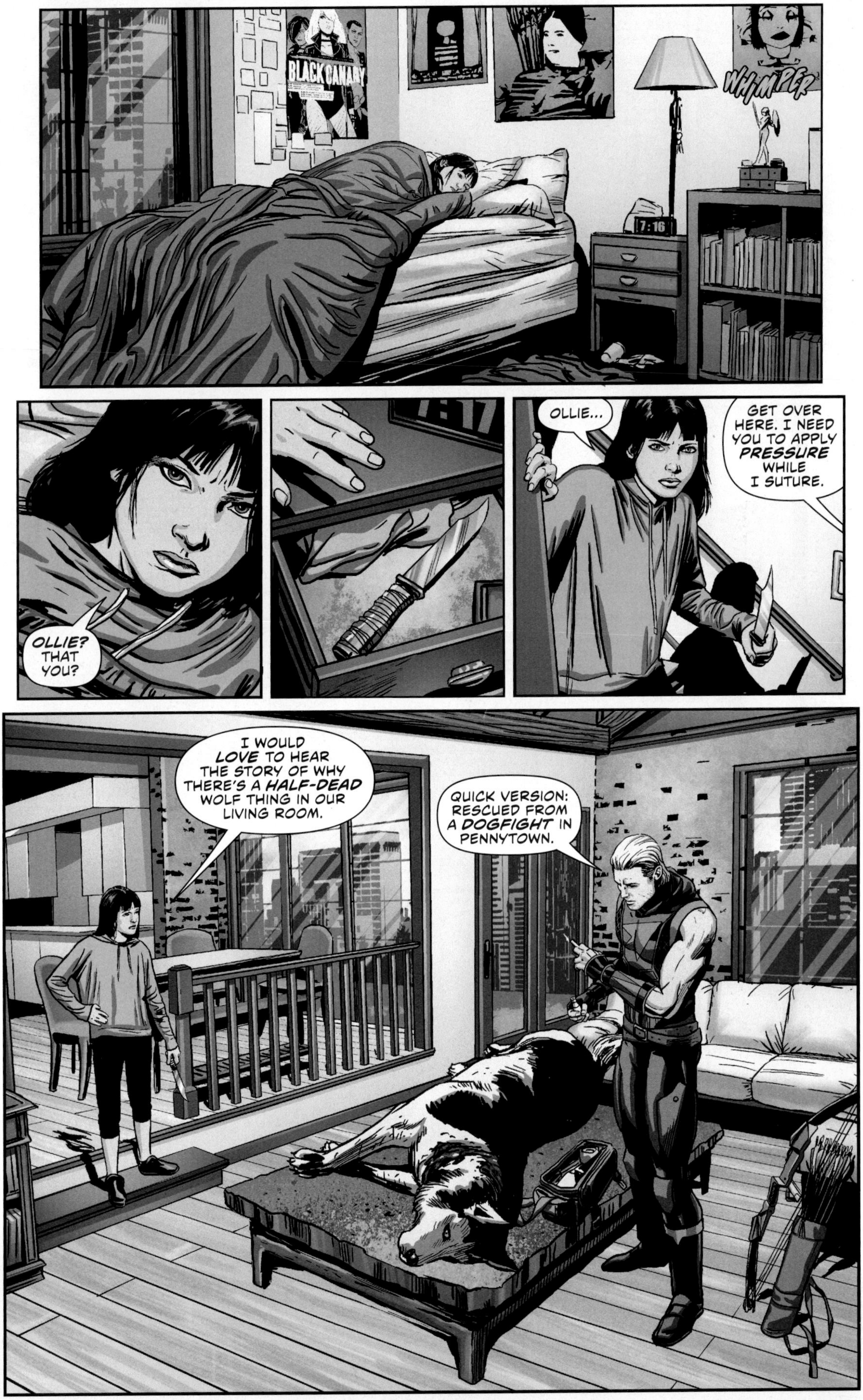
BLACK CANARY
WHIMPER
7:16
OLLIE? THAT YOU?
OLLIE...
GET OVER HERE. I NEED YOU TO APPLY PRESSURE WHILE I SUTURE.
I WOULD LOVE TO HEAR THE STORY OF WHY THERE'S A HALF-DEAD WOLF THING IN OUR LIVING ROOM.
QUICK VERSION: RESCUED FROM A DOGFIGHT IN PENNYTOWN.

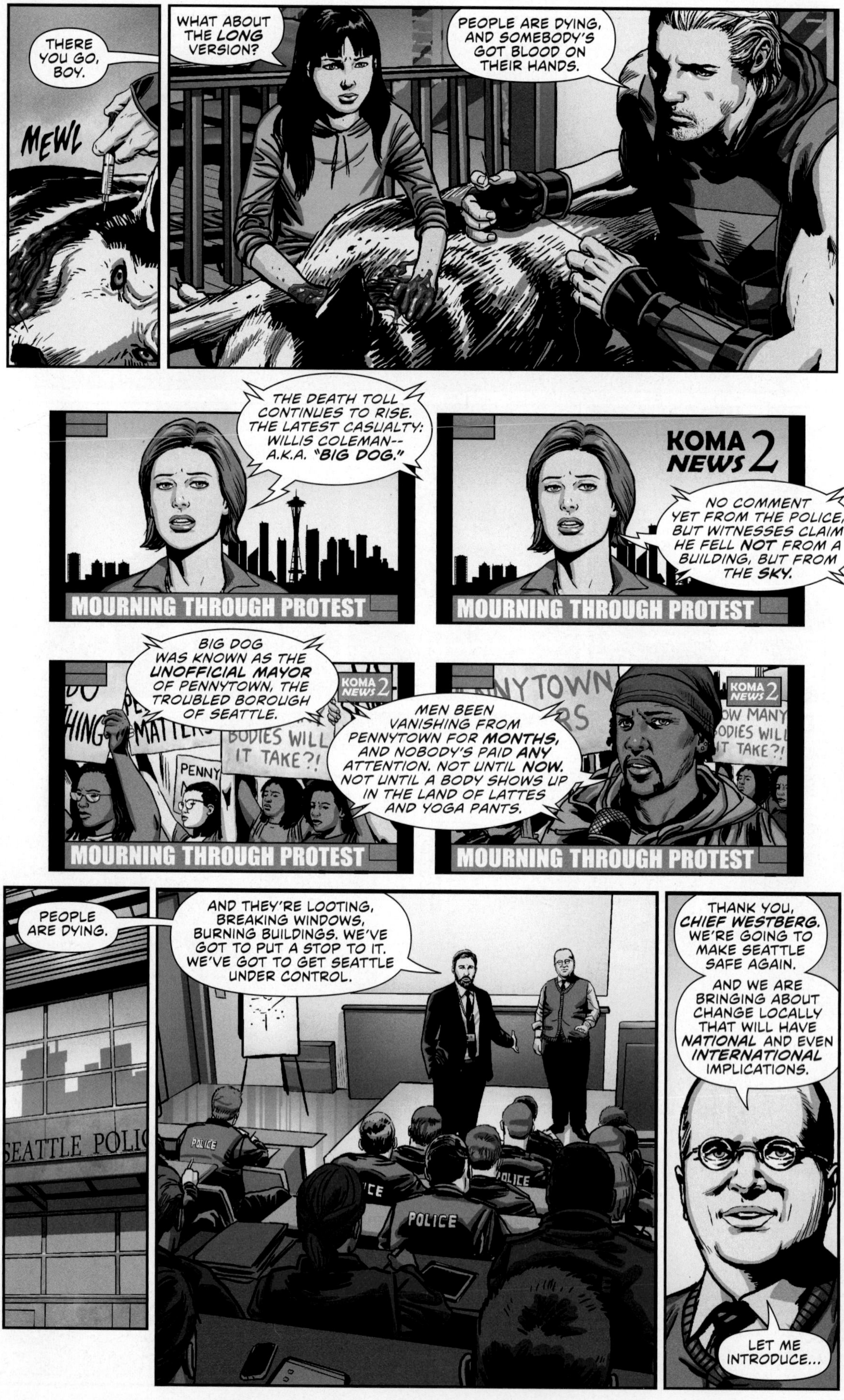

THERE YOU GO, BOY.
MEWL
WHAT ABOUT THE LONG VERSION?
PEOPLE ARE DYING, AND SOMEBODY'S GOT BLOOD ON THEIR HANDS.
THE DEATH TOLL CONTINUES TO RISE. THE LATEST CASUALTY: WILLIS COLEMAN-- A.K.A. "BIG DOG."
MOURNING THROUGH PROTEST
KOMA NEWS 2
NO COMMENT YET FROM THE POLICE, BUT WITNESSES CLAIM HE FELL NOT FROM A BUILDING, BUT FROM THE SKY.
MOURNING THROUGH PROTEST
BIG DOG WAS KNOWN AS THE UNOFFICIAL MAYOR OF PENNYTOWN, THE TROUBLED BOROUGH OF SEATTLE.
KOMA NEWS 2
BODIES WILL IT TAKE?!
MOURNING THROUGH PROTEST
MEN BEEN VANISHING FROM PENNYTOWN FOR MONTHS, AND NOBODY'S PAID ANY ATTENTION. NOT UNTIL NOW. NOT UNTIL A BODY SHOWS UP IN THE LAND OF LATTES AND YOGA PANTS.
KOMA NEWS 2
MOURNING THROUGH PROTEST
PEOPLE ARE DYING.
SEATTLE POLI
AND THEY'RE LOOTING, BREAKING WINDOWS, BURNING BUILDINGS. WE'VE GOT TO PUT A STOP TO IT. WE'VE GOT TO GET SEATTLE UNDER CONTROL.
POLICE
POLICE
THANK YOU, CHIEF WESTBERG. WE'RE GOING TO MAKE SEATTLE SAFE AGAIN.
AND WE ARE BRINGING ABOUT CHANGE LOCALLY THAT WILL HAVE NATIONAL AND EVEN INTERNATIONAL IMPLICATIONS.
LET ME INTRODUCE...

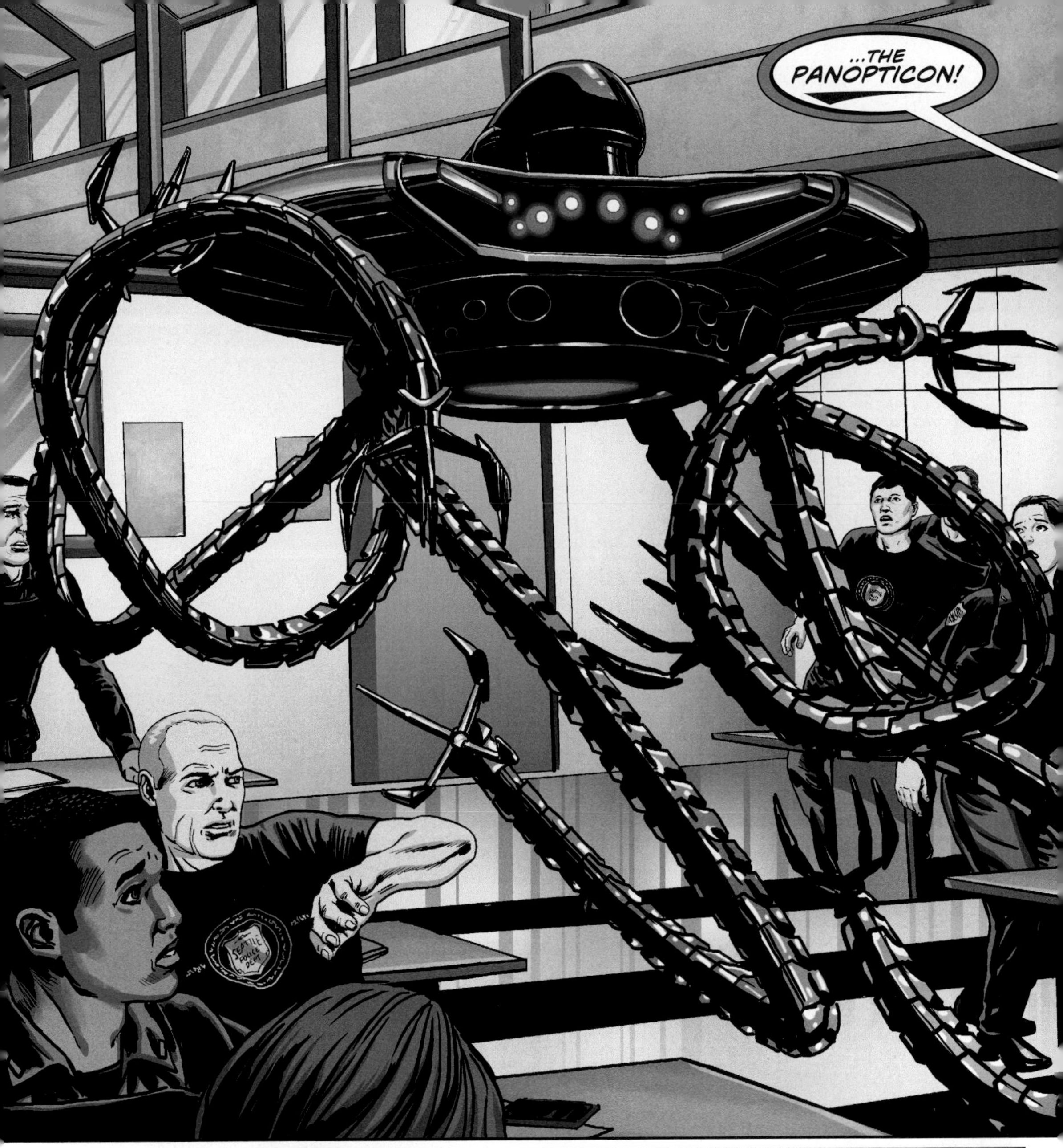
...THE PANOPTICON!
SEATTLE POLICE DEPT

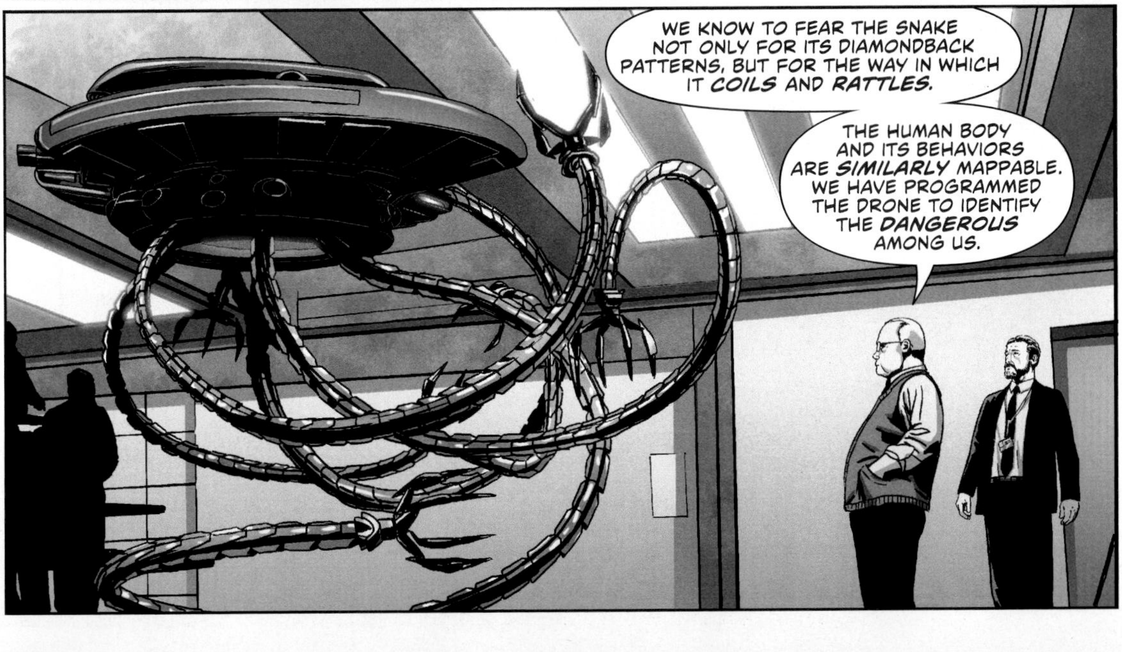
WE KNOW TO FEAR THE SNAKE NOT ONLY FOR ITS DIAMONDBACK PATTERNS, BUT FOR THE WAY IN WHICH IT COILS AND RATTLES.
THE HUMAN BODY AND ITS BEHAVIORS ARE SIMILARLY MAPPABLE. WE HAVE PROGRAMMED THE DRONE TO IDENTIFY THE DANGEROUS AMONG US.

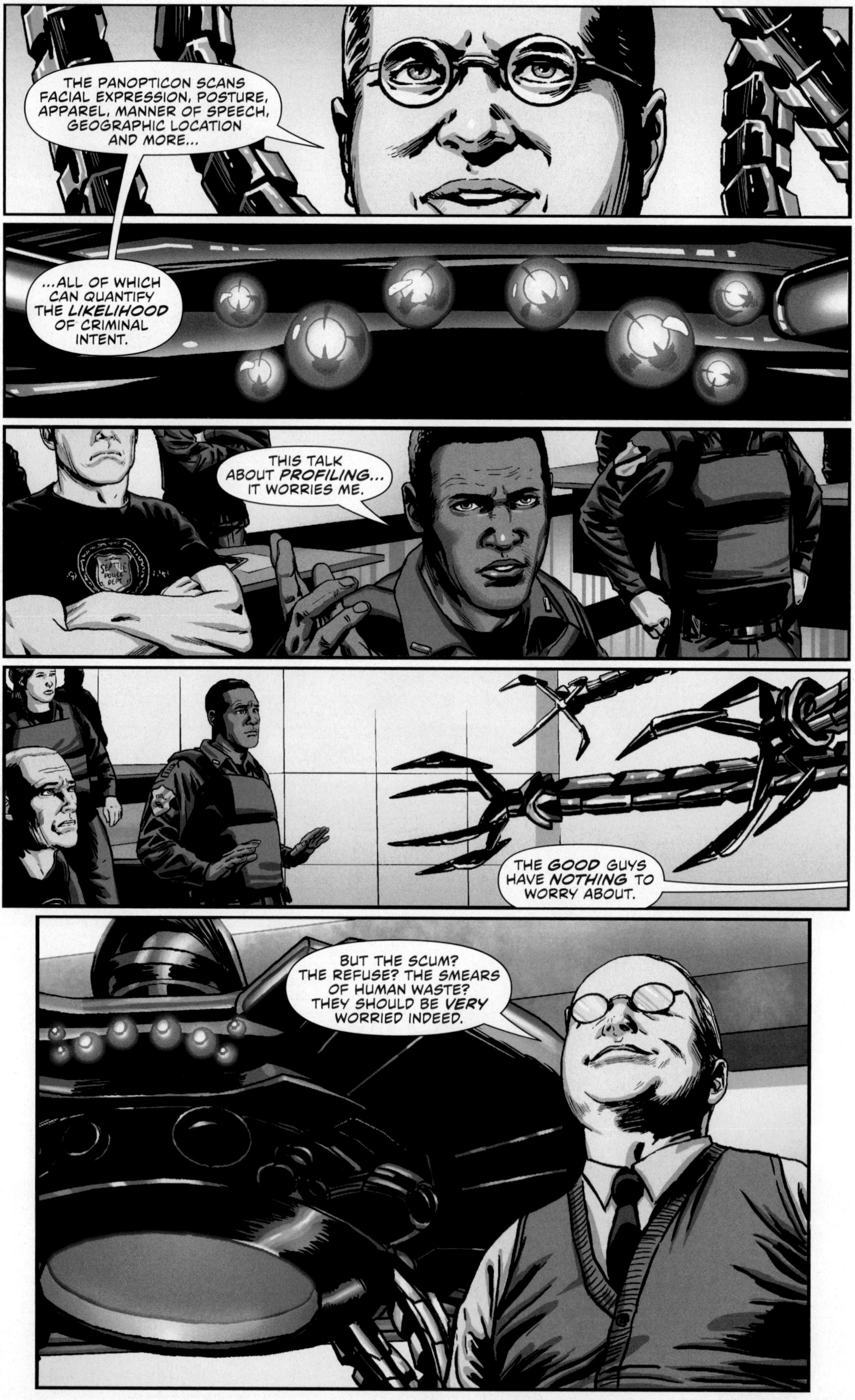
THE PANOPTICON SCANS FACIAL EXPRESSION, POSTURE, APPAREL, MANNER OF SPEECH, GEOGRAPHIC LOCATION AND MORE...
...ALL OF WHICH CAN QUANTIFY THE *LIKELIHOOD* OF CRIMINAL INTENT.
THIS TALK ABOUT *PROFILING...* IT WORRIES ME.
SEATTLE POLICE DEPT
THE *GOOD* GUYS HAVE *NOTHING* TO WORRY ABOUT.
BUT THE SCUM? THE REFUSE? THE SMEARS OF HUMAN WASTE? THEY SHOULD BE *VERY* WORRIED INDEED.

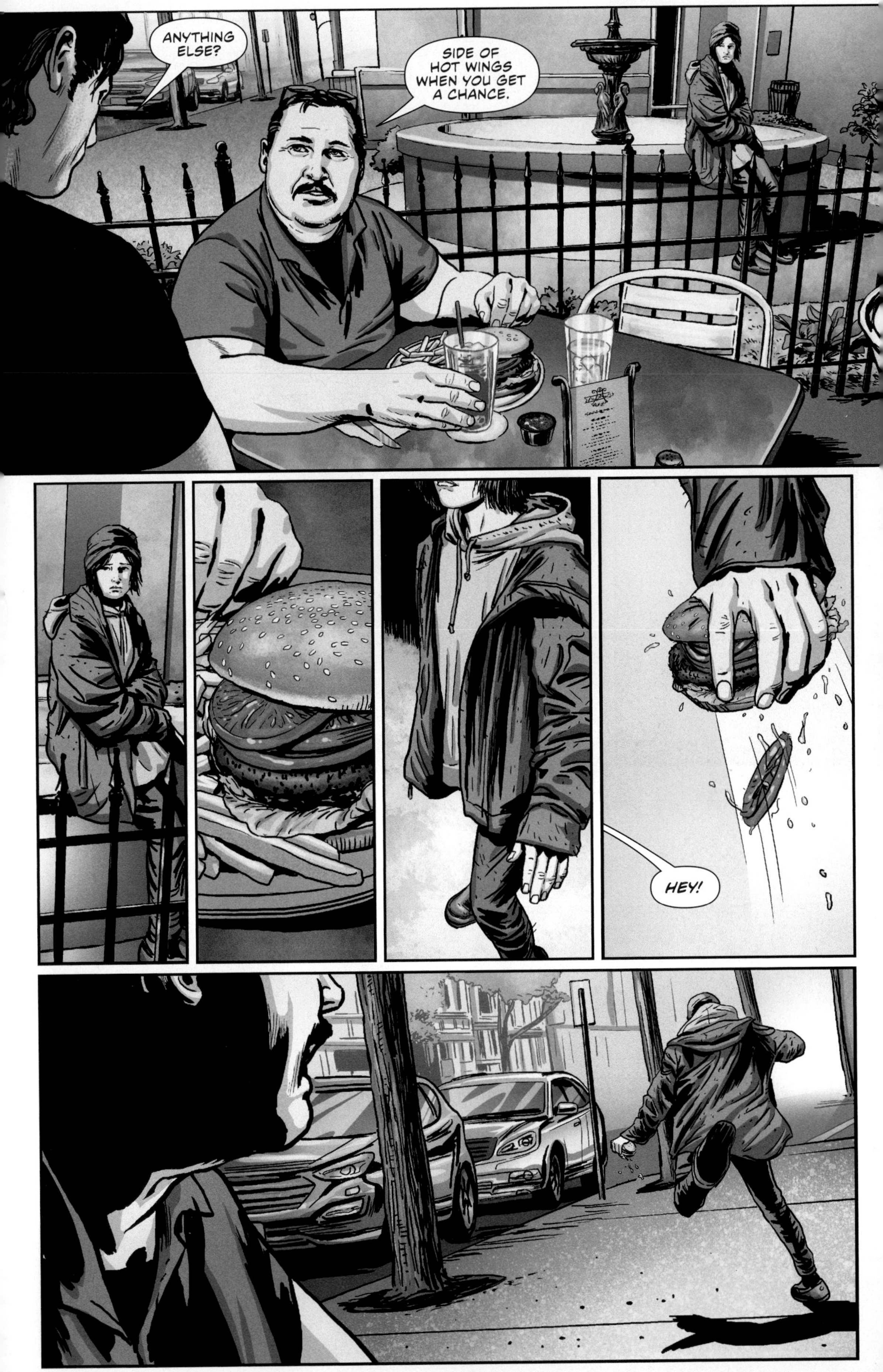
ANYTHING ELSE?
SIDE OF HOT WINGS WHEN YOU GET A CHANCE.
HEY!

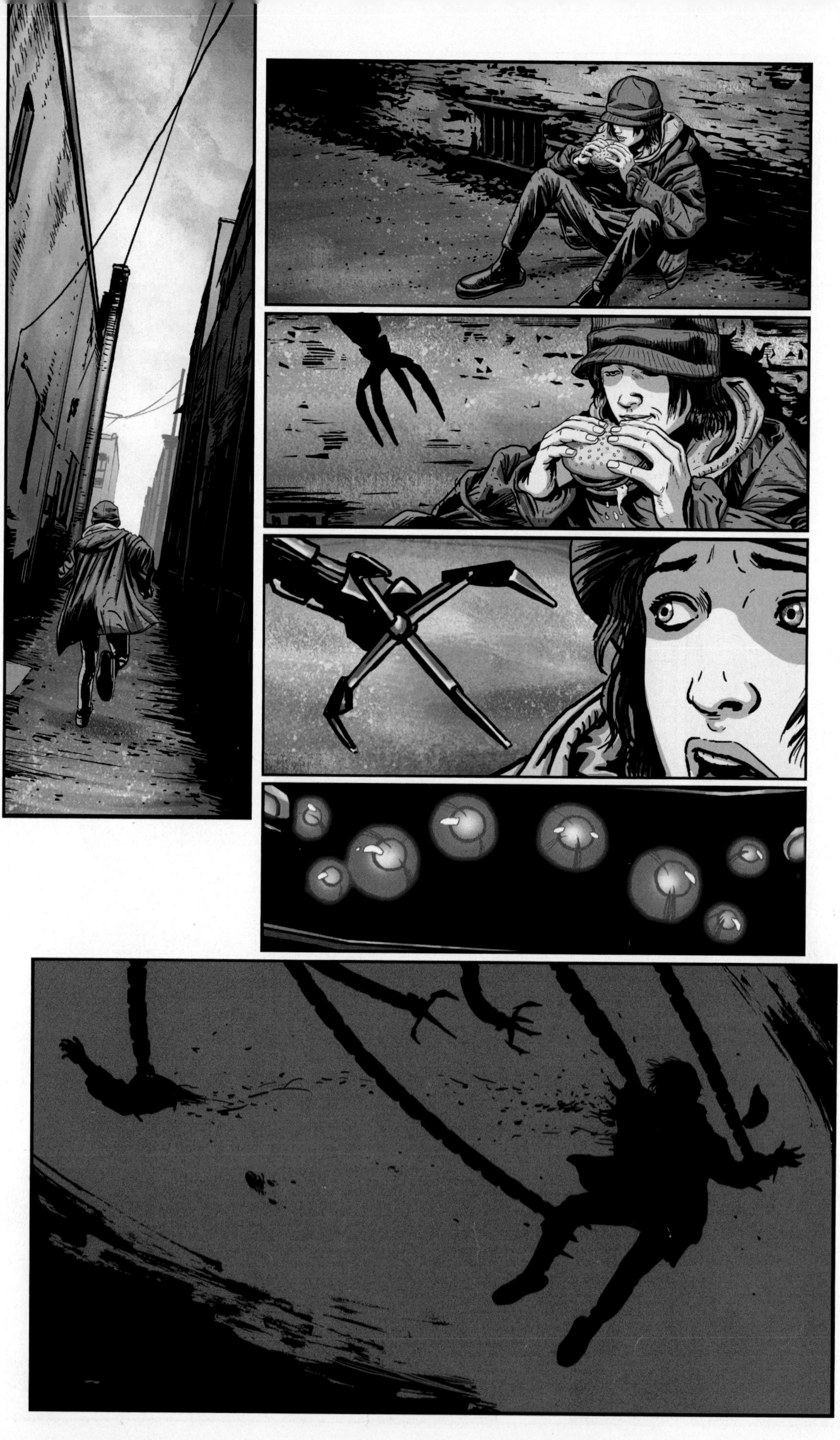

WHAT DOES THAT EVEN MEAN? "PANOPTICON"?

SOUNDS LIKE SOMETHING A HIGH-SCORING JERK WOULD SPELL ON *WORDS WITH FRIENDS.*

IT'S A PRISON CONCEPT DESIGNED BY AN 18th CENTURY PHILOSOPHER. DUH.

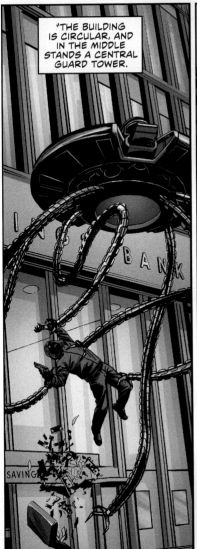

"THE BUILDING IS CIRCULAR, AND IN THE MIDDLE STANDS A CENTRAL GUARD TOWER.

BANK

SAVINGS

"THE TOWER IS SHIELDED IN SUCH A WAY THAT *NO ONE* CAN TELL WHEN A GUARD IS LOOKING AT THEIR CELL.

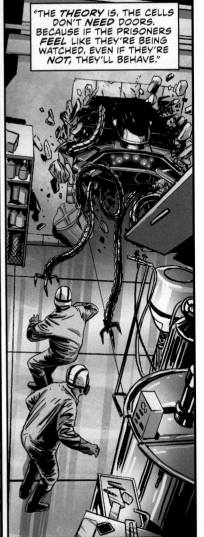

"THE *THEORY* IS, THE CELLS DON'T *NEED* DOORS. BECAUSE IF THE PRISONERS *FEEL* LIKE THEY'RE BEING WATCHED, EVEN IF THEY'RE *NOT,* THEY'LL BEHAVE."

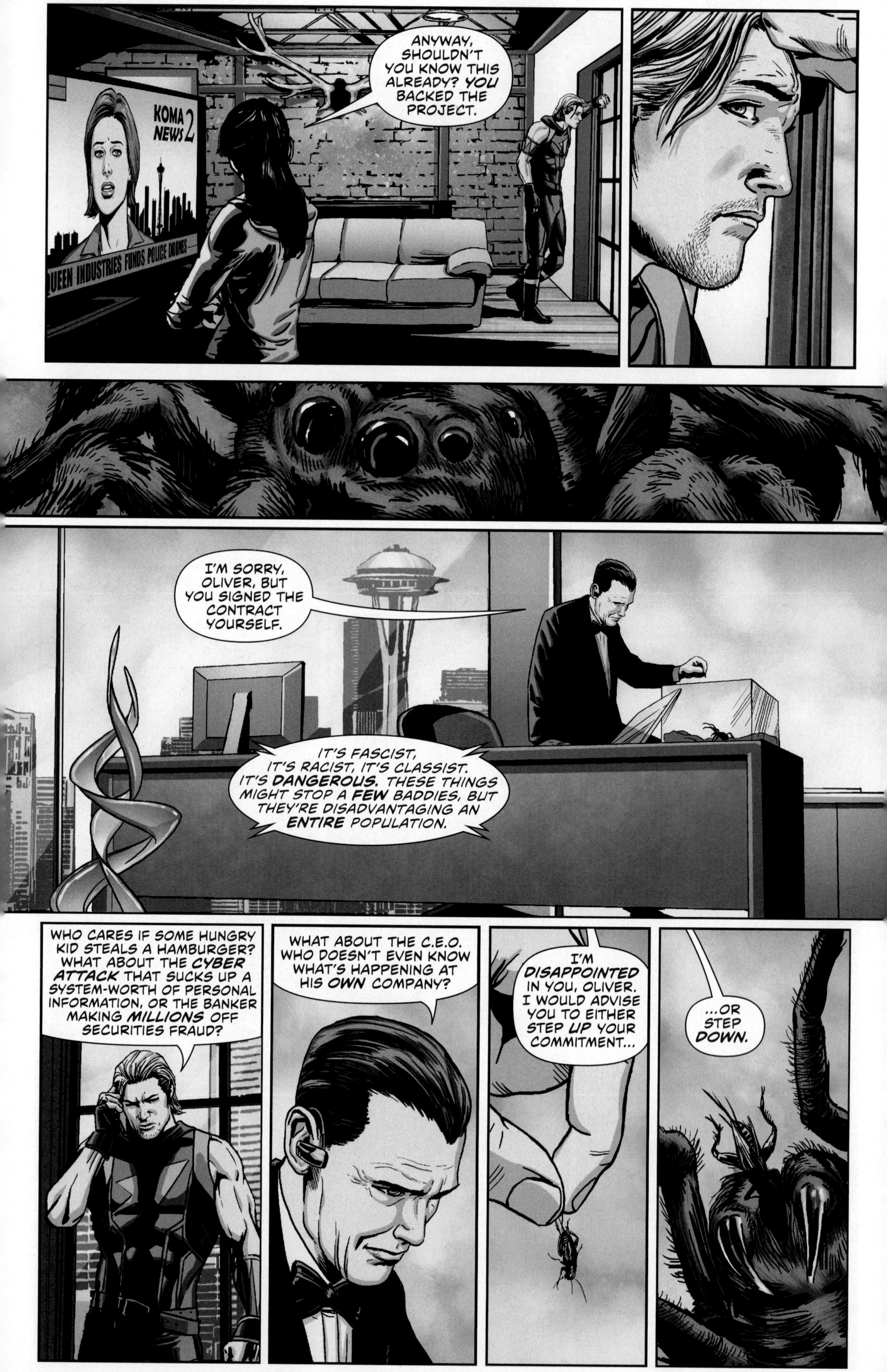
KOMA NEWS 2
QUEEN INDUSTRIES FUNDS POLICE DRONES
ANYWAY, SHOULDN'T YOU KNOW THIS ALREADY? YOU BACKED THE PROJECT.
I'M SORRY, OLIVER, BUT YOU SIGNED THE CONTRACT YOURSELF.
IT'S FASCIST, IT'S RACIST, IT'S CLASSIST. IT'S DANGEROUS. THESE THINGS MIGHT STOP A FEW BADDIES, BUT THEY'RE DISADVANTAGING AN ENTIRE POPULATION.
WHO CARES IF SOME HUNGRY KID STEALS A HAMBURGER? WHAT ABOUT THE CYBER ATTACK THAT SUCKS UP A SYSTEM-WORTH OF PERSONAL INFORMATION, OR THE BANKER MAKING MILLIONS OFF SECURITIES FRAUD?
WHAT ABOUT THE C.E.O. WHO DOESN'T EVEN KNOW WHAT'S HAPPENING AT HIS OWN COMPANY?
I'M DISAPPOINTED IN YOU, OLIVER. I WOULD ADVISE YOU TO EITHER STEP UP YOUR COMMITMENT...
...OR STEP DOWN.

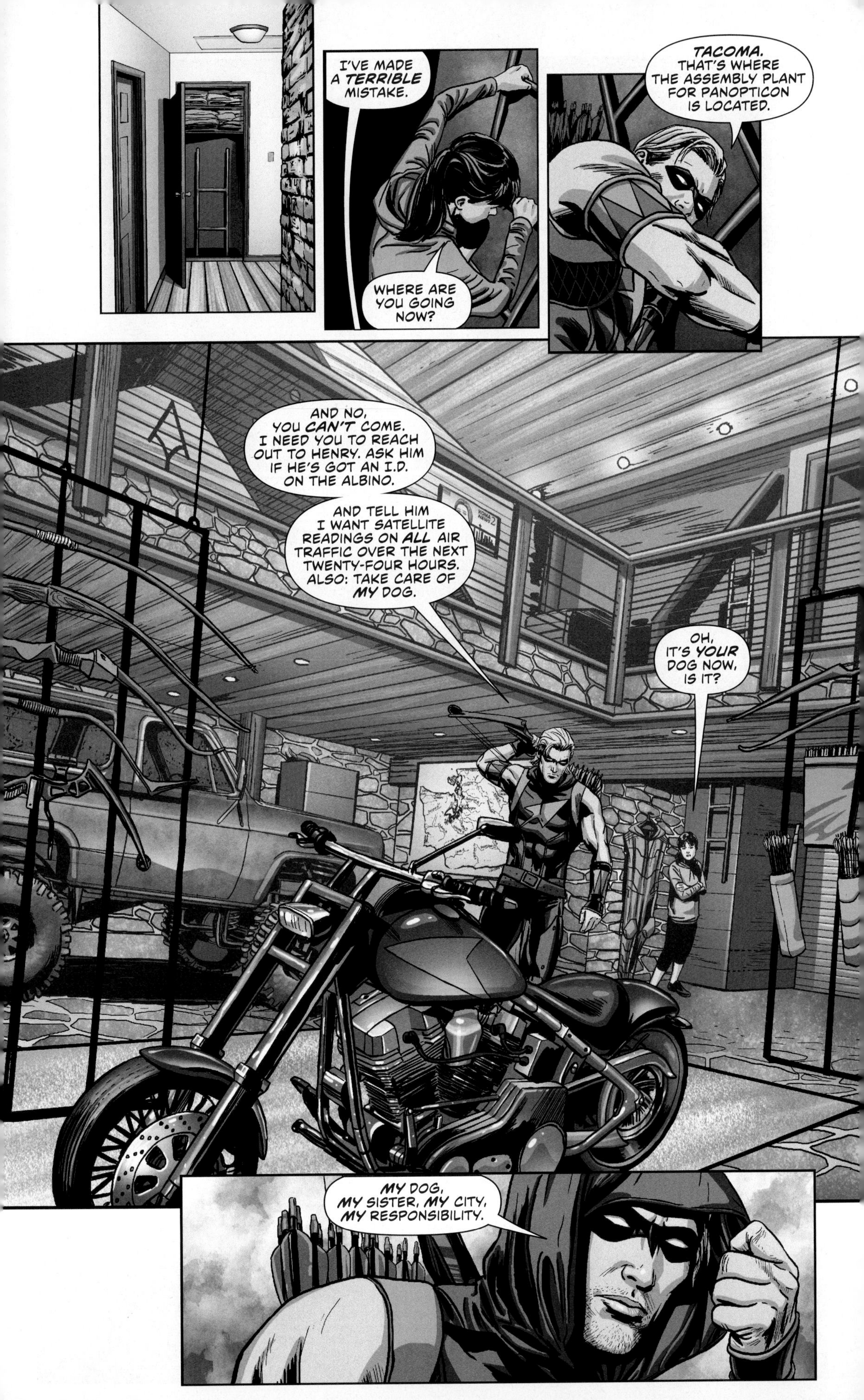

I'VE MADE A TERRIBLE MISTAKE.
WHERE ARE YOU GOING NOW?
TACOMA. THAT'S WHERE THE ASSEMBLY PLANT FOR PANOPTICON IS LOCATED.
AND NO, YOU CAN'T COME. I NEED YOU TO REACH OUT TO HENRY. ASK HIM IF HE'S GOT AN I.D. ON THE ALBINO.
AND TELL HIM I WANT SATELLITE READINGS ON ALL AIR TRAFFIC OVER THE NEXT TWENTY-FOUR HOURS. ALSO: TAKE CARE OF MY DOG.
OH, IT'S YOUR DOG NOW, IS IT?
MY DOG, MY SISTER, MY CITY, MY RESPONSIBILITY.

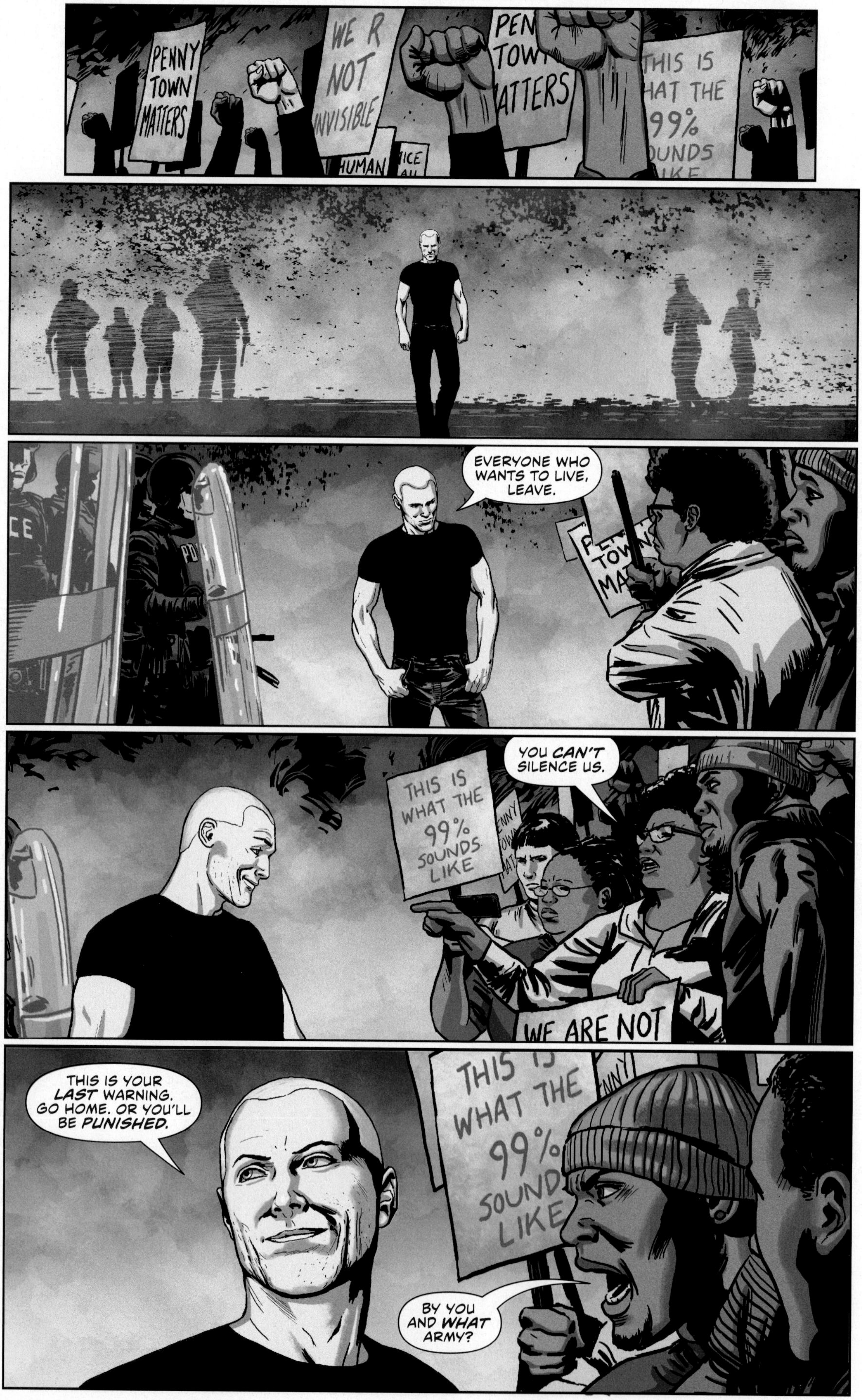
PENNY TOWN MATTERS
WE R NOT INVISIBLE
HUMAN
EVERYONE WHO WANTS TO LIVE, LEAVE.
THIS IS WHAT THE 99% SOUNDS LIKE
YOU *CAN'T* SILENCE US.
WE ARE NOT
THIS IS YOUR *LAST* WARNING. GO HOME. OR YOU'LL BE *PUNISHED*.
BY YOU AND *WHAT* ARMY?

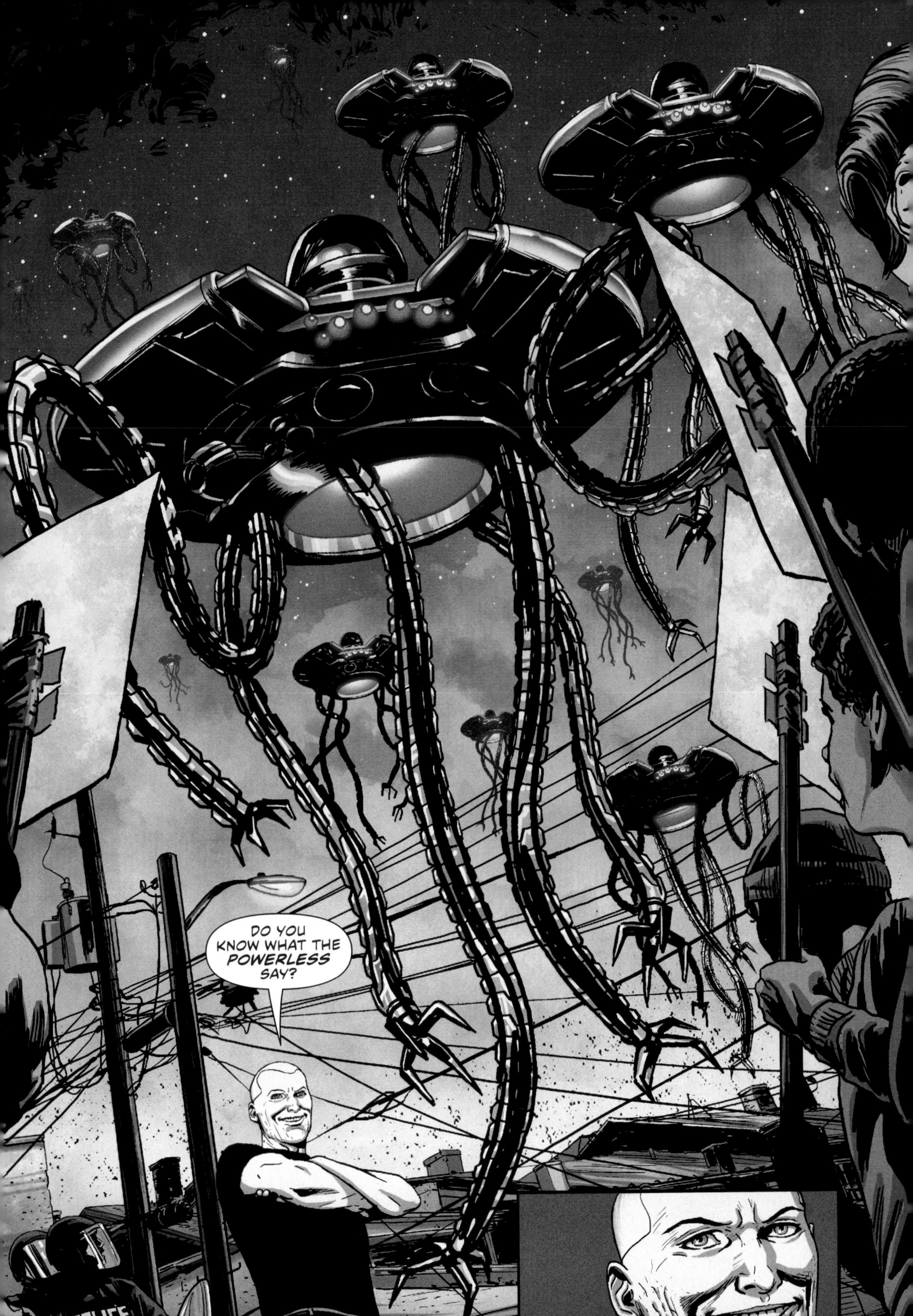
DO YOU KNOW WHAT THE POWERLESS SAY?
POLICE

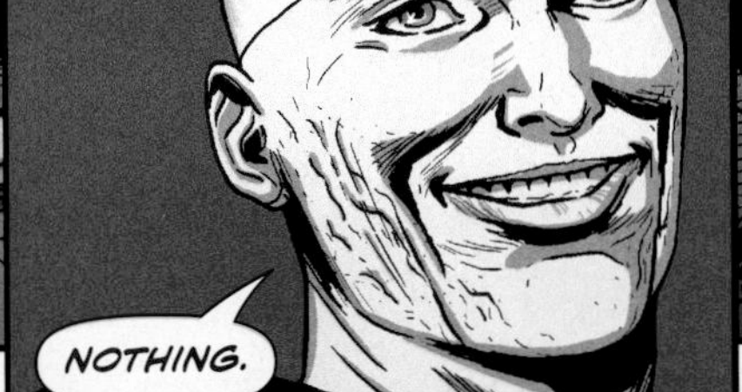
NOTHING.

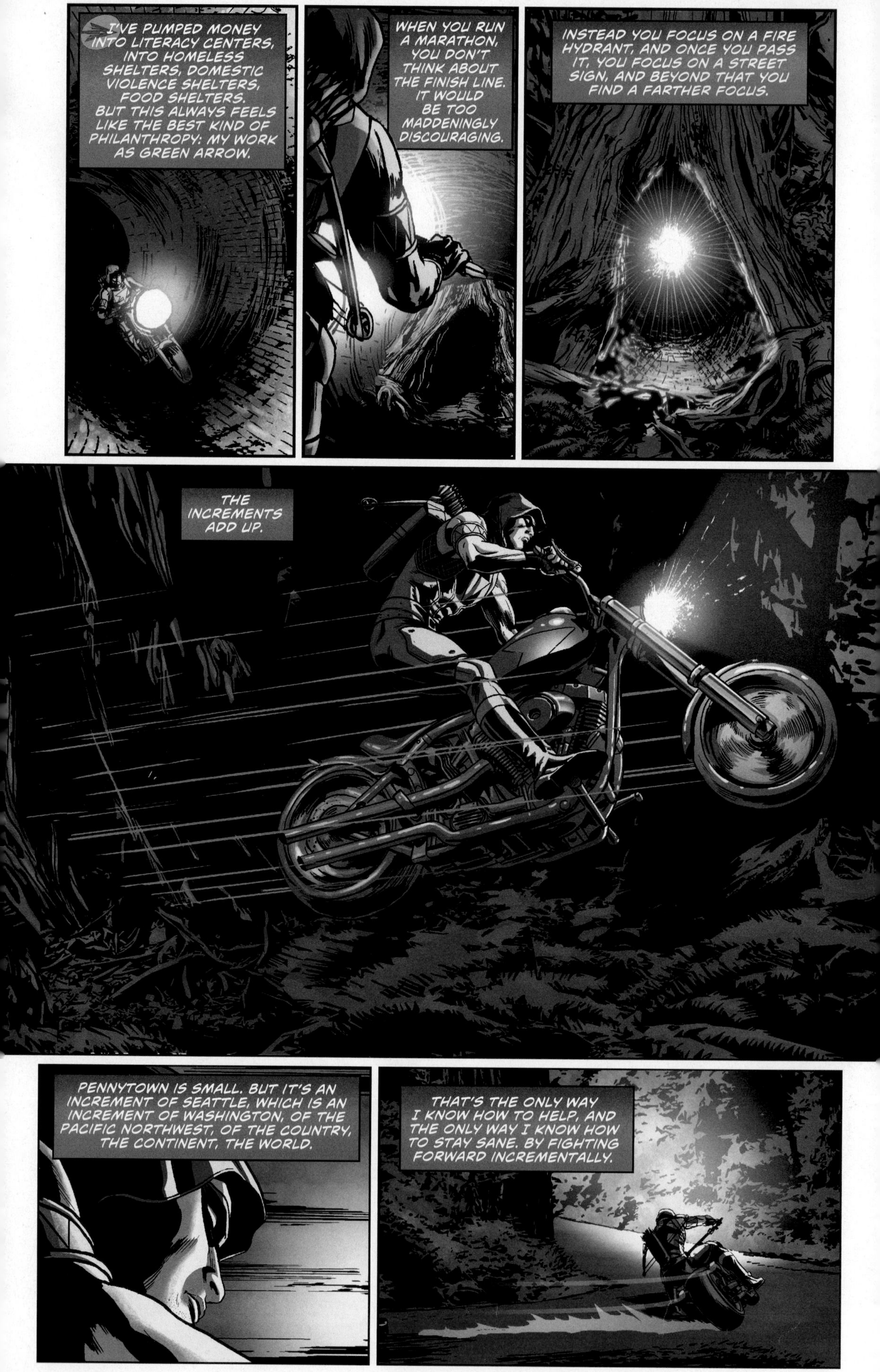
I'VE PUMPED MONEY INTO LITERACY CENTERS, INTO HOMELESS SHELTERS, DOMESTIC VIOLENCE SHELTERS, FOOD SHELTERS. BUT THIS ALWAYS FEELS LIKE THE BEST KIND OF PHILANTHROPY: MY WORK AS GREEN ARROW.
WHEN YOU RUN A MARATHON, YOU DON'T THINK ABOUT THE FINISH LINE. IT WOULD BE TOO MADDENINGLY DISCOURAGING.
INSTEAD YOU FOCUS ON A FIRE HYDRANT, AND ONCE YOU PASS IT, YOU FOCUS ON A STREET SIGN, AND BEYOND THAT YOU FIND A FARTHER FOCUS.
THE INCREMENTS ADD UP.
PENNYTOWN IS SMALL. BUT IT'S AN INCREMENT OF SEATTLE, WHICH IS AN INCREMENT OF WASHINGTON, OF THE PACIFIC NORTHWEST, OF THE COUNTRY, THE CONTINENT, THE WORLD.
THAT'S THE ONLY WAY I KNOW HOW TO HELP, AND THE ONLY WAY I KNOW HOW TO STAY SANE. BY FIGHTING FORWARD INCREMENTALLY.

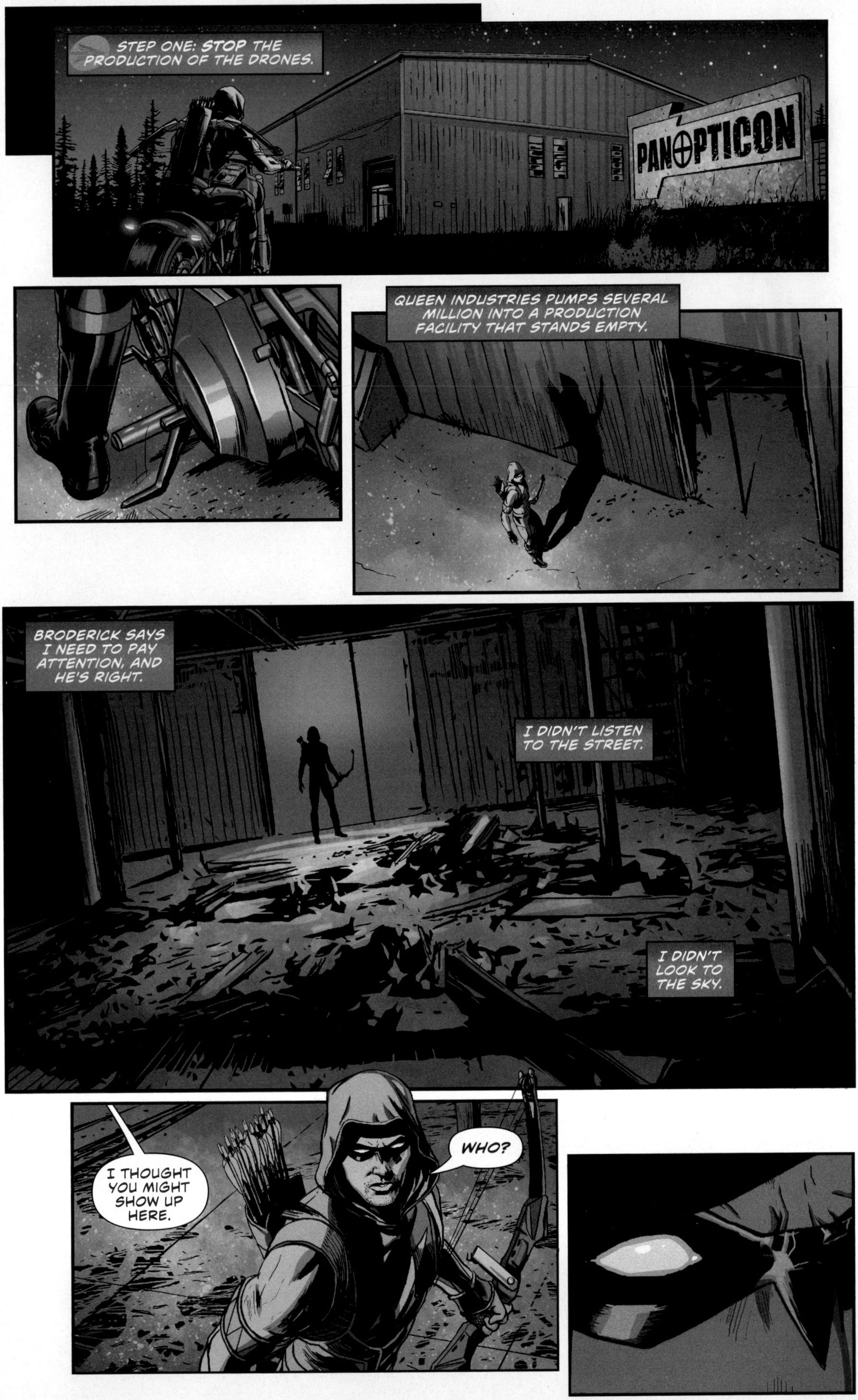

STEP ONE: STOP THE PRODUCTION OF THE DRONES.
PANOPTICON
QUEEN INDUSTRIES PUMPS SEVERAL MILLION INTO A PRODUCTION FACILITY THAT STANDS EMPTY.
BRODERICK SAYS I NEED TO PAY ATTENTION, AND HE'S RIGHT.
I DIDN'T LISTEN TO THE STREET.
I DIDN'T LOOK TO THE SKY.
I THOUGHT YOU MIGHT SHOW UP HERE.
WHO?

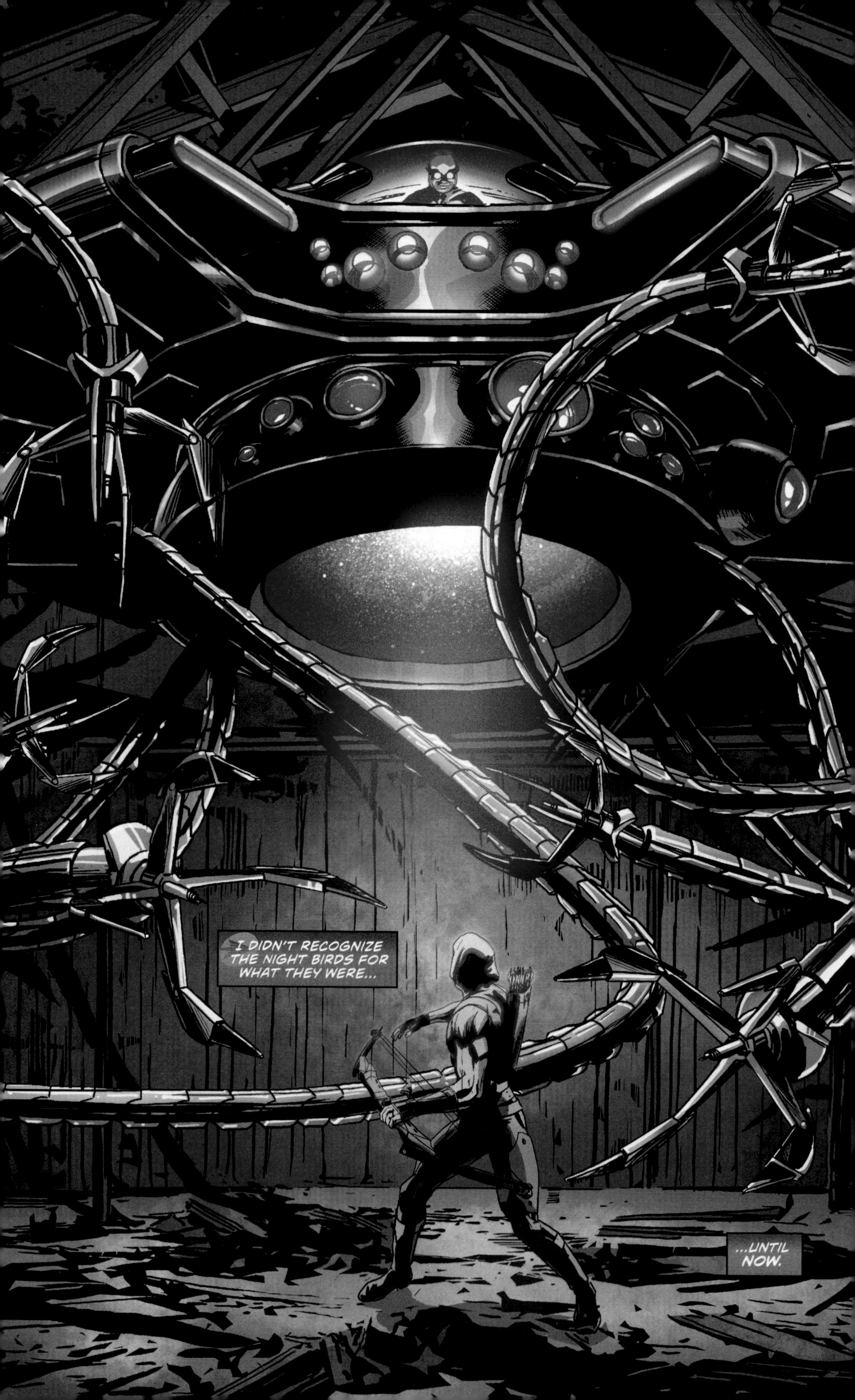
I DIDN'T RECOGNIZE THE NIGHT BIRDS FOR WHAT THEY WERE...
...UNTIL NOW.

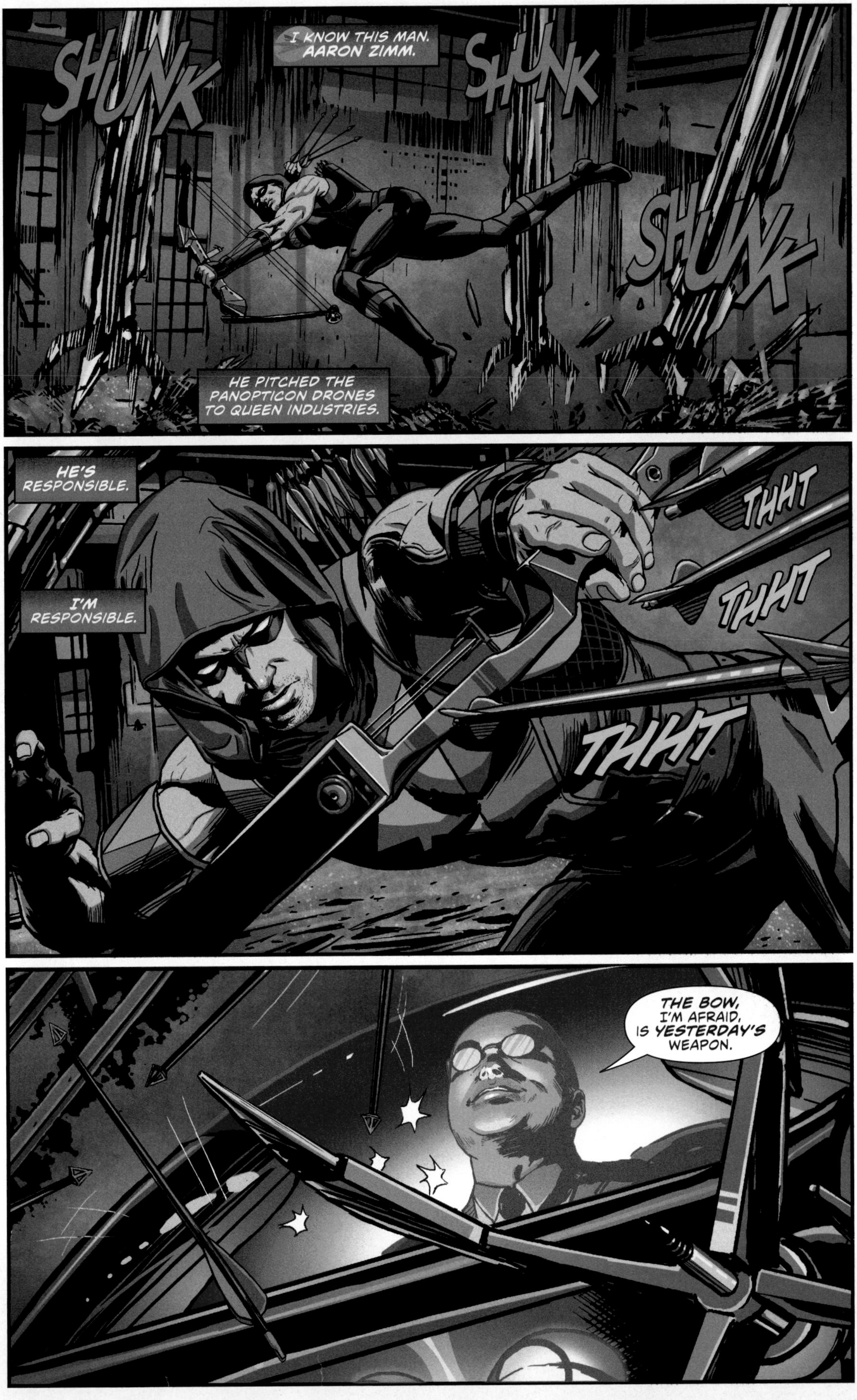

I KNOW THIS MAN. AARON ZIMM.
SHUNK
SHUNK
SHUNK
HE PITCHED THE PANOPTICON DRONES TO QUEEN INDUSTRIES.
HE'S RESPONSIBLE.
I'M RESPONSIBLE.
THHT
THHT
THHT
THE BOW, I'M AFRAID, IS YESTERDAY'S WEAPON.

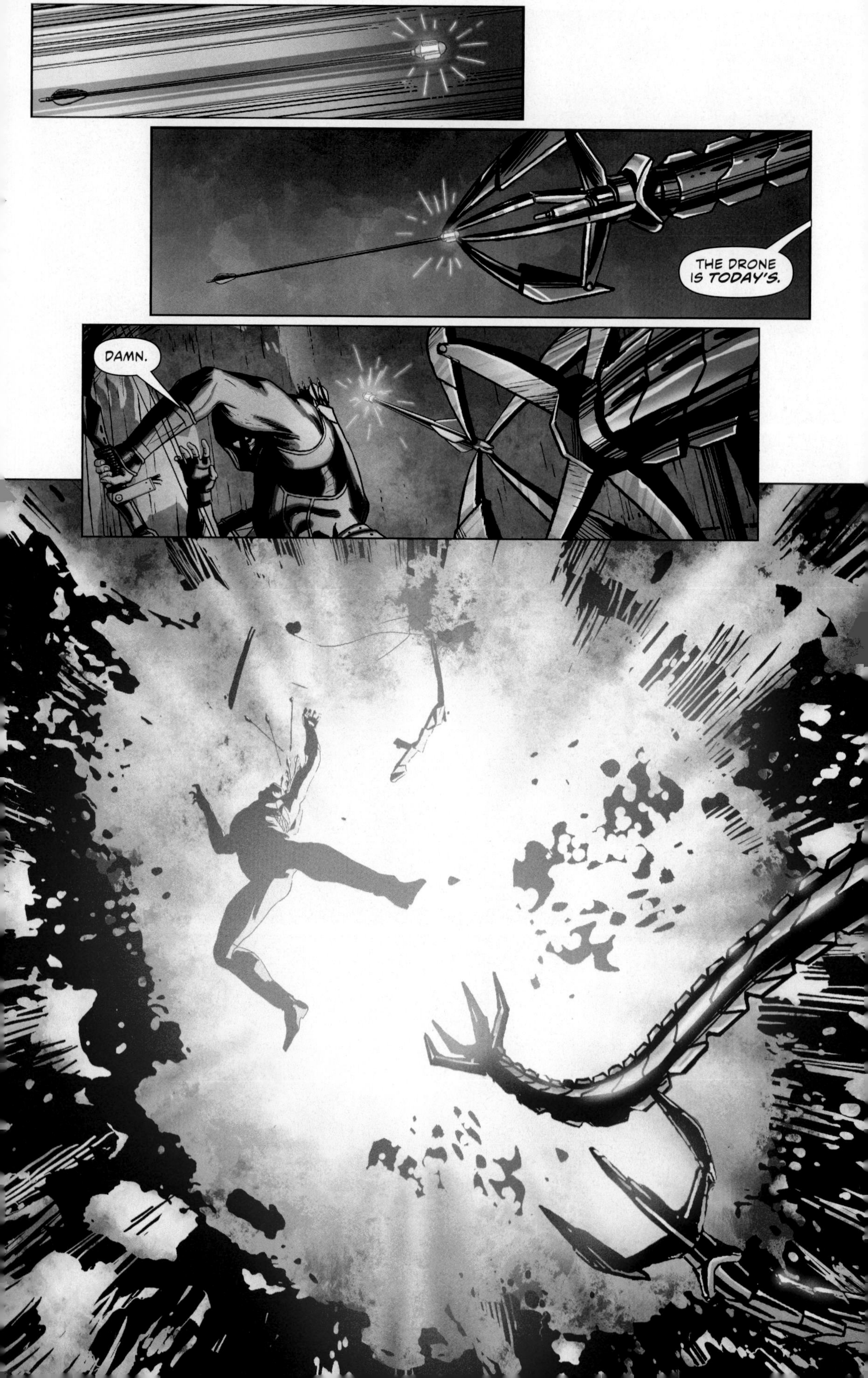
THE DRONE IS TODAY'S.
DAMN.

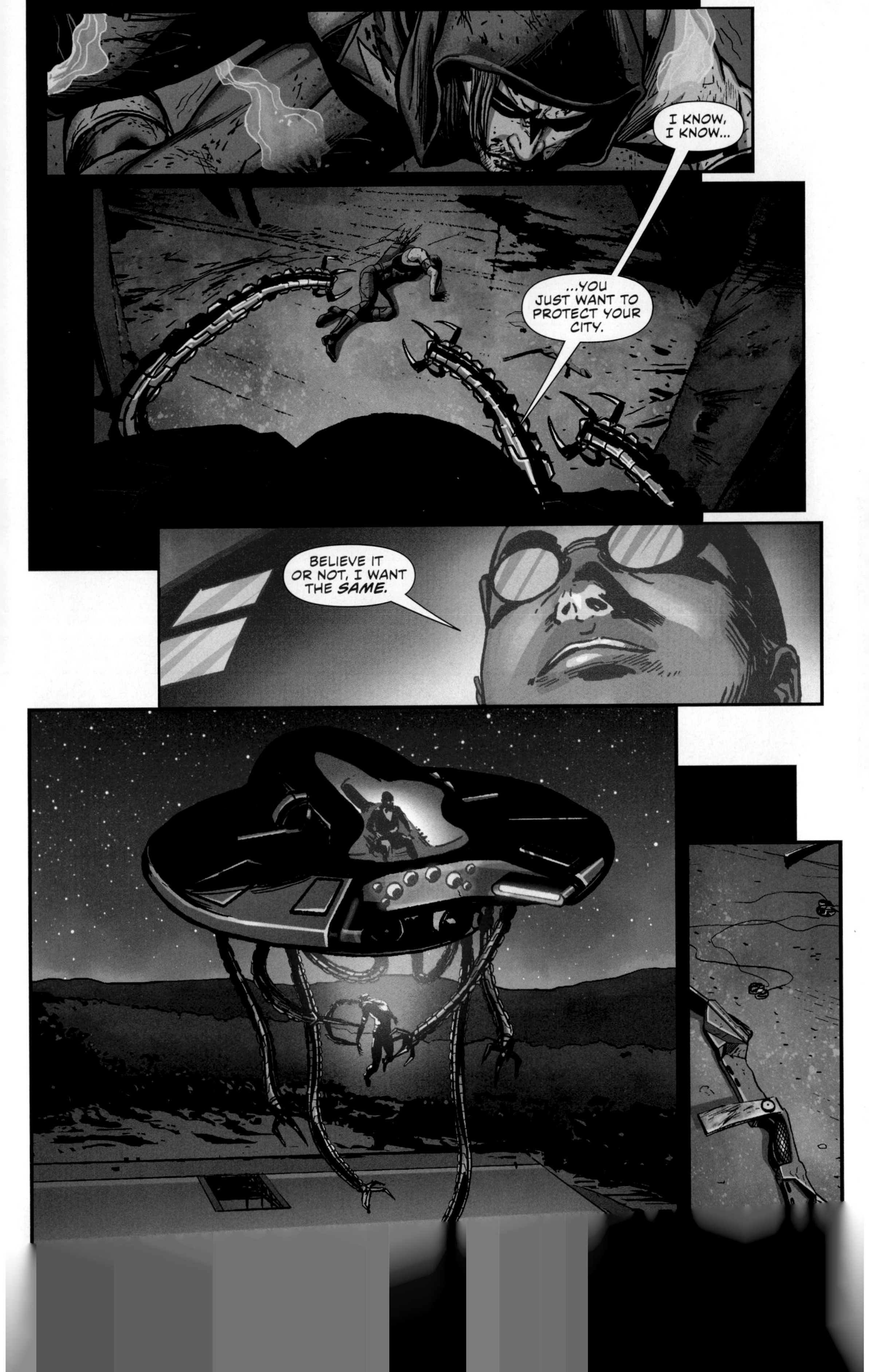

I KNOW, I KNOW...
...YOU JUST WANT TO PROTECT YOUR CITY.
BELIEVE IT OR NOT, I WANT THE SAME.

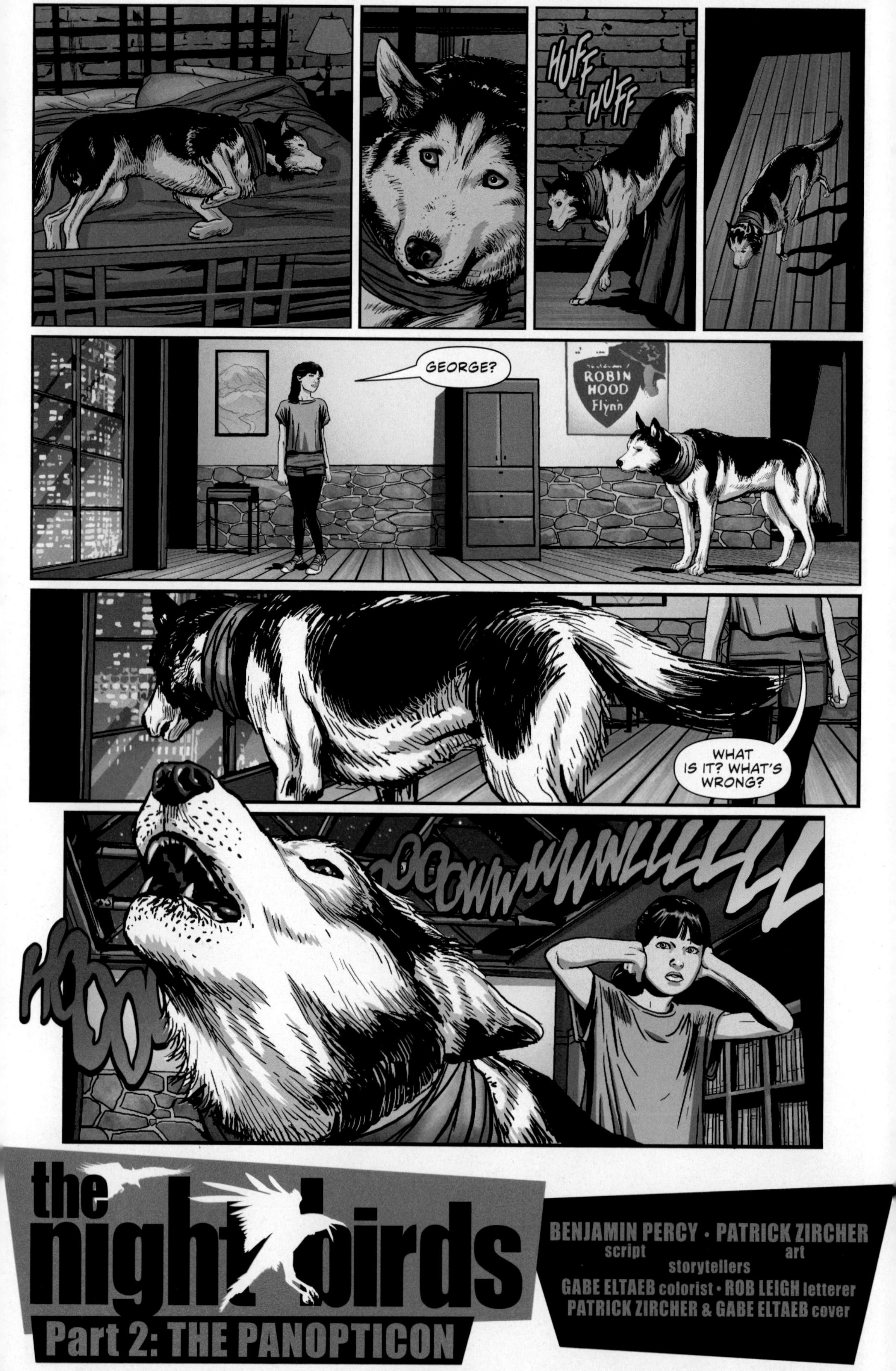

HUFF
HUFF
GEORGE?
ROBIN HOOD Flynn
WHAT IS IT? WHAT'S WRONG?
HOOO
OOOWWWWWLLLLLLLL

the night birds

Part 2: THE PANOPTICON

BENJAMIN PERCY script · PATRICK ZIRCHER art
storytellers
GABE ELTAEB colorist · ROB LEIGH letterer
PATRICK ZIRCHER & GABE ELTAEB cover

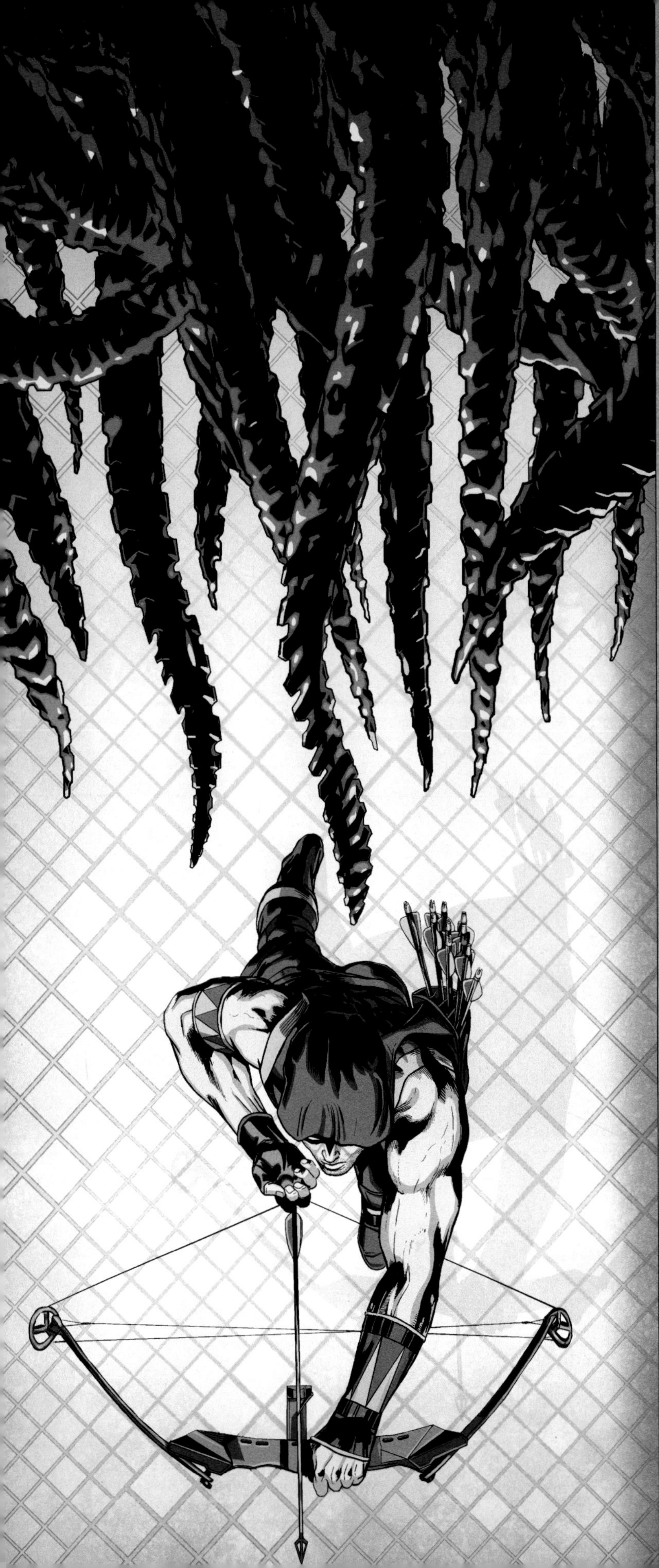

WHEN NIGHTBIRDS GATHER

INVISIBILITY IS
AN ILLUSION.

SOMEONE'S
ALWAYS
WATCHING.

Annaya Youkai repeated
Adam P. Knave //adampknave - 4hr
What year is this, 1984? *Orwell *Pennytown
> << 14 ♥ 31

EVERYTHING
IS RECORDED.

Schizorabbit1 //schizorabbit1 -1hr
Green Arrow MIA or AWOL or DOA?
*Seattle needs you.
> << 35 ♥ 42

Nelson Blake II //nelsonblake2 - 1hr
Check out this vid of drone assault: bit.ly/3AMngXj
*Pennytown is bleeding.
View video
♥ 231

KOMA
NEWS 2

NOTHING IS
NOT SEEN.

PROPERTY DAMAGE IN THE MILLIONS AFTER PROTEST

10:16 am

The Seattle TIMES

AND THE MANNER IN WHICH
YOU ARE SEEN IS A WEAPON.
A COMMERCIAL OR SEXUAL OR
POLITICAL OR CRIMINAL WEAPON.

Riots Result in Five-Alarm Fire

Pennytown residents clash with Seattle Police over the use of new drones

By Andrew Scott
August 5

Fires continue to burn in the Pennytown neighborhood of Seattle after, at approximately 8:10 pm, Residents reacted to the conflict with

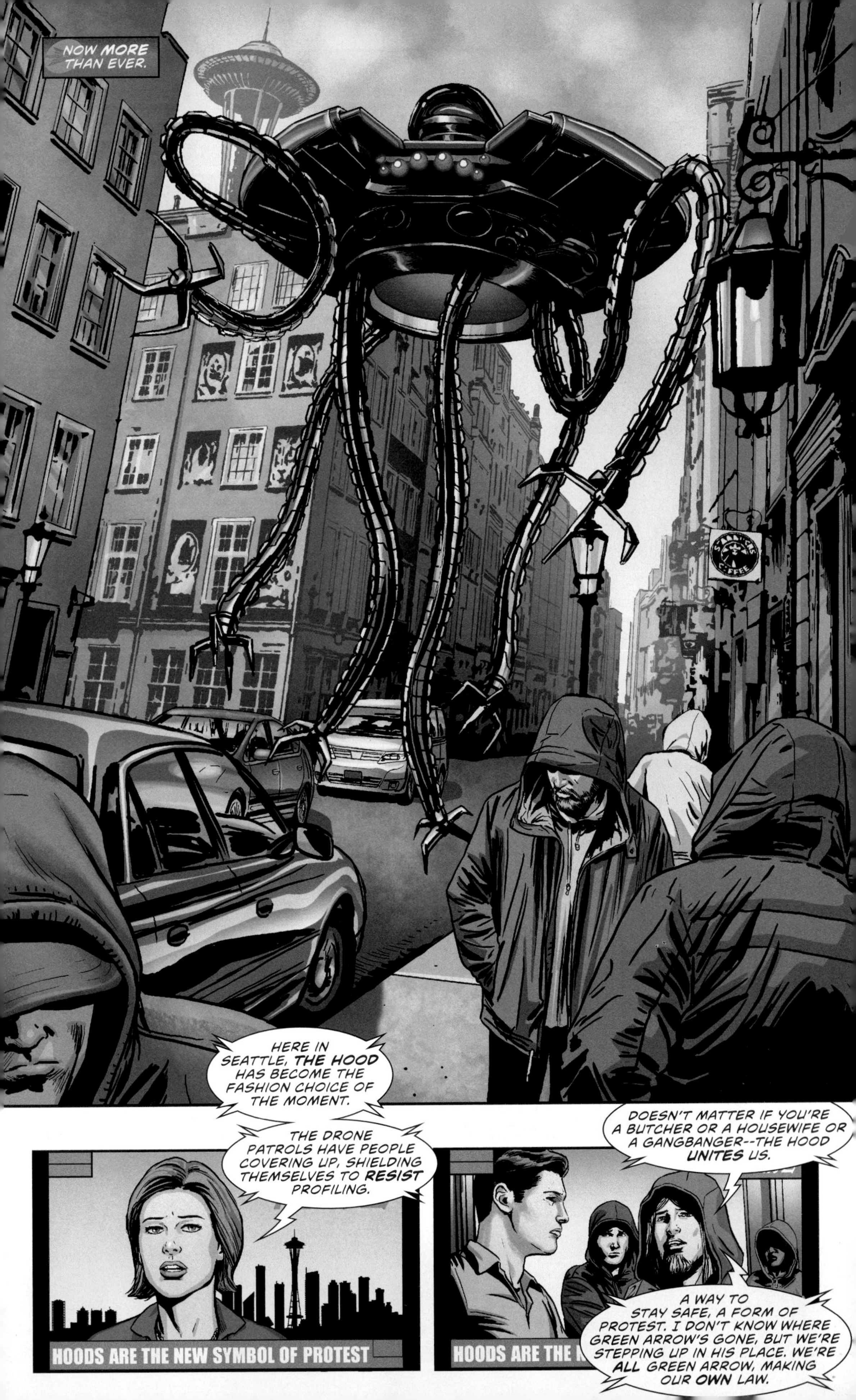
NOW MORE THAN EVER.
HERE IN SEATTLE, THE HOOD HAS BECOME THE FASHION CHOICE OF THE MOMENT.
THE DRONE PATROLS HAVE PEOPLE COVERING UP, SHIELDING THEMSELVES TO RESIST PROFILING.
HOODS ARE THE NEW SYMBOL OF PROTEST
DOESN'T MATTER IF YOU'RE A BUTCHER OR A HOUSEWIFE OR A GANGBANGER--THE HOOD UNITES US.
A WAY TO STAY SAFE, A FORM OF PROTEST. I DON'T KNOW WHERE GREEN ARROW'S GONE, BUT WE'RE STEPPING UP IN HIS PLACE. WE'RE ALL GREEN ARROW, MAKING OUR OWN LAW.
HOODS ARE THE N

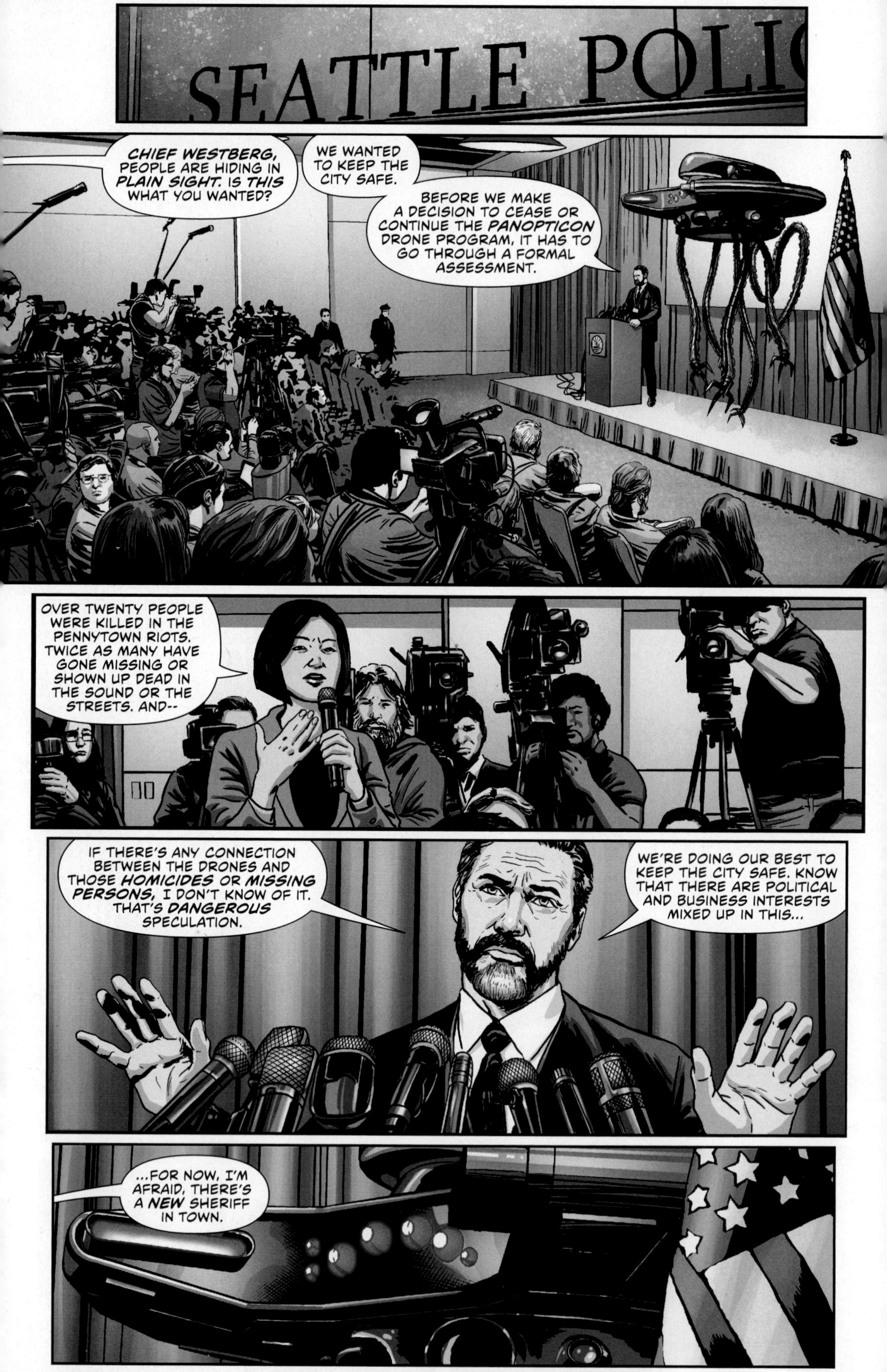
SEATTLE POLI
CHIEF WESTBERG, PEOPLE ARE HIDING IN PLAIN SIGHT. IS THIS WHAT YOU WANTED?
WE WANTED TO KEEP THE CITY SAFE.
BEFORE WE MAKE A DECISION TO CEASE OR CONTINUE THE PANOPTICON DRONE PROGRAM, IT HAS TO GO THROUGH A FORMAL ASSESSMENT.
OVER TWENTY PEOPLE WERE KILLED IN THE PENNYTOWN RIOTS. TWICE AS MANY HAVE GONE MISSING OR SHOWN UP DEAD IN THE SOUND OR THE STREETS. AND--
IF THERE'S ANY CONNECTION BETWEEN THE DRONES AND THOSE HOMICIDES OR MISSING PERSONS, I DON'T KNOW OF IT. THAT'S DANGEROUS SPECULATION.
WE'RE DOING OUR BEST TO KEEP THE CITY SAFE. KNOW THAT THERE ARE POLITICAL AND BUSINESS INTERESTS MIXED UP IN THIS...
...FOR NOW, I'M AFRAID, THERE'S A NEW SHERIFF IN TOWN.

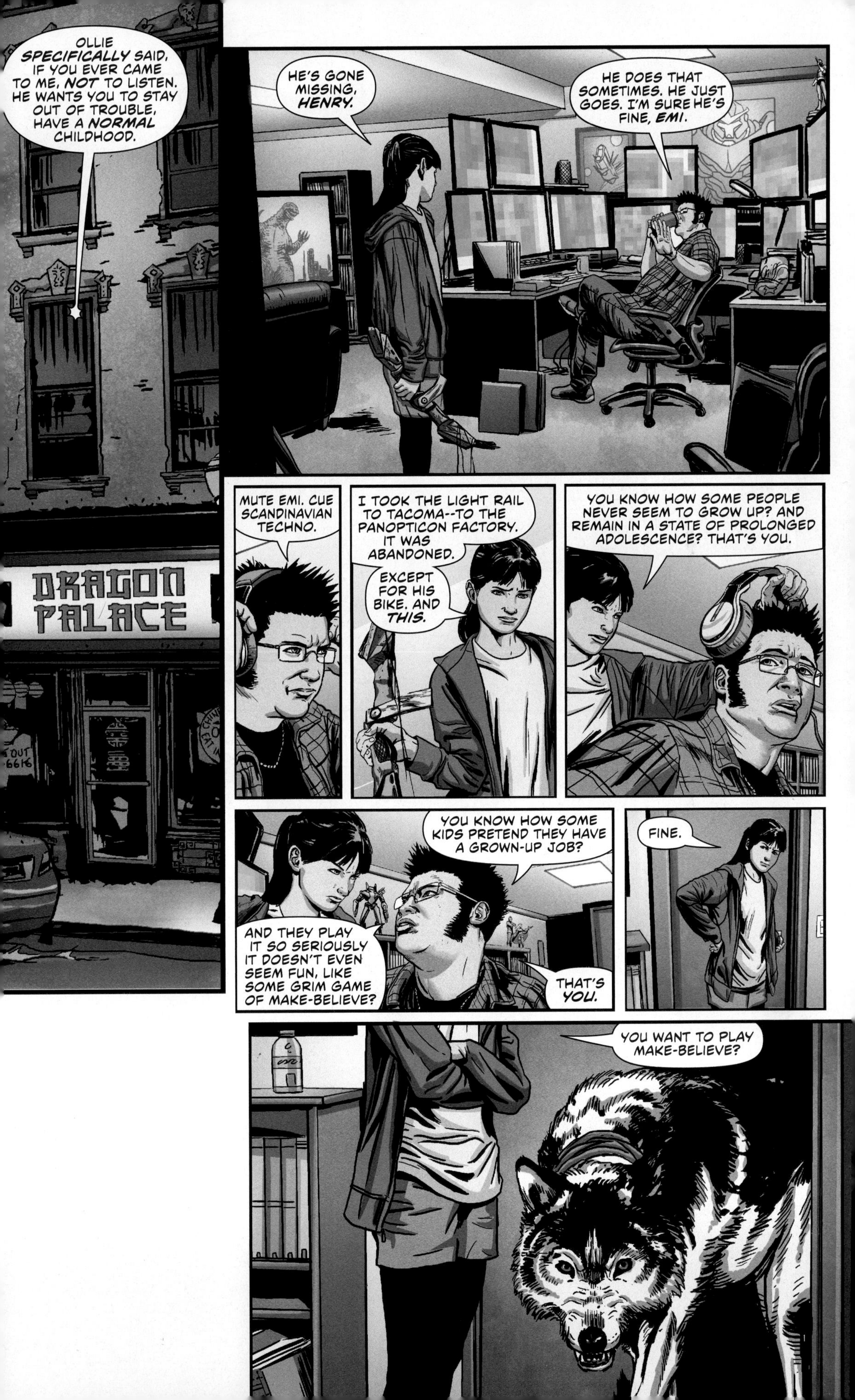
OLLIE SPECIFICALLY SAID, IF YOU EVER CAME TO ME, NOT TO LISTEN. HE WANTS YOU TO STAY OUT OF TROUBLE, HAVE A NORMAL CHILDHOOD.
DRAGON PALACE
HE'S GONE MISSING, HENRY.
HE DOES THAT SOMETIMES. HE JUST GOES. I'M SURE HE'S FINE, EMI.
MUTE EMI. CUE SCANDINAVIAN TECHNO.
I TOOK THE LIGHT RAIL TO TACOMA--TO THE PANOPTICON FACTORY. IT WAS ABANDONED.
EXCEPT FOR HIS BIKE. AND THIS.
YOU KNOW HOW SOME PEOPLE NEVER SEEM TO GROW UP? AND REMAIN IN A STATE OF PROLONGED ADOLESCENCE? THAT'S YOU.
YOU KNOW HOW SOME KIDS PRETEND THEY HAVE A GROWN-UP JOB?
AND THEY PLAY IT SO SERIOUSLY IT DOESN'T EVEN SEEM FUN, LIKE SOME GRIM GAME OF MAKE-BELIEVE?
THAT'S YOU.
FINE.
YOU WANT TO PLAY MAKE-BELIEVE?

MEET THE BIG BAD WOLF.

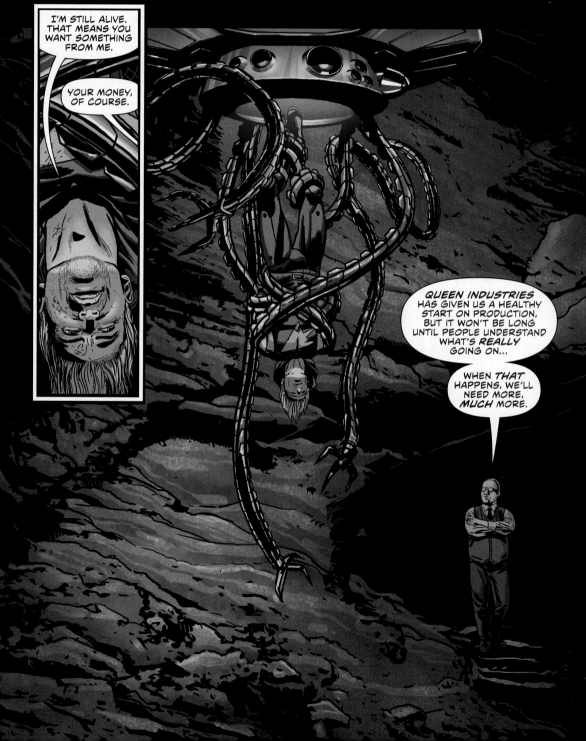

I'M STILL ALIVE. THAT MEANS YOU WANT SOMETHING FROM ME.

YOUR MONEY, OF COURSE.

QUEEN INDUSTRIES HAS GIVEN US A HEALTHY START ON PRODUCTION, BUT IT WON'T BE LONG UNTIL PEOPLE UNDERSTAND WHAT'S *REALLY* GOING ON...

WHEN *THAT* HAPPENS, WE'LL NEED MORE, *MUCH* MORE.

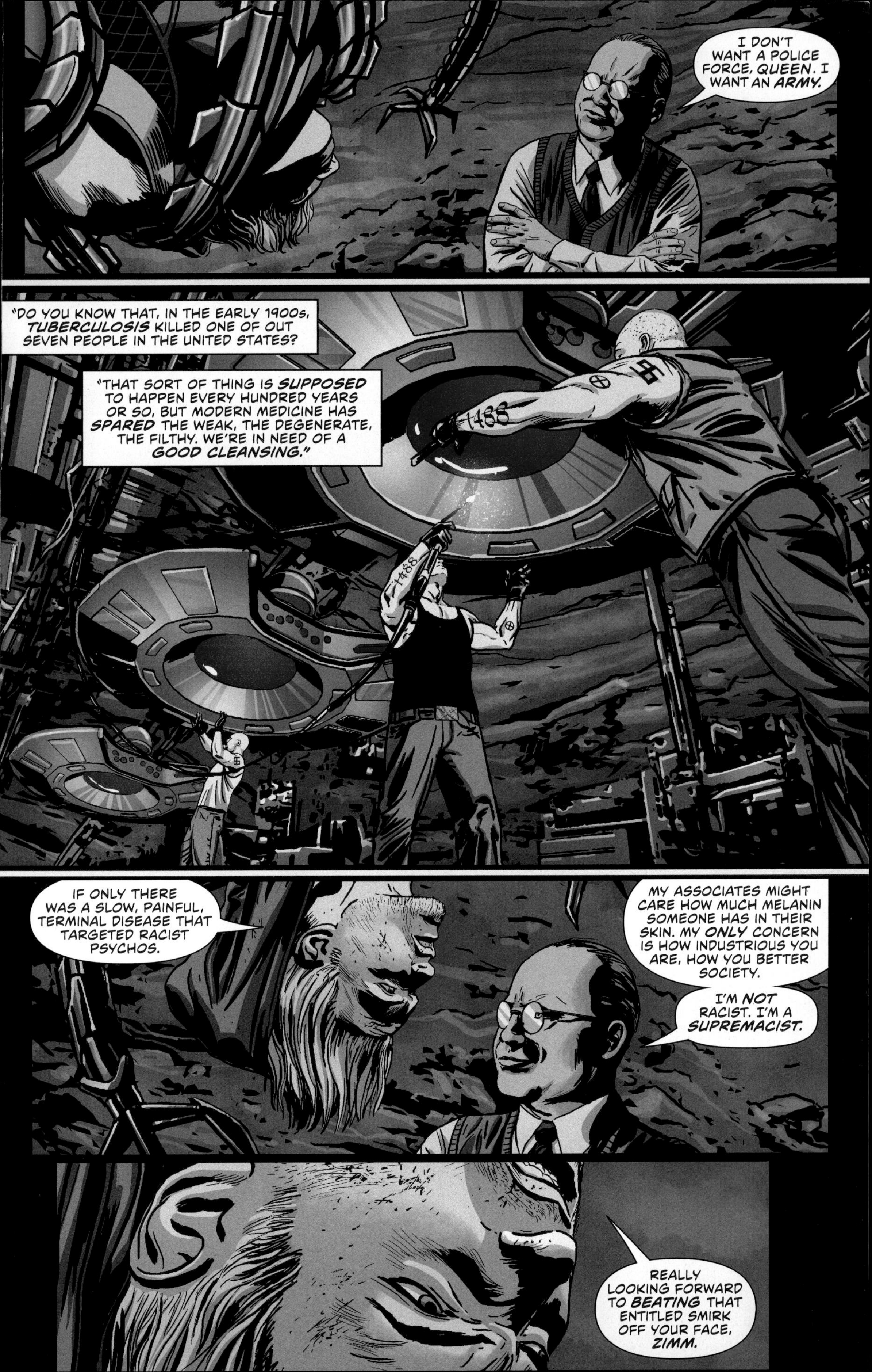
I DON'T WANT A POLICE FORCE, QUEEN. I WANT AN ARMY.
"DO YOU KNOW THAT, IN THE EARLY 1900s, TUBERCULOSIS KILLED ONE OF OUT SEVEN PEOPLE IN THE UNITED STATES?
"THAT SORT OF THING IS SUPPOSED TO HAPPEN EVERY HUNDRED YEARS OR SO, BUT MODERN MEDICINE HAS SPARED THE WEAK, THE DEGENERATE, THE FILTHY. WE'RE IN NEED OF A GOOD CLEANSING."
IF ONLY THERE WAS A SLOW, PAINFUL, TERMINAL DISEASE THAT TARGETED RACIST PSYCHOS.
MY ASSOCIATES MIGHT CARE HOW MUCH MELANIN SOMEONE HAS IN THEIR SKIN. MY ONLY CONCERN IS HOW INDUSTRIOUS YOU ARE, HOW YOU BETTER SOCIETY.
I'M NOT RACIST. I'M A SUPREMACIST.
REALLY LOOKING FORWARD TO BEATING THAT ENTITLED SMIRK OFF YOUR FACE, ZIMM.

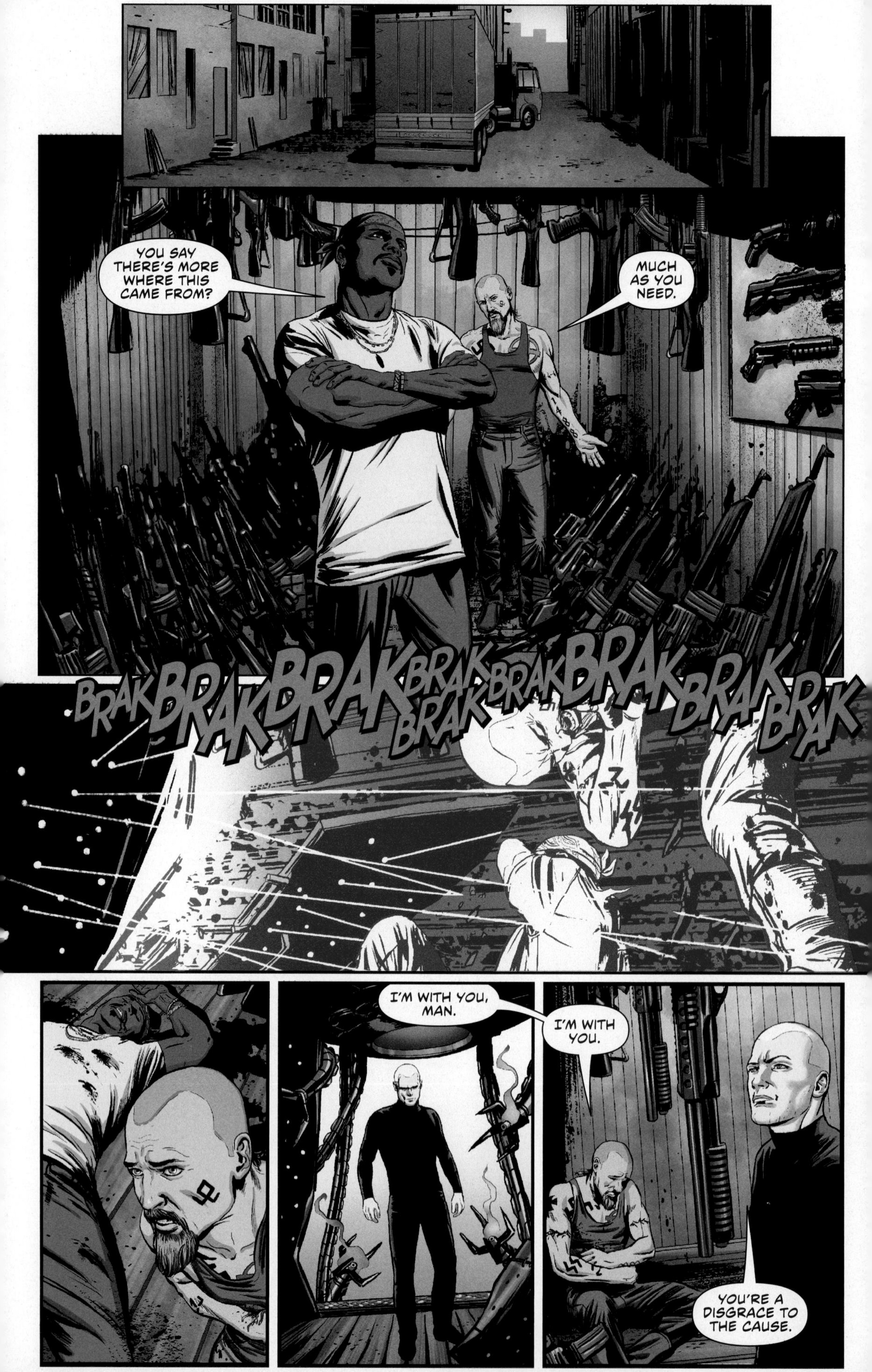
YOU SAY THERE'S MORE WHERE THIS CAME FROM?
MUCH AS YOU NEED.
BRAK BRAK BRAK BRAK BRAK BRAK BRAK BRAK BRAK BRAK
I'M WITH YOU, MAN.
I'M WITH YOU.
YOU'RE A DISGRACE TO THE CAUSE.

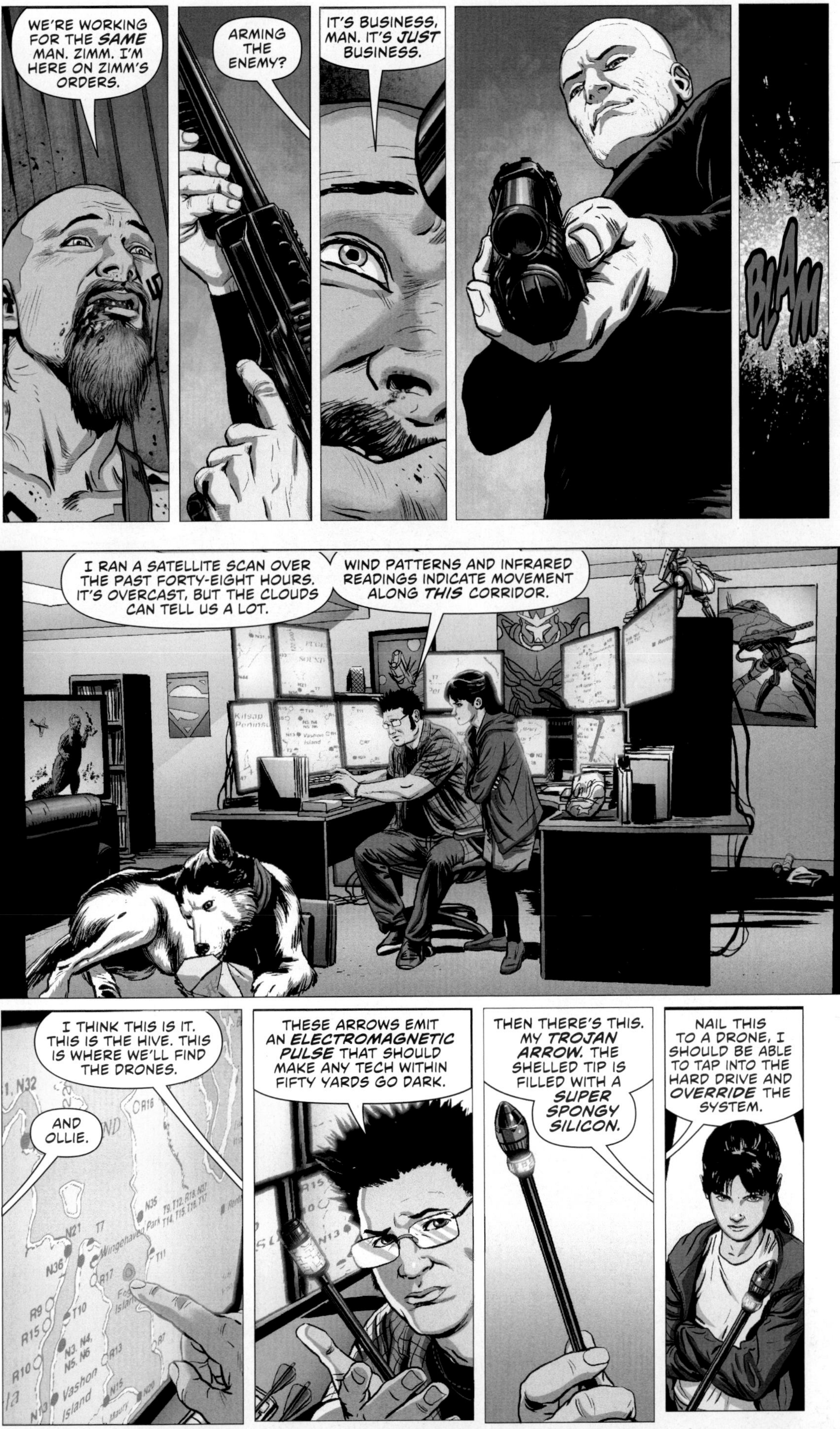
WE'RE WORKING FOR THE SAME MAN. ZIMM. I'M HERE ON ZIMM'S ORDERS.
ARMING THE ENEMY?
IT'S BUSINESS, MAN. IT'S JUST BUSINESS.
BLAM
I RAN A SATELLITE SCAN OVER THE PAST FORTY-EIGHT HOURS. IT'S OVERCAST, BUT THE CLOUDS CAN TELL US A LOT.
WIND PATTERNS AND INFRARED READINGS INDICATE MOVEMENT ALONG THIS CORRIDOR.
I THINK THIS IS IT. THIS IS THE HIVE. THIS IS WHERE WE'LL FIND THE DRONES.
AND OLLIE.
THESE ARROWS EMIT AN ELECTROMAGNETIC PULSE THAT SHOULD MAKE ANY TECH WITHIN FIFTY YARDS GO DARK.
THEN THERE'S THIS. MY TROJAN ARROW. THE SHELLED TIP IS FILLED WITH A SUPER SPONGY SILICON.
NAIL THIS TO A DRONE, I SHOULD BE ABLE TO TAP INTO THE HARD DRIVE AND OVERRIDE THE SYSTEM.

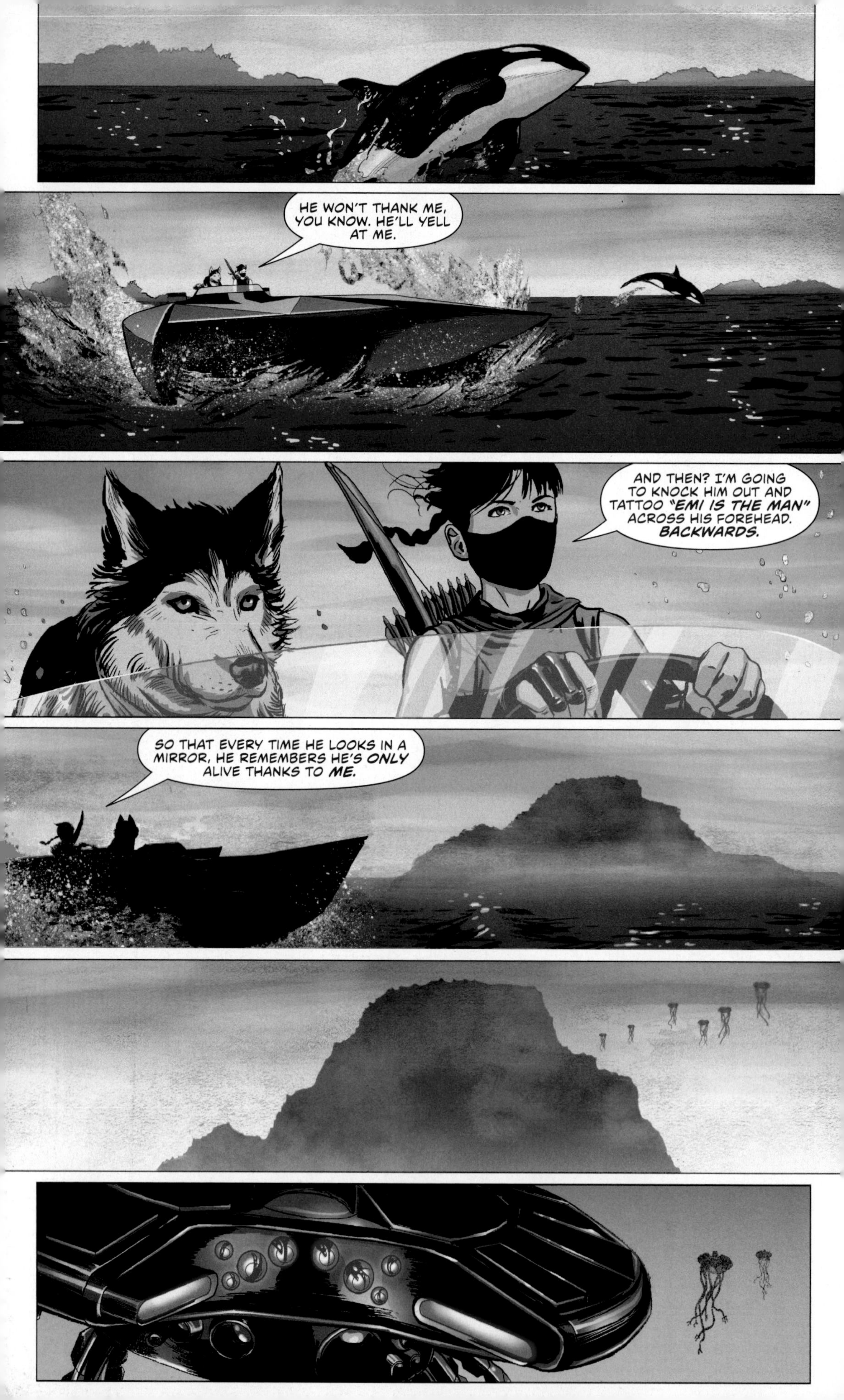
HE WON'T THANK ME, YOU KNOW. HE'LL YELL AT ME.
AND THEN? I'M GOING TO KNOCK HIM OUT AND TATTOO "EMI IS THE MAN" ACROSS HIS FOREHEAD. BACKWARDS.
SO THAT EVERY TIME HE LOOKS IN A MIRROR, HE REMEMBERS HE'S ONLY ALIVE THANKS TO ME.

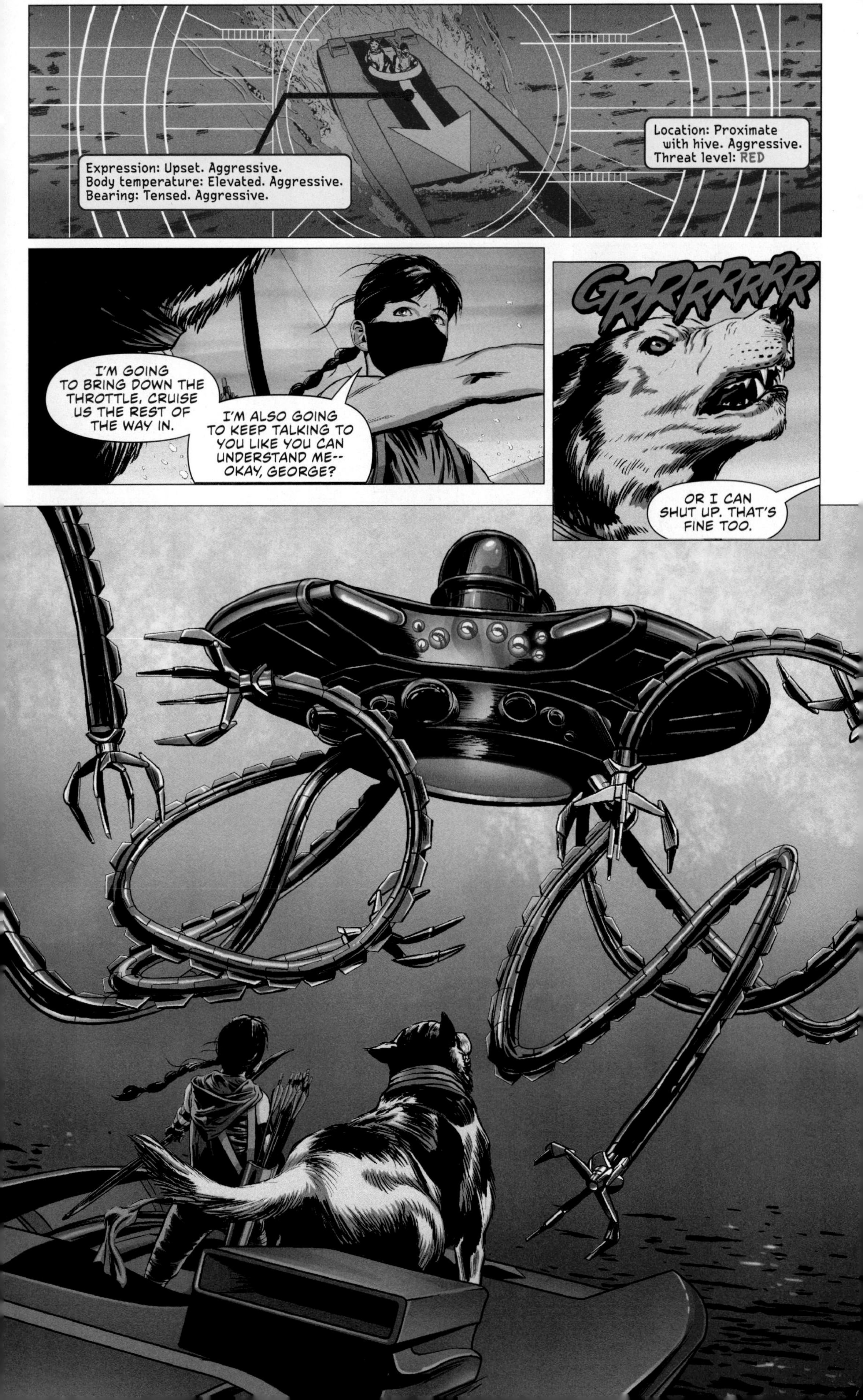
Expression: Upset. Aggressive.
Body temperature: Elevated. Aggressive.
Bearing: Tensed. Aggressive.
Location: Proximate with hive. Aggressive.
Threat level: RED
I'M GOING TO BRING DOWN THE THROTTLE, CRUISE US THE REST OF THE WAY IN.
I'M ALSO GOING TO KEEP TALKING TO YOU LIKE YOU CAN UNDERSTAND ME-- OKAY, GEORGE?
GRRRRRRR
OR I CAN SHUT UP. THAT'S FINE TOO.

AHH!

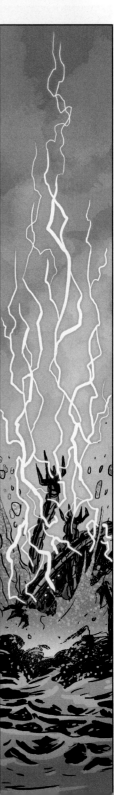

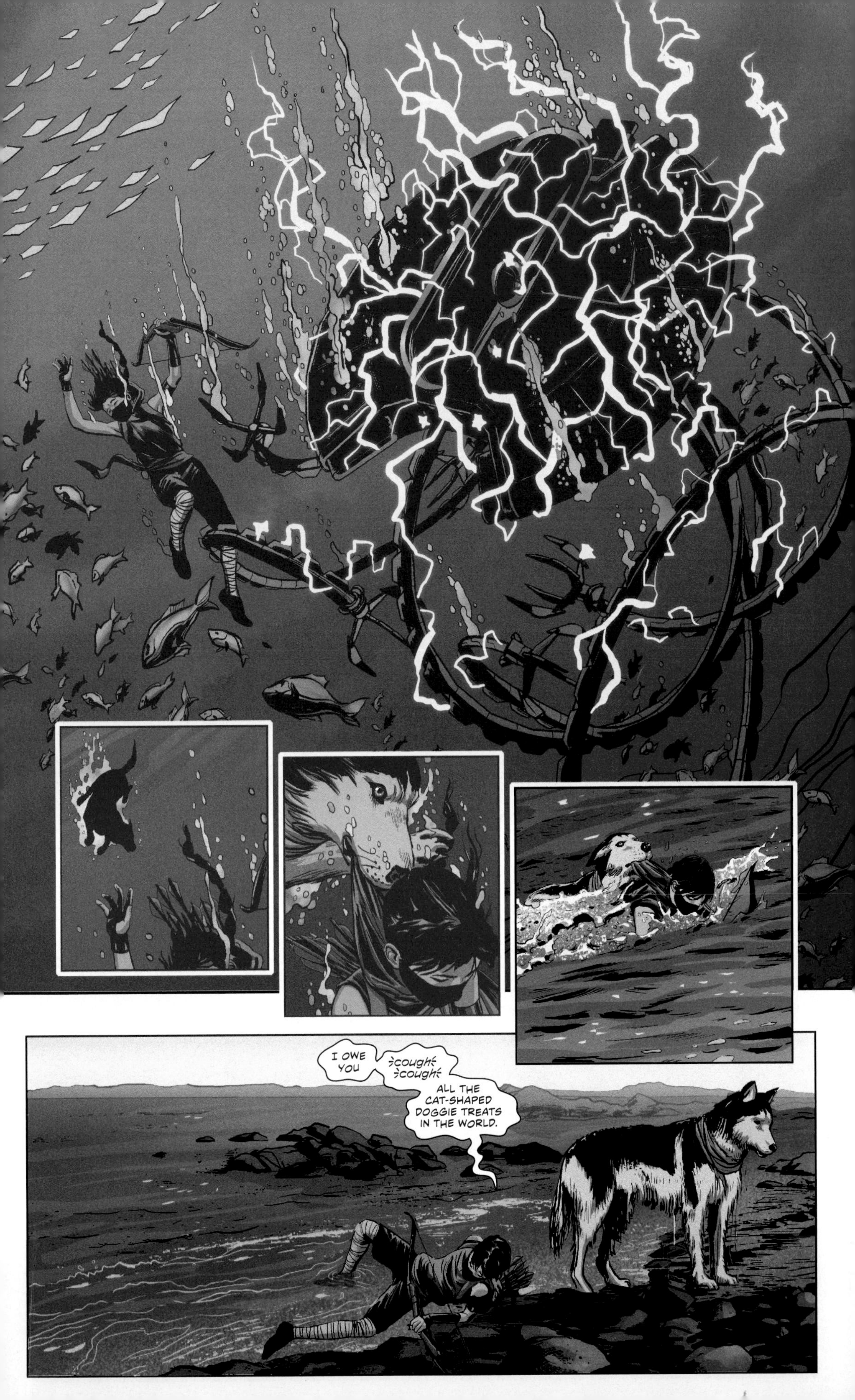
I OWE YOU
cough *cough*
ALL THE CAT-SHAPED DOGGIE TREATS IN THE WORLD.

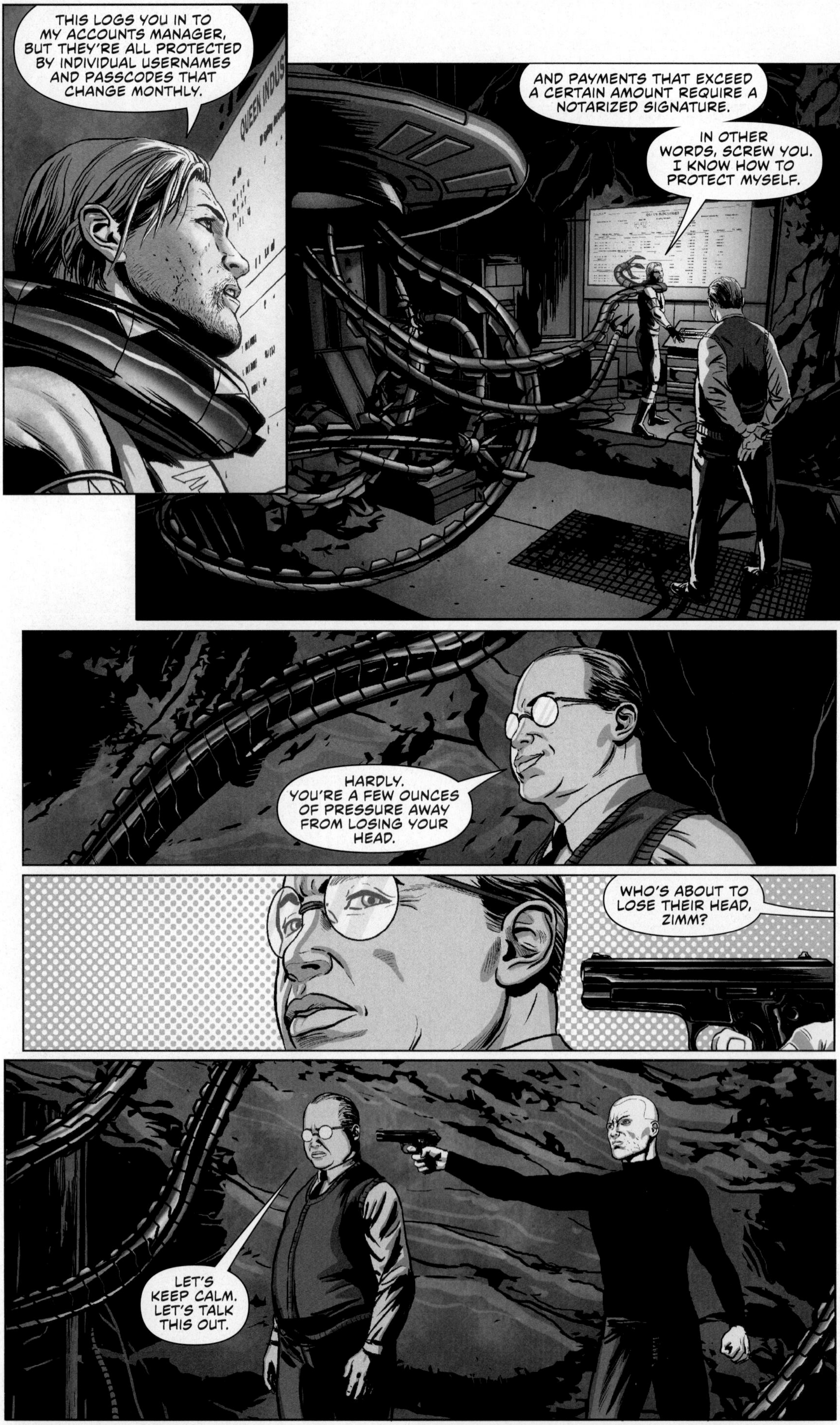
THIS LOGS YOU IN TO MY ACCOUNTS MANAGER, BUT THEY'RE ALL PROTECTED BY INDIVIDUAL USERNAMES AND PASSCODES THAT CHANGE MONTHLY.
AND PAYMENTS THAT EXCEED A CERTAIN AMOUNT REQUIRE A NOTARIZED SIGNATURE.
IN OTHER WORDS, SCREW YOU. I KNOW HOW TO PROTECT MYSELF.
HARDLY. YOU'RE A FEW OUNCES OF PRESSURE AWAY FROM LOSING YOUR HEAD.
WHO'S ABOUT TO LOSE THEIR HEAD, ZIMM?
LET'S KEEP CALM. LET'S TALK THIS OUT.

I DIDN'T WANT TO BELIEVE IT. BUT THE GUNRUNNING LED ME TO A *DRUG LAB* LED ME TO A *PROSTITUTION RING.*

THESE WERE NECESSARY FOR *START-UP* FUNDS. AND BY HELPING CRIME WE CREATED THE CITYWIDE NEED FOR THE DRONES.

THERE'S NO MORE *WE.*

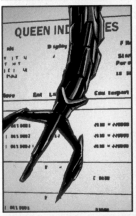

SOMETIMES A SOLDIER *CAN'T* UNDERSTAND THE DECISIONS MADE BY A GENERAL...

...BUT HE *HAS TO* TRUST THAT THE GENERAL *KNOWS BEST.*

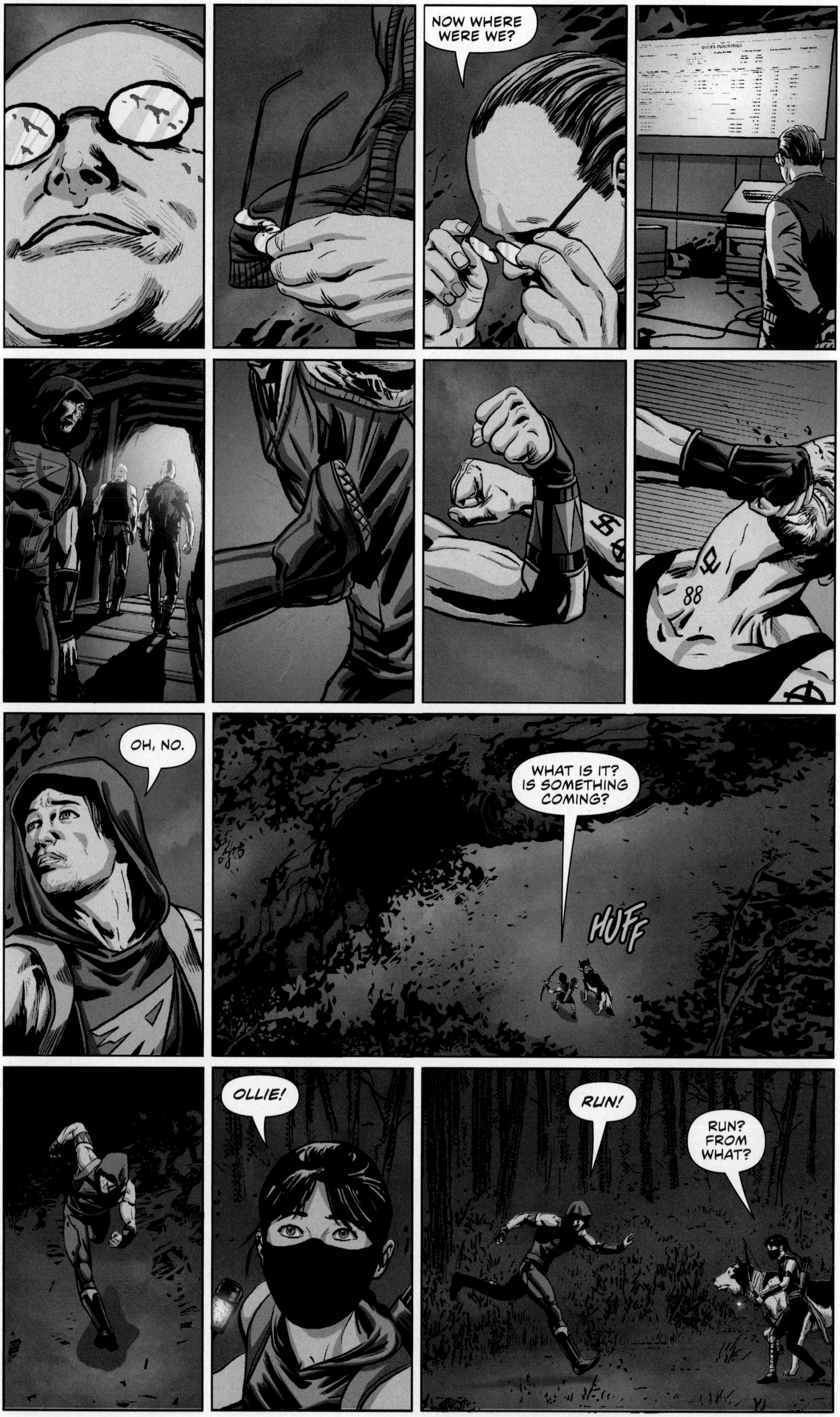
NOW WHERE WERE WE?
OH, NO.
WHAT IS IT? IS SOMETHING COMING?
HUFF
OLLIE!
RUN!
RUN? FROM WHAT?

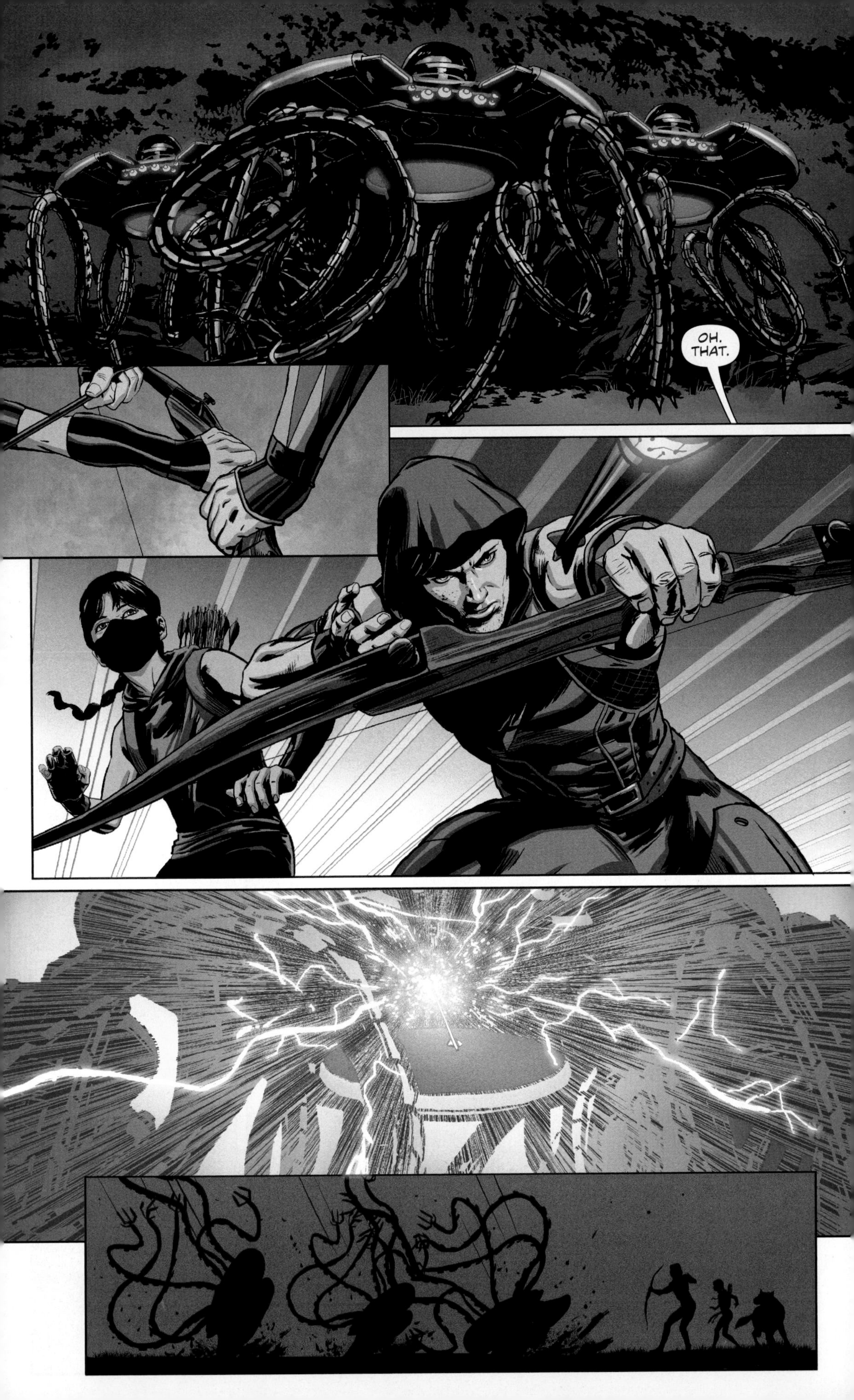
OH. THAT.

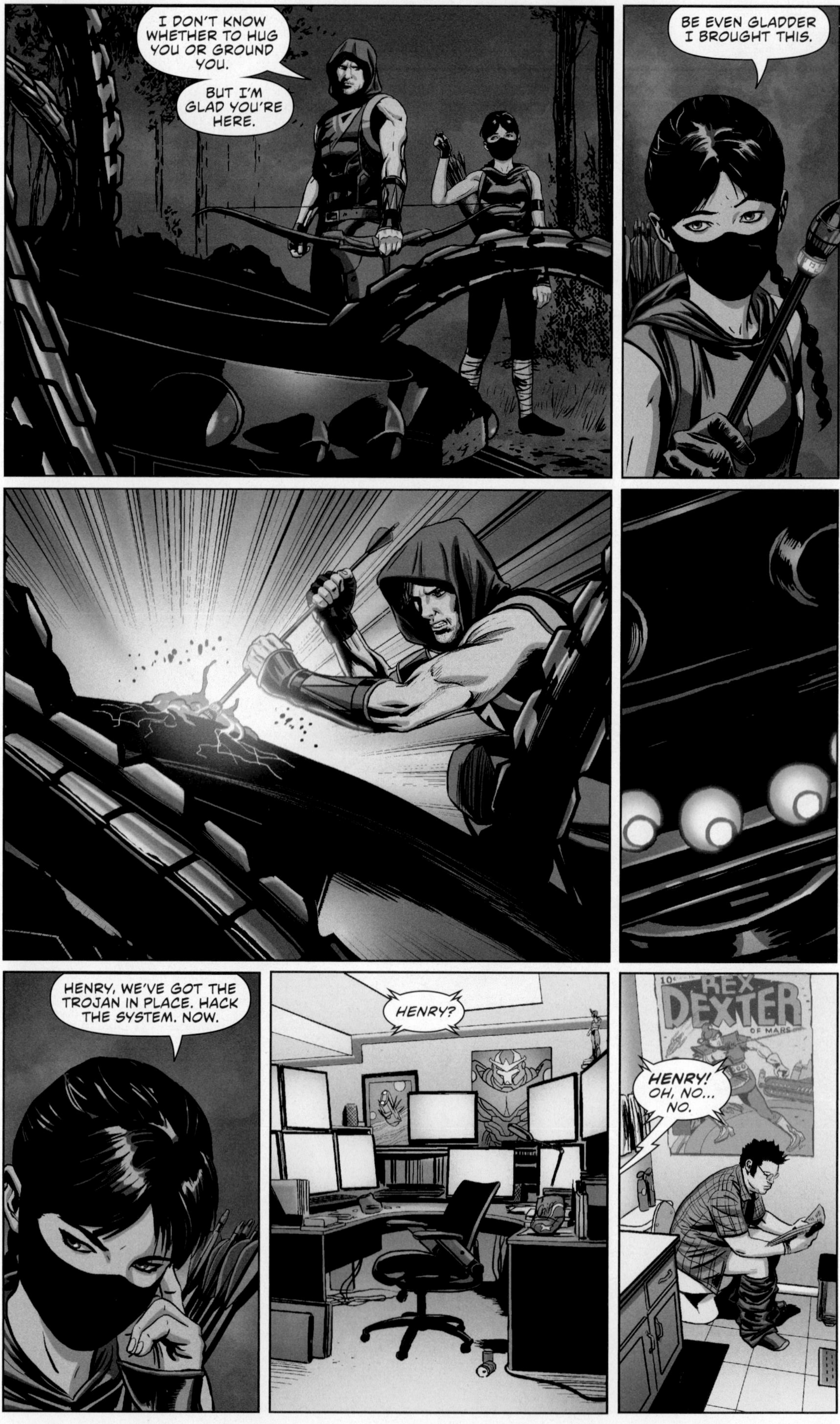
I DON'T KNOW WHETHER TO HUG YOU OR GROUND YOU.
BUT I'M GLAD YOU'RE HERE.
BE EVEN GLADDER I BROUGHT THIS.
HENRY, WE'VE GOT THE TROJAN IN PLACE. HACK THE SYSTEM. NOW.
HENRY?
REX DEXTER OF MARS
HENRY! OH, NO... NO.

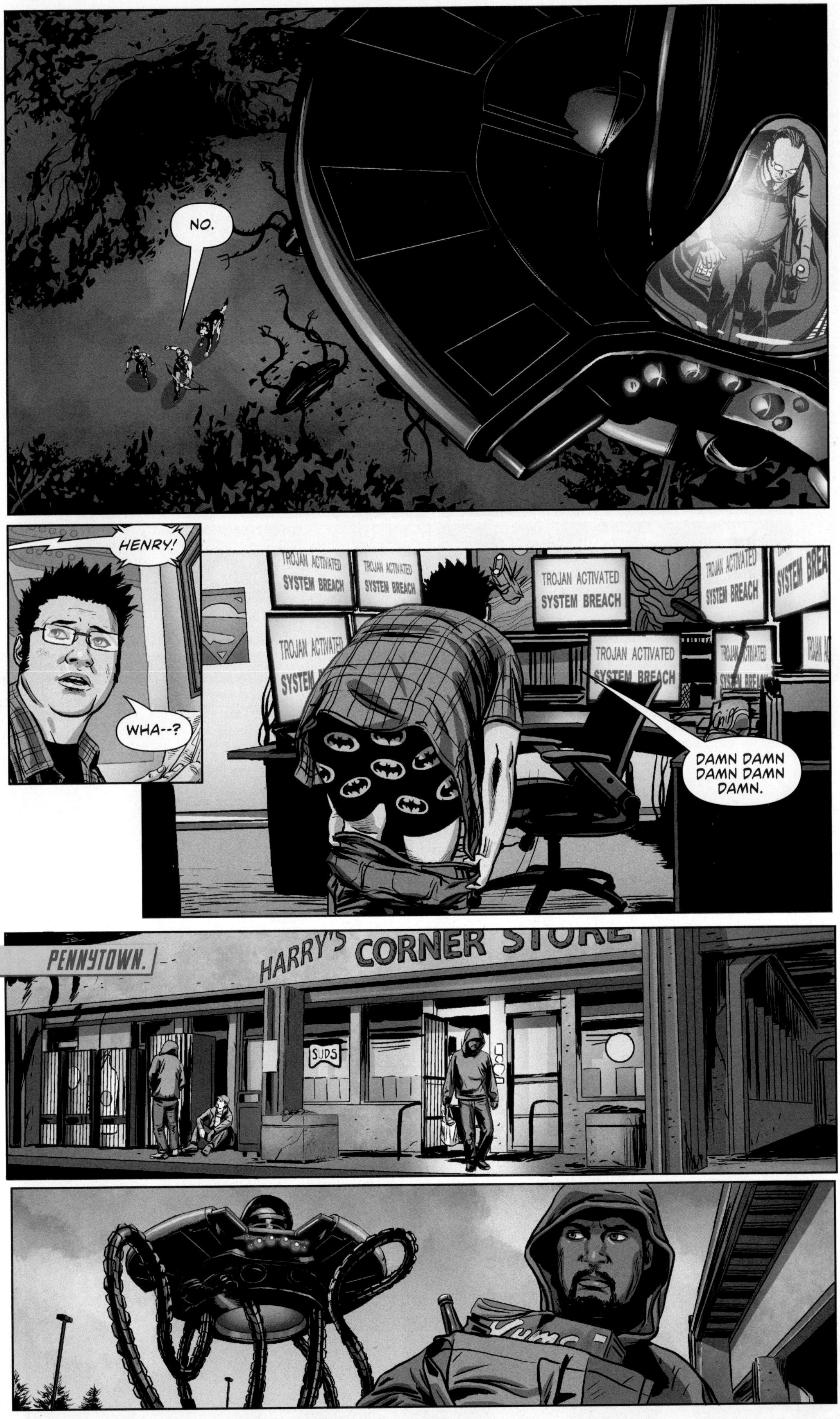
NO.
HENRY!
WHA--?
TROJAN ACTIVATED
SYSTEM BREACH
DAMN DAMN DAMN DAMN DAMN.
PENNYTOWN.
HARRY'S CORNER STORE
SUDS

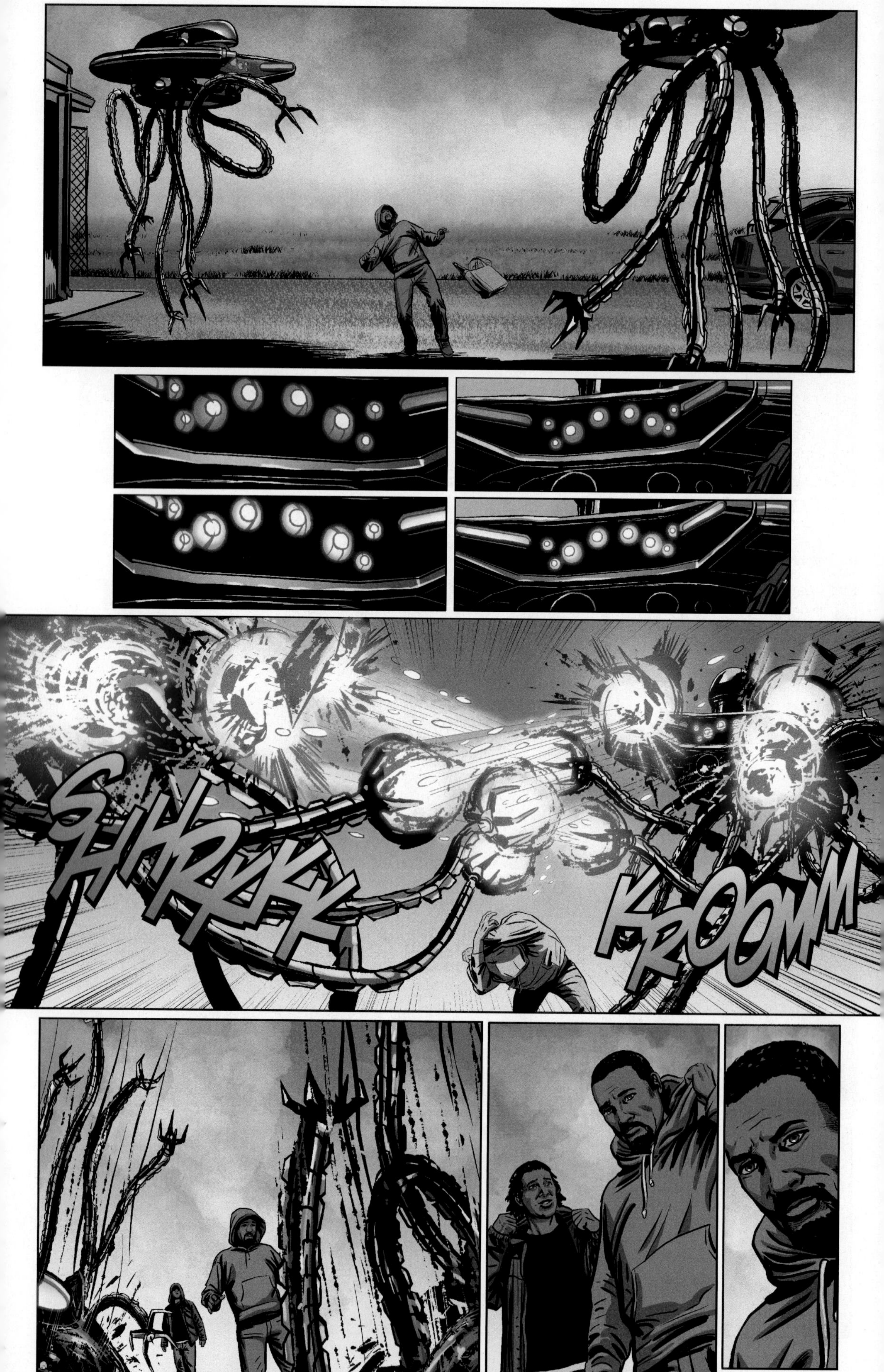
SHRKKK
KROOMM

RIGHT ABOUT NOW, I'M REALIZING THAT I CAN'T DO THIS ALONE, THAT I NEED TO TRUST AND RELY ON OTHERS, THAT A QUIVER CARRIES MANY ARROWS.

RIGHT ABOUT NOW, THE SUN IS BURNING THROUGH THE CLOUDS, AND SEATTLE IS PULLING BACK ITS HOOD.

RIGHT ABOUT NOW, THE MOTHER DRONE IS TOUCHING BOTTOM, WHERE THE SALT WILL SLOWLY CLAIM IT.

RIGHT ABOUT NOW, ITS METAL AND GLASS WILL MOCK AARON ZIMM WITH A WARPED VERSION OF HIS OWN REFLECTION.

AND RIGHT ABOUT NOW, THE BLACKFISH--

--THE HUNTERS OF THE SOUND, PROPELLED BY THEIR SEETHING HUNGER--WILL HAVE FOUND HIM...

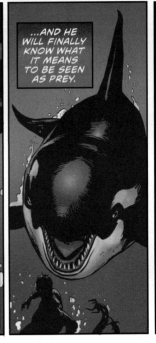

...AND HE WILL FINALLY KNOW WHAT IT MEANS TO BE SEEN AS PREY.

the night birds

Part 3: THE HOOD

BENJAMIN PERCY · PATRICK ZIRCHER
script   art
storytellers

GABE ELTAEB colorist · ROB LEIGH letterer
PATRICK ZIRCHER & GABE ELTAEB cover

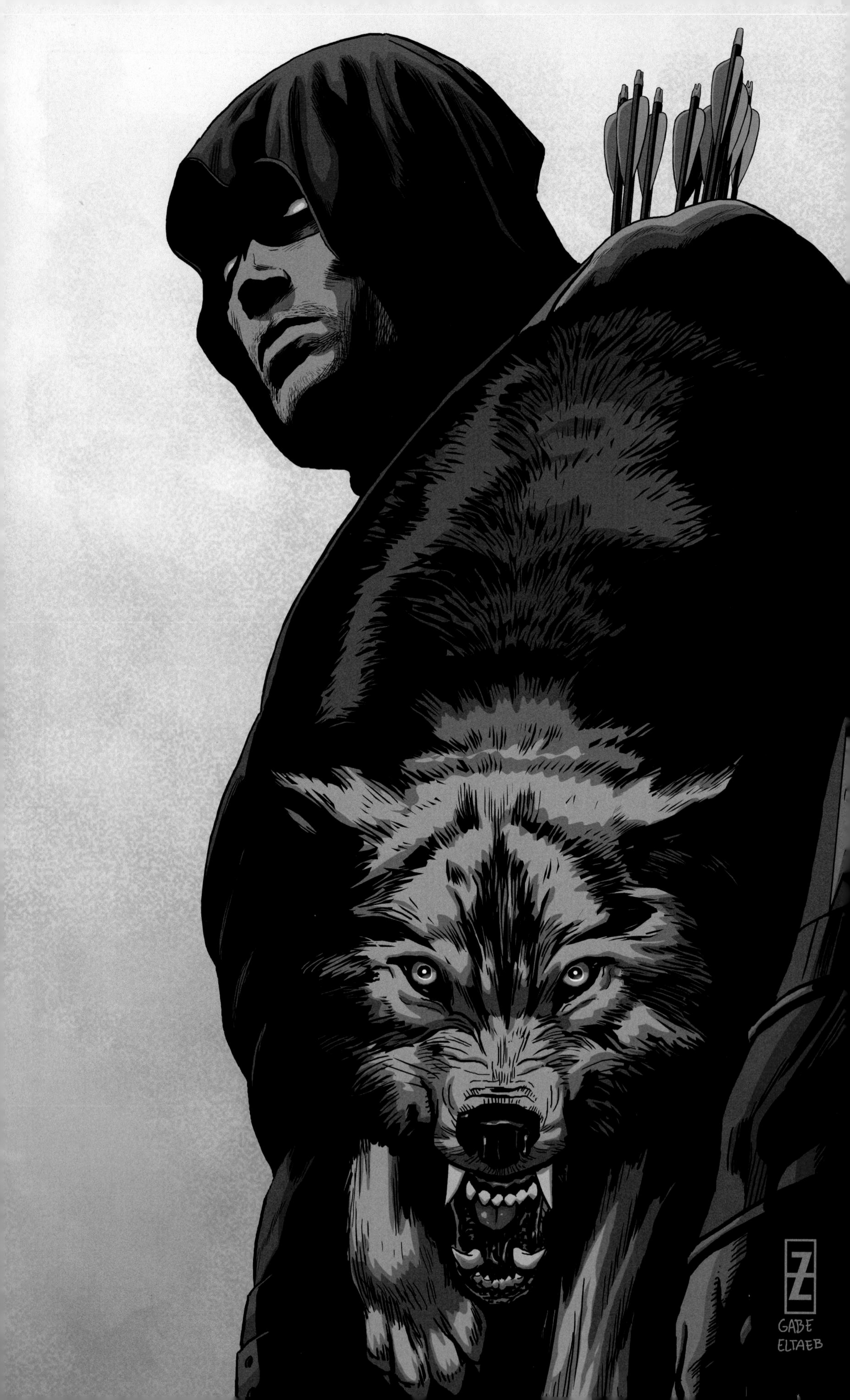
GABE
ELTAEB

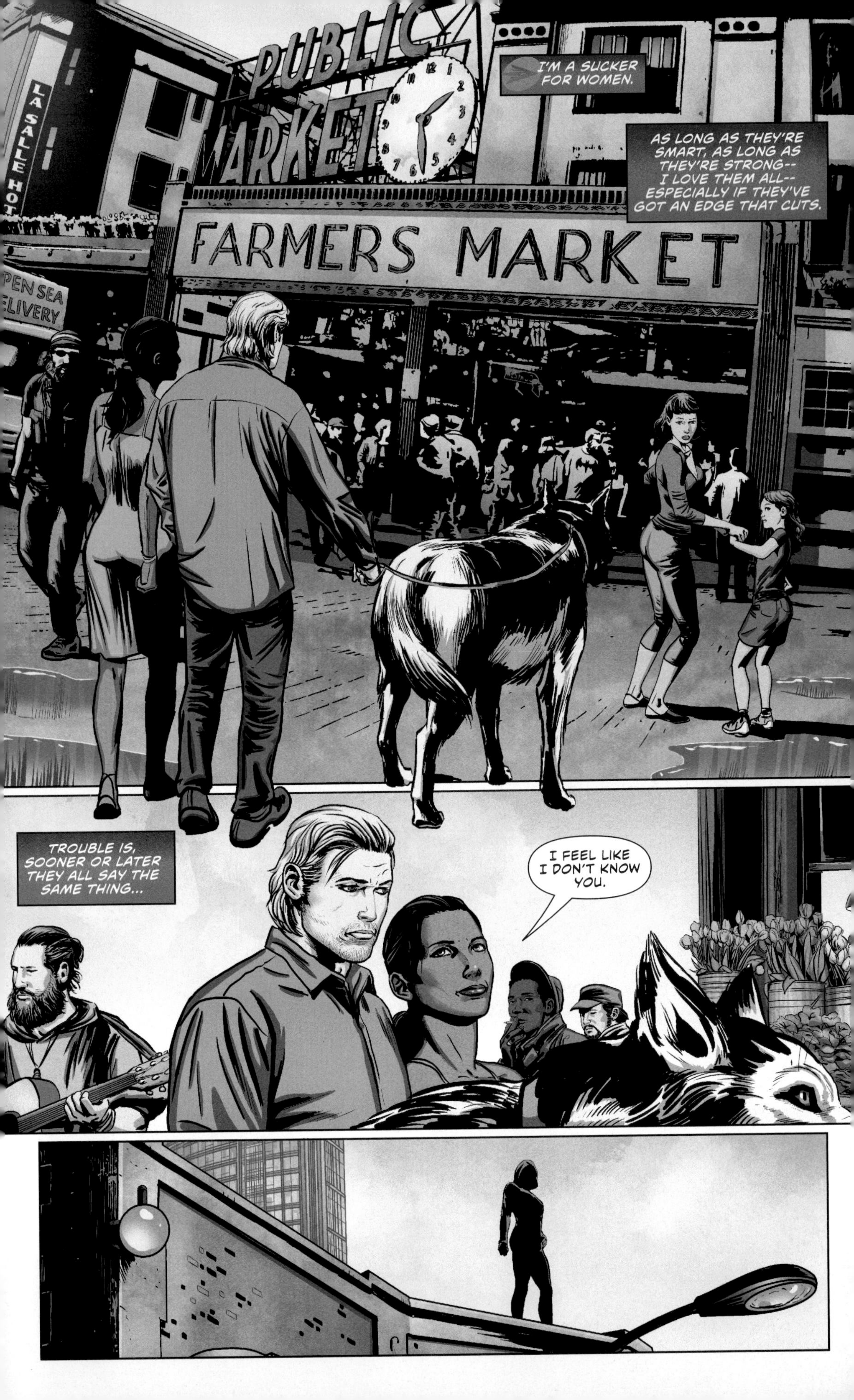
PUBLIC MARKET
LA SALLE HOT
PEN SEA
LIVERY
FARMERS MARKET
I'M A SUCKER FOR WOMEN.
AS LONG AS THEY'RE SMART, AS LONG AS THEY'RE STRONG-- I LOVE THEM ALL-- ESPECIALLY IF THEY'VE GOT AN EDGE THAT CUTS.
TROUBLE IS, SOONER OR LATER THEY ALL SAY THE SAME THING...
I FEEL LIKE I DON'T KNOW YOU.

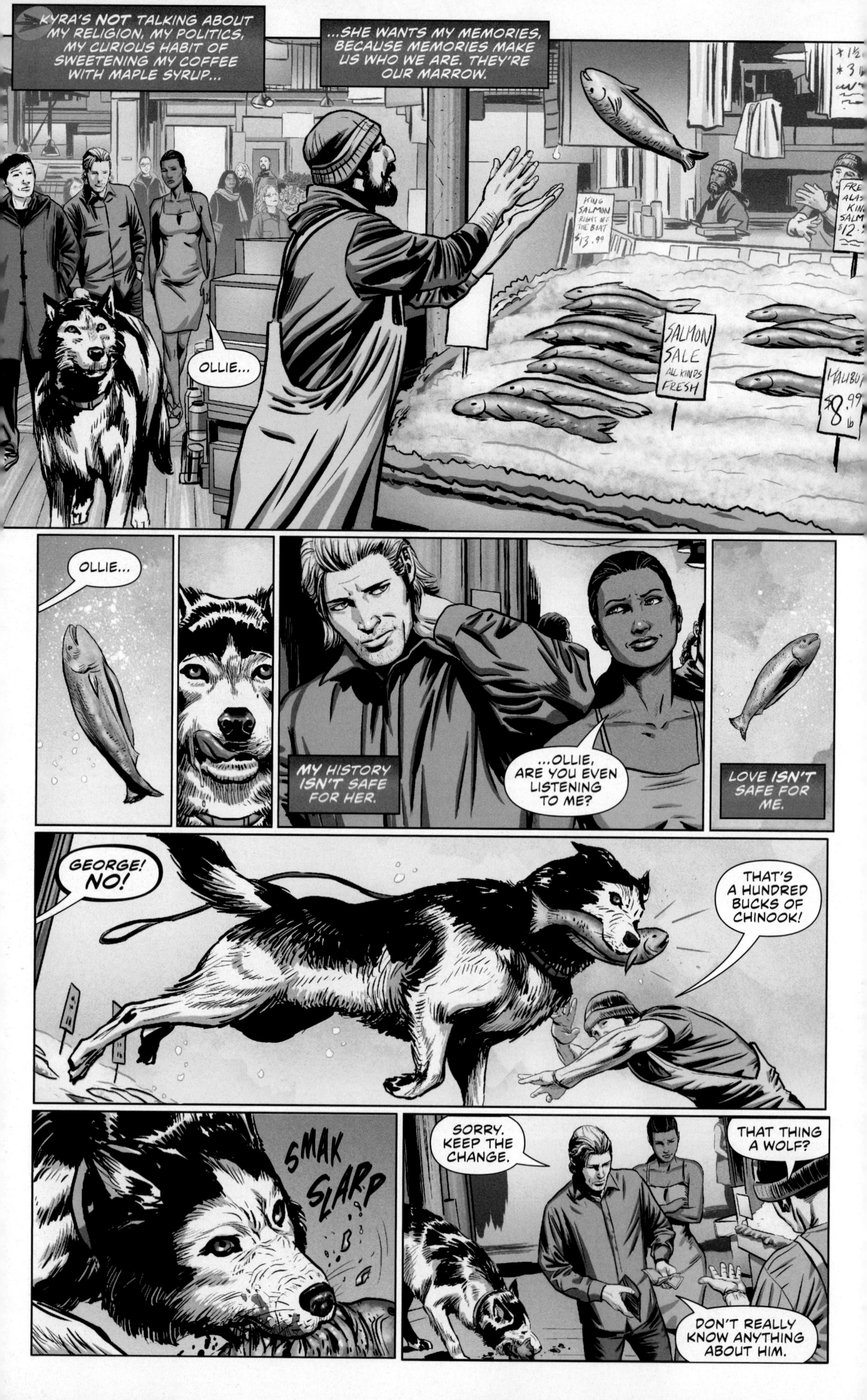
KYRA'S NOT TALKING ABOUT MY RELIGION, MY POLITICS, MY CURIOUS HABIT OF SWEETENING MY COFFEE WITH MAPLE SYRUP...
...SHE WANTS MY MEMORIES, BECAUSE MEMORIES MAKE US WHO WE ARE. THEY'RE OUR MARROW.
KING SALMON RIGHT OFF THE BOAT $13.99
SALMON SALE ALL KINDS FRESH
HALIBUT $8.99 lb
OLLIE...
OLLIE...
MY HISTORY ISN'T SAFE FOR HER.
...OLLIE, ARE YOU EVEN LISTENING TO ME?
LOVE ISN'T SAFE FOR ME.
GEORGE! NO!
THAT'S A HUNDRED BUCKS OF CHINOOK!
SMAK
SLARP
SORRY. KEEP THE CHANGE.
THAT THING A WOLF?
DON'T REALLY KNOW ANYTHING ABOUT HIM.

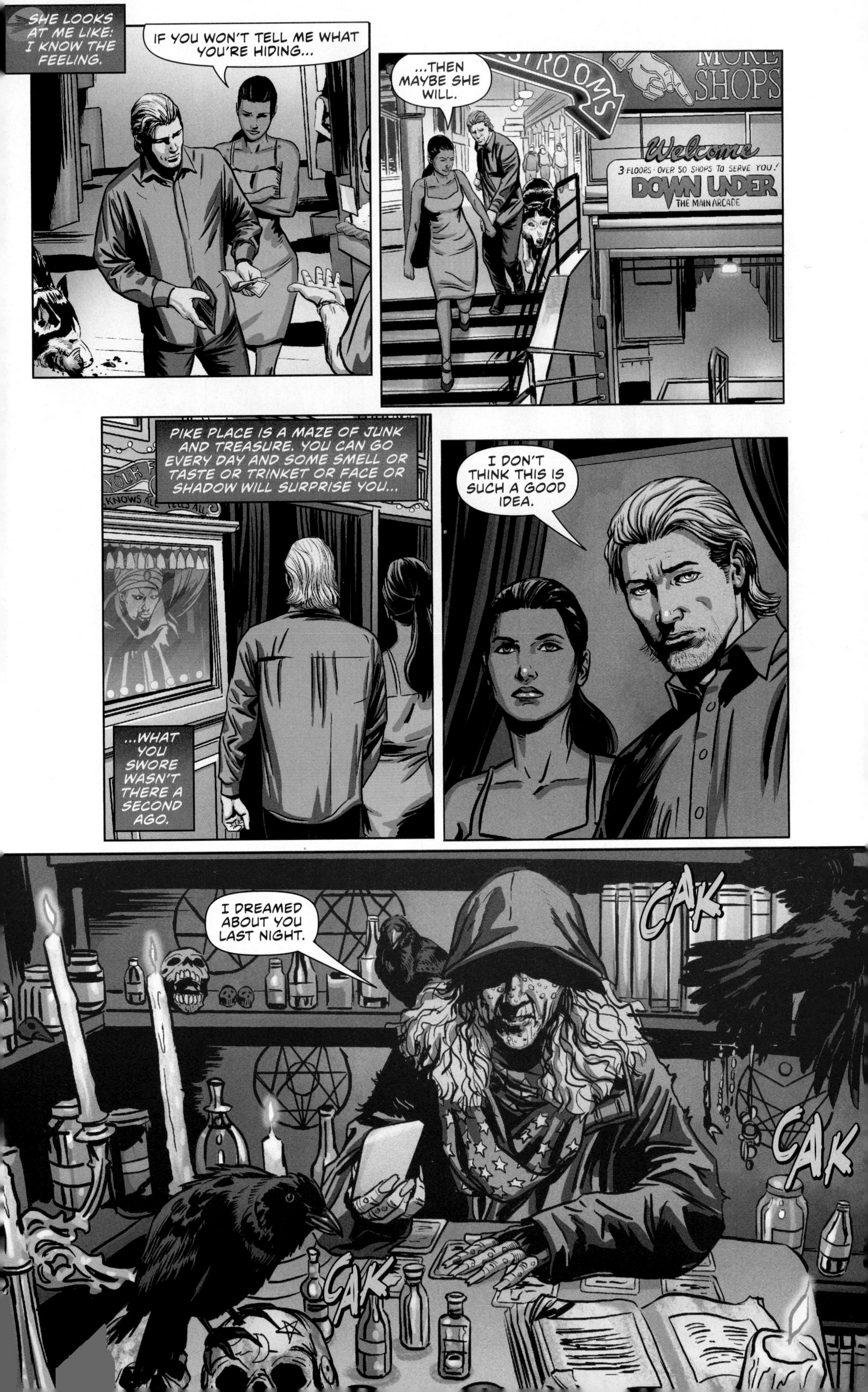
SHE LOOKS AT ME LIKE: I KNOW THE FEELING.
IF YOU WON'T TELL ME WHAT YOU'RE HIDING...
...THEN MAYBE SHE WILL.
RESTROOMS
MORE SHOPS
Welcome
3 FLOORS · OVER 50 SHOPS TO SERVE YOU!
DOWN UNDER
THE MAIN ARCADE
PIKE PLACE IS A MAZE OF JUNK AND TREASURE. YOU CAN GO EVERY DAY AND SOME SMELL OR TASTE OR TRINKET OR FACE OR SHADOW WILL SURPRISE YOU...
KNOWS ALL TELLS ALL
...WHAT YOU SWORE WASN'T THERE A SECOND AGO.
I DON'T THINK THIS IS SUCH A GOOD IDEA.
I DREAMED ABOUT YOU LAST NIGHT.
CAK
CAK
CAK

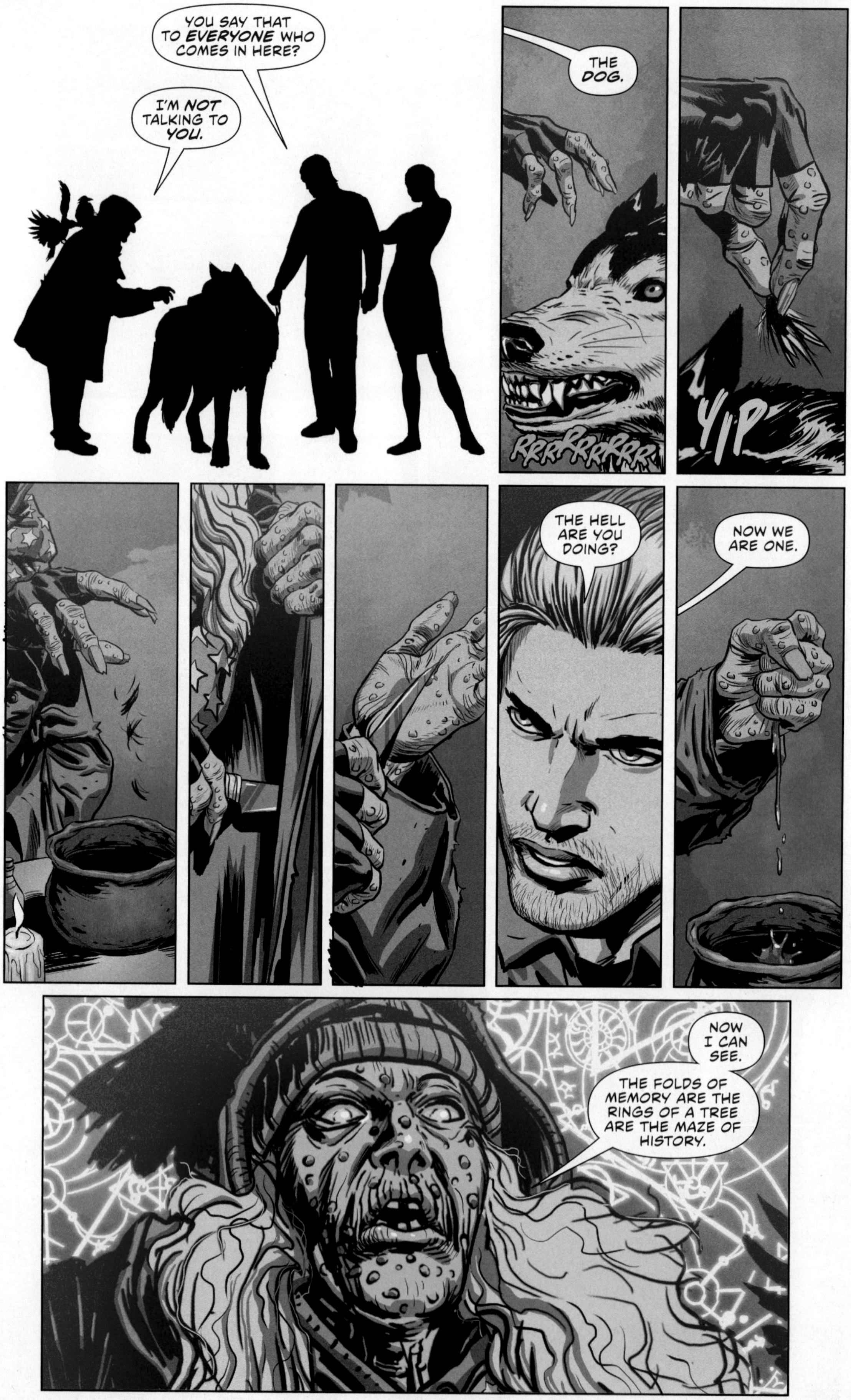
YOU SAY THAT TO EVERYONE WHO COMES IN HERE?
I'M NOT TALKING TO YOU.
THE DOG.
RRRRRRRRR
YIP
THE HELL ARE YOU DOING?
NOW WE ARE ONE.
NOW I CAN SEE.
THE FOLDS OF MEMORY ARE THE RINGS OF A TREE ARE THE MAZE OF HISTORY.

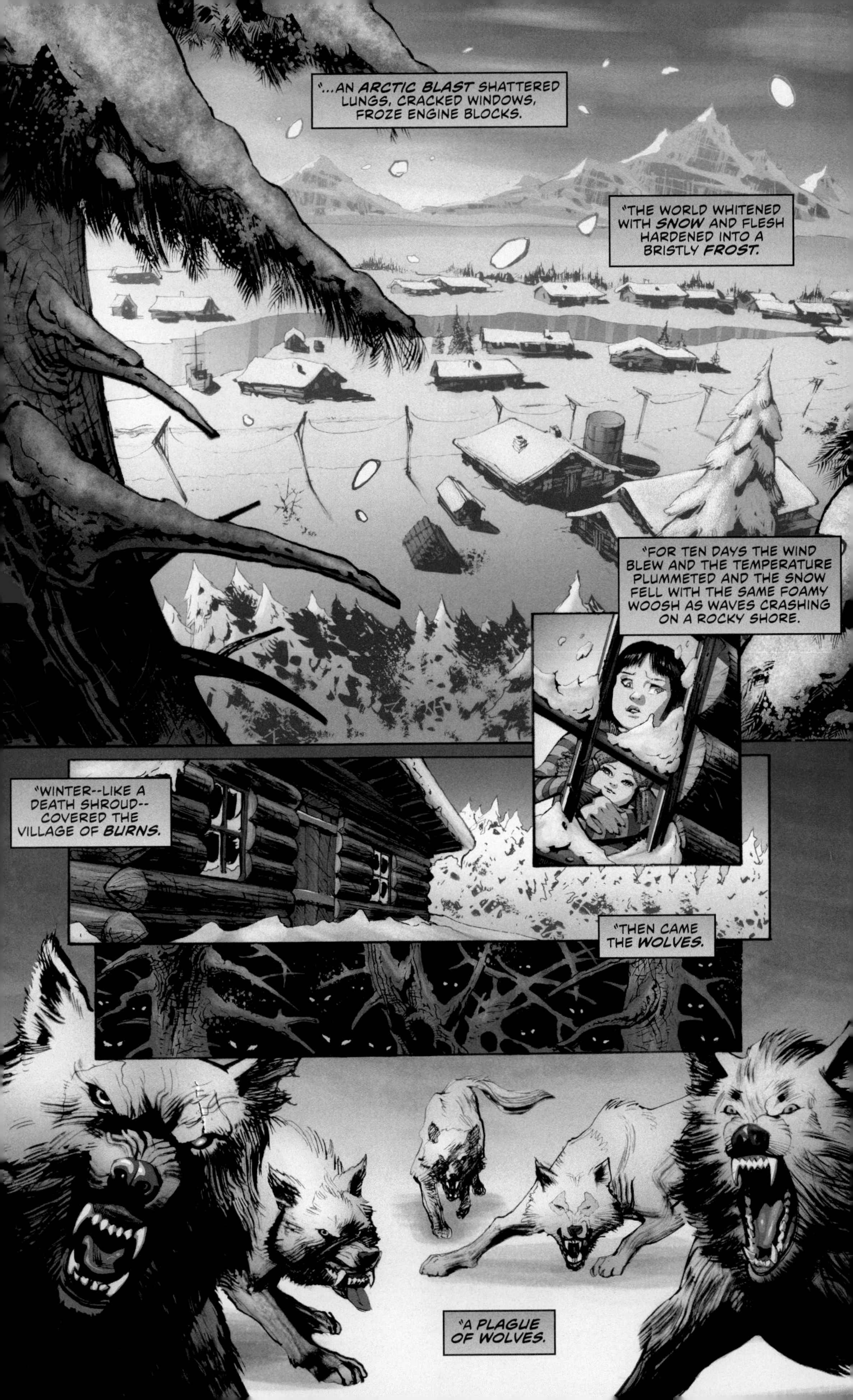
"...AN ARCTIC BLAST SHATTERED LUNGS, CRACKED WINDOWS, FROZE ENGINE BLOCKS.
"THE WORLD WHITENED WITH SNOW AND FLESH HARDENED INTO A BRISTLY FROST.
"FOR TEN DAYS THE WIND BLEW AND THE TEMPERATURE PLUMMETED AND THE SNOW FELL WITH THE SAME FOAMY WOOSH AS WAVES CRASHING ON A ROCKY SHORE.
"WINTER--LIKE A DEATH SHROUD--COVERED THE VILLAGE OF BURNS.
"THEN CAME THE WOLVES.
"A PLAGUE OF WOLVES.

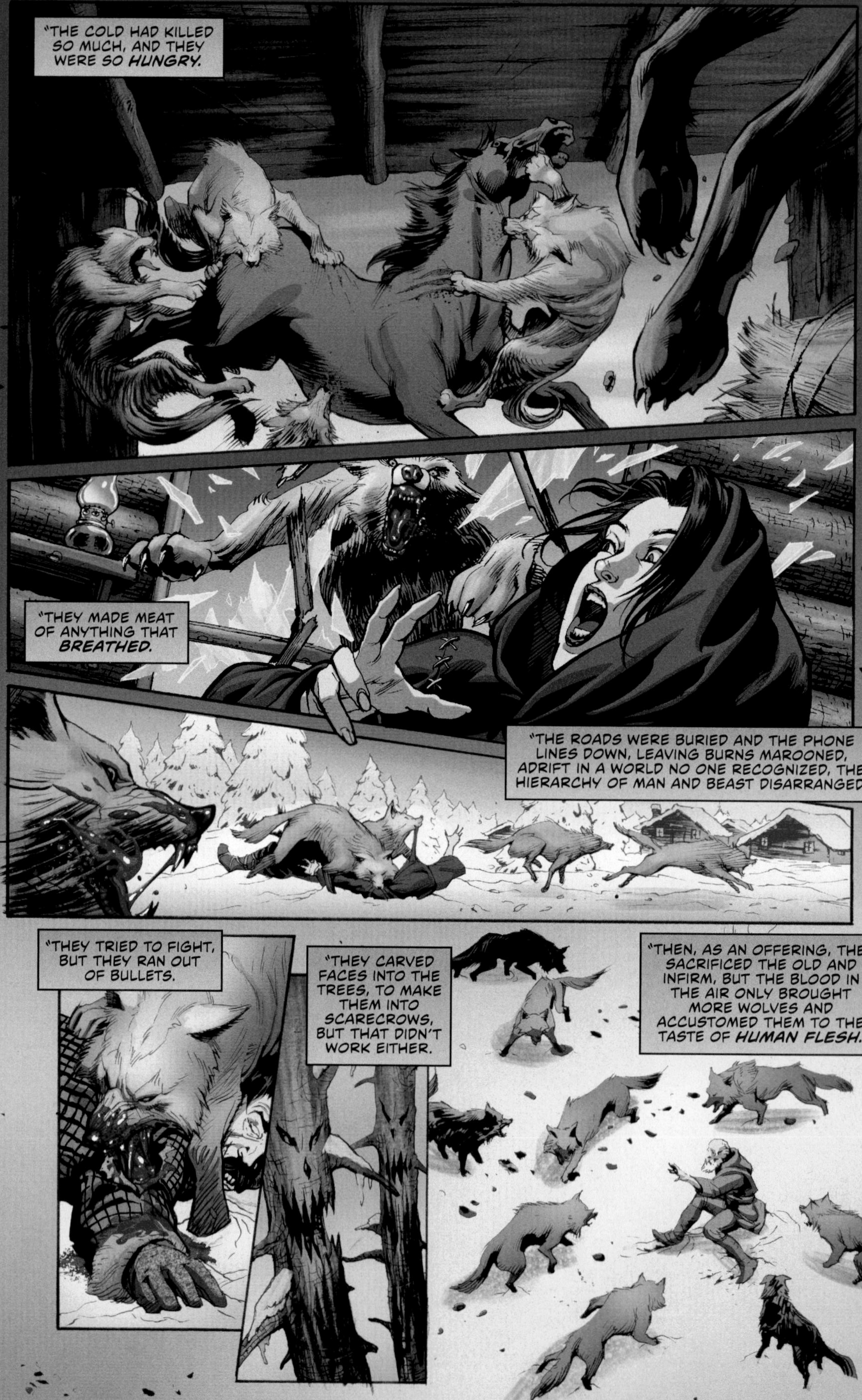
"THE COLD HAD KILLED SO MUCH, AND THEY WERE SO HUNGRY.
"THEY MADE MEAT OF ANYTHING THAT BREATHED.
"THE ROADS WERE BURIED AND THE PHONE LINES DOWN, LEAVING BURNS MAROONED, ADRIFT IN A WORLD NO ONE RECOGNIZED, THE HIERARCHY OF MAN AND BEAST DISARRANGED.
"THEY TRIED TO FIGHT, BUT THEY RAN OUT OF BULLETS.
"THEY CARVED FACES INTO THE TREES, TO MAKE THEM INTO SCARECROWS, BUT THAT DIDN'T WORK EITHER.
"THEN, AS AN OFFERING, THEY SACRIFICED THE OLD AND INFIRM, BUT THE BLOOD IN THE AIR ONLY BROUGHT MORE WOLVES AND ACCUSTOMED THEM TO THE TASTE OF HUMAN FLESH.

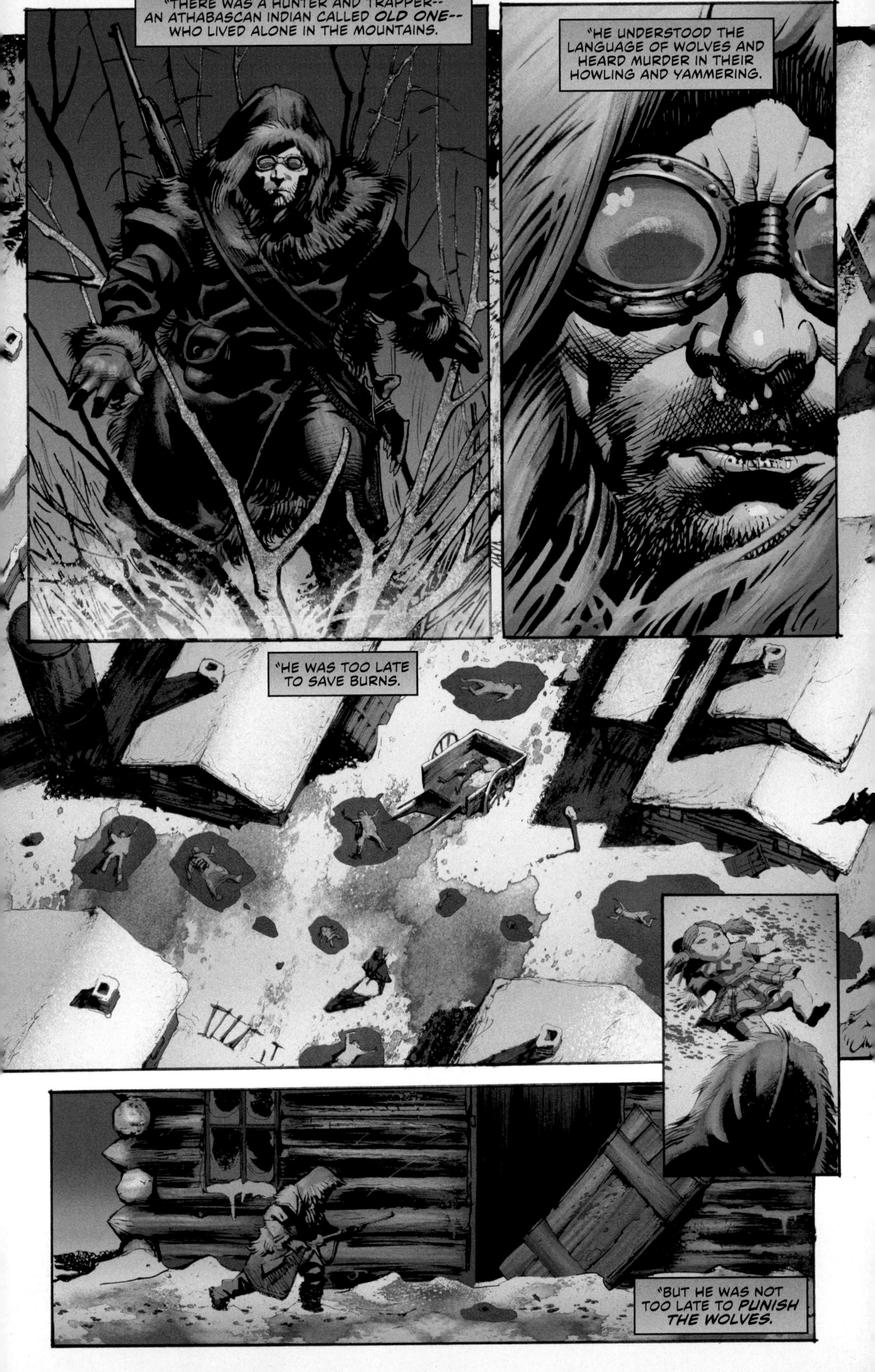
"THERE WAS A HUNTER AND TRAPPER-- AN ATHABASCAN INDIAN CALLED *OLD ONE*-- WHO LIVED ALONE IN THE MOUNTAINS.
"HE UNDERSTOOD THE LANGUAGE OF WOLVES AND HEARD MURDER IN THEIR HOWLING AND YAMMERING.
"HE WAS TOO LATE TO SAVE BURNS.
"BUT HE WAS NOT TOO LATE TO *PUNISH THE WOLVES.*

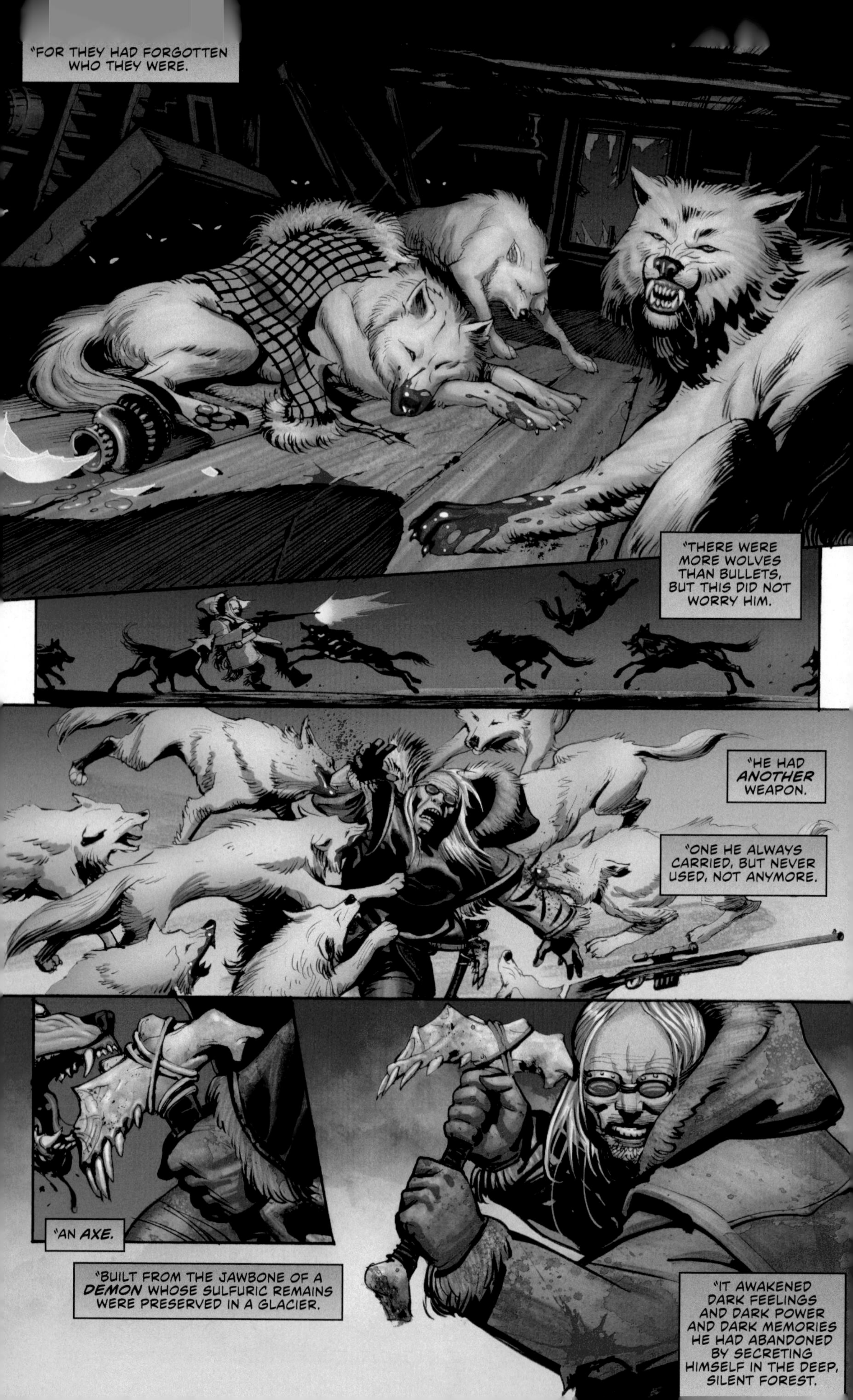
"FOR THEY HAD FORGOTTEN WHO THEY WERE.
"THERE WERE MORE WOLVES THAN BULLETS, BUT THIS DID NOT WORRY HIM.
"HE HAD ANOTHER WEAPON.
"ONE HE ALWAYS CARRIED, BUT NEVER USED, NOT ANYMORE.
"AN AXE.
"BUILT FROM THE JAWBONE OF A DEMON WHOSE SULFURIC REMAINS WERE PRESERVED IN A GLACIER.
"IT AWAKENED DARK FEELINGS AND DARK POWER AND DARK MEMORIES HE HAD ABANDONED BY SECRETING HIMSELF IN THE DEEP, SILENT FOREST.

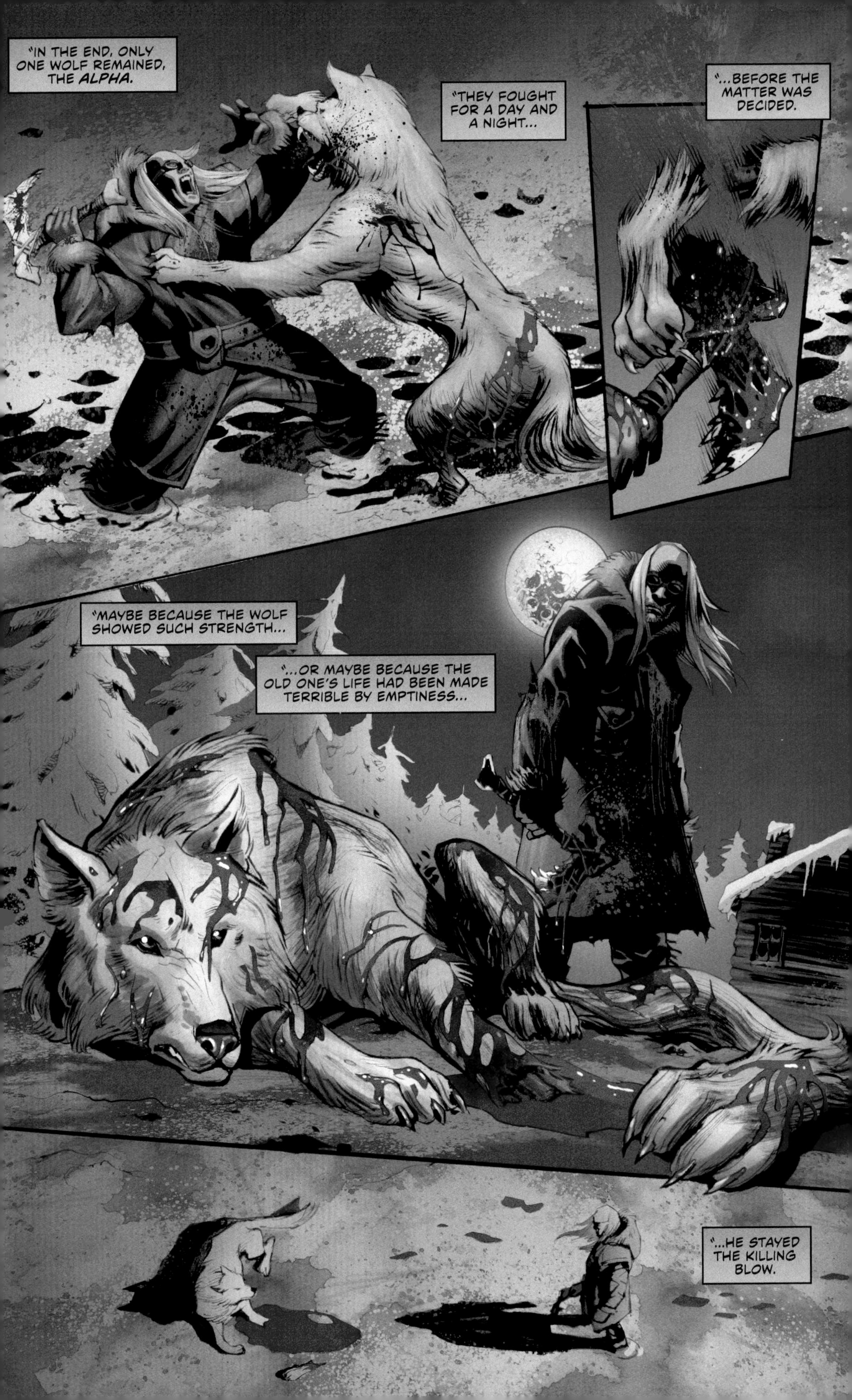
"IN THE END, ONLY ONE WOLF REMAINED, THE *ALPHA*.
"THEY FOUGHT FOR A DAY AND A NIGHT...
"...BEFORE THE MATTER WAS DECIDED.
"MAYBE BECAUSE THE WOLF SHOWED SUCH STRENGTH...
"...OR MAYBE BECAUSE THE OLD ONE'S LIFE HAD BEEN MADE TERRIBLE BY EMPTINESS...
"...HE STAYED THE KILLING BLOW.

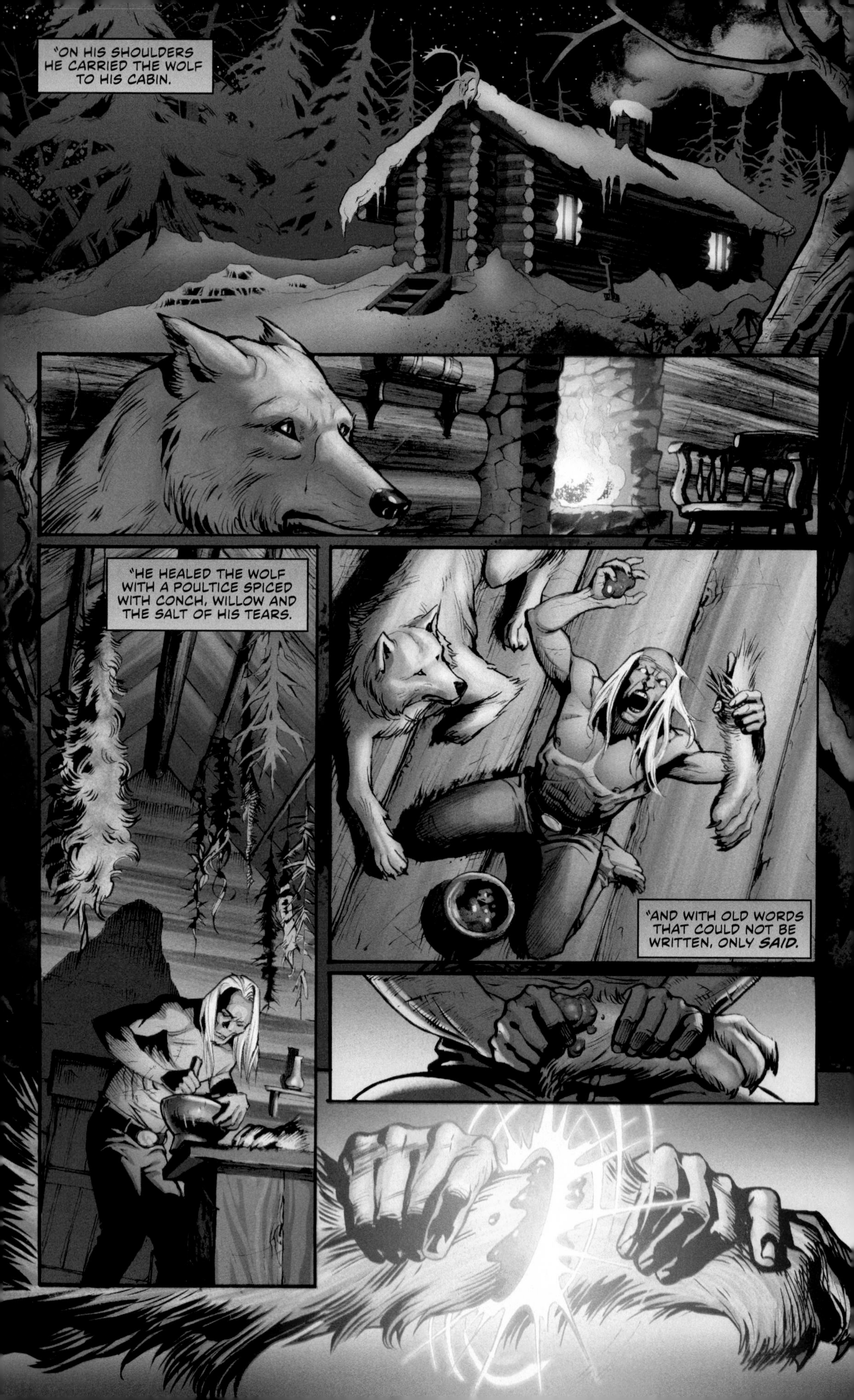
"ON HIS SHOULDERS HE CARRIED THE WOLF TO HIS CABIN.
"HE HEALED THE WOLF WITH A POULTICE SPICED WITH CONCH, WILLOW AND THE SALT OF HIS TEARS.
"AND WITH OLD WORDS THAT COULD NOT BE WRITTEN, ONLY SAID.

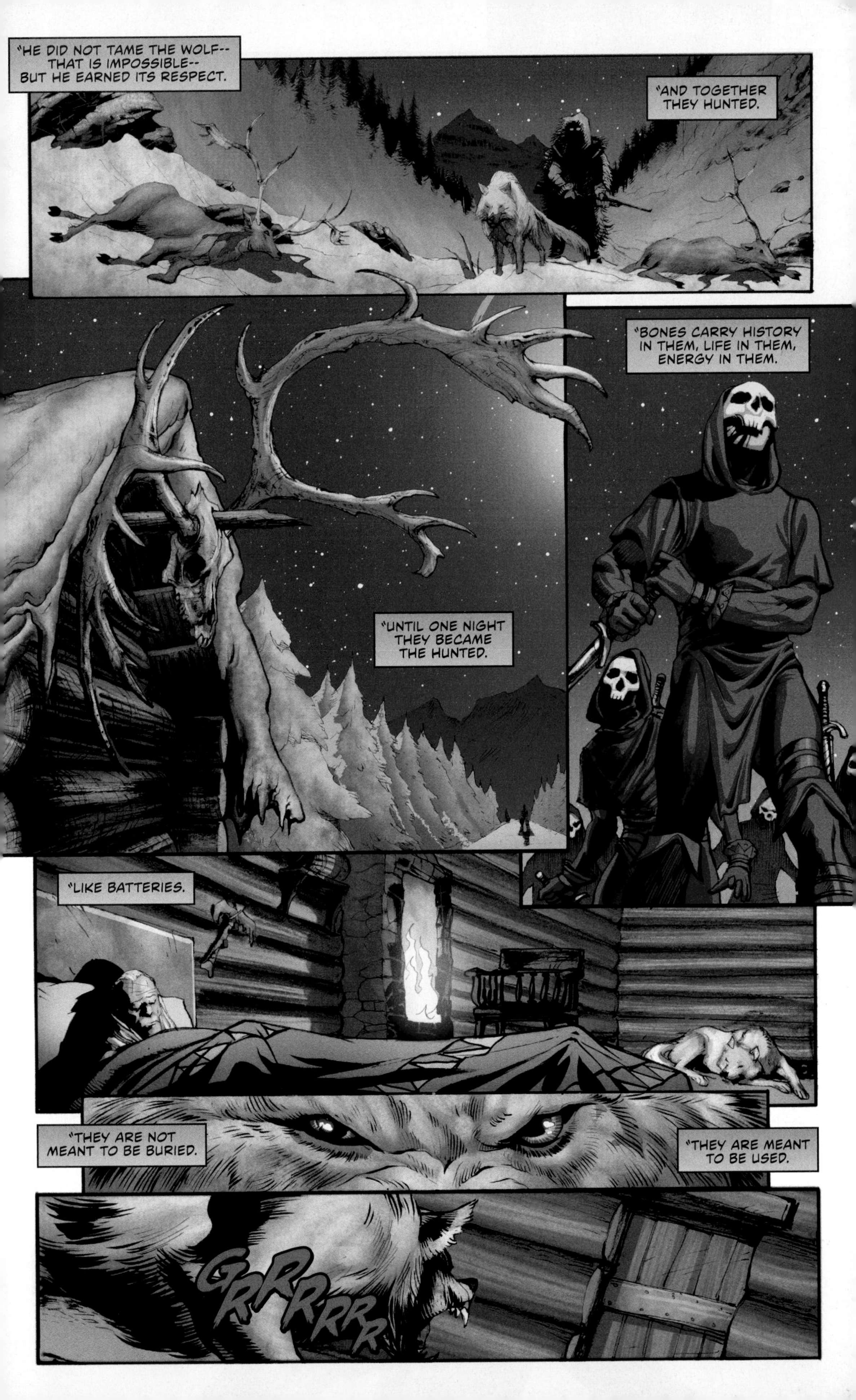
"HE DID NOT TAME THE WOLF-- THAT IS IMPOSSIBLE-- BUT HE EARNED ITS RESPECT.
"AND TOGETHER THEY HUNTED.
"UNTIL ONE NIGHT THEY BECAME THE HUNTED.
"BONES CARRY HISTORY IN THEM, LIFE IN THEM, ENERGY IN THEM.
"LIKE BATTERIES.
"THEY ARE NOT MEANT TO BE BURIED.
"THEY ARE MEANT TO BE USED.
GRRRRRR

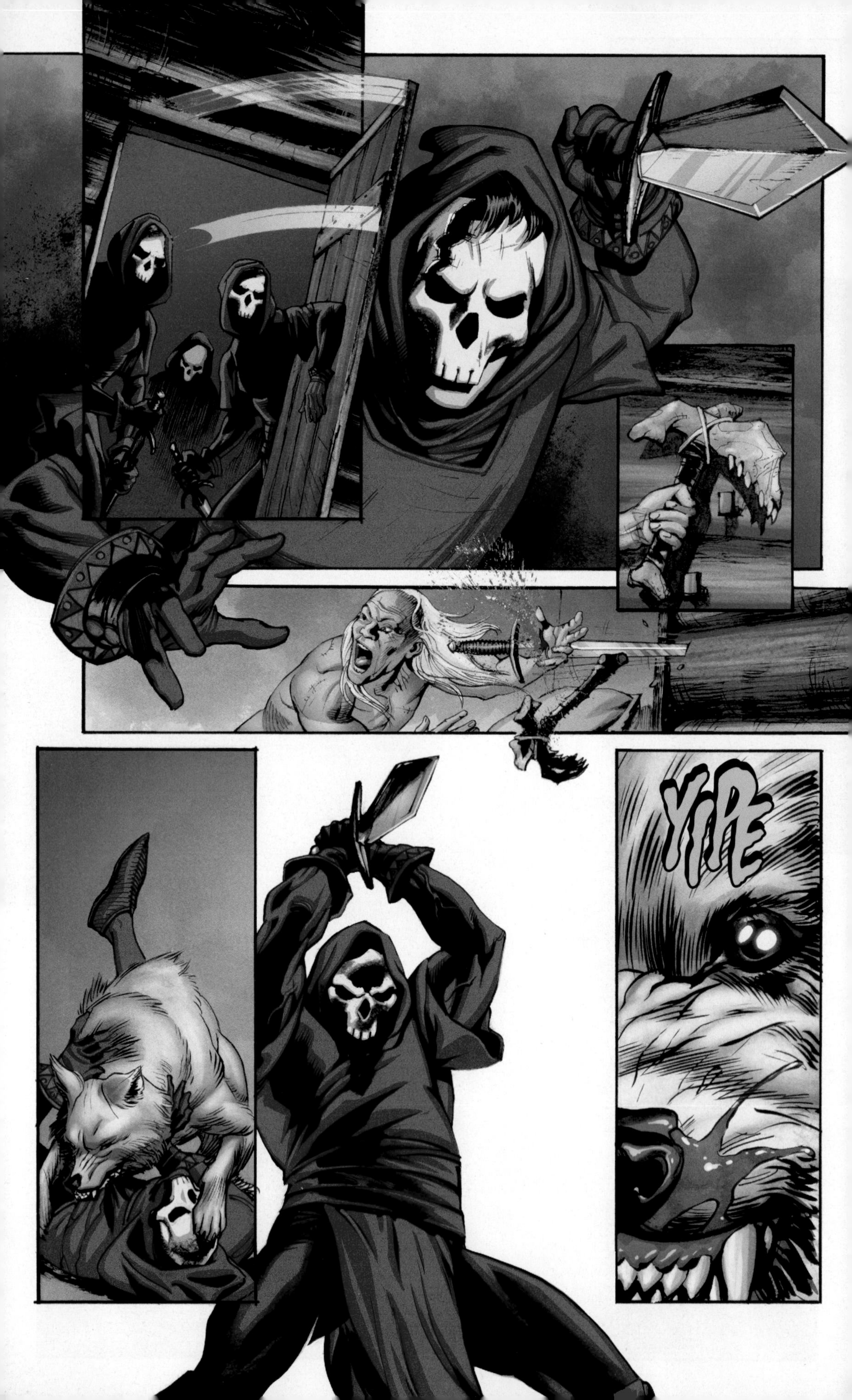
YIPE

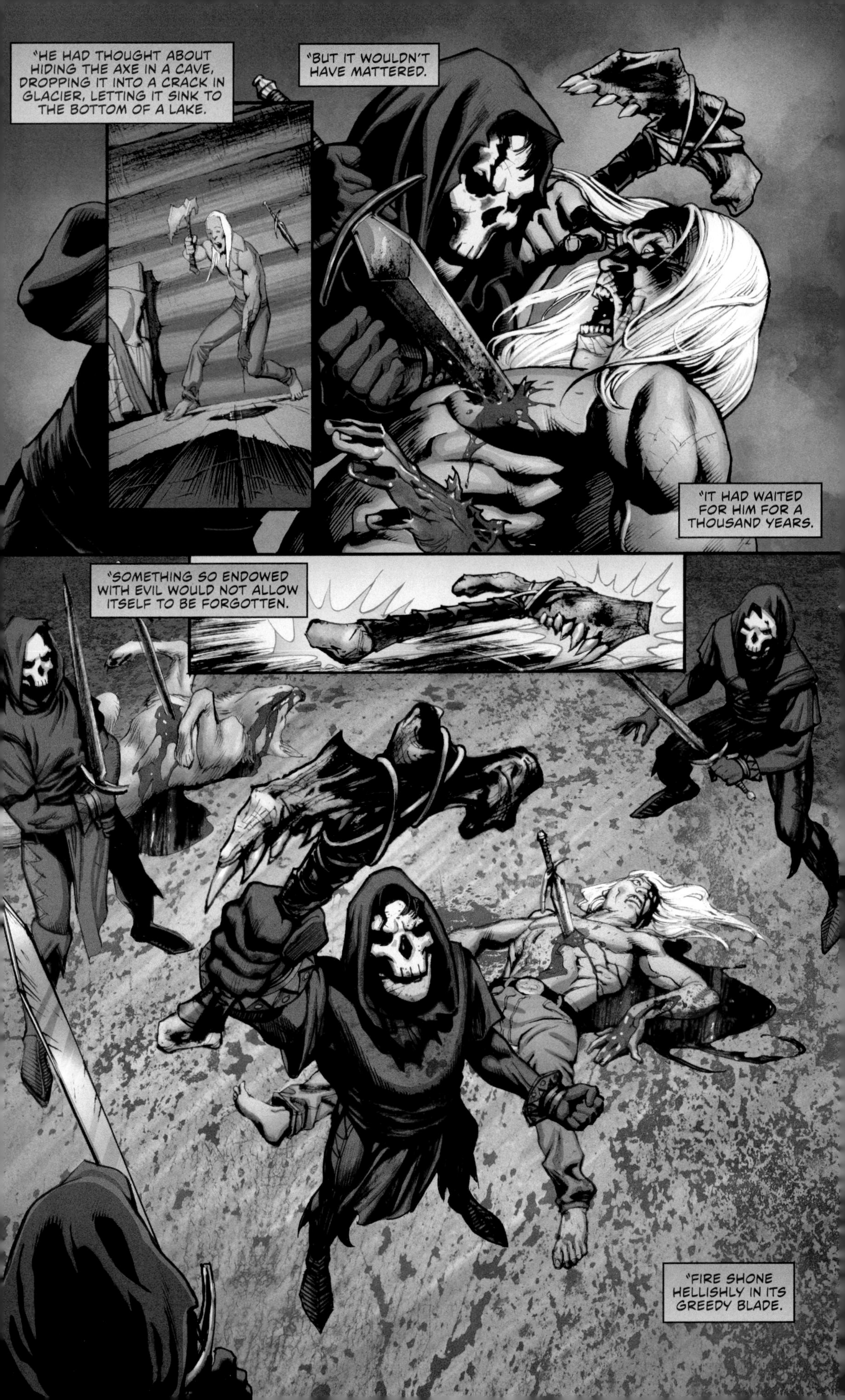
"HE HAD THOUGHT ABOUT HIDING THE AXE IN A CAVE, DROPPING IT INTO A CRACK IN GLACIER, LETTING IT SINK TO THE BOTTOM OF A LAKE.
"BUT IT WOULDN'T HAVE MATTERED.
"IT HAD WAITED FOR HIM FOR A THOUSAND YEARS.
"SOMETHING SO ENDOWED WITH EVIL WOULD NOT ALLOW ITSELF TO BE FORGOTTEN.
"FIRE SHONE HELLISHLY IN ITS GREEDY BLADE.

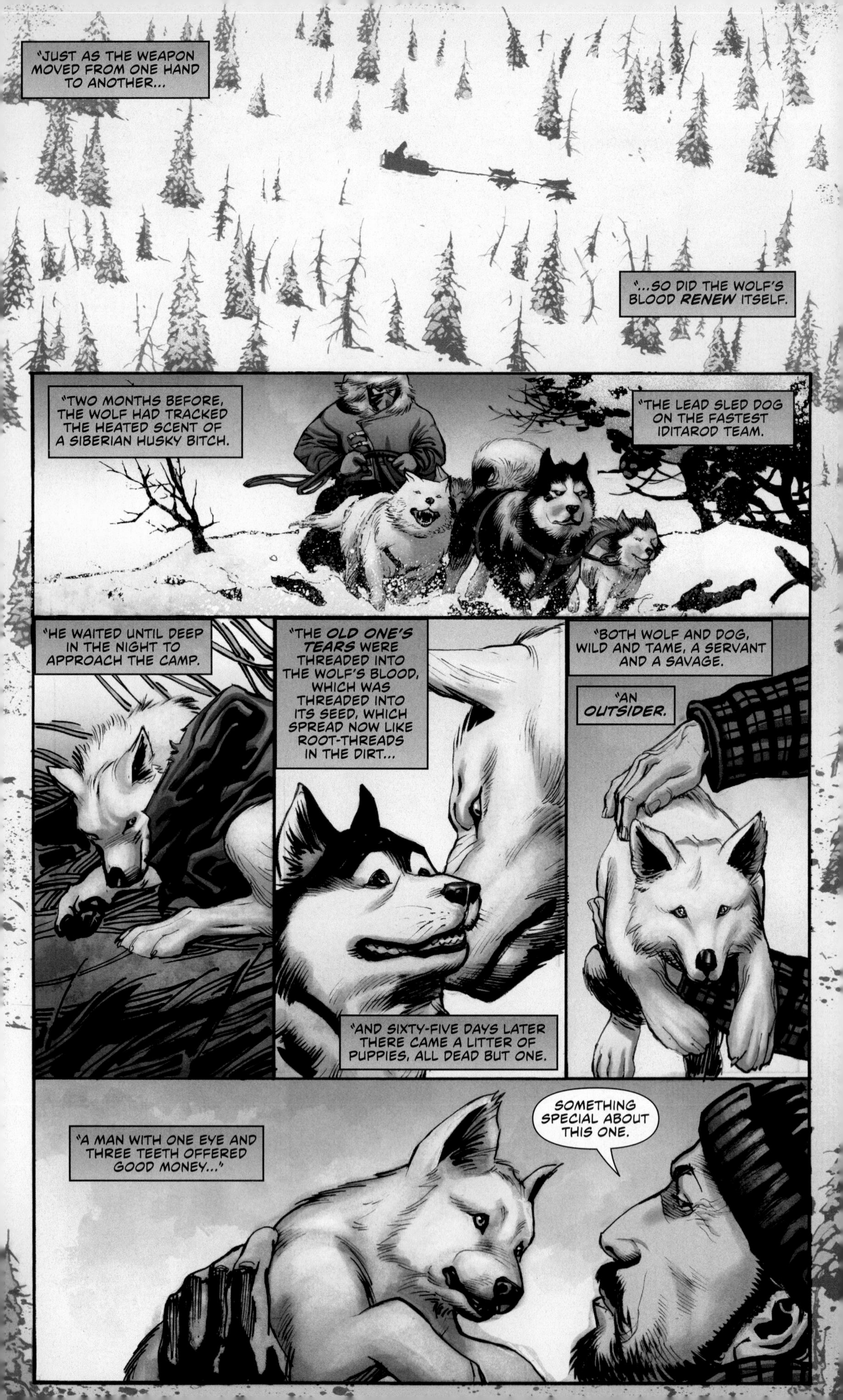
"JUST AS THE WEAPON MOVED FROM ONE HAND TO ANOTHER...
"...SO DID THE WOLF'S BLOOD *RENEW* ITSELF.
"TWO MONTHS BEFORE, THE WOLF HAD TRACKED THE HEATED SCENT OF A SIBERIAN HUSKY BITCH.
"THE LEAD SLED DOG ON THE FASTEST IDITAROD TEAM.
"HE WAITED UNTIL DEEP IN THE NIGHT TO APPROACH THE CAMP.
"THE *OLD ONE'S TEARS* WERE THREADED INTO THE WOLF'S BLOOD, WHICH WAS THREADED INTO ITS SEED, WHICH SPREAD NOW LIKE ROOT-THREADS IN THE DIRT...
"AND SIXTY-FIVE DAYS LATER THERE CAME A LITTER OF PUPPIES, ALL DEAD BUT ONE.
"BOTH WOLF AND DOG, WILD AND TAME, A SERVANT AND A SAVAGE.
"AN *OUTSIDER*.
"A MAN WITH ONE EYE AND THREE TEETH OFFERED GOOD MONEY..."
SOMETHING SPECIAL ABOUT THIS ONE.

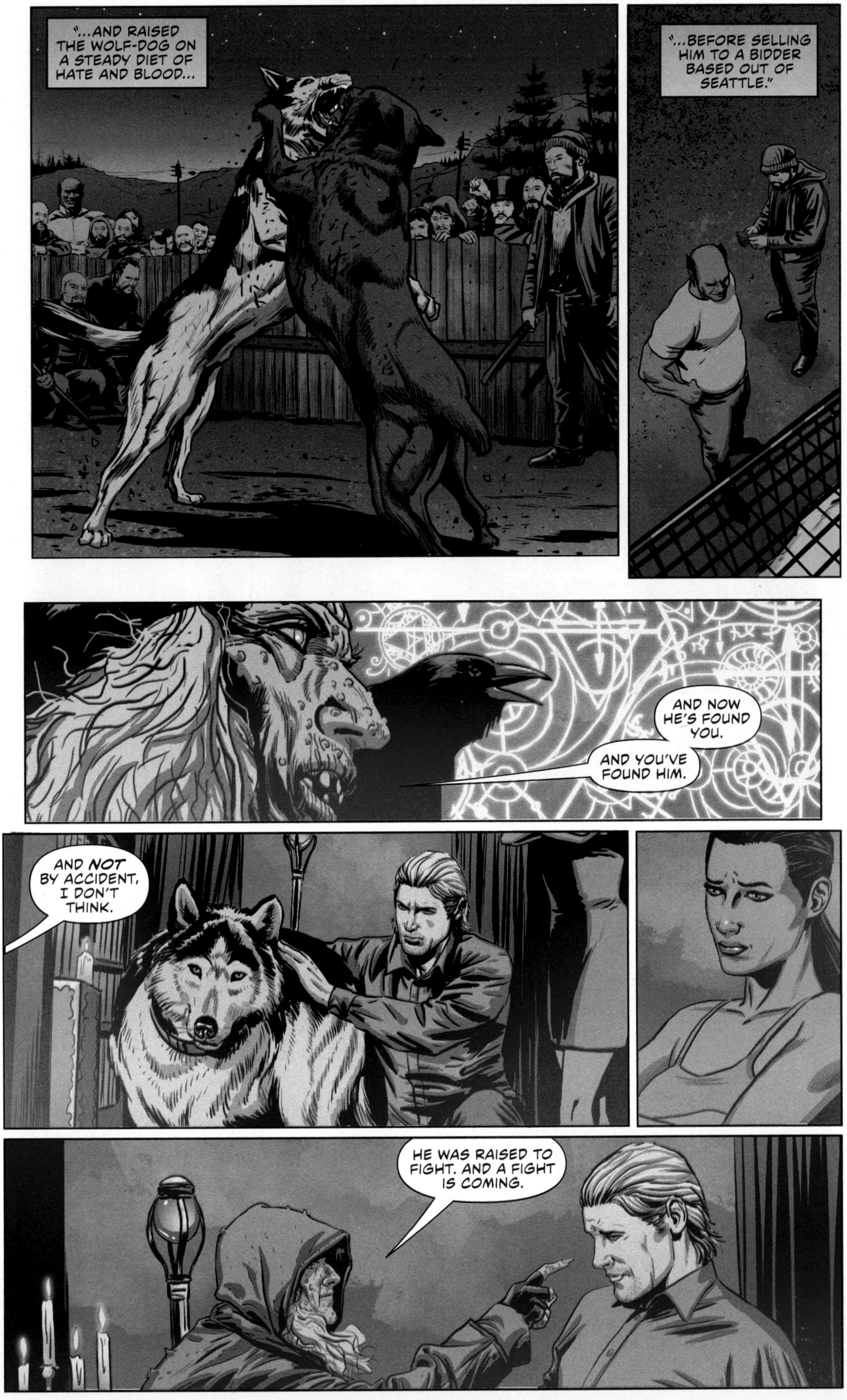
"...AND RAISED THE WOLF-DOG ON A STEADY DIET OF HATE AND BLOOD...
"...BEFORE SELLING HIM TO A BIDDER BASED OUT OF SEATTLE."
AND NOW HE'S FOUND YOU.
AND YOU'VE FOUND HIM.
AND NOT BY ACCIDENT, I DON'T THINK.
HE WAS RAISED TO FIGHT. AND A FIGHT IS COMING.

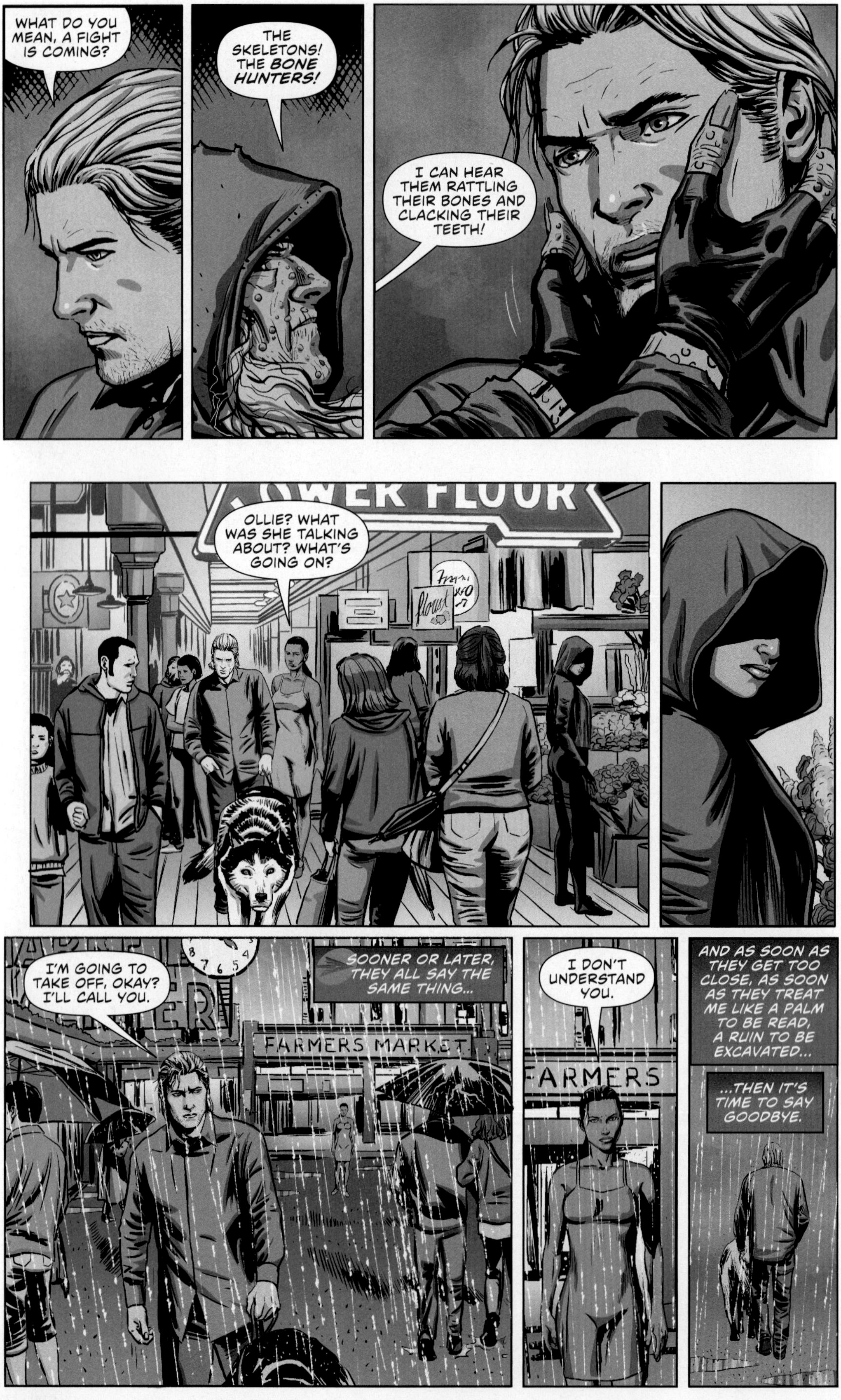
WHAT DO YOU MEAN, A FIGHT IS COMING?
THE SKELETONS! THE BONE HUNTERS!
I CAN HEAR THEM RATTLING THEIR BONES AND CLACKING THEIR TEETH!
OWER FLOOR
OLLIE? WHAT WAS SHE TALKING ABOUT? WHAT'S GOING ON?
I'M GOING TO TAKE OFF, OKAY? I'LL CALL YOU.
SOONER OR LATER, THEY ALL SAY THE SAME THING...
FARMERS MARKET
I DON'T UNDERSTAND YOU.
FARMERS
AND AS SOON AS THEY GET TOO CLOSE, AS SOON AS THEY TREAT ME LIKE A PALM TO BE READ, A RUIN TO BE EXCAVATED...
...THEN IT'S TIME TO SAY GOODBYE.

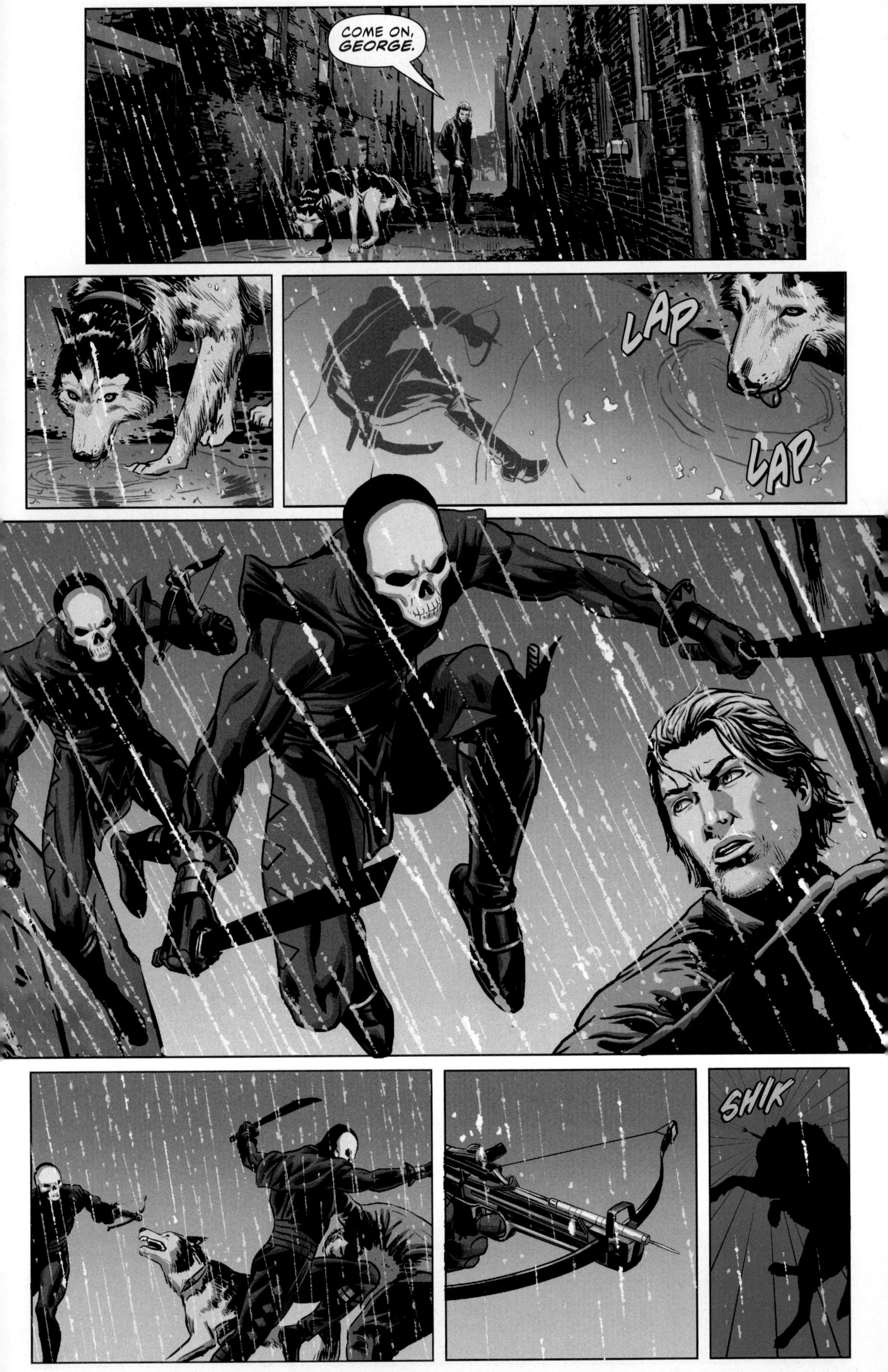
COME ON, GEORGE.
LAP
LAP
SHIK

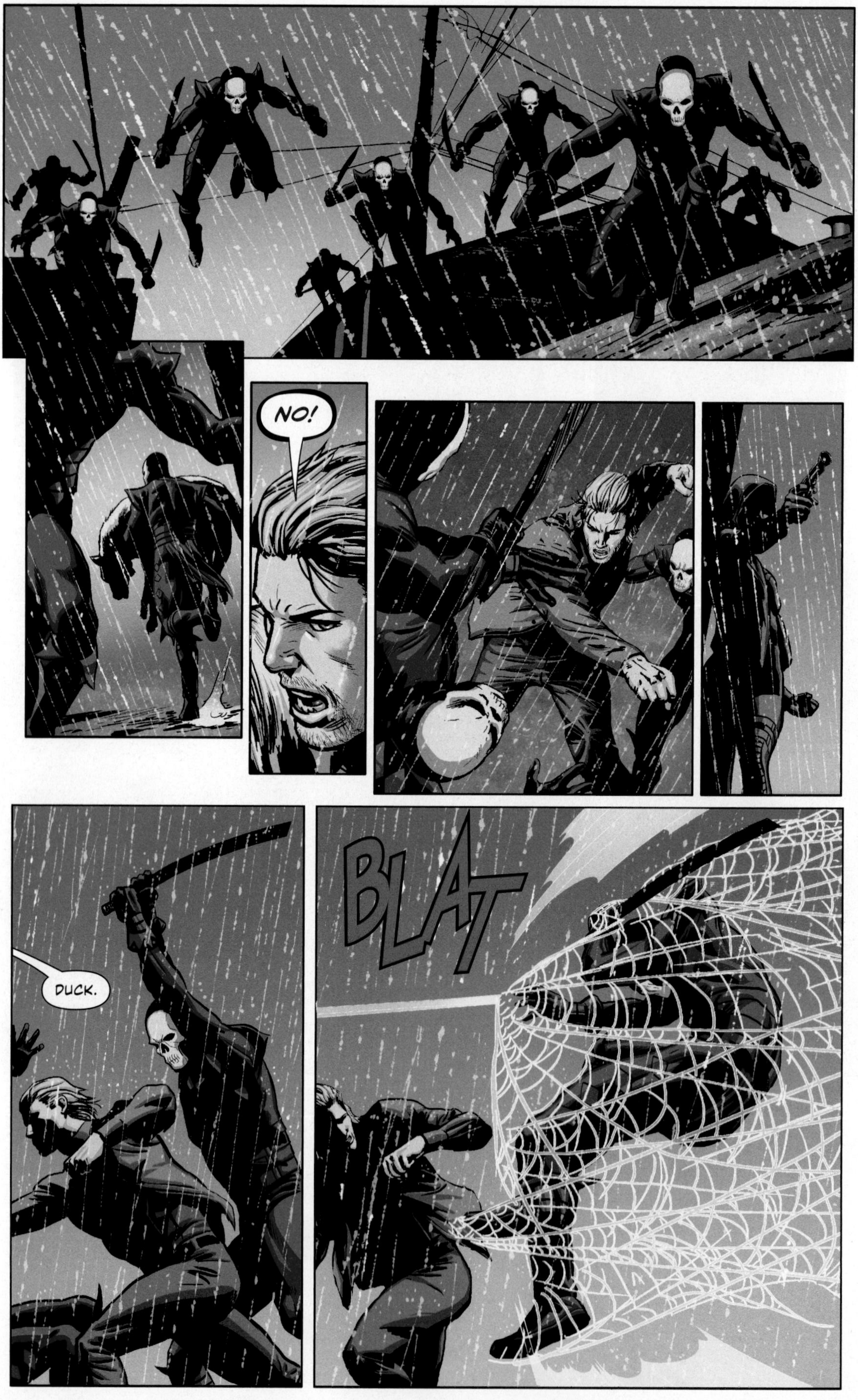
NO!
DUCK.
BLAT

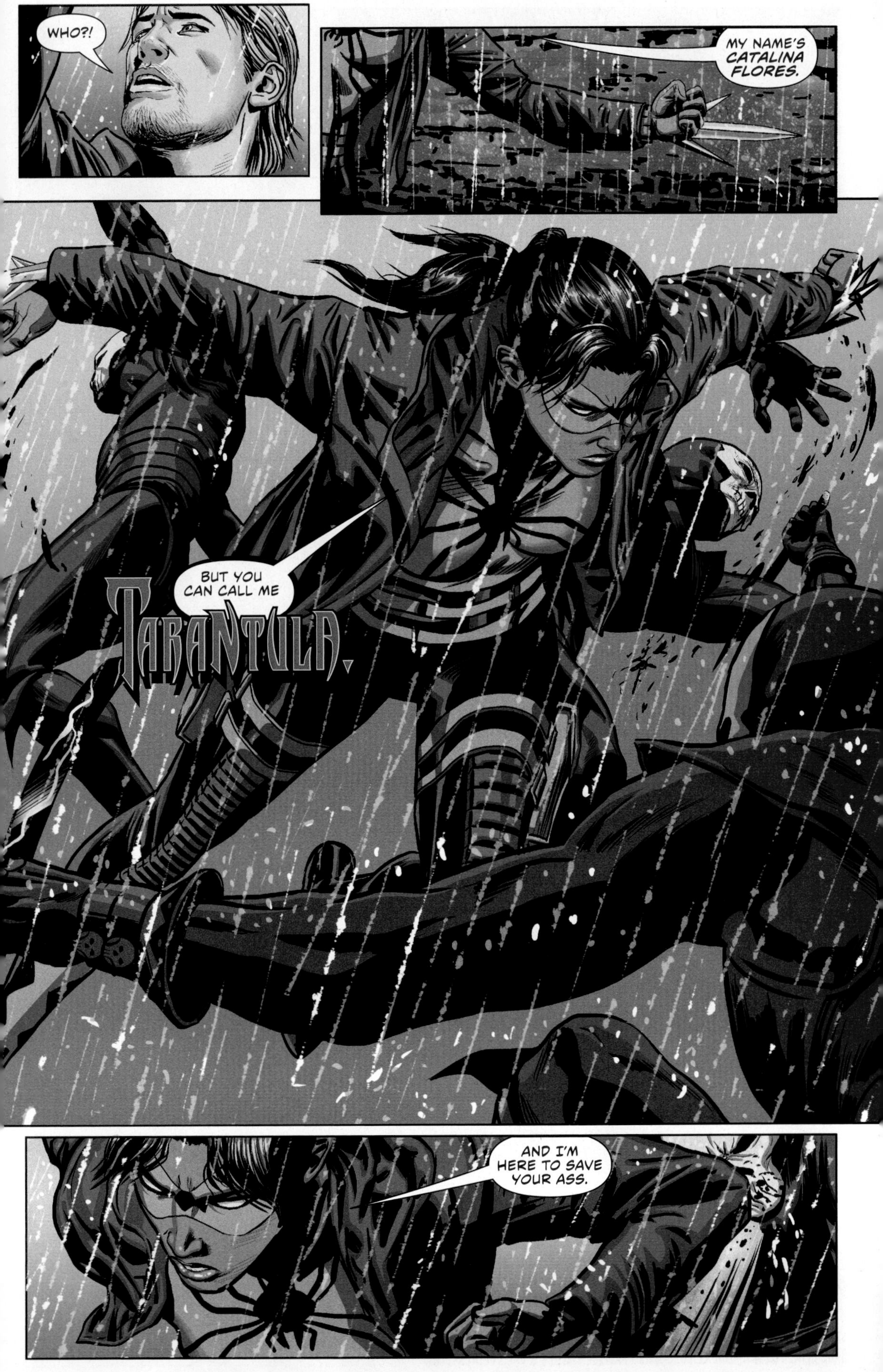
WHO?!
MY NAME'S CATALINA FLORES.
BUT YOU CAN CALL ME
TARANTULA.
AND I'M HERE TO SAVE YOUR ASS.

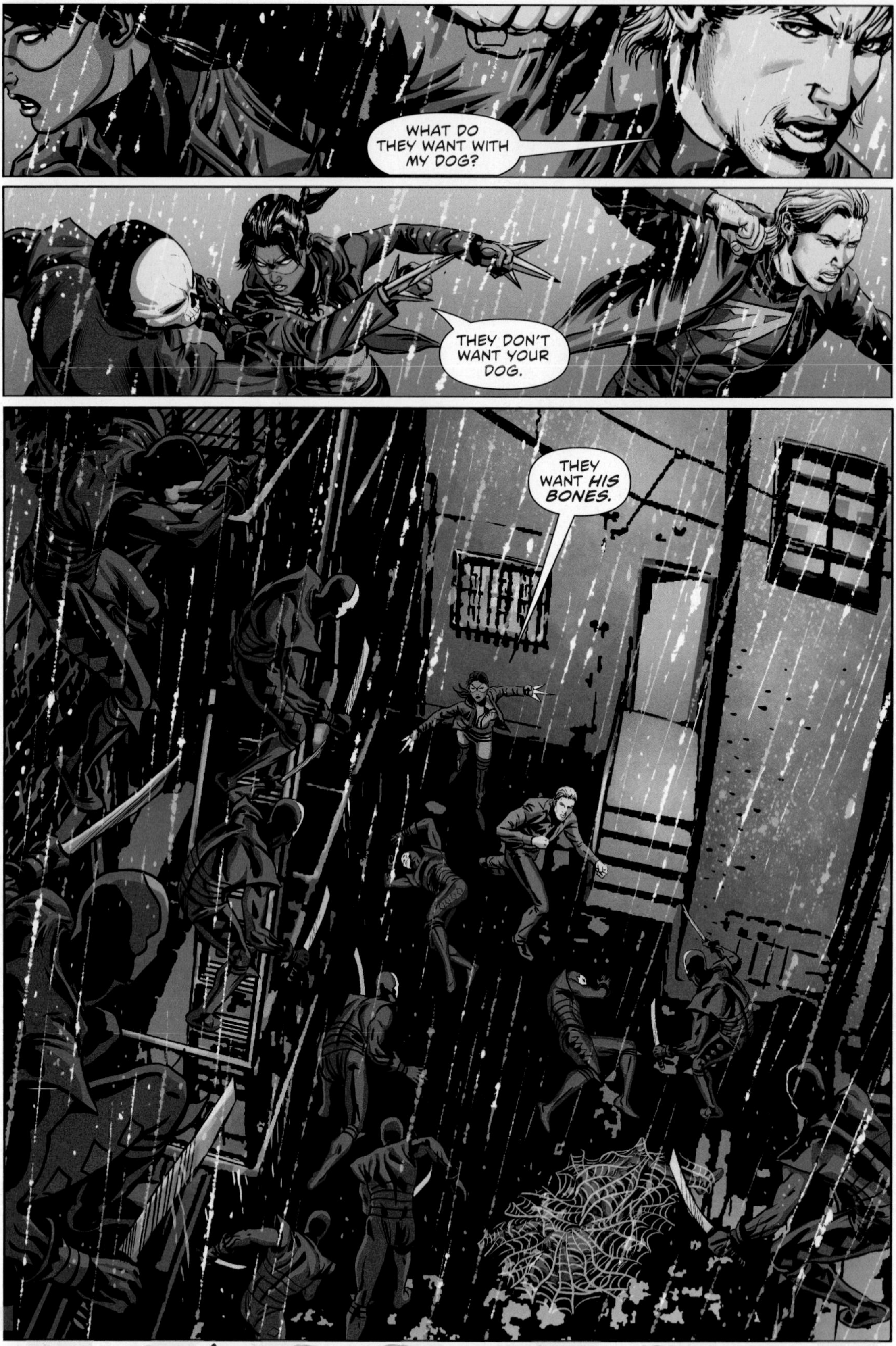
WHAT DO THEY WANT WITH MY DOG?
THEY DON'T WANT YOUR DOG.
THEY WANT *HIS* BONES.

secret of the WOLF

STORYTELLERS: **BENJAMIN PERCY** SCRIPT • **PATRICK ZIRCHER & FABRIZIO FIORENTINO** ART
GABE ELTAEB COLORIST • **ROB LEIGH** LETTERER • **PATRICK ZIRCHER & GABE ELTAEB** COVER

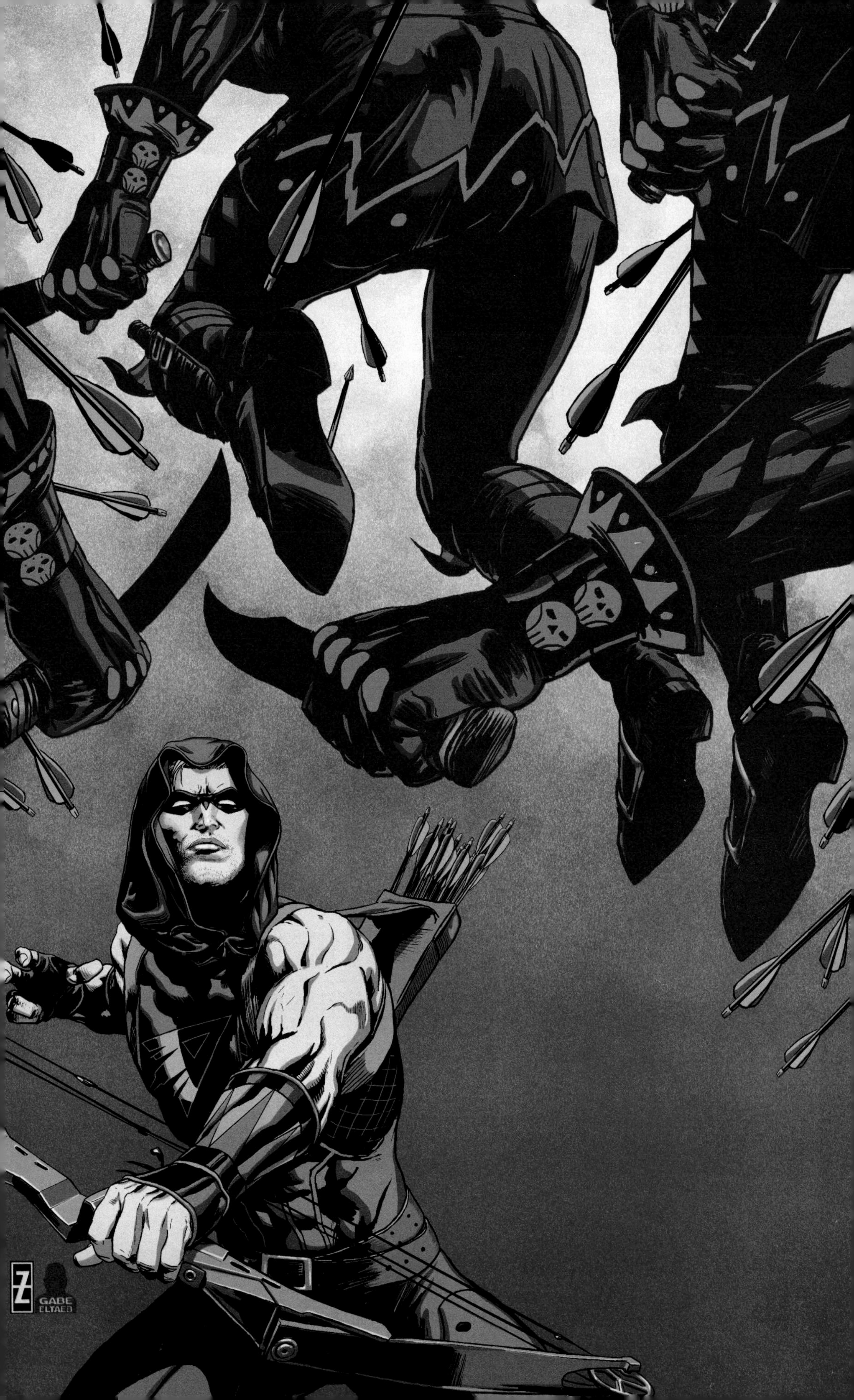
GABE
ELTAEB

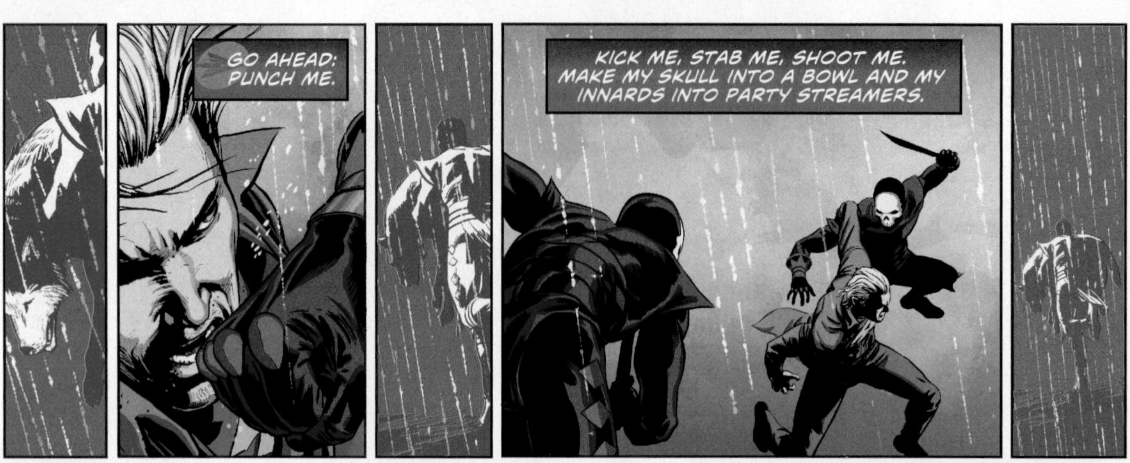
GO AHEAD: PUNCH ME.
KICK ME, STAB ME, SHOOT ME. MAKE MY SKULL INTO A BOWL AND MY INNARDS INTO PARTY STREAMERS.

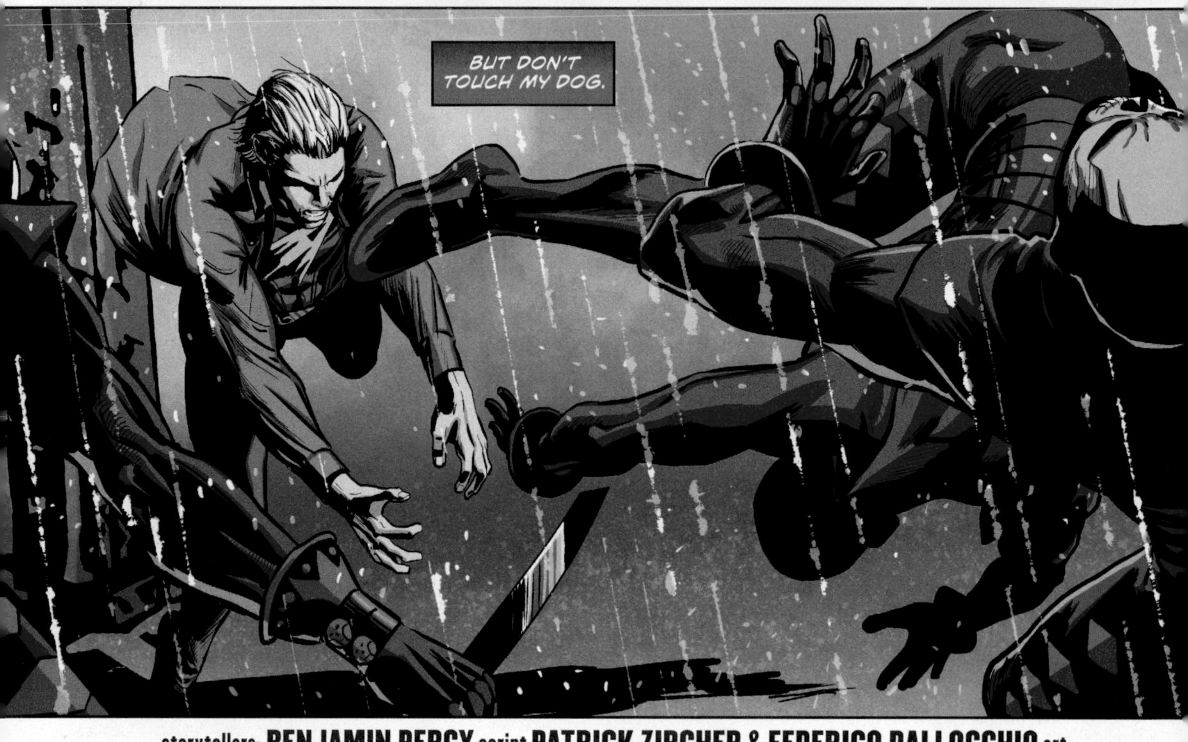
BUT DON'T TOUCH MY DOG.

storytellers: **BENJAMIN PERCY** script **PATRICK ZIRCHER & FEDERICO DALLOCCHIO** art

The Bone Hunters

GABE ELTAEB colorist **ROB LEIGH** letterer **ZIRCHER & ELTAEB** cover

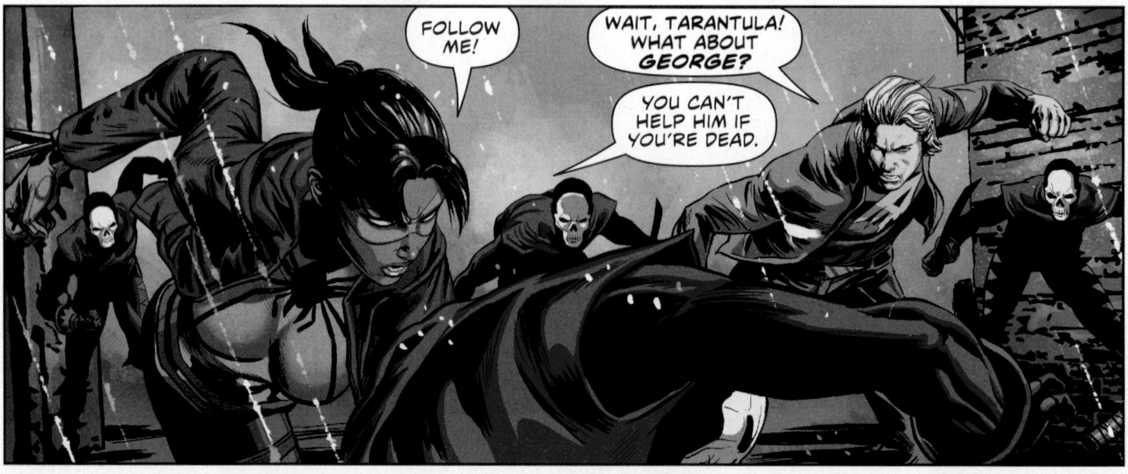
FOLLOW ME!
WAIT, TARANTULA! WHAT ABOUT *GEORGE?*
YOU CAN'T HELP HIM IF YOU'RE DEAD.

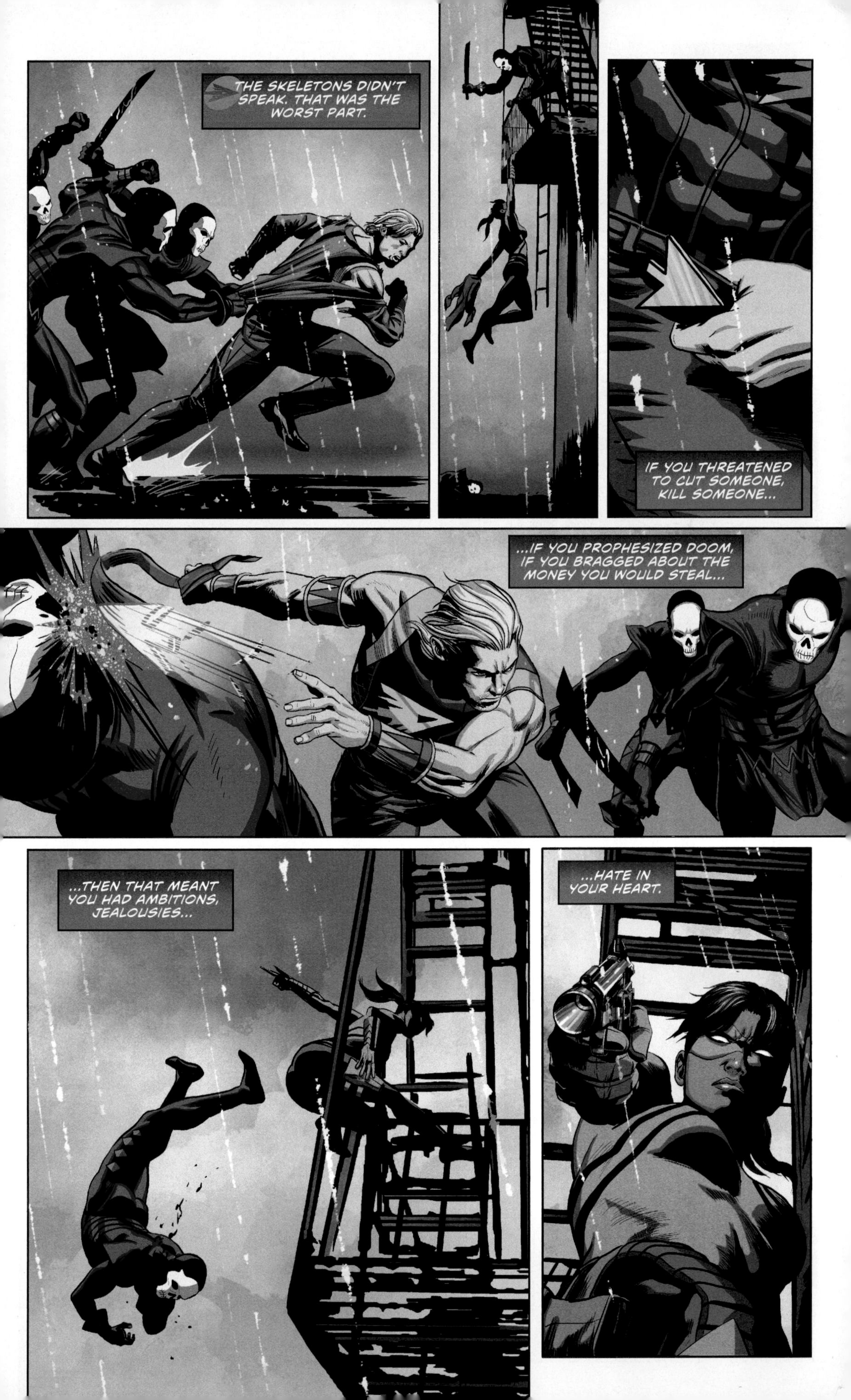
THE SKELETONS DIDN'T SPEAK. THAT WAS THE WORST PART.
IF YOU THREATENED TO CUT SOMEONE, KILL SOMEONE...
...IF YOU PROPHESIZED DOOM, IF YOU BRAGGED ABOUT THE MONEY YOU WOULD STEAL...
...THEN THAT MEANT YOU HAD AMBITIONS, JEALOUSIES...
...HATE IN YOUR HEART.

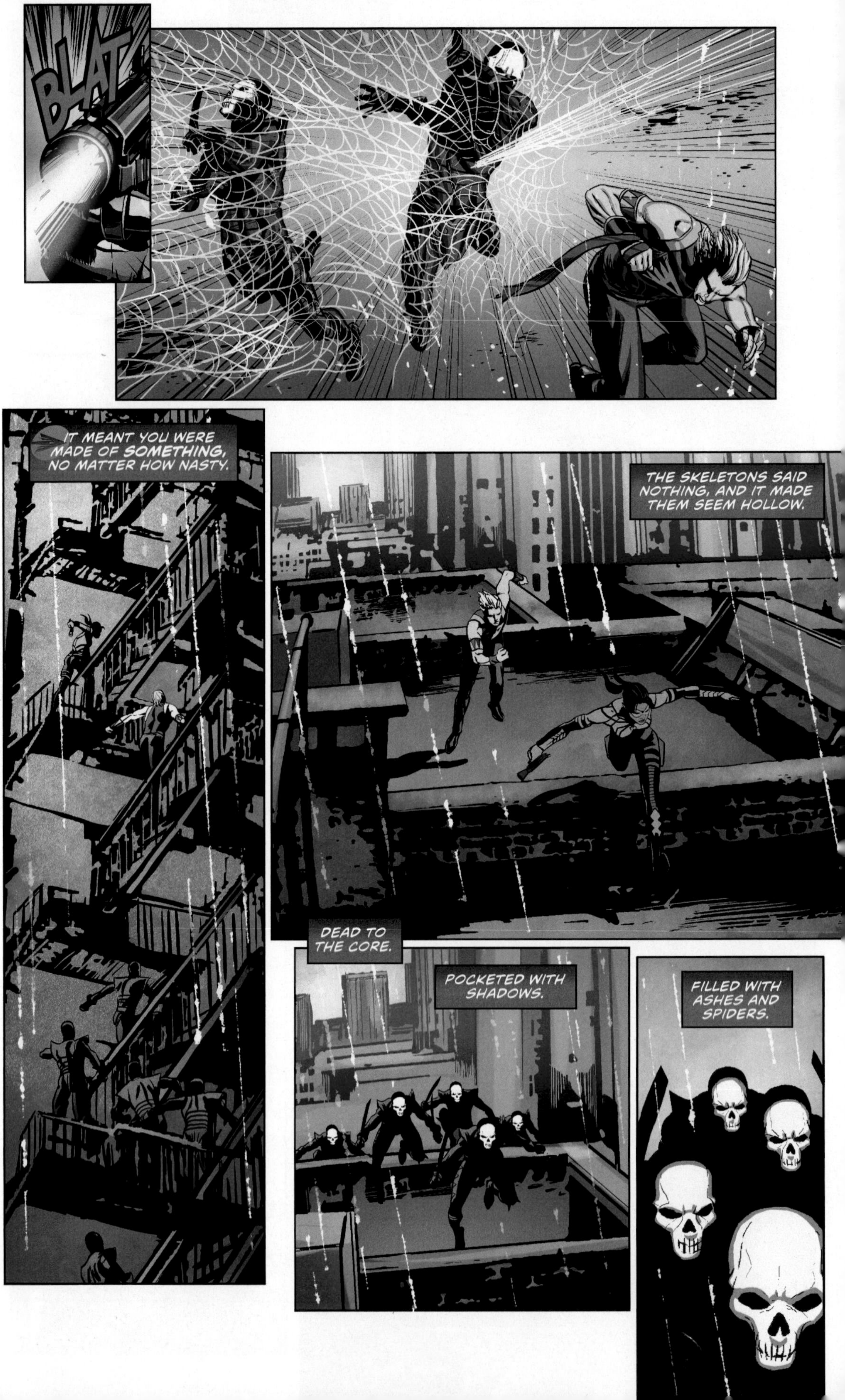
BLAT
IT MEANT YOU WERE MADE OF SOMETHING, NO MATTER HOW NASTY.
THE SKELETONS SAID NOTHING, AND IT MADE THEM SEEM HOLLOW.
DEAD TO THE CORE.
POCKETED WITH SHADOWS.
FILLED WITH ASHES AND SPIDERS.

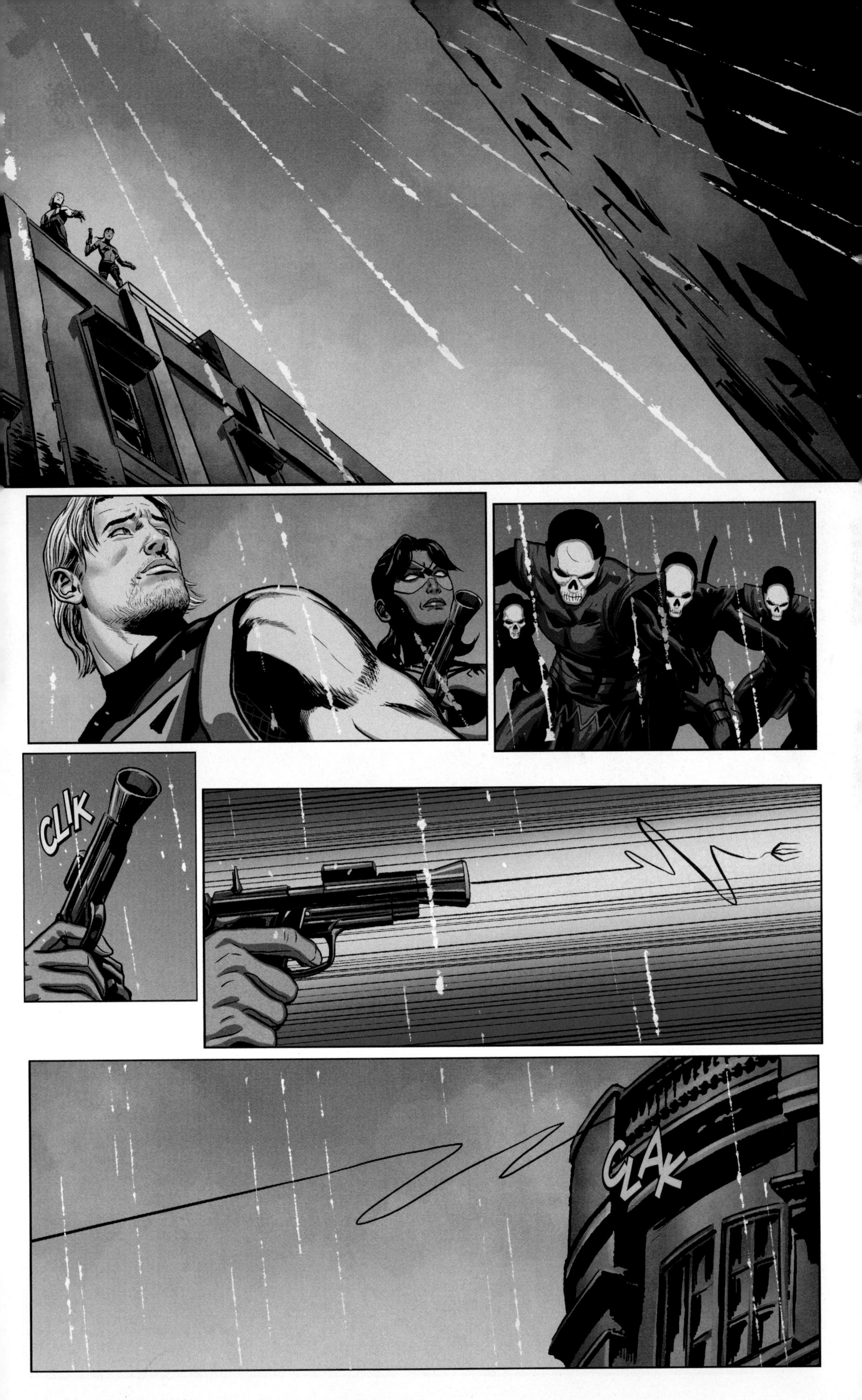
CLIK
CLAK

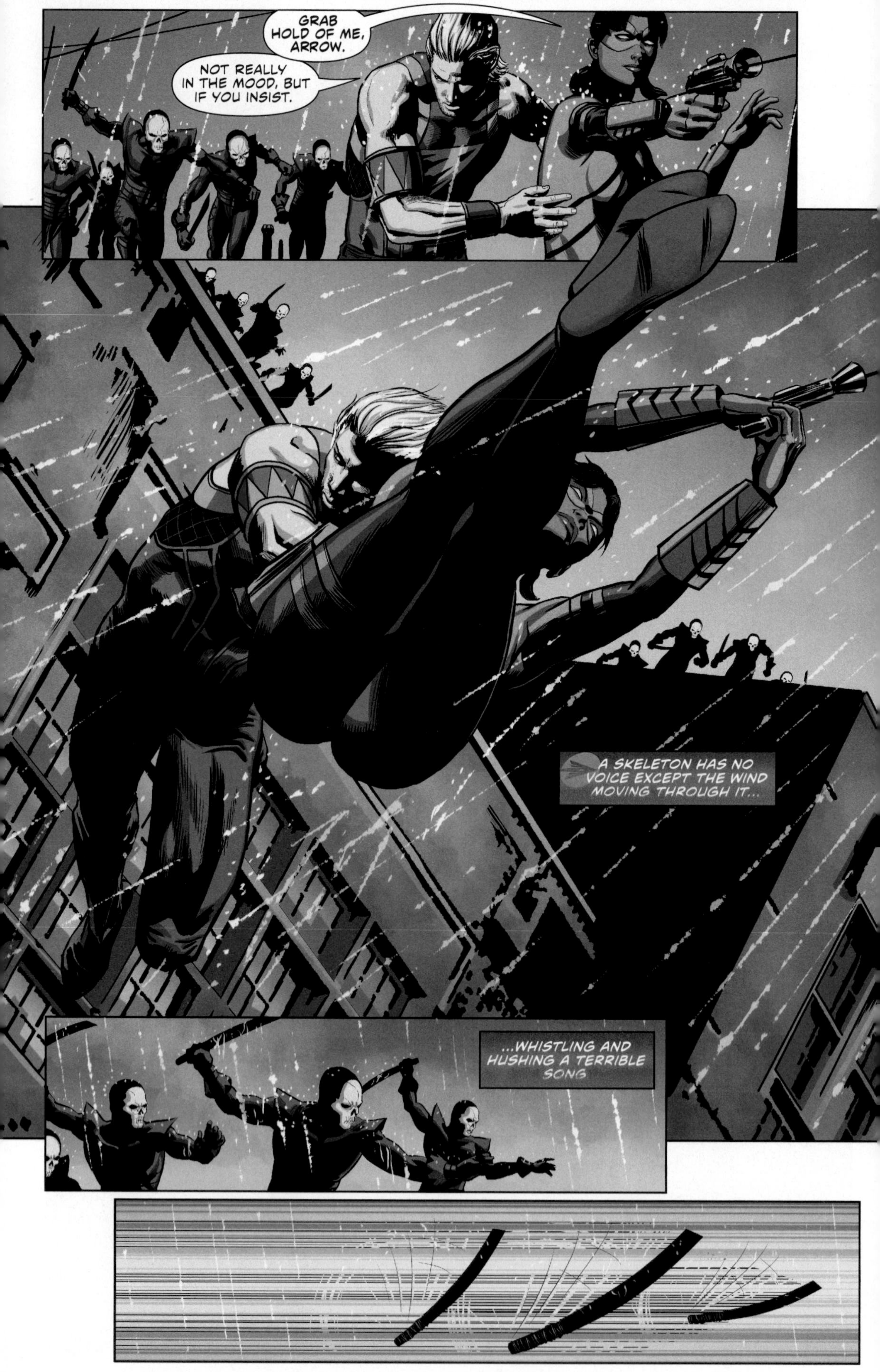
GRAB HOLD OF ME, ARROW.
NOT REALLY IN THE MOOD, BUT IF YOU INSIST.
A SKELETON HAS NO VOICE EXCEPT THE WIND MOVING THROUGH IT...
...WHISTLING AND HUSHING A TERRIBLE SONG

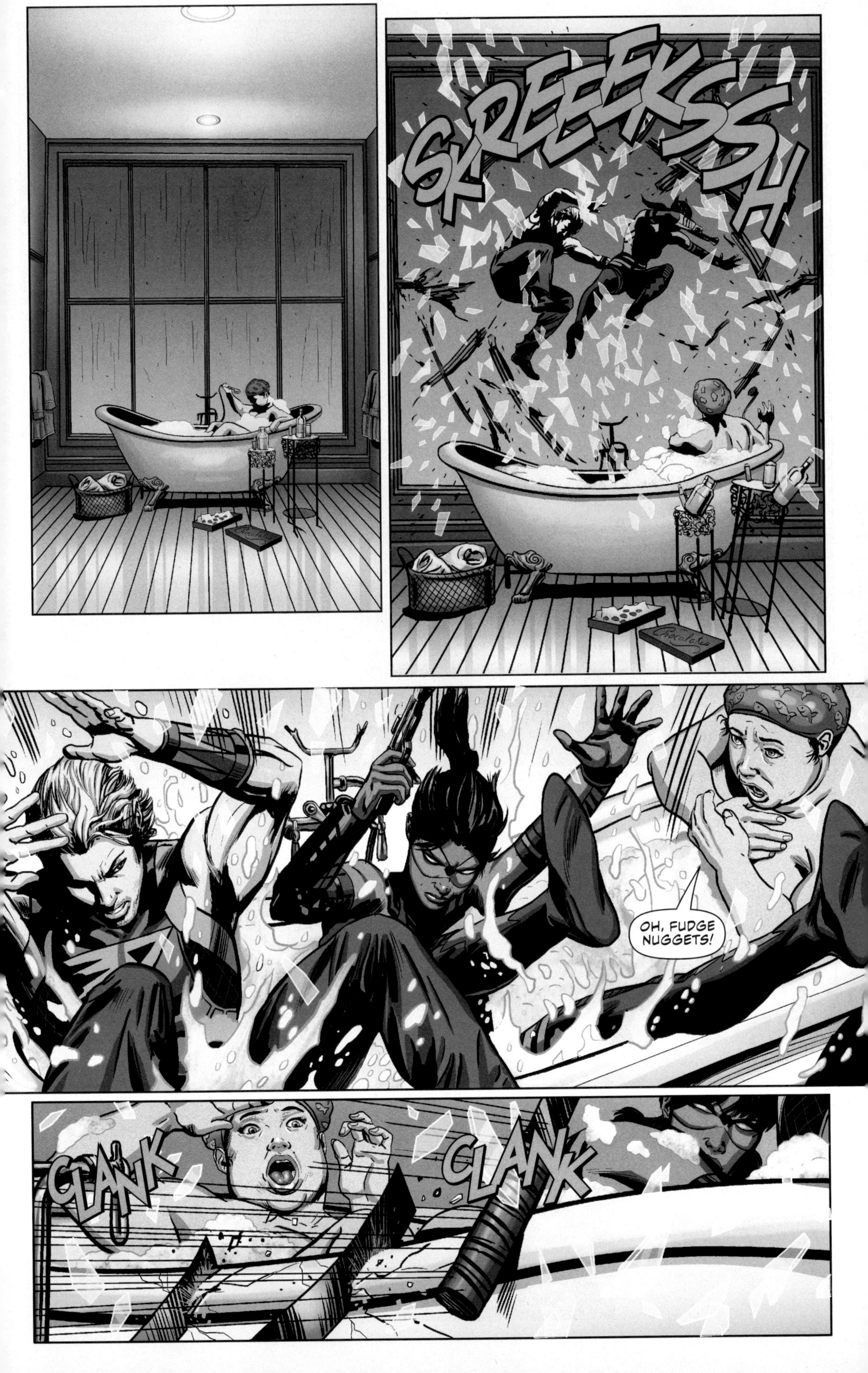
SKREEEKSSH
OH, FUDGE NUGGETS!
CLANK
CLANK

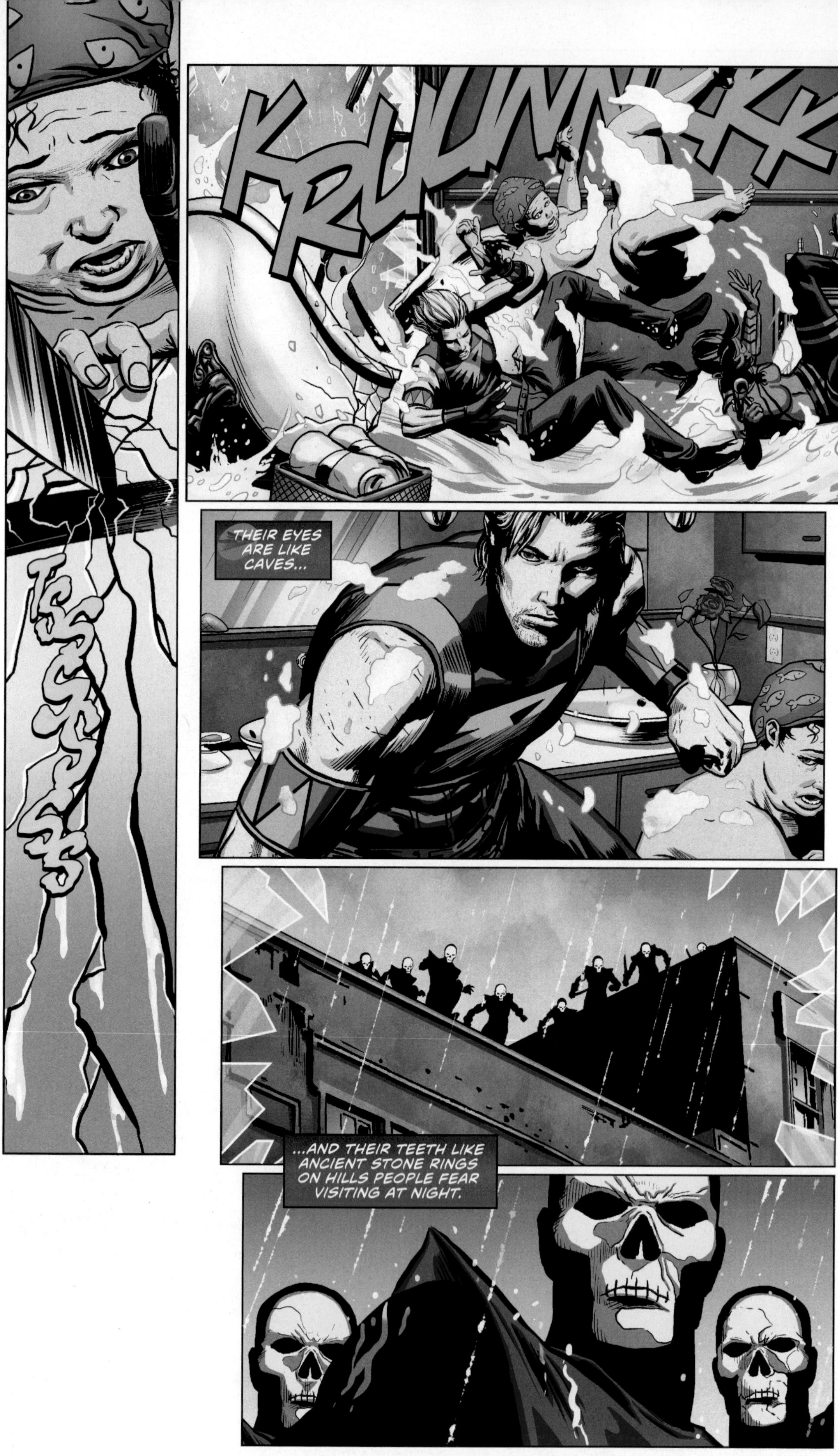
TSSSSSS
KRUUNNKK
THEIR EYES ARE LIKE CAVES...
...AND THEIR TEETH LIKE ANCIENT STONE RINGS ON HILLS PEOPLE FEAR VISITING AT NIGHT.

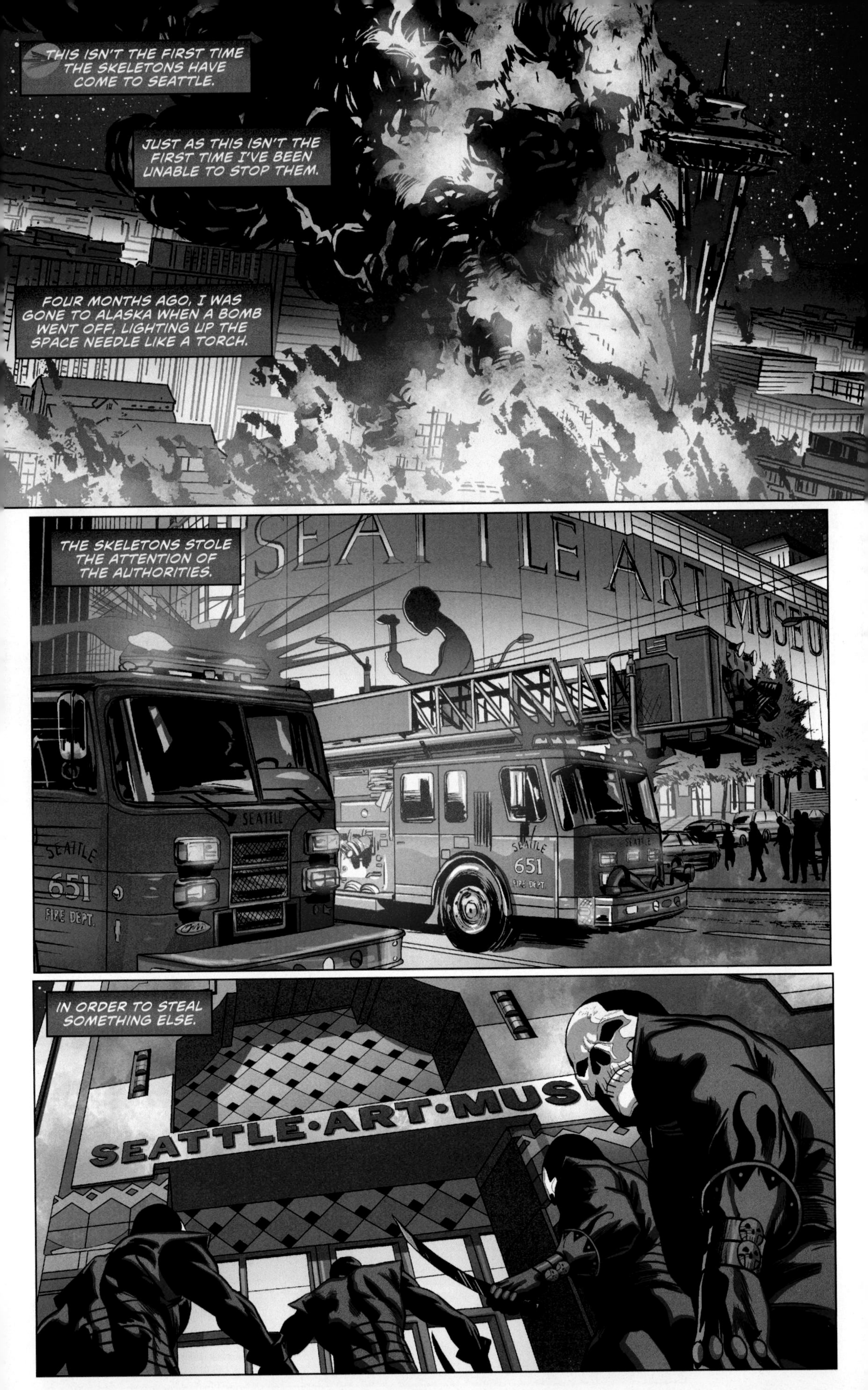
THIS ISN'T THE FIRST TIME THE SKELETONS HAVE COME TO SEATTLE.
JUST AS THIS ISN'T THE FIRST TIME I'VE BEEN UNABLE TO STOP THEM.
FOUR MONTHS AGO, I WAS GONE TO ALASKA WHEN A BOMB WENT OFF, LIGHTING UP THE SPACE NEEDLE LIKE A TORCH.
THE SKELETONS STOLE THE ATTENTION OF THE AUTHORITIES.
SEATTLE ART MUSEU
SEATTLE
SEATTLE
651
FIRE DEPT.
SEATTLE
651
FIRE DEPT.
IN ORDER TO STEAL SOMETHING ELSE.
SEATTLE·ART·MUS

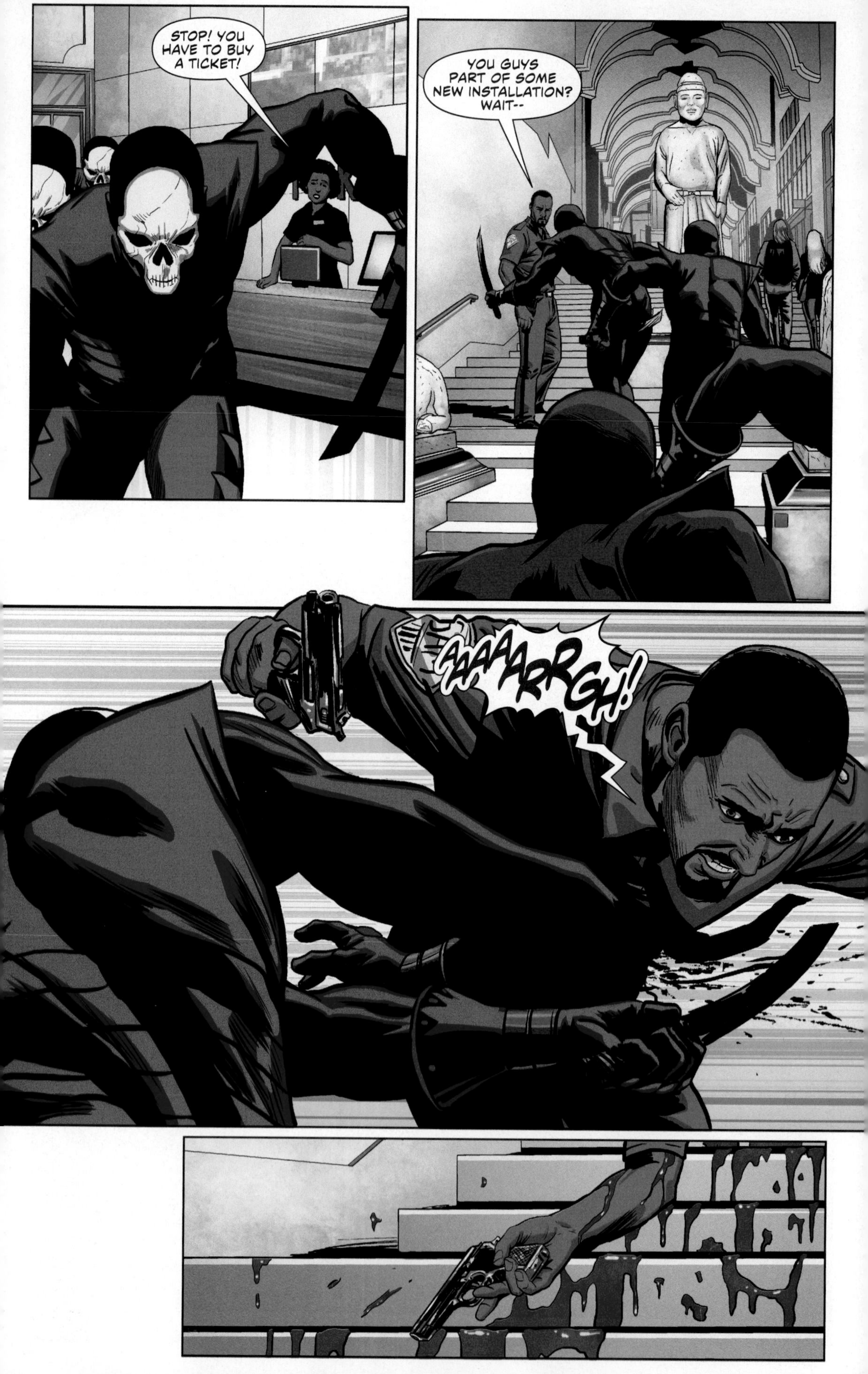
STOP! YOU HAVE TO BUY A TICKET!
YOU GUYS PART OF SOME NEW INSTALLATION? WAIT--
AAAAARRGH!

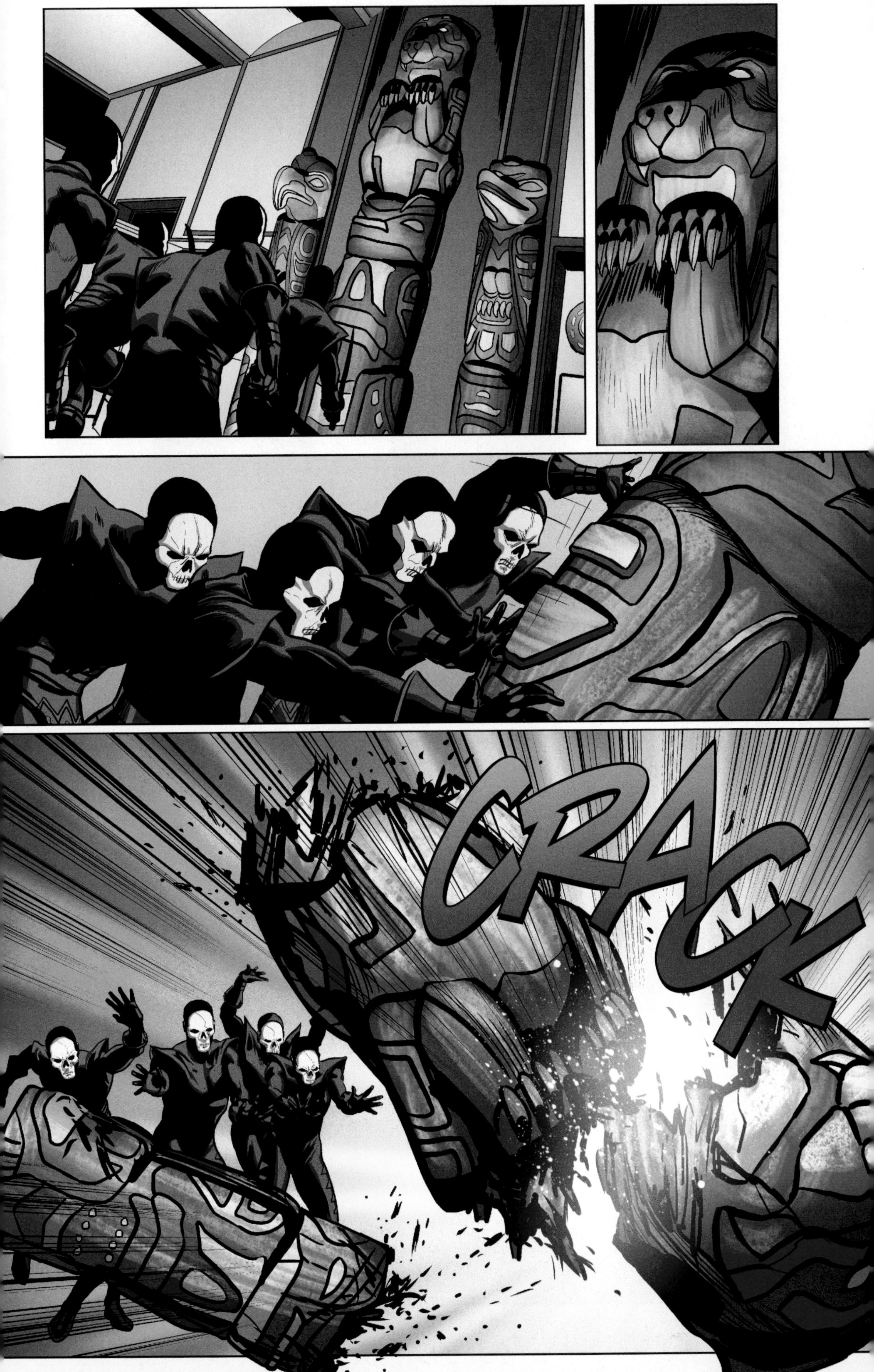
CRACK

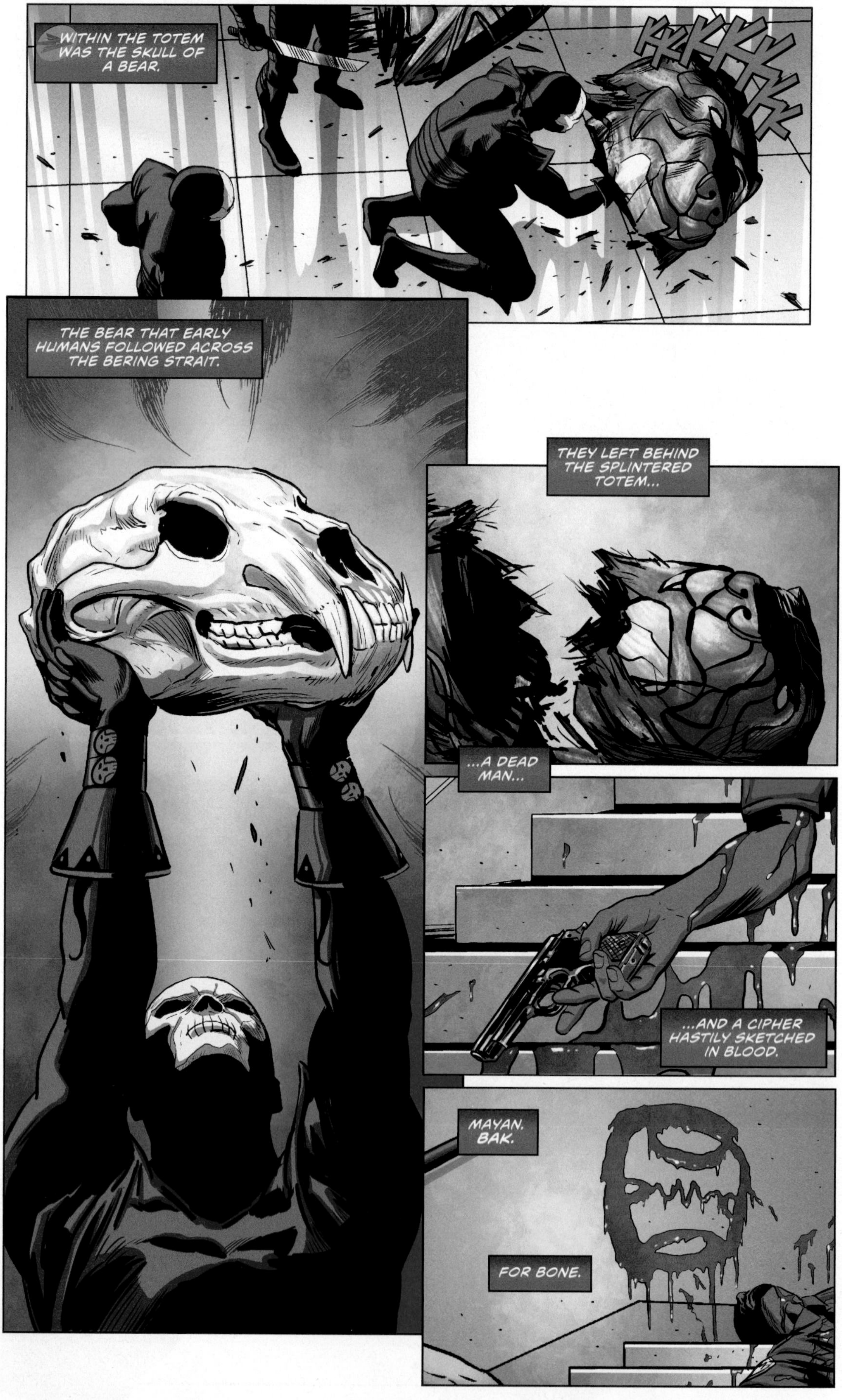
WITHIN THE TOTEM WAS THE SKULL OF A BEAR.
KKKKKKK
THE BEAR THAT EARLY HUMANS FOLLOWED ACROSS THE BERING STRAIT.
THEY LEFT BEHIND THE SPLINTERED TOTEM...
...A DEAD MAN...
...AND A CIPHER HASTILY SKETCHED IN BLOOD.
MAYAN. BAK.
FOR BONE.

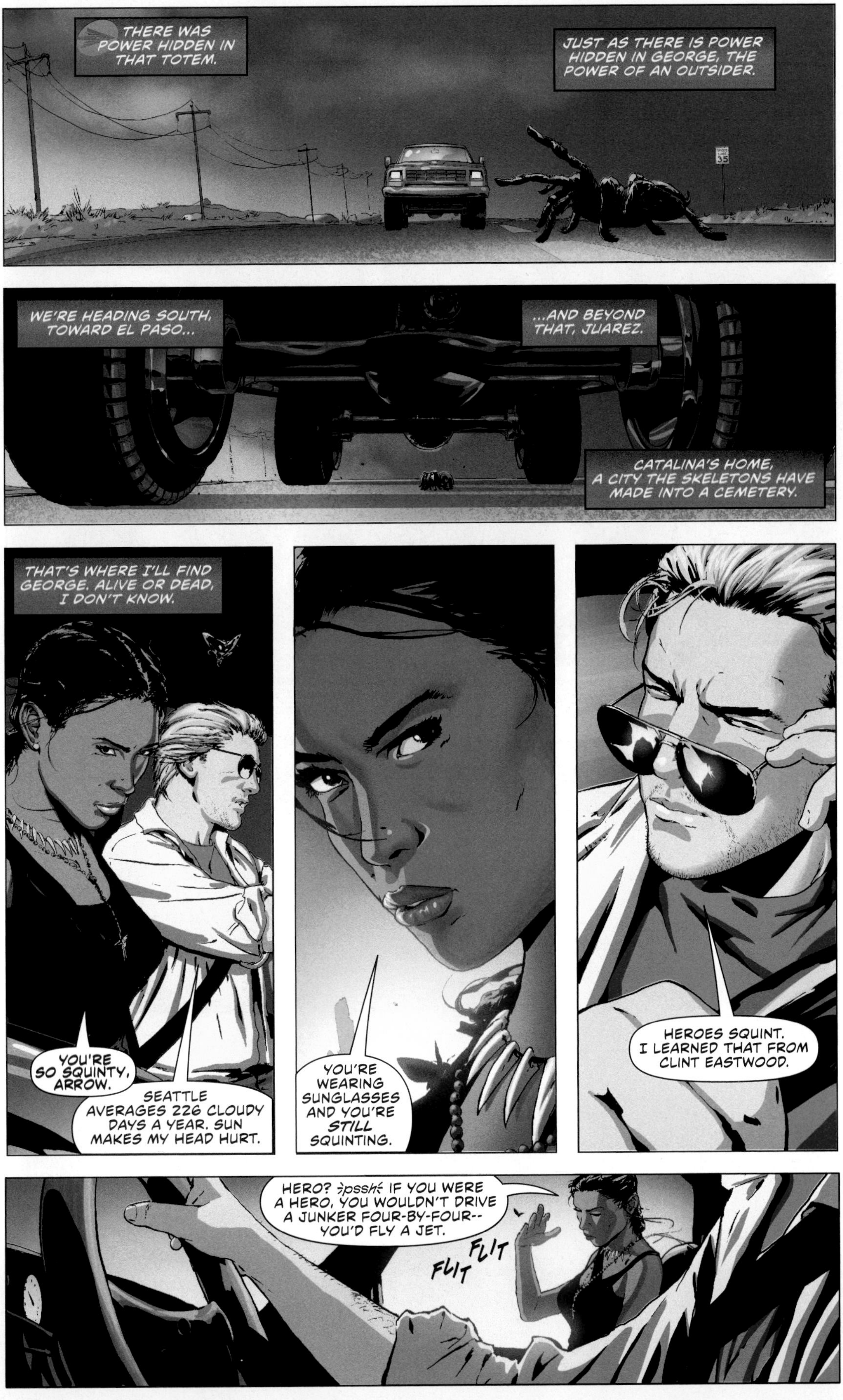

THERE WAS POWER HIDDEN IN THAT TOTEM.
JUST AS THERE IS POWER HIDDEN IN GEORGE, THE POWER OF AN OUTSIDER.
WE'RE HEADING SOUTH, TOWARD EL PASO...
...AND BEYOND THAT, JUAREZ.
CATALINA'S HOME, A CITY THE SKELETONS HAVE MADE INTO A CEMETERY.
THAT'S WHERE I'LL FIND GEORGE. ALIVE OR DEAD, I DON'T KNOW.
YOU'RE SO SQUINTY, ARROW.
SEATTLE AVERAGES 226 CLOUDY DAYS A YEAR. SUN MAKES MY HEAD HURT.
YOU'RE WEARING SUNGLASSES AND YOU'RE STILL SQUINTING.
HEROES SQUINT. I LEARNED THAT FROM CLINT EASTWOOD.
HERO? pssh IF YOU WERE A HERO, YOU WOULDN'T DRIVE A JUNKER FOUR-BY-FOUR-- YOU'D FLY A JET.
FLIT FLIT FLIT

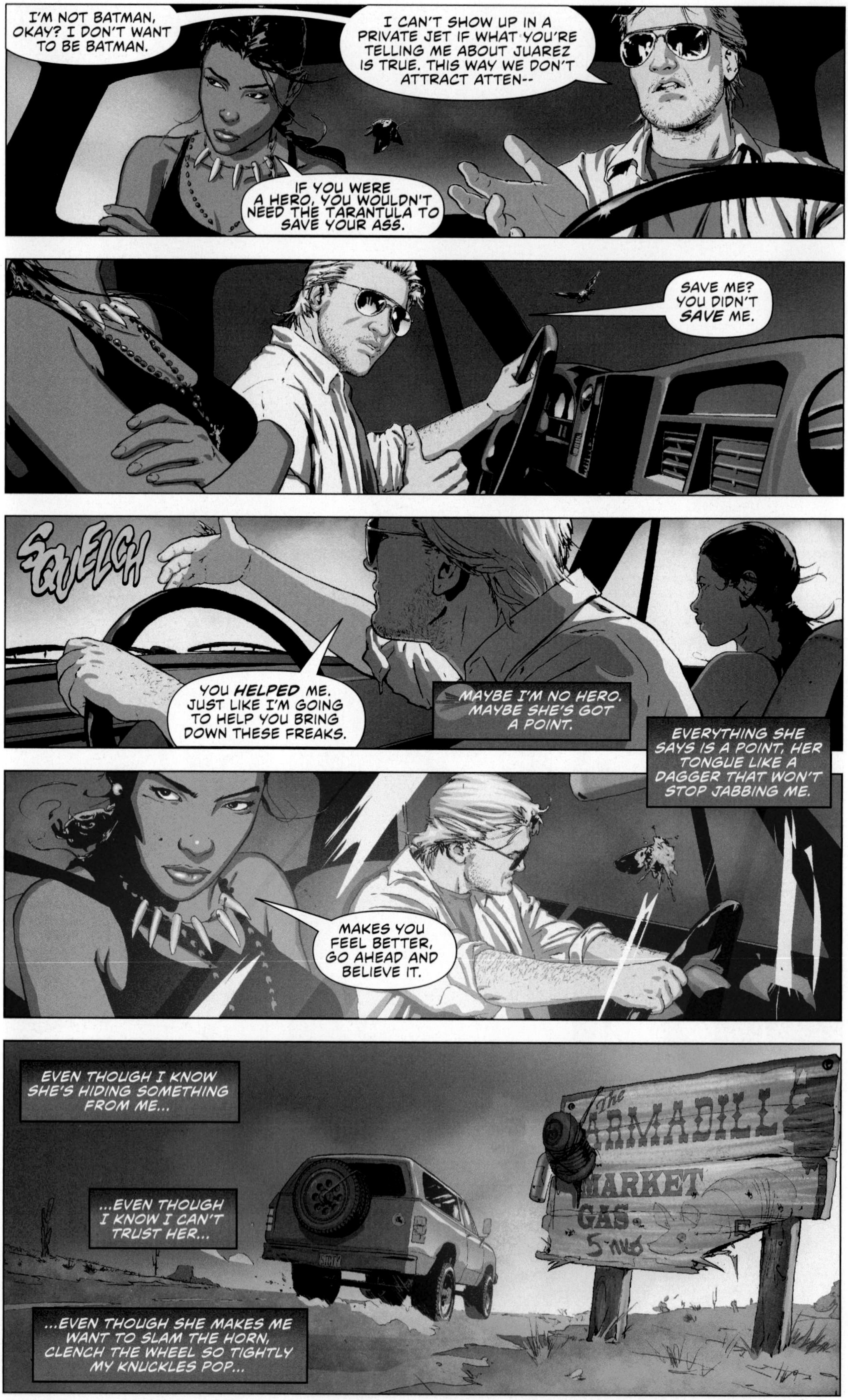
I'M NOT BATMAN, OKAY? I DON'T WANT TO BE BATMAN.
I CAN'T SHOW UP IN A PRIVATE JET IF WHAT YOU'RE TELLING ME ABOUT JUAREZ IS TRUE. THIS WAY WE DON'T ATTRACT ATTEN--
IF YOU WERE A HERO, YOU WOULDN'T NEED THE TARANTULA TO SAVE YOUR ASS.
SAVE ME? YOU DIDN'T SAVE ME.
SQUELCH
YOU HELPED ME. JUST LIKE I'M GOING TO HELP YOU BRING DOWN THESE FREAKS.
MAYBE I'M NO HERO. MAYBE SHE'S GOT A POINT.
EVERYTHING SHE SAYS IS A POINT, HER TONGUE LIKE A DAGGER THAT WON'T STOP JABBING ME.
MAKES YOU FEEL BETTER, GO AHEAD AND BELIEVE IT.
EVEN THOUGH I KNOW SHE'S HIDING SOMETHING FROM ME...
The ARMADILL
MARKET
GAS
...EVEN THOUGH I KNOW I CAN'T TRUST HER...
...EVEN THOUGH SHE MAKES ME WANT TO SLAM THE HORN, CLENCH THE WHEEL SO TIGHTLY MY KNUCKLES POP...

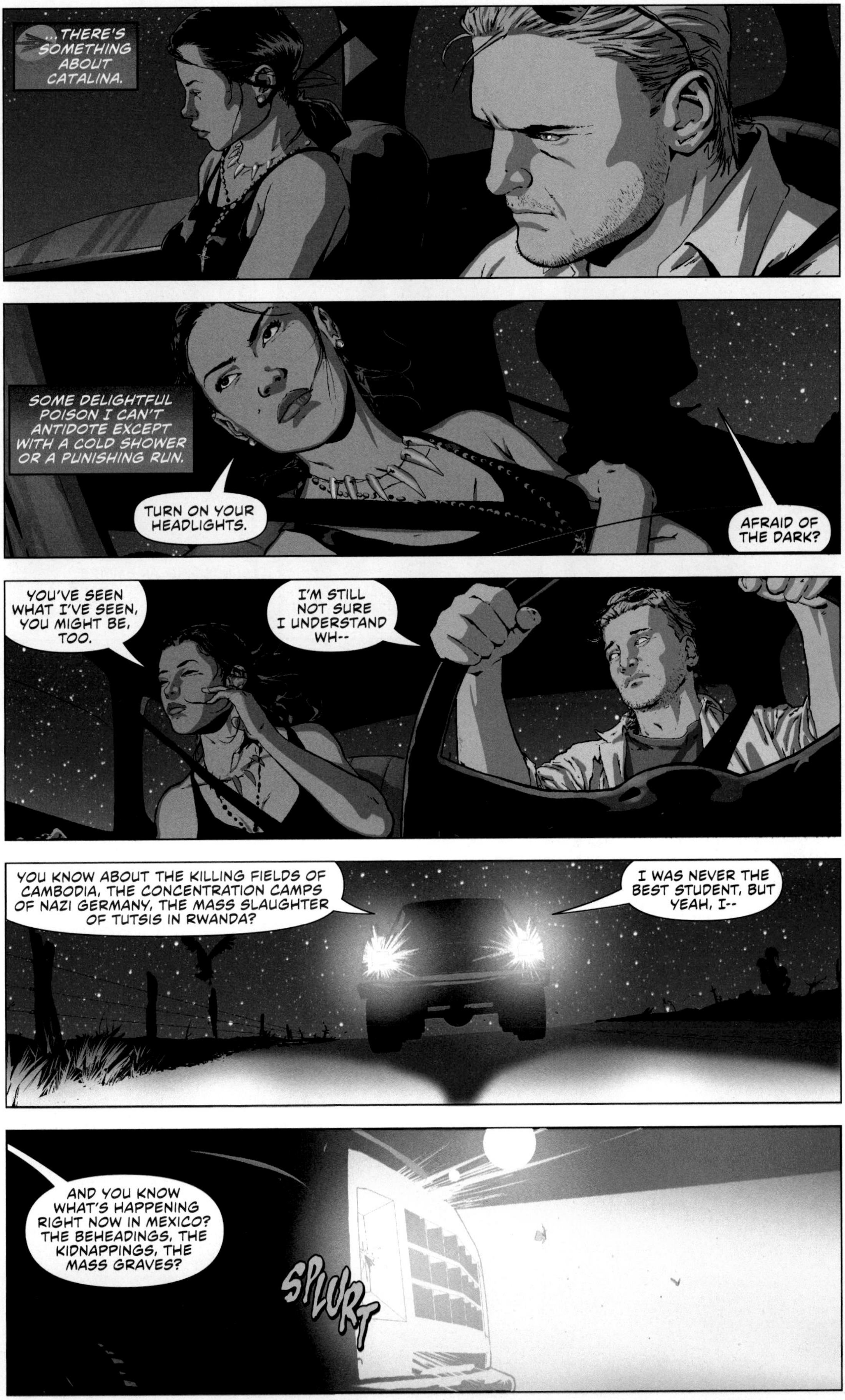
...THERE'S SOMETHING ABOUT CATALINA.
SOME DELIGHTFUL POISON I CAN'T ANTIDOTE EXCEPT WITH A COLD SHOWER OR A PUNISHING RUN.
TURN ON YOUR HEADLIGHTS.
AFRAID OF THE DARK?
YOU'VE SEEN WHAT I'VE SEEN, YOU MIGHT BE, TOO.
I'M STILL NOT SURE I UNDERSTAND WH--
YOU KNOW ABOUT THE KILLING FIELDS OF CAMBODIA, THE CONCENTRATION CAMPS OF NAZI GERMANY, THE MASS SLAUGHTER OF TUTSIS IN RWANDA?
I WAS NEVER THE BEST STUDENT, BUT YEAH, I--
AND YOU KNOW WHAT'S HAPPENING RIGHT NOW IN MEXICO? THE BEHEADINGS, THE KIDNAPPINGS, THE MASS GRAVES?
SPLURT

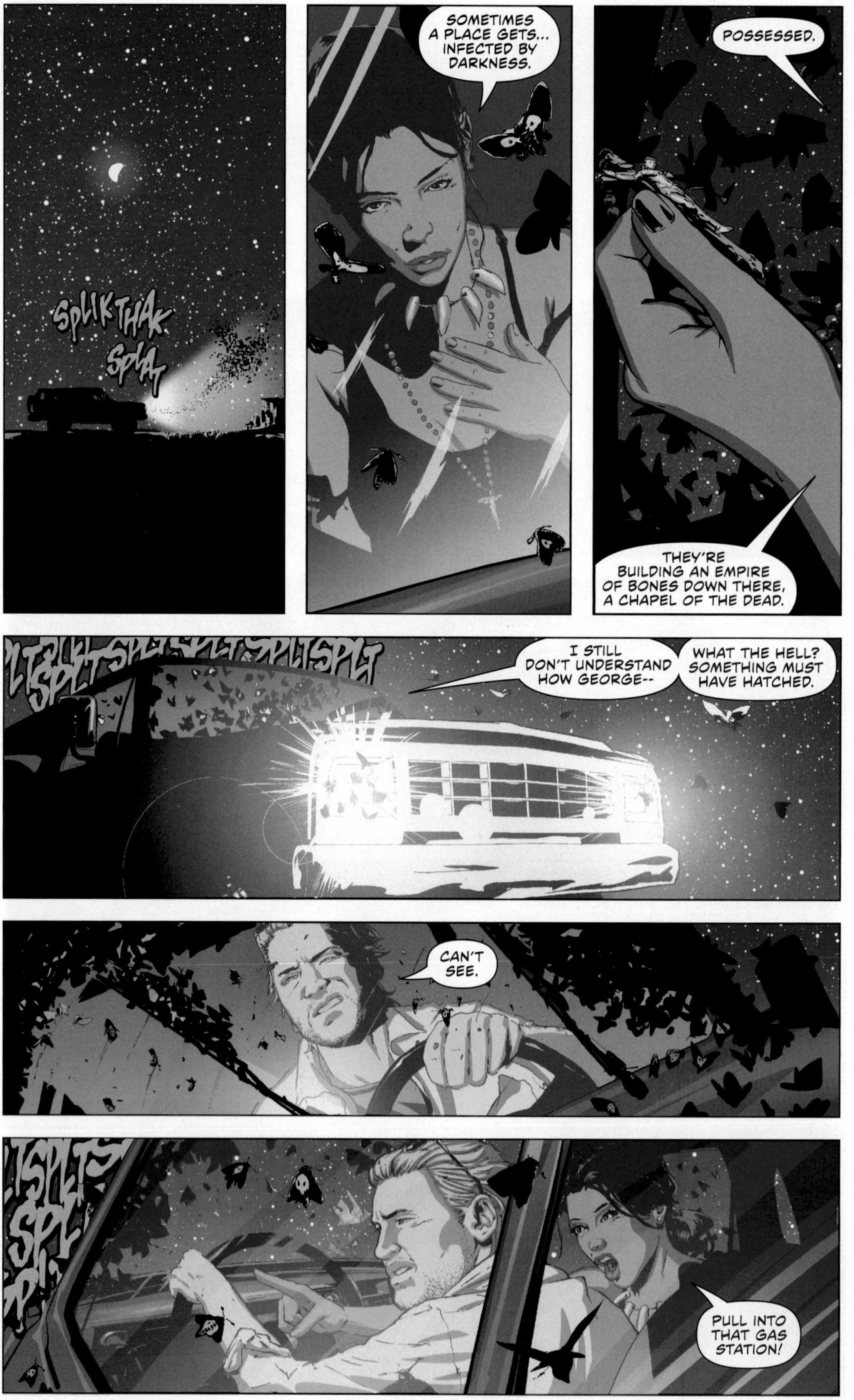
SPLIKTHAK
SPLAT
SOMETIMES A PLACE GETS... INFECTED BY DARKNESS.
POSSESSED.
THEY'RE BUILDING AN EMPIRE OF BONES DOWN THERE, A CHAPEL OF THE DEAD.
SPLT SPLT SPLT SPLT SPLT SPLT
I STILL DON'T UNDERSTAND HOW GEORGE--
WHAT THE HELL? SOMETHING MUST HAVE HATCHED.
CAN'T SEE.
SPLTSPLTS SPLT SPLT
PULL INTO THAT GAS STATION!

THIS IS KIND OF BIBLICAL.

WHAT ARE YOU DOING?

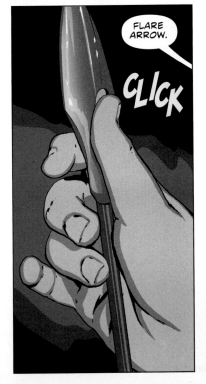

FLARE ARROW.

CLICK

LIKE MOTHS TO FLAME.

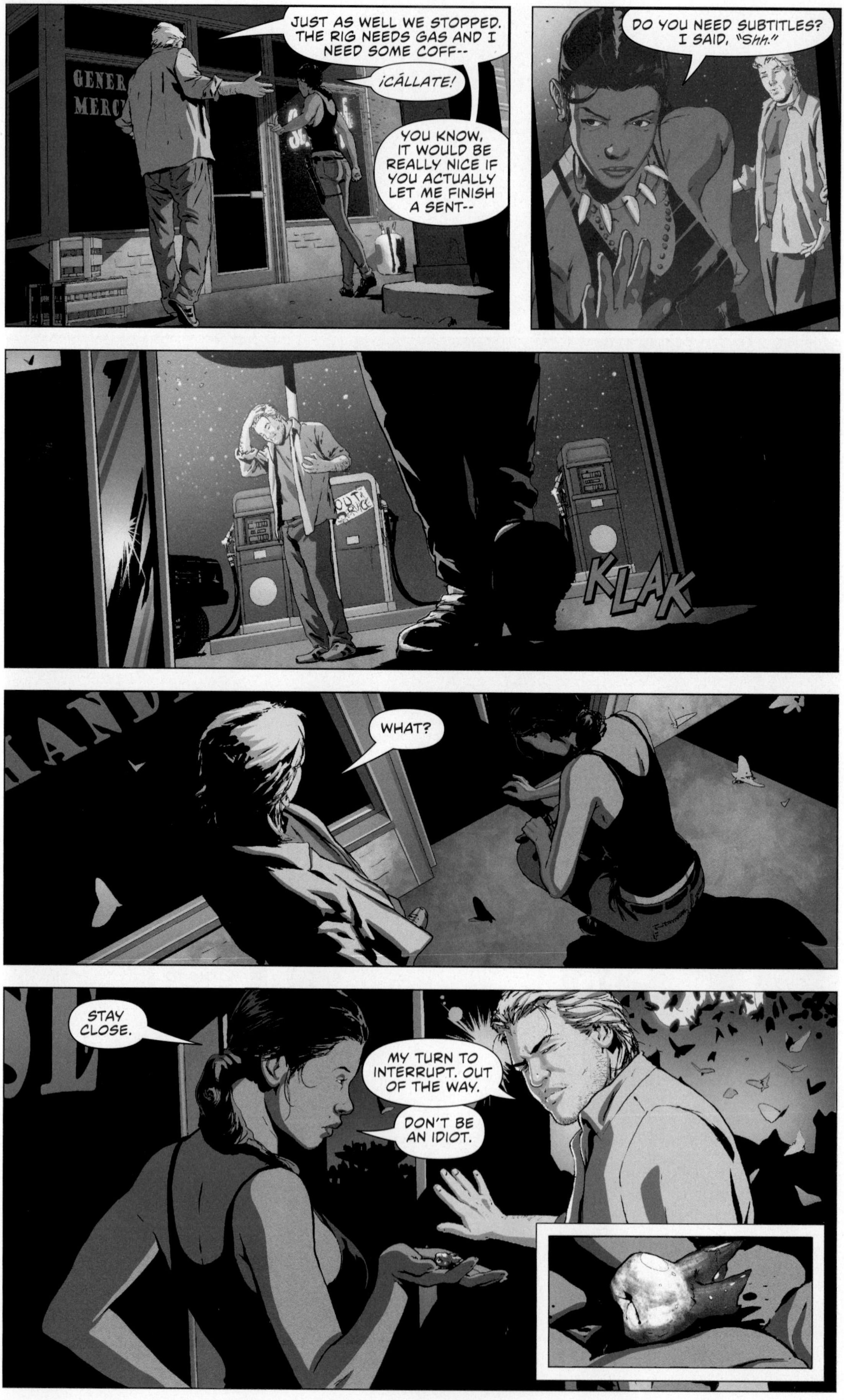
JUST AS WELL WE STOPPED. THE RIG NEEDS GAS AND I NEED SOME COFF--
¡CÁLLATE!
YOU KNOW, IT WOULD BE REALLY NICE IF YOU ACTUALLY LET ME FINISH A SENT--
DO YOU NEED SUBTITLES? I SAID, "Shh."
KLAK
WHAT?
STAY CLOSE.
MY TURN TO INTERRUPT. OUT OF THE WAY.
DON'T BE AN IDIOT.

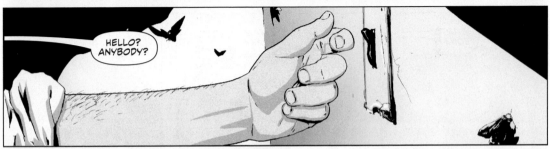

HELLO? ANYBODY?

MY GOD.

NO. NOT YOURS. AND NOT MINE EITHER.

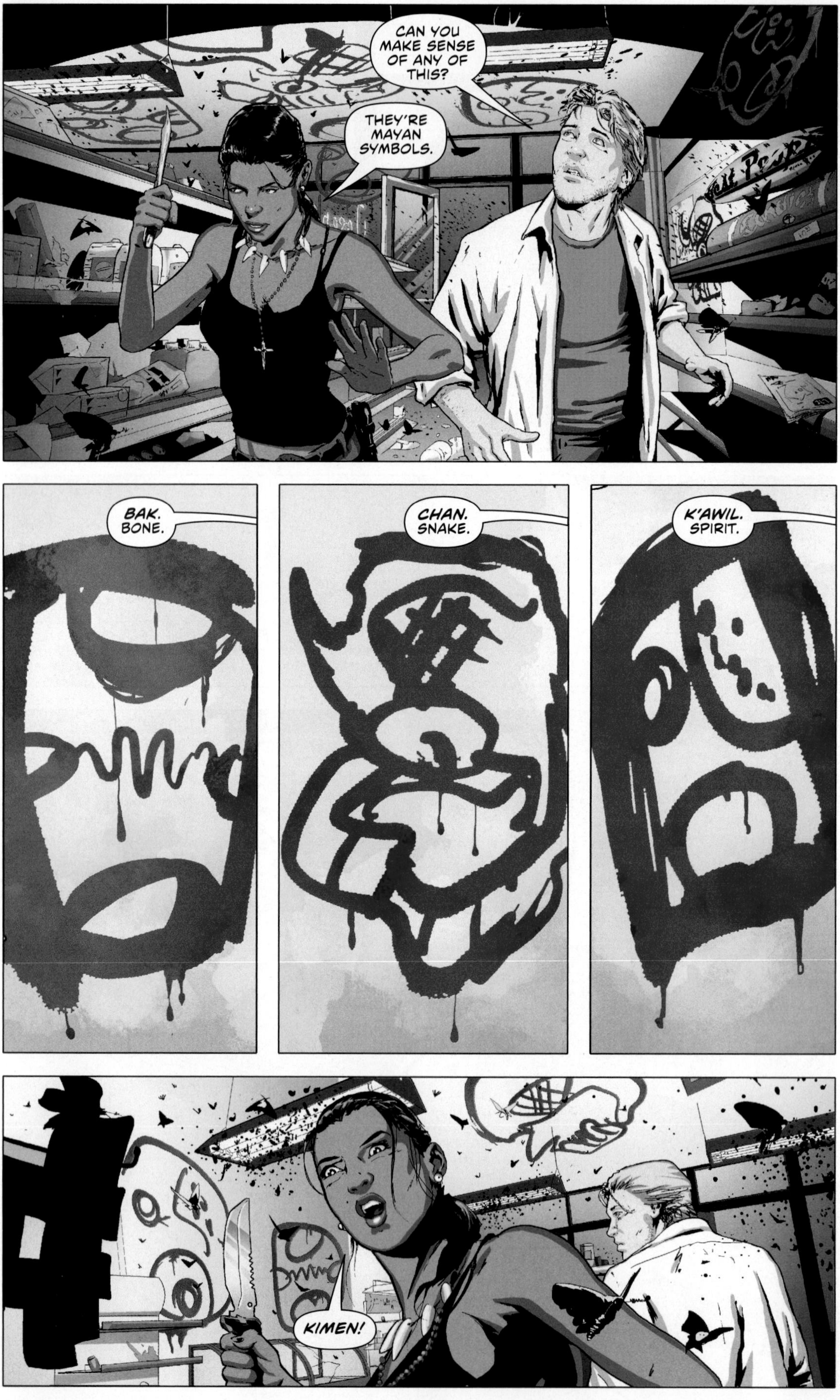
CAN YOU MAKE SENSE OF ANY OF THIS?
THEY'RE MAYAN SYMBOLS.
BAK. BONE.
CHAN. SNAKE.
K'AWIL. SPIRIT.
KIMEN!

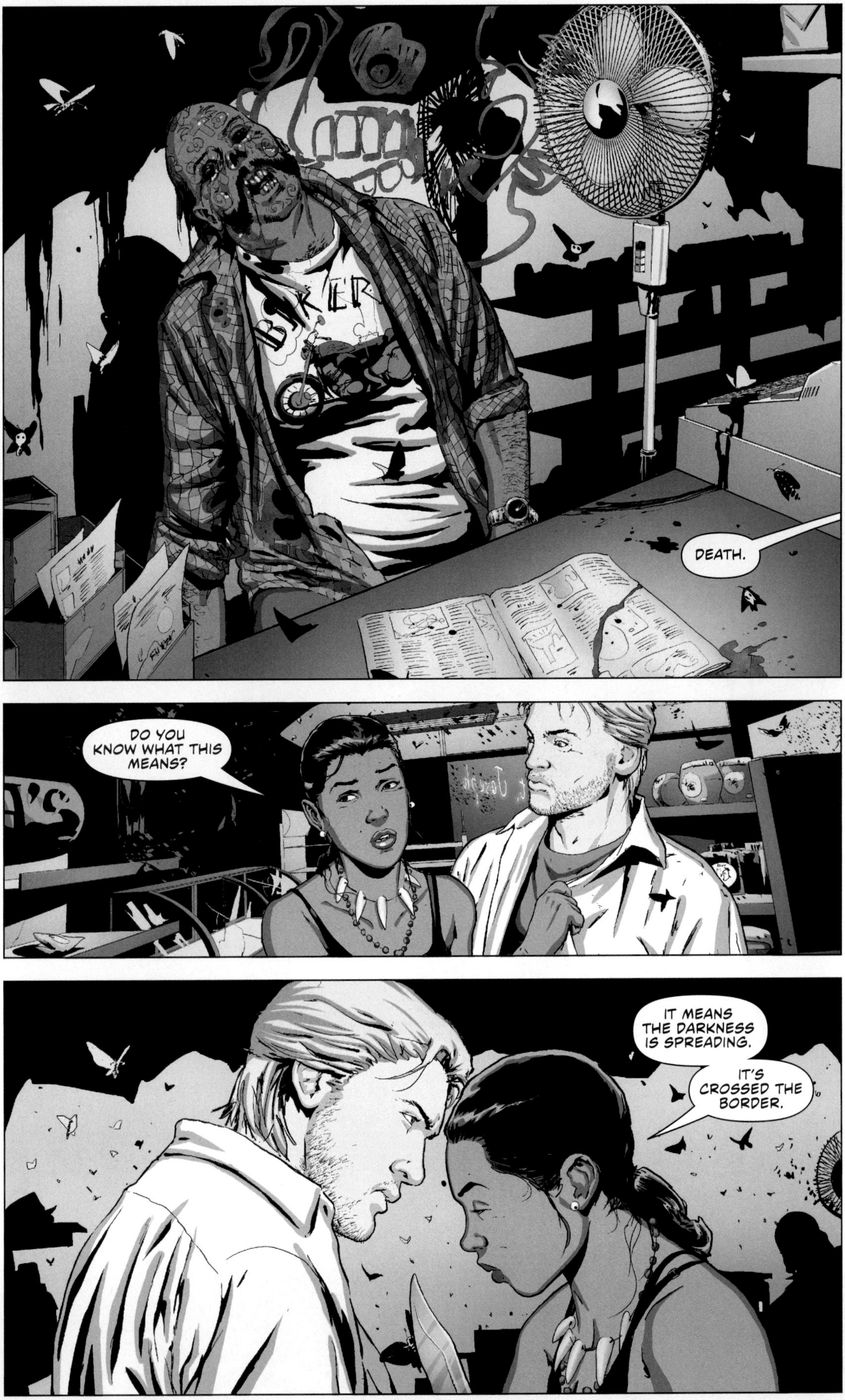
DEATH.
DO YOU KNOW WHAT THIS MEANS?
IT MEANS THE DARKNESS IS SPREADING.
IT'S CROSSED THE BORDER.

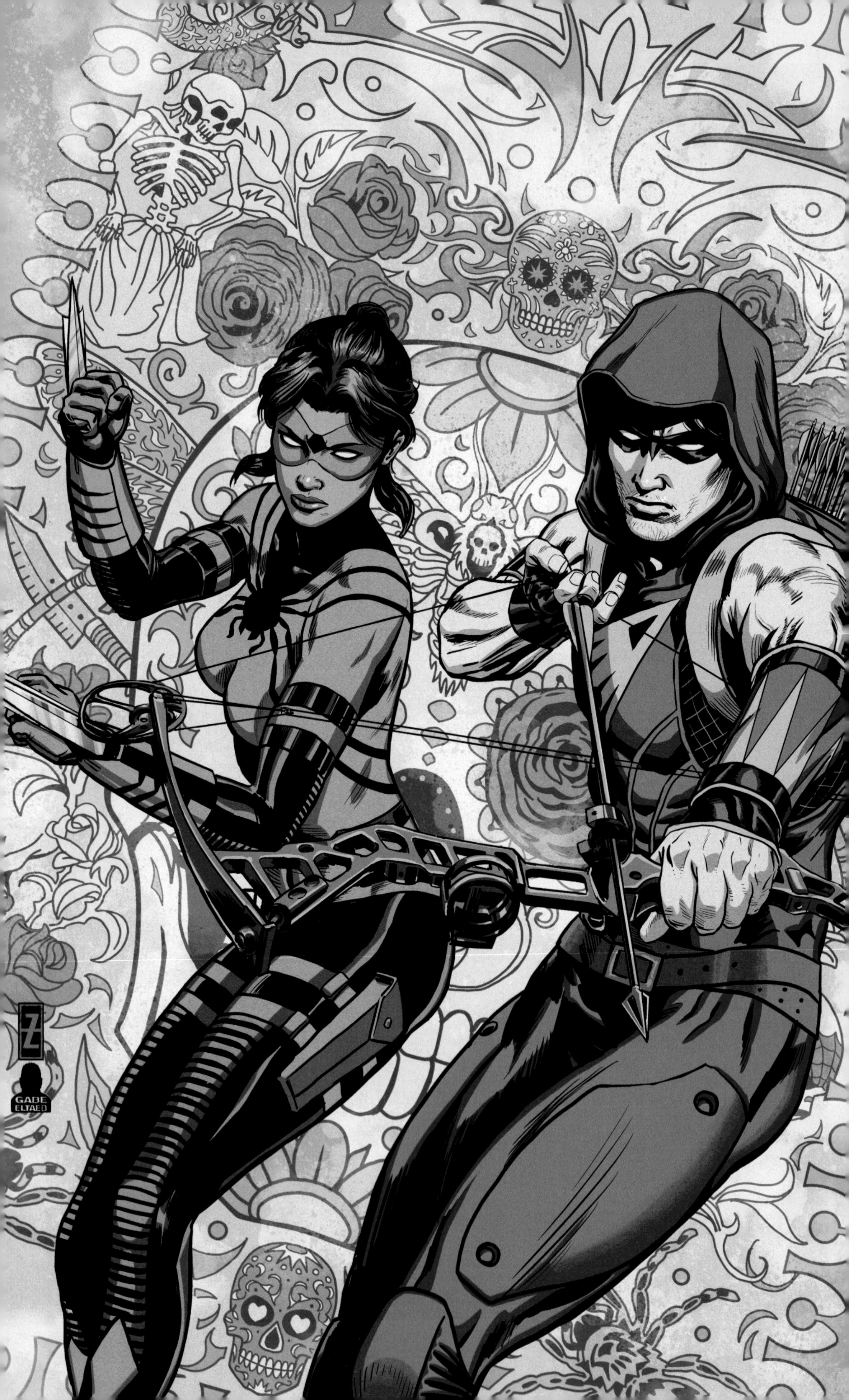
GABE
ELTAEB

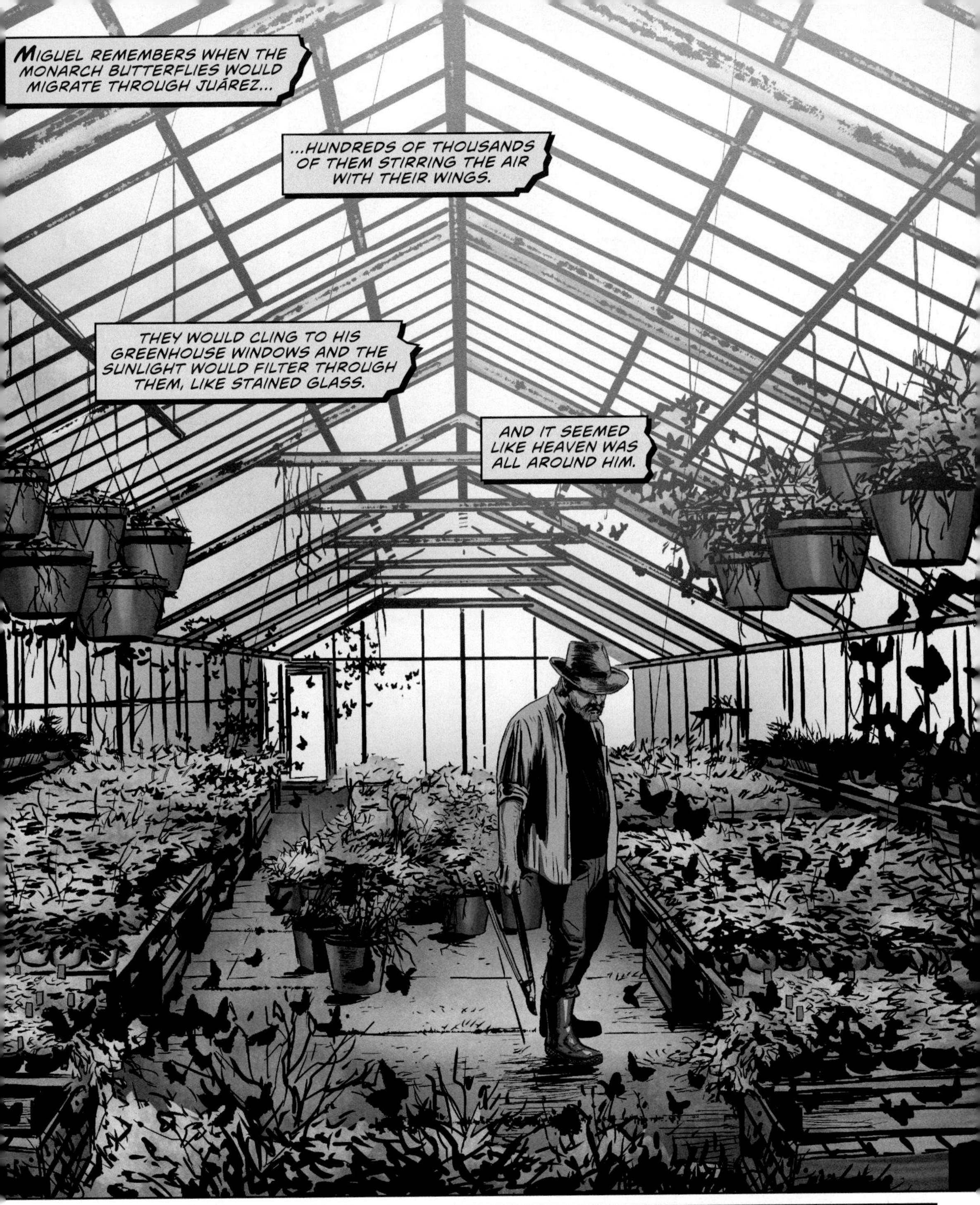
MIGUEL REMEMBERS WHEN THE MONARCH BUTTERFLIES WOULD MIGRATE THROUGH JUÁREZ...
...HUNDREDS OF THOUSANDS OF THEM STIRRING THE AIR WITH THEIR WINGS.
THEY WOULD CLING TO HIS GREENHOUSE WINDOWS AND THE SUNLIGHT WOULD FILTER THROUGH THEM, LIKE STAINED GLASS.
AND IT SEEMED LIKE HEAVEN WAS ALL AROUND HIM.

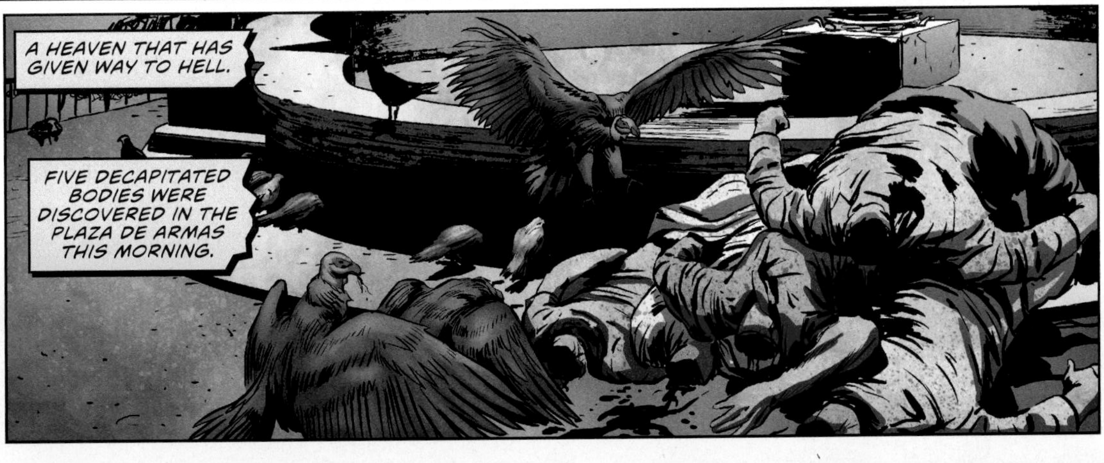
A HEAVEN THAT HAS GIVEN WAY TO HELL.
FIVE DECAPITATED BODIES WERE DISCOVERED IN THE PLAZA DE ARMAS THIS MORNING.

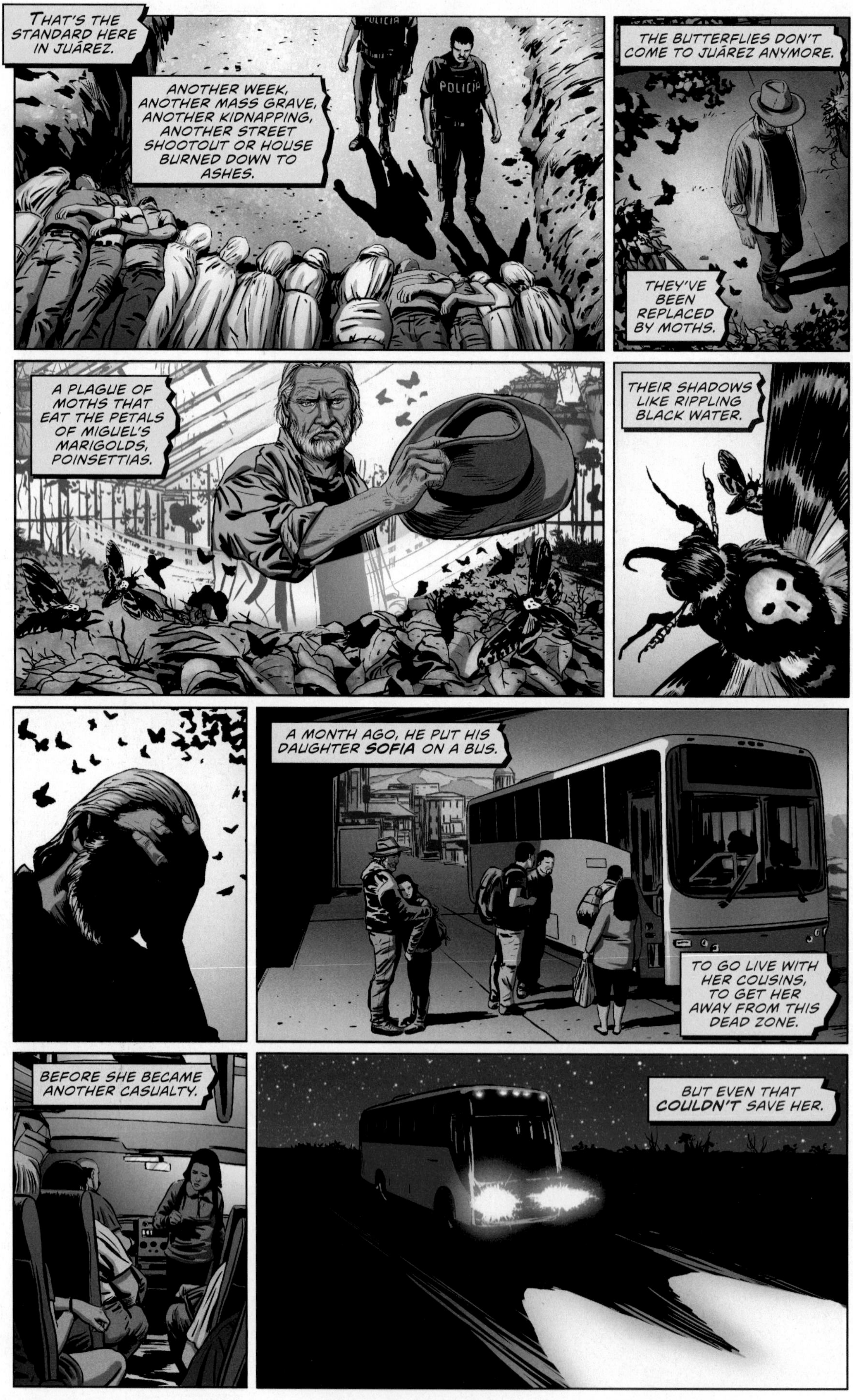
THAT'S THE STANDARD HERE IN JUÁREZ.
POLICIA
ANOTHER WEEK, ANOTHER MASS GRAVE, ANOTHER KIDNAPPING, ANOTHER STREET SHOOTOUT OR HOUSE BURNED DOWN TO ASHES.
THE BUTTERFLIES DON'T COME TO JUÁREZ ANYMORE.
THEY'VE BEEN REPLACED BY MOTHS.
A PLAGUE OF MOTHS THAT EAT THE PETALS OF MIGUEL'S MARIGOLDS, POINSETTIAS.
THEIR SHADOWS LIKE RIPPLING BLACK WATER.
A MONTH AGO, HE PUT HIS DAUGHTER SOFIA ON A BUS.
TO GO LIVE WITH HER COUSINS, TO GET HER AWAY FROM THIS DEAD ZONE.
BEFORE SHE BECAME ANOTHER CASUALTY.
BUT EVEN THAT COULDN'T SAVE HER.

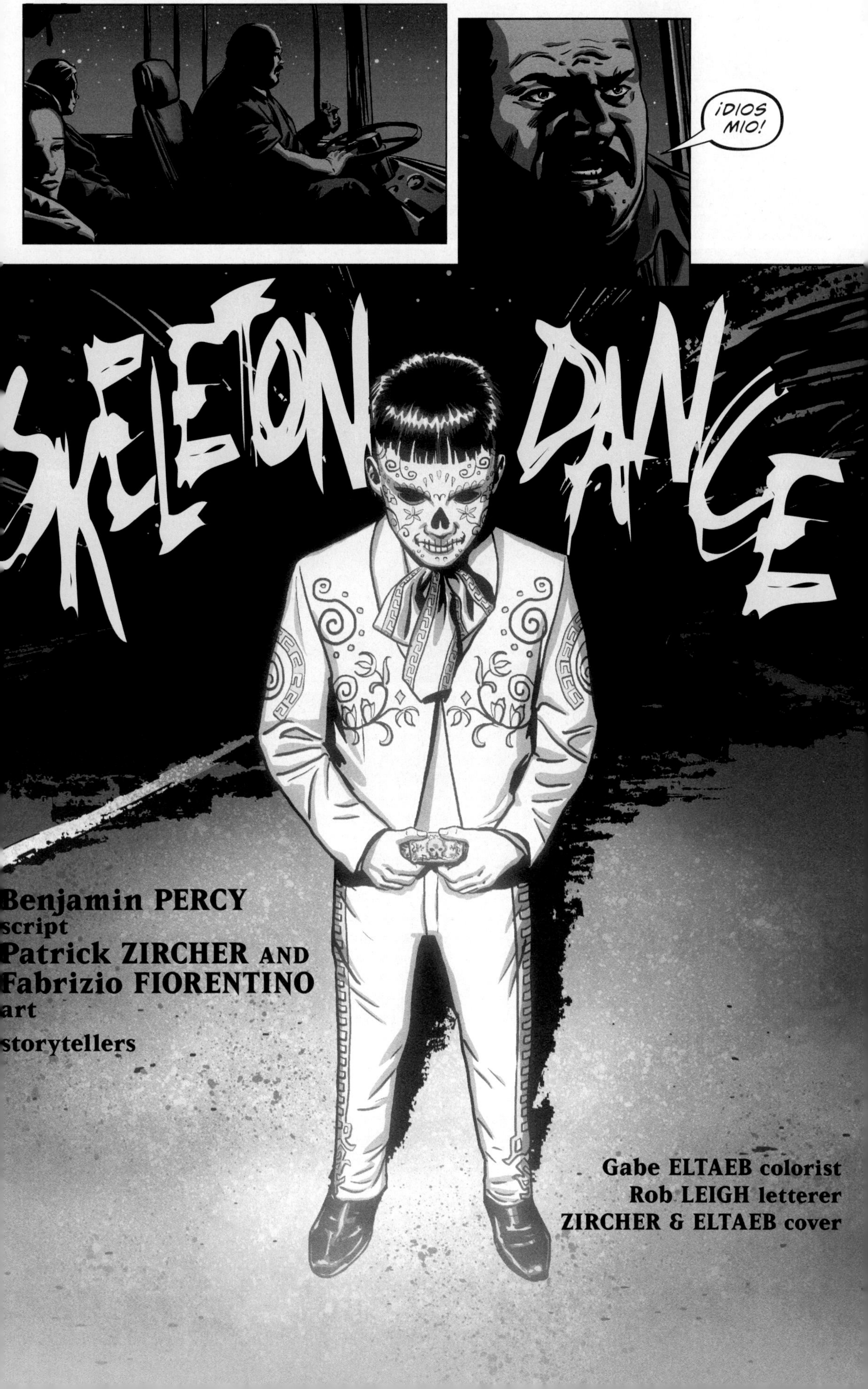
¡DIOS MIO!
SKELETON DANCE
Benjamin PERCY script
Patrick ZIRCHER AND Fabrizio FIORENTINO art
storytellers
Gabe ELTAEB colorist
Rob LEIGH letterer
ZIRCHER & ELTAEB cover

SCREEEEEECH

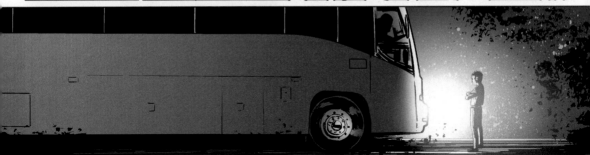

PEOPLE BLAME THE TROUBLE IN JUÁREZ ON DRUGS...

¡QUÉ DEMONIOS!

BUT BEHIND THE DRUGS, THERE'S SOMETHING ELSE AT WORK.

THE SKELETONS MADE EVERYONE LIE DOWN ON THE PAVEMENT BEFORE THE BUS.

ALL BUT ONE.

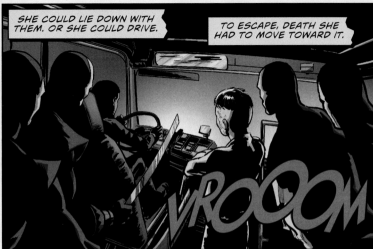

SHE COULD LIE DOWN WITH THEM. OR SHE COULD DRIVE.

TO ESCAPE, DEATH SHE HAD TO MOVE TOWARD IT.

VROOOM

SHE HASN'T BEEN SEEN SINCE.

THE SKELETONS TOOK HER.

POR FAVOR, CATALINA...

...SAVE MY DAUGHTER. SAVE OUR FAMILY. SAVE JUÁREZ.

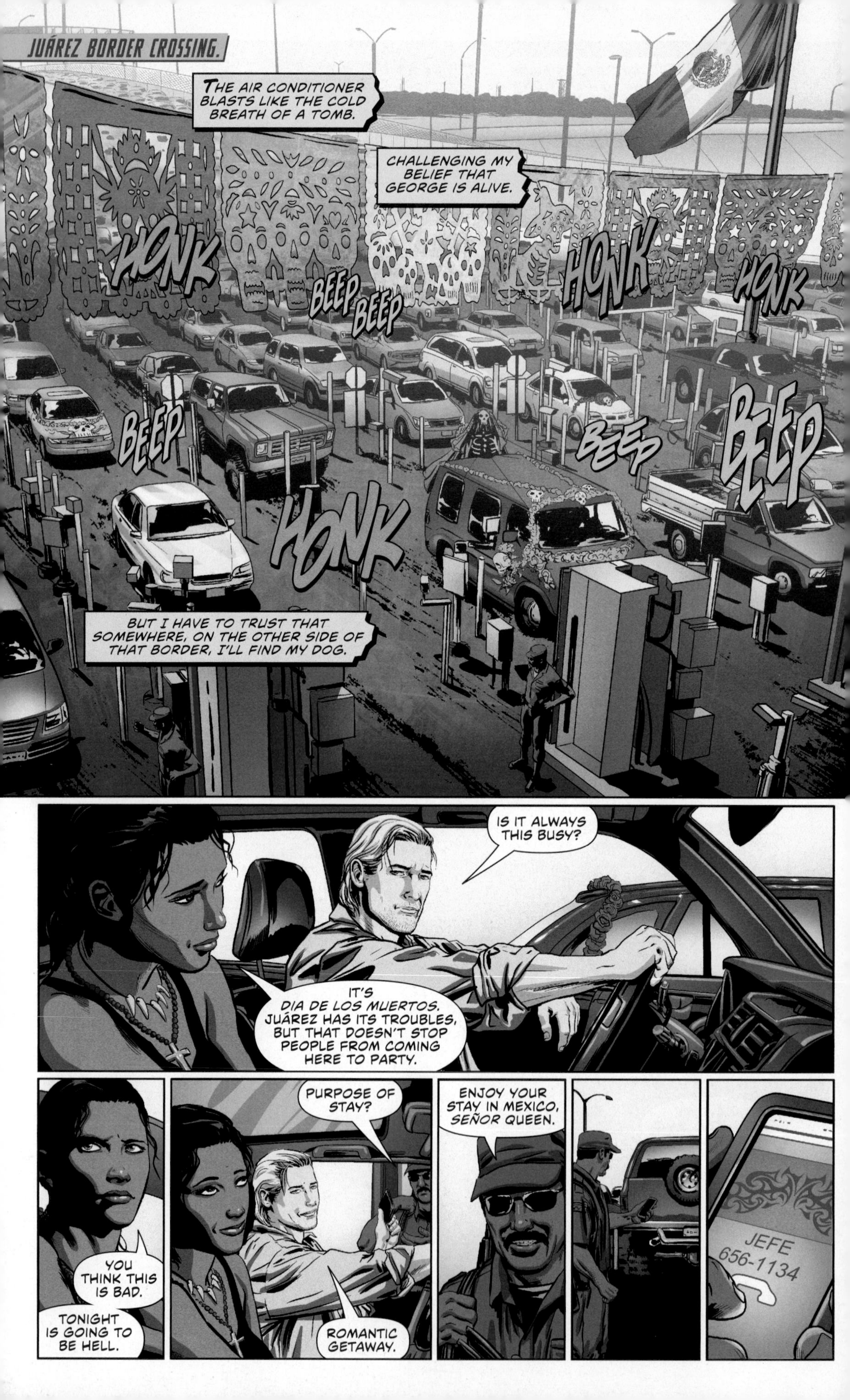
JUÁREZ BORDER CROSSING.
THE AIR CONDITIONER BLASTS LIKE THE COLD BREATH OF A TOMB.
CHALLENGING MY BELIEF THAT GEORGE IS ALIVE.
HONK
BEEP BEEP
HONK
HONK
BEEP
BEEP
BEEP
HONK
BUT I HAVE TO TRUST THAT SOMEWHERE, ON THE OTHER SIDE OF THAT BORDER, I'LL FIND MY DOG.
IS IT ALWAYS THIS BUSY?
IT'S DIA DE LOS MUERTOS. JUÁREZ HAS ITS TROUBLES, BUT THAT DOESN'T STOP PEOPLE FROM COMING HERE TO PARTY.
YOU THINK THIS IS BAD.
TONIGHT IS GOING TO BE HELL.
PURPOSE OF STAY?
ROMANTIC GETAWAY.
ENJOY YOUR STAY IN MEXICO, SEÑOR QUEEN.
JEFE
656-1134

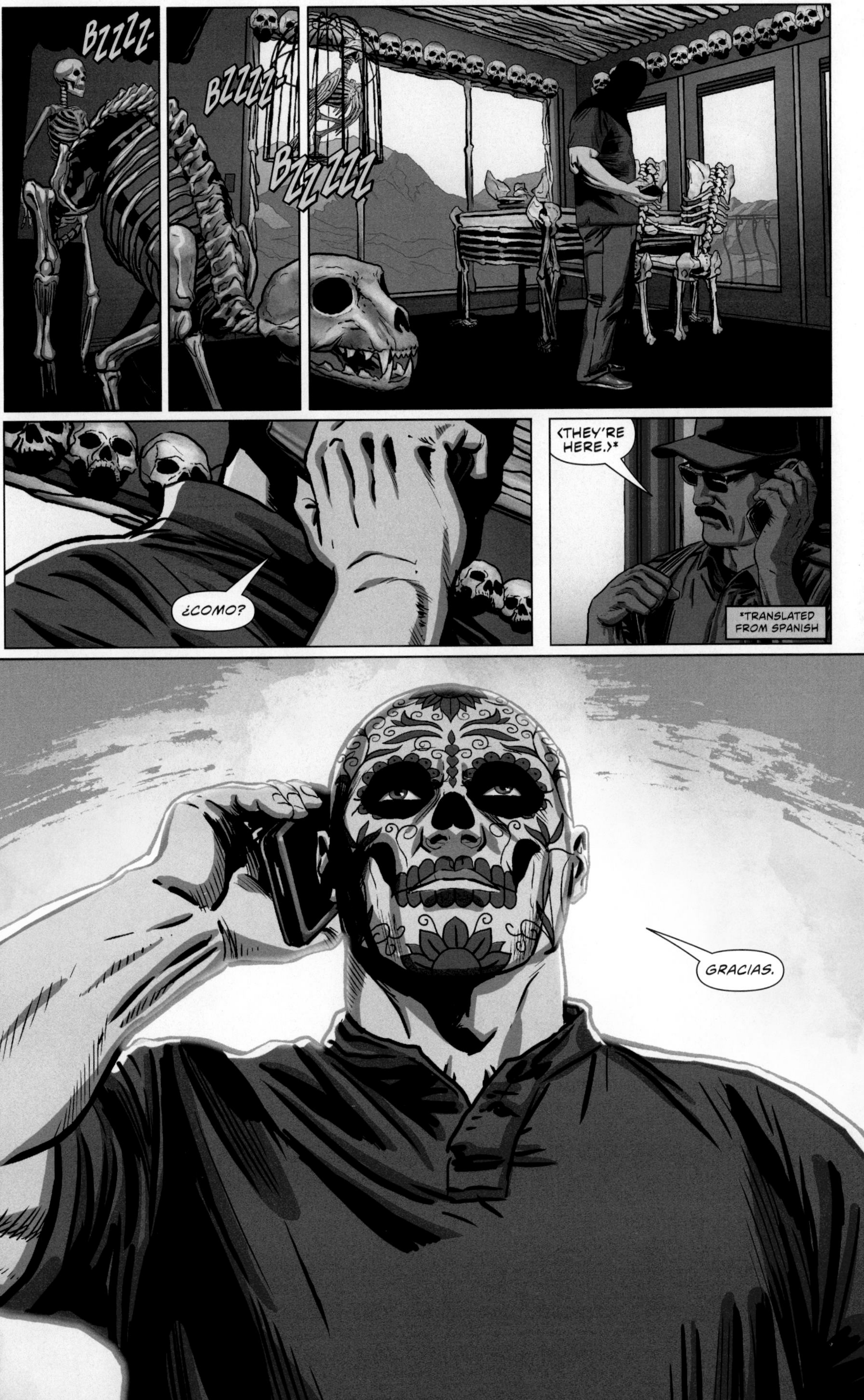
BZZZZ-
BZZZZ-
BZZZZZ
¿COMO?
<THEY'RE HERE.>*
*TRANSLATED FROM SPANISH
GRACIAS.

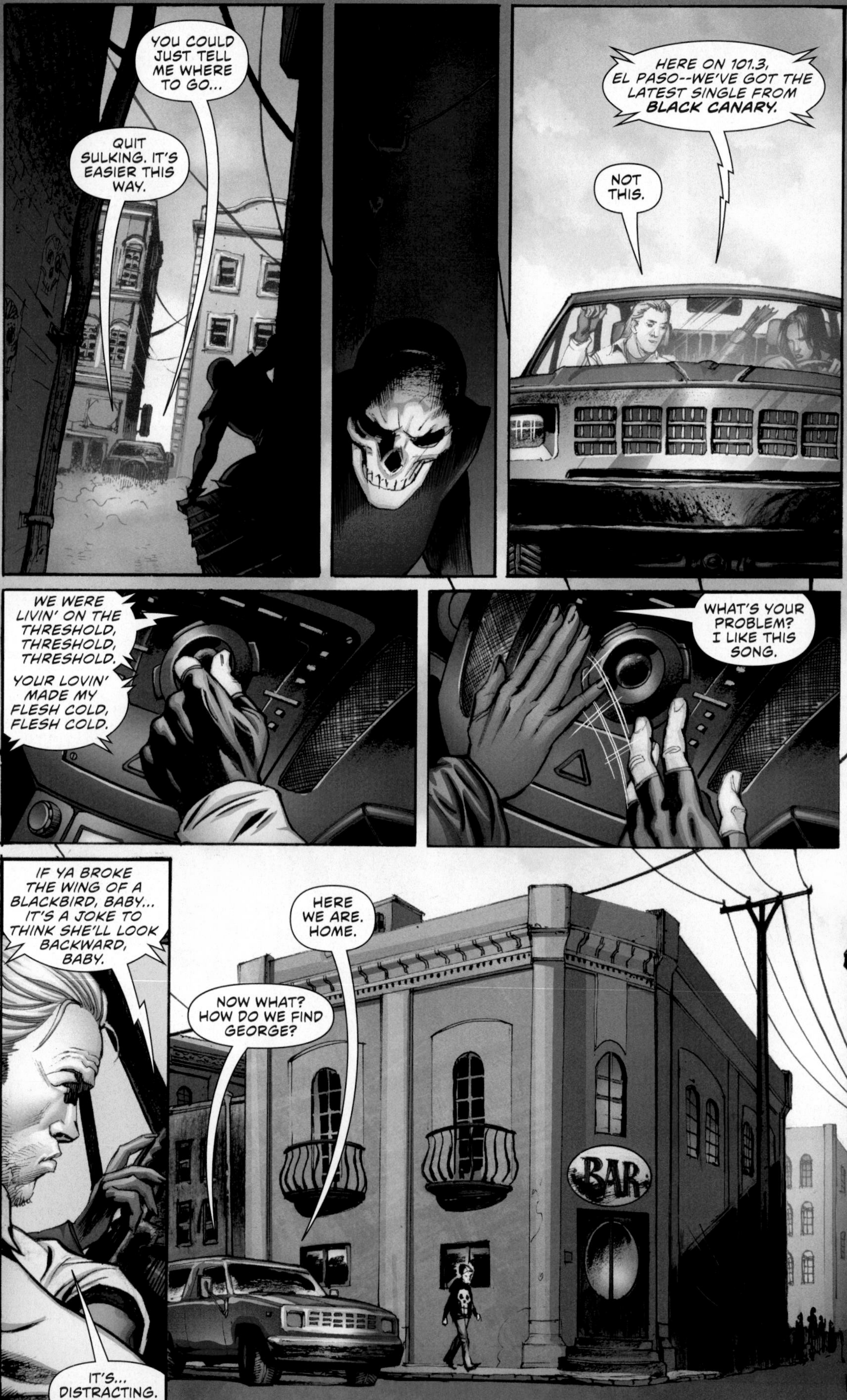

YOU COULD JUST TELL ME WHERE TO GO...
QUIT SULKING. IT'S EASIER THIS WAY.
HERE ON 101.3, EL PASO--WE'VE GOT THE LATEST SINGLE FROM BLACK CANARY.
NOT THIS.
WE WERE LIVIN' ON THE THRESHOLD, THRESHOLD, THRESHOLD.
YOUR LOVIN' MADE MY FLESH COLD, FLESH COLD.
WHAT'S YOUR PROBLEM? I LIKE THIS SONG.
IF YA BROKE THE WING OF A BLACKBIRD, BABY... IT'S A JOKE TO THINK SHE'LL LOOK BACKWARD, BABY.
HERE WE ARE. HOME.
NOW WHAT? HOW DO WE FIND GEORGE?
IT'S... DISTRACTING.
BAR

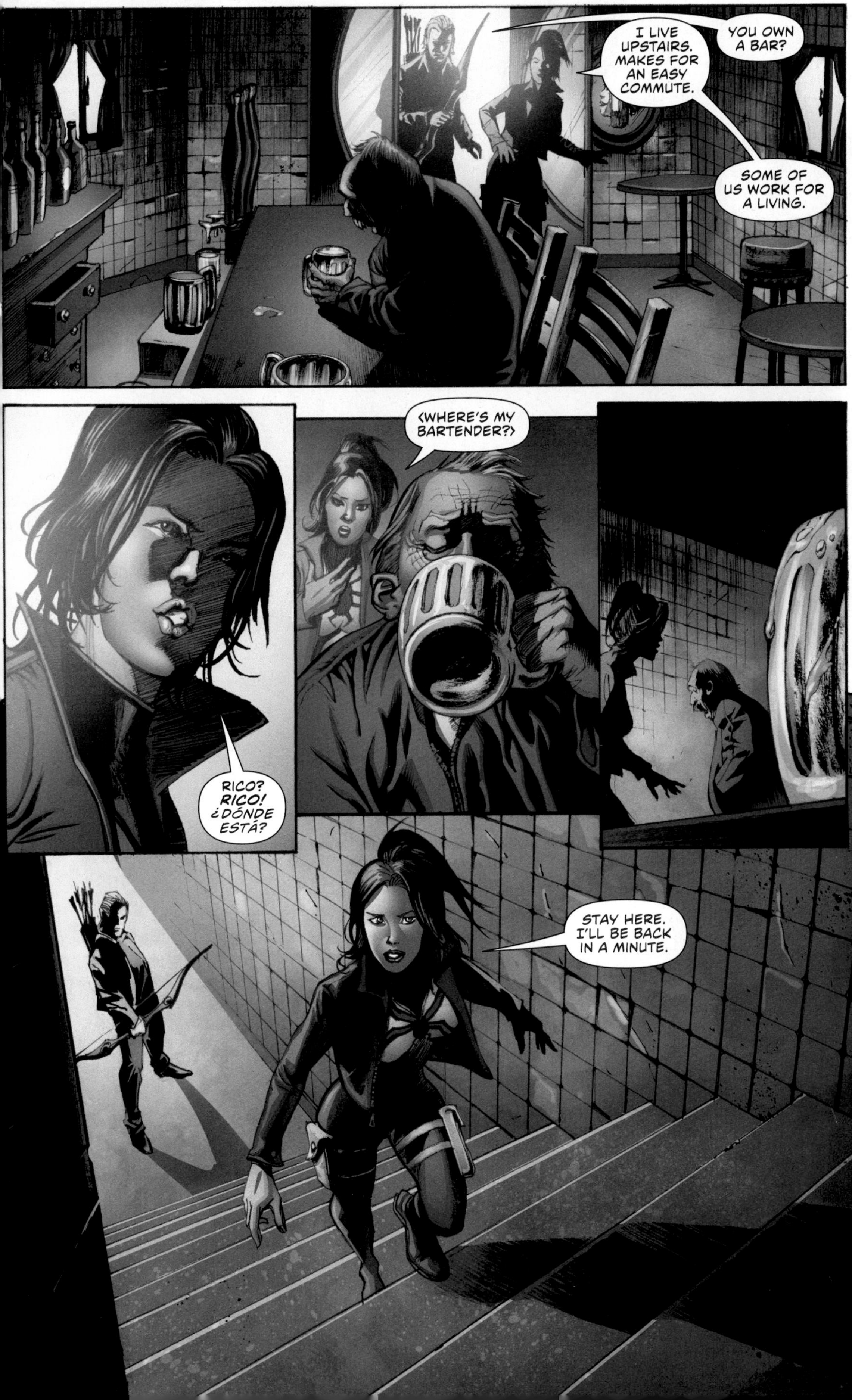
YOU OWN A BAR?
I LIVE UPSTAIRS. MAKES FOR AN EASY COMMUTE.
SOME OF US WORK FOR A LIVING.
RICO? RICO! ¿DÓNDE ESTÁ?
<WHERE'S MY BARTENDER?>
STAY HERE. I'LL BE BACK IN A MINUTE.

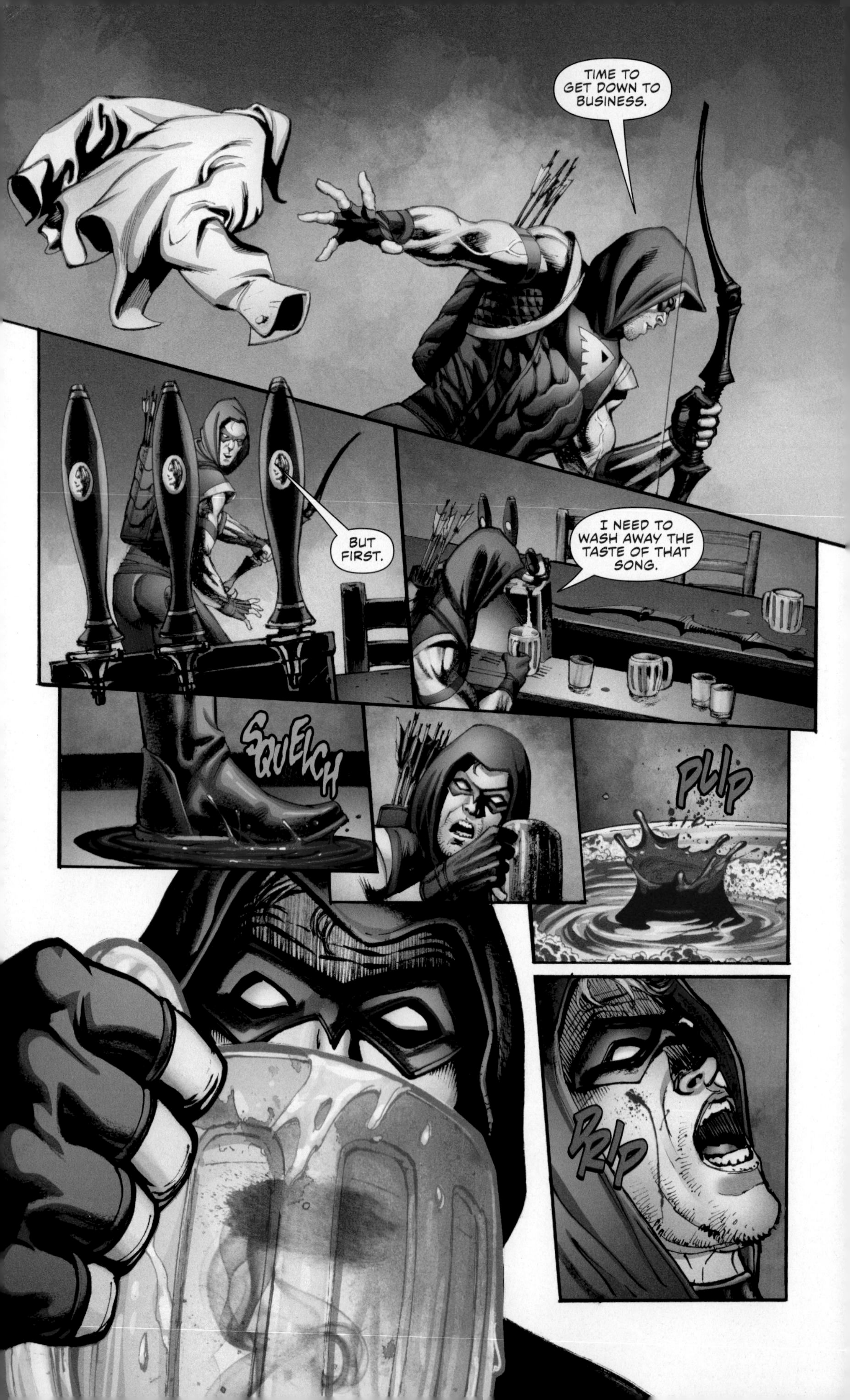
TIME TO GET DOWN TO BUSINESS.
BUT FIRST.
I NEED TO WASH AWAY THE TASTE OF THAT SONG.
SQUELCH
PLIP
DRIP

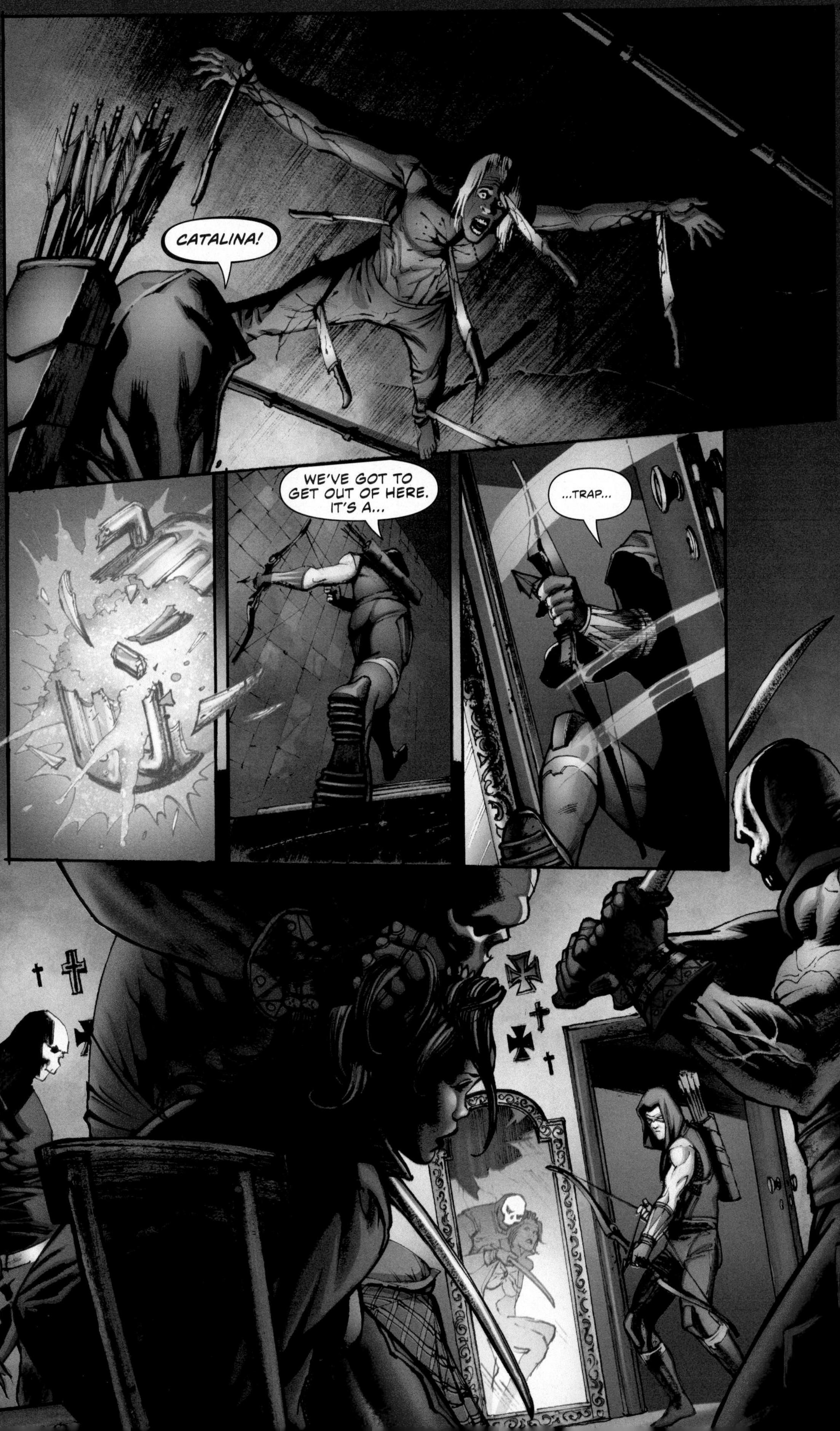
CATALINA!
WE'VE GOT TO GET OUT OF HERE. IT'S A...
...TRAP...

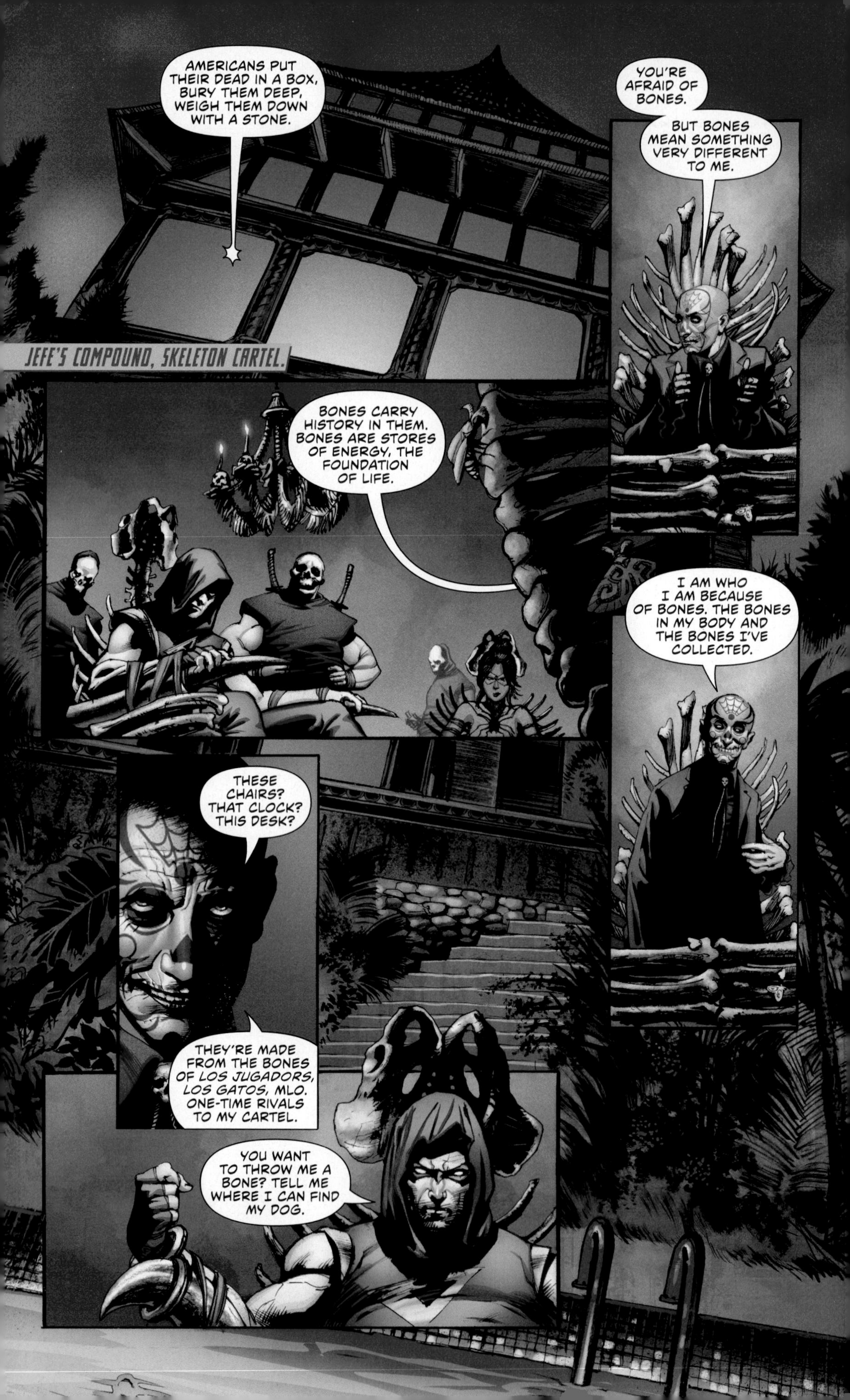
AMERICANS PUT THEIR DEAD IN A BOX, BURY THEM DEEP, WEIGH THEM DOWN WITH A STONE.
YOU'RE AFRAID OF BONES.
BUT BONES MEAN SOMETHING VERY DIFFERENT TO ME.
JEFE'S COMPOUND, SKELETON CARTEL.
BONES CARRY HISTORY IN THEM. BONES ARE STORES OF ENERGY, THE FOUNDATION OF LIFE.
I AM WHO I AM BECAUSE OF BONES. THE BONES IN MY BODY AND THE BONES I'VE COLLECTED.
THESE CHAIRS? THAT CLOCK? THIS DESK?
THEY'RE MADE FROM THE BONES OF *LOS JUGADORS*, *LOS GATOS*, MLO. ONE-TIME RIVALS TO MY CARTEL.
YOU WANT TO THROW ME A BONE? TELL ME WHERE I CAN FIND MY DOG.

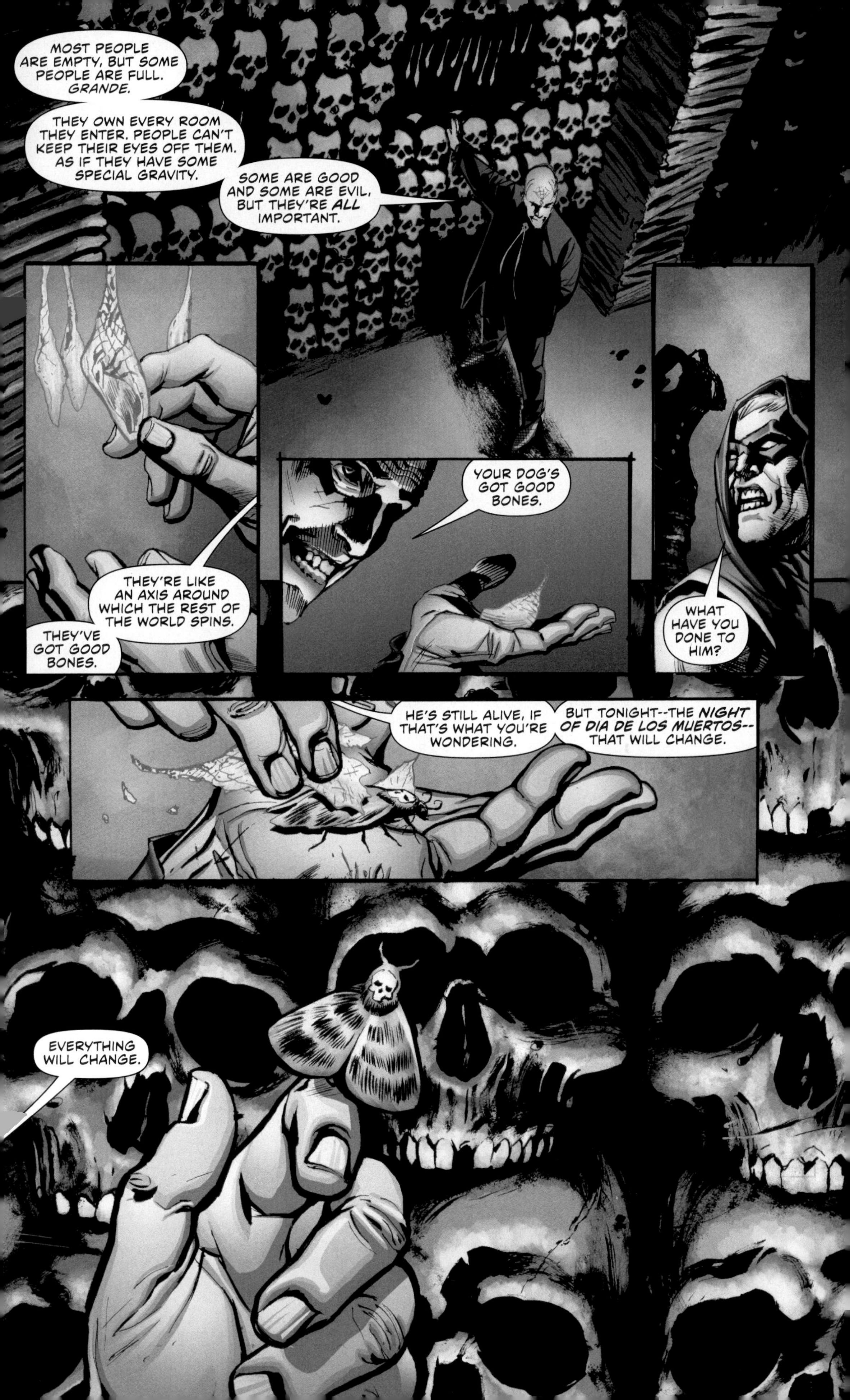
MOST PEOPLE ARE EMPTY, BUT SOME PEOPLE ARE FULL. *GRANDE.*
THEY OWN EVERY ROOM THEY ENTER. PEOPLE CAN'T KEEP THEIR EYES OFF THEM. AS IF THEY HAVE SOME SPECIAL GRAVITY.
SOME ARE GOOD AND SOME ARE EVIL, BUT THEY'RE *ALL* IMPORTANT.
THEY'RE LIKE AN AXIS AROUND WHICH THE REST OF THE WORLD SPINS.
THEY'VE GOT GOOD BONES.
YOUR DOG'S GOT GOOD BONES.
WHAT HAVE YOU DONE TO HIM?
HE'S STILL ALIVE, IF THAT'S WHAT YOU'RE WONDERING.
BUT TONIGHT--THE *NIGHT OF DIA DE LOS MUERTOS*--THAT WILL CHANGE.
EVERYTHING WILL CHANGE.

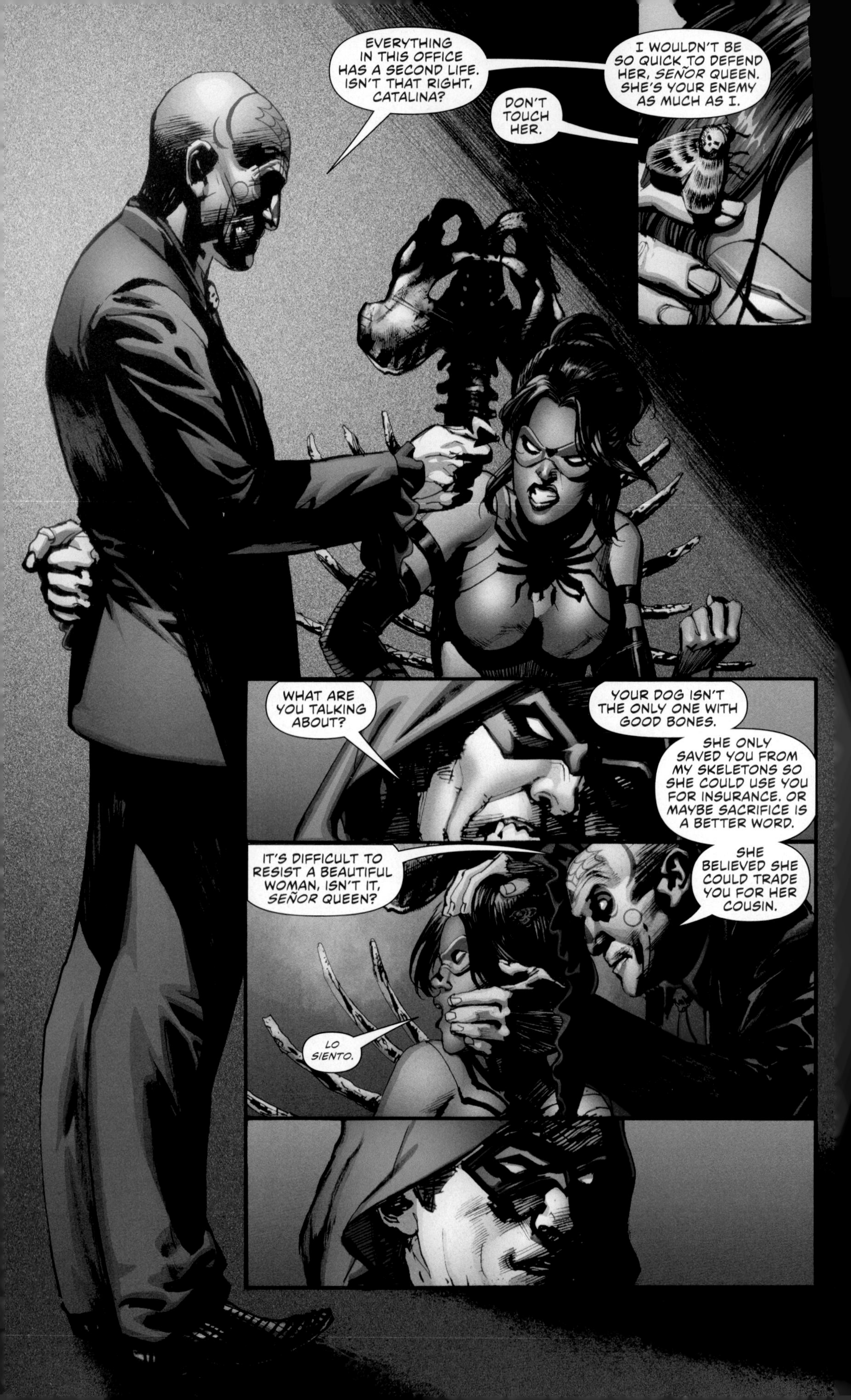
EVERYTHING IN THIS OFFICE HAS A SECOND LIFE. ISN'T THAT RIGHT, CATALINA?
I WOULDN'T BE SO QUICK TO DEFEND HER, SEÑOR QUEEN. SHE'S YOUR ENEMY AS MUCH AS I.
DON'T TOUCH HER.
WHAT ARE YOU TALKING ABOUT?
YOUR DOG ISN'T THE ONLY ONE WITH GOOD BONES.
SHE ONLY SAVED YOU FROM MY SKELETONS SO SHE COULD USE YOU FOR INSURANCE. OR MAYBE SACRIFICE IS A BETTER WORD.
IT'S DIFFICULT TO RESIST A BEAUTIFUL WOMAN, ISN'T IT, SEÑOR QUEEN?
SHE BELIEVED SHE COULD TRADE YOU FOR HER COUSIN.
LO SIENTO.

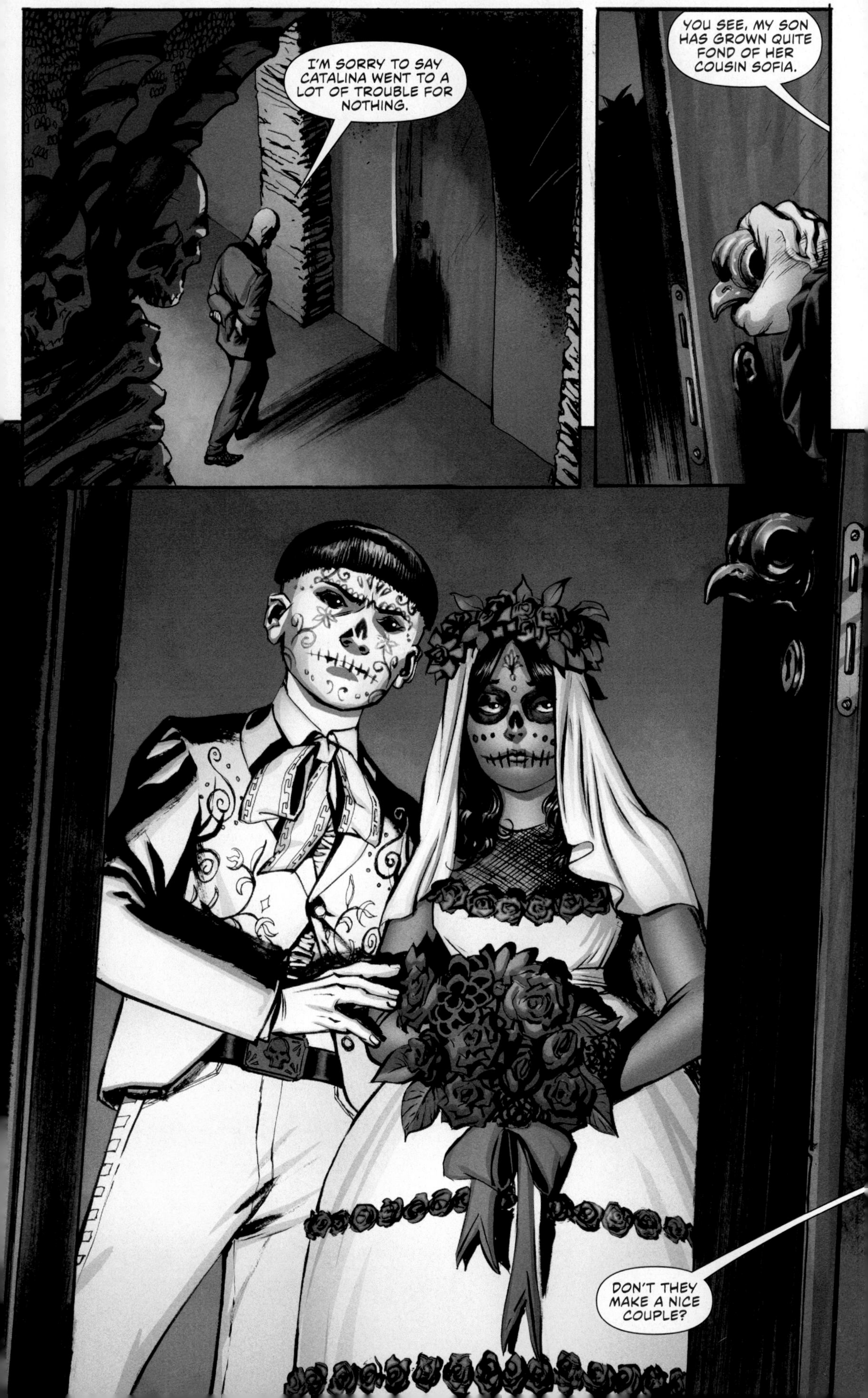
I'M SORRY TO SAY CATALINA WENT TO A LOT OF TROUBLE FOR NOTHING.
YOU SEE, MY SON HAS GROWN QUITE FOND OF HER COUSIN SOFIA.
DON'T THEY MAKE A NICE COUPLE?

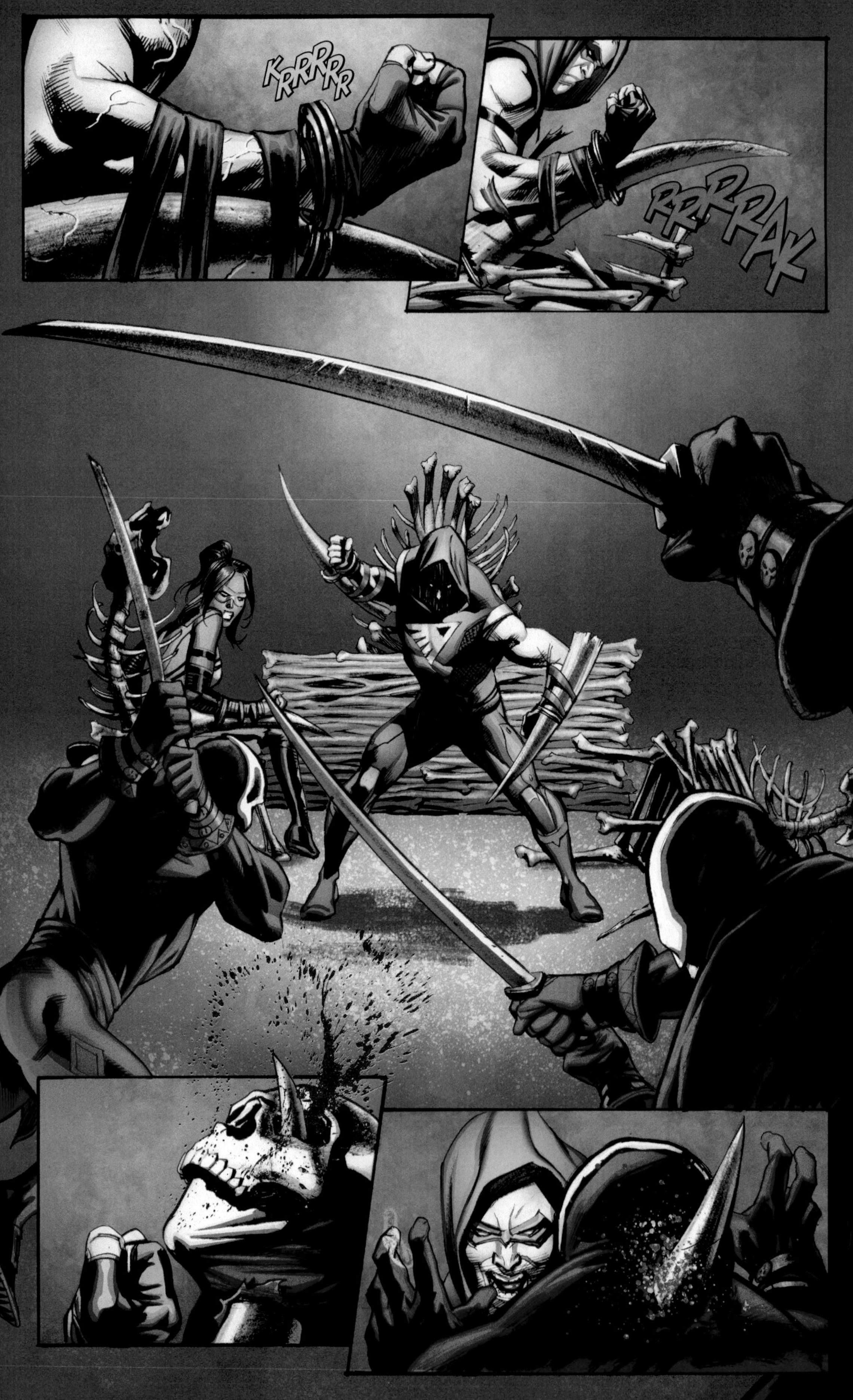
KRRRRR
RRRRAK

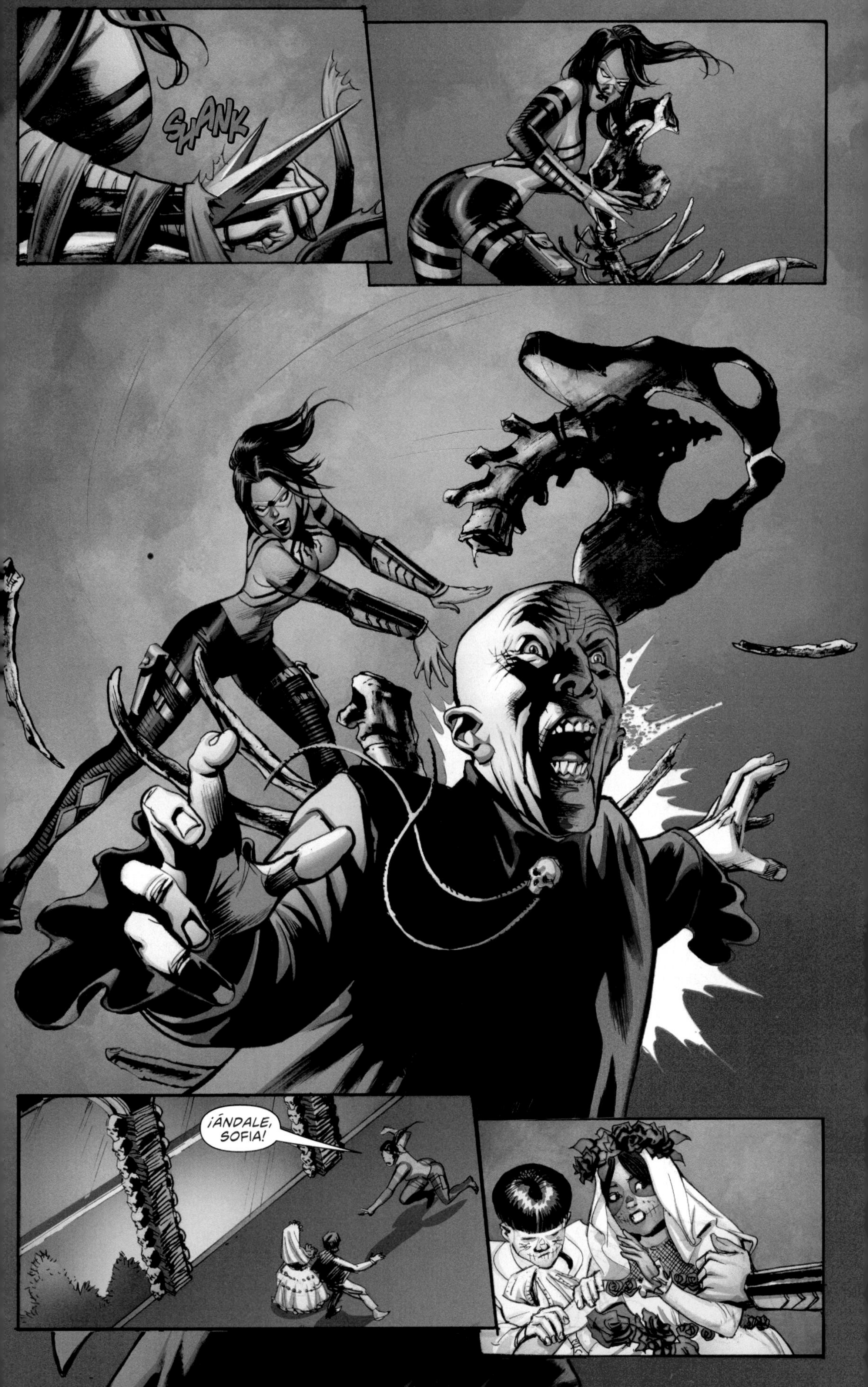
SHANK
¡ÁNDALE, SOFIA!

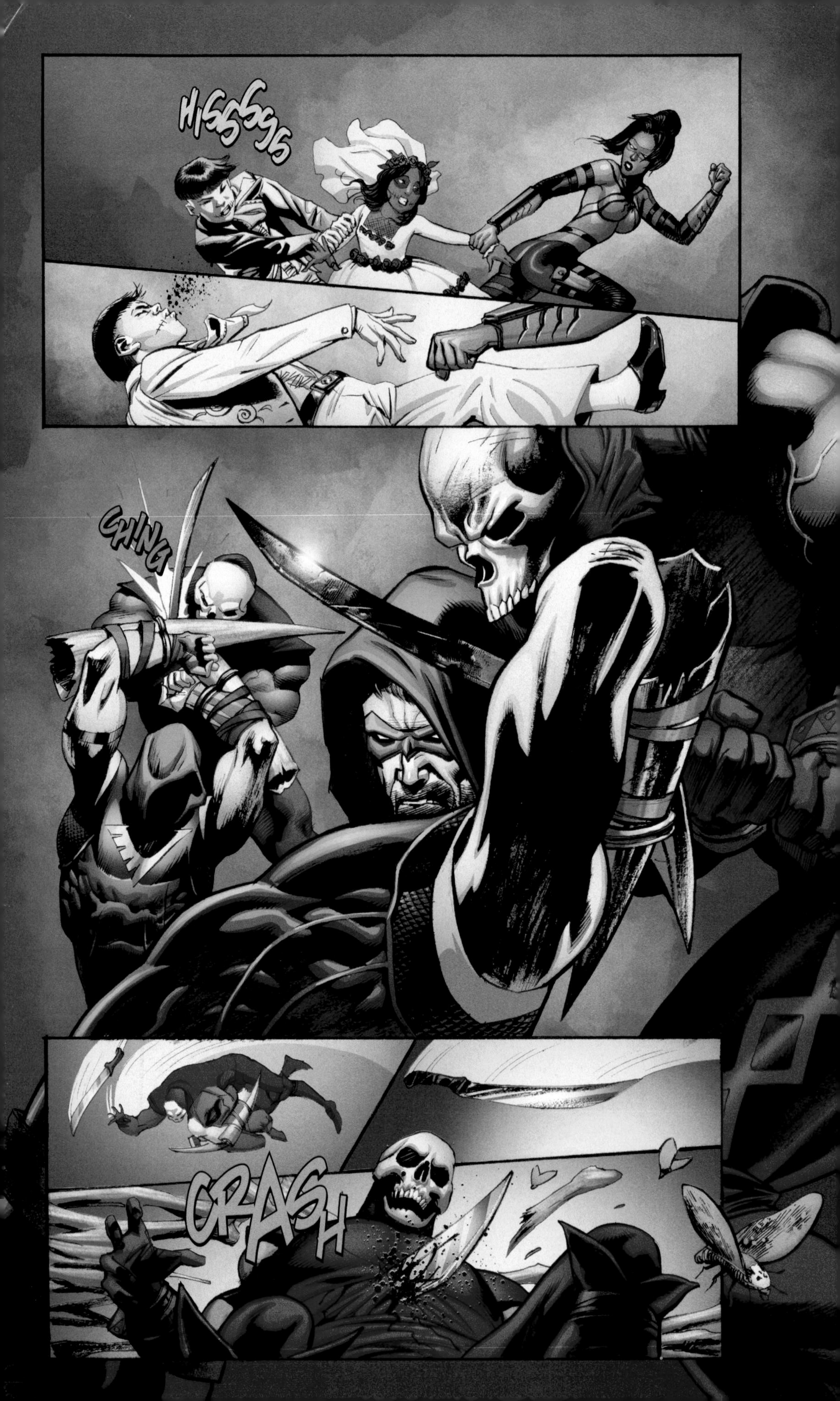
HISSSSSS
CHING
CRASH

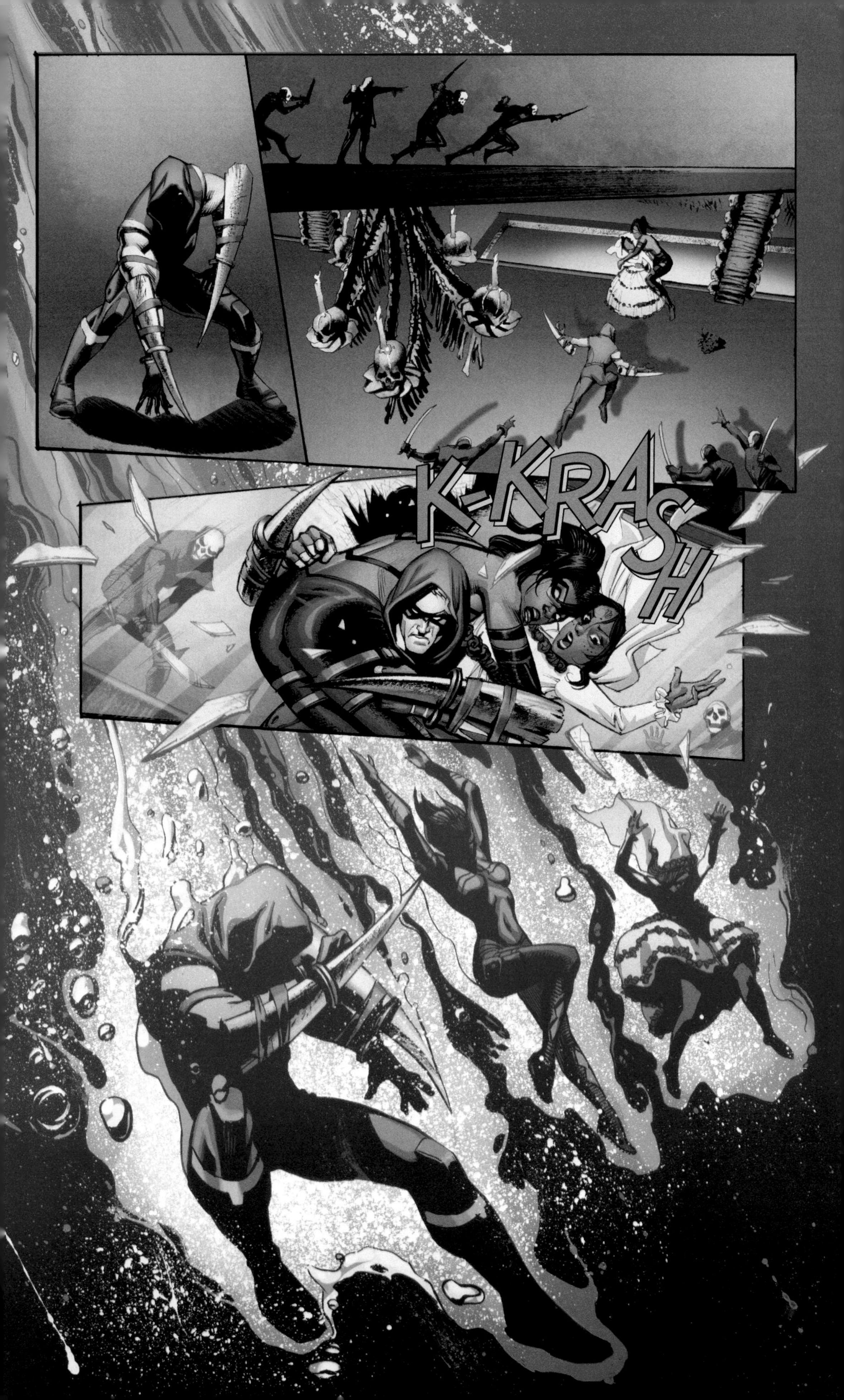
K-KRASH

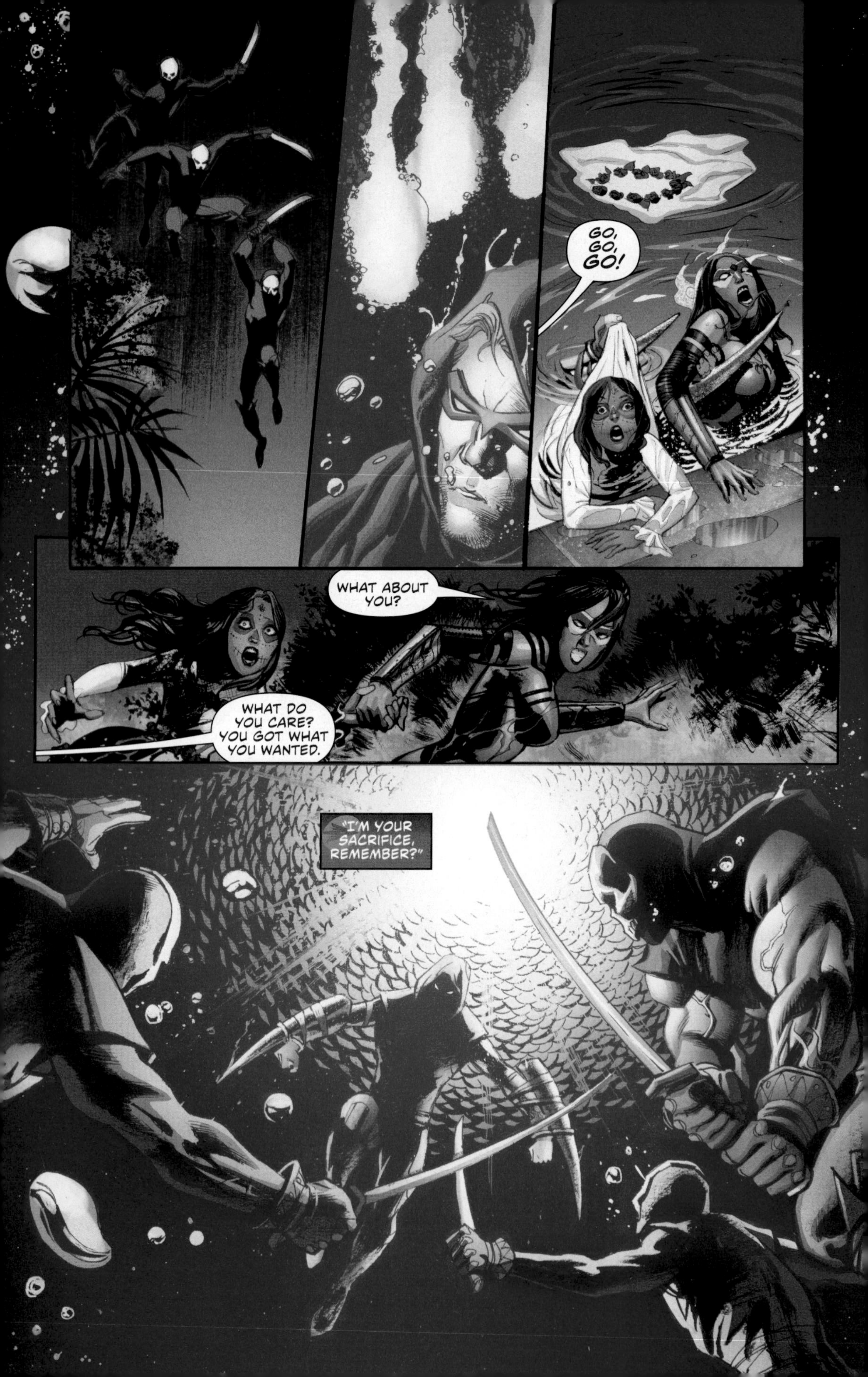

GO, GO, GO!
WHAT ABOUT YOU?
WHAT DO YOU CARE? YOU GOT WHAT YOU WANTED.
"I'M YOUR SACRIFICE, REMEMBER?"

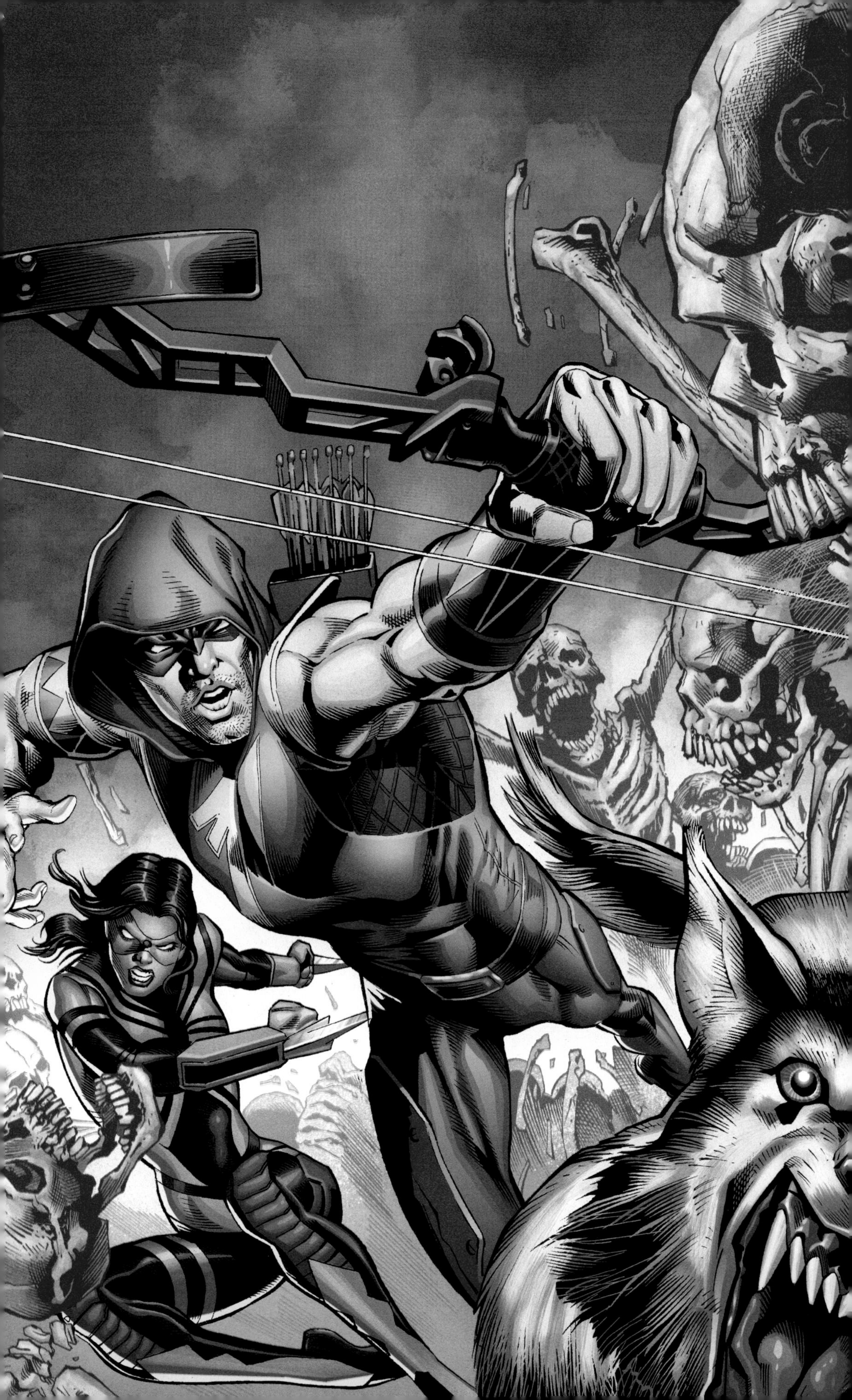

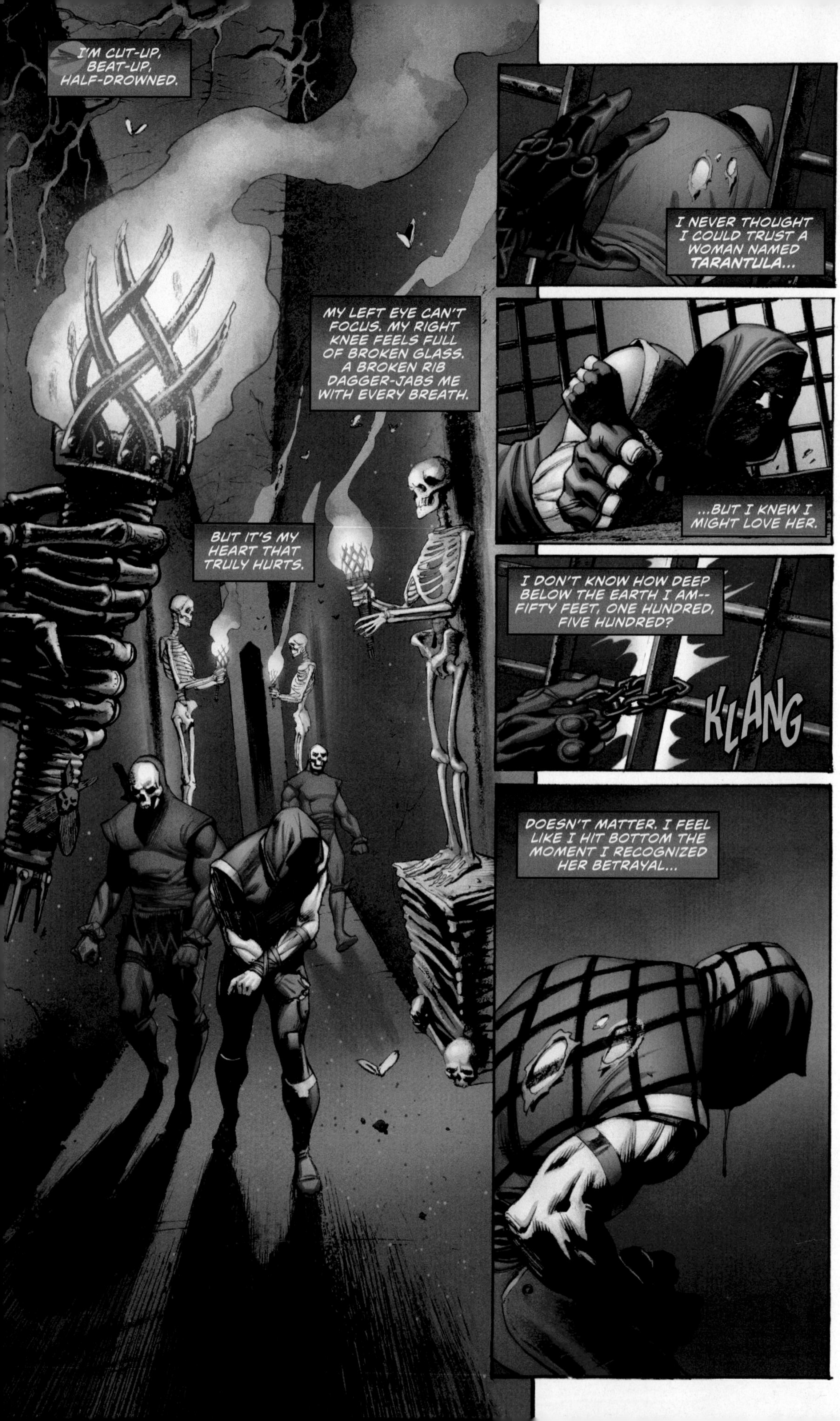
I'M CUT-UP, BEAT-UP, HALF-DROWNED.
MY LEFT EYE CAN'T FOCUS. MY RIGHT KNEE FEELS FULL OF BROKEN GLASS. A BROKEN RIB DAGGER-JABS ME WITH EVERY BREATH.
BUT IT'S MY HEART THAT TRULY HURTS.
I NEVER THOUGHT I COULD TRUST A WOMAN NAMED TARANTULA...
...BUT I KNEW I MIGHT LOVE HER.
I DON'T KNOW HOW DEEP BELOW THE EARTH I AM-- FIFTY FEET, ONE HUNDRED, FIVE HUNDRED?
K-LANG
DOESN'T MATTER. I FEEL LIKE I HIT BOTTOM THE MOMENT I RECOGNIZED HER BETRAYAL...

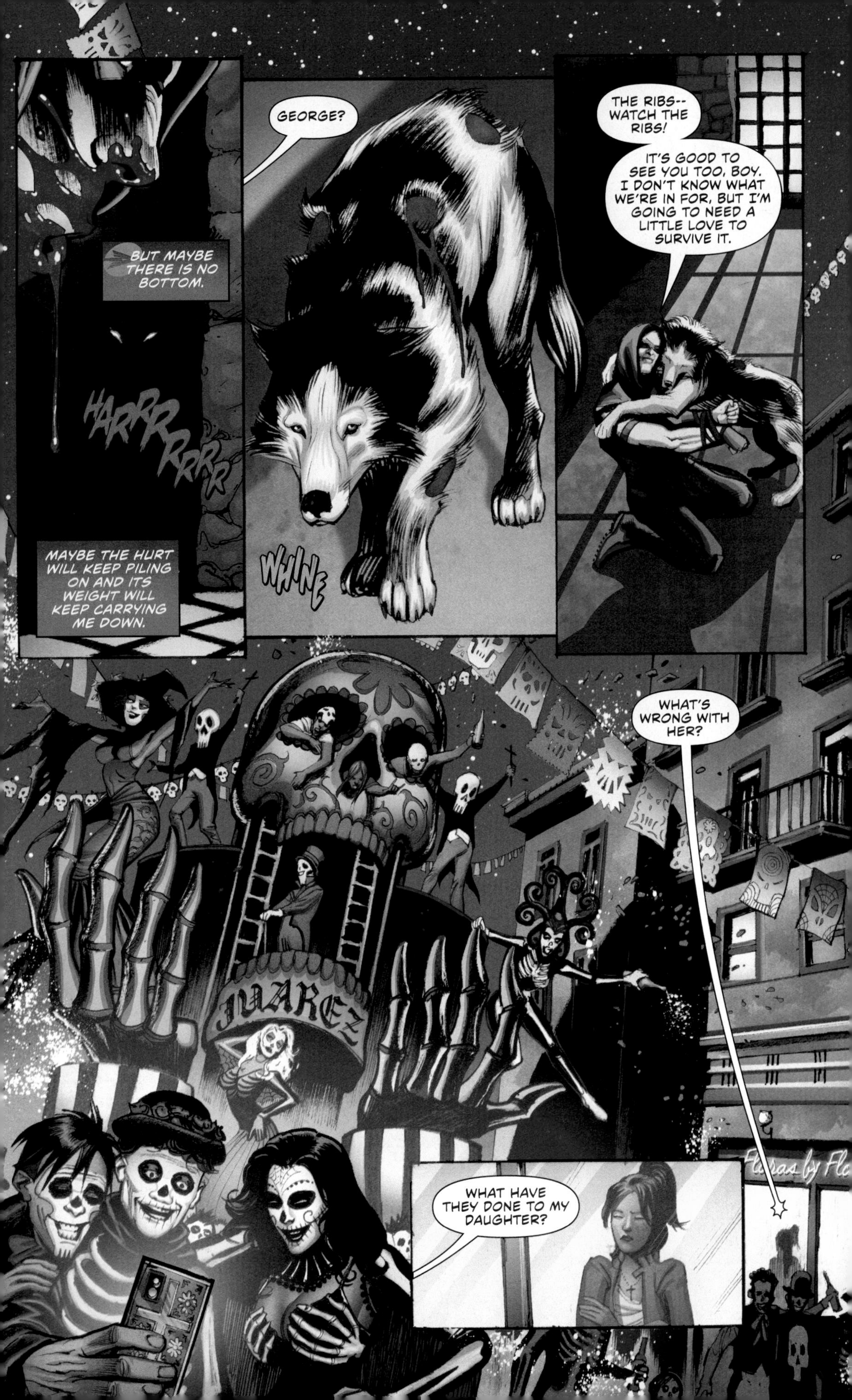

BUT MAYBE THERE IS NO BOTTOM.
HARRRRRRR
MAYBE THE HURT WILL KEEP PILING ON AND ITS WEIGHT WILL KEEP CARRYING ME DOWN.
GEORGE?
WHINE
THE RIBS-- WATCH THE RIBS!
IT'S GOOD TO SEE YOU TOO, BOY. I DON'T KNOW WHAT WE'RE IN FOR, BUT I'M GOING TO NEED A LITTLE LOVE TO SURVIVE IT.
JUAREZ
WHAT'S WRONG WITH HER?
WHAT HAVE THEY DONE TO MY DAUGHTER?

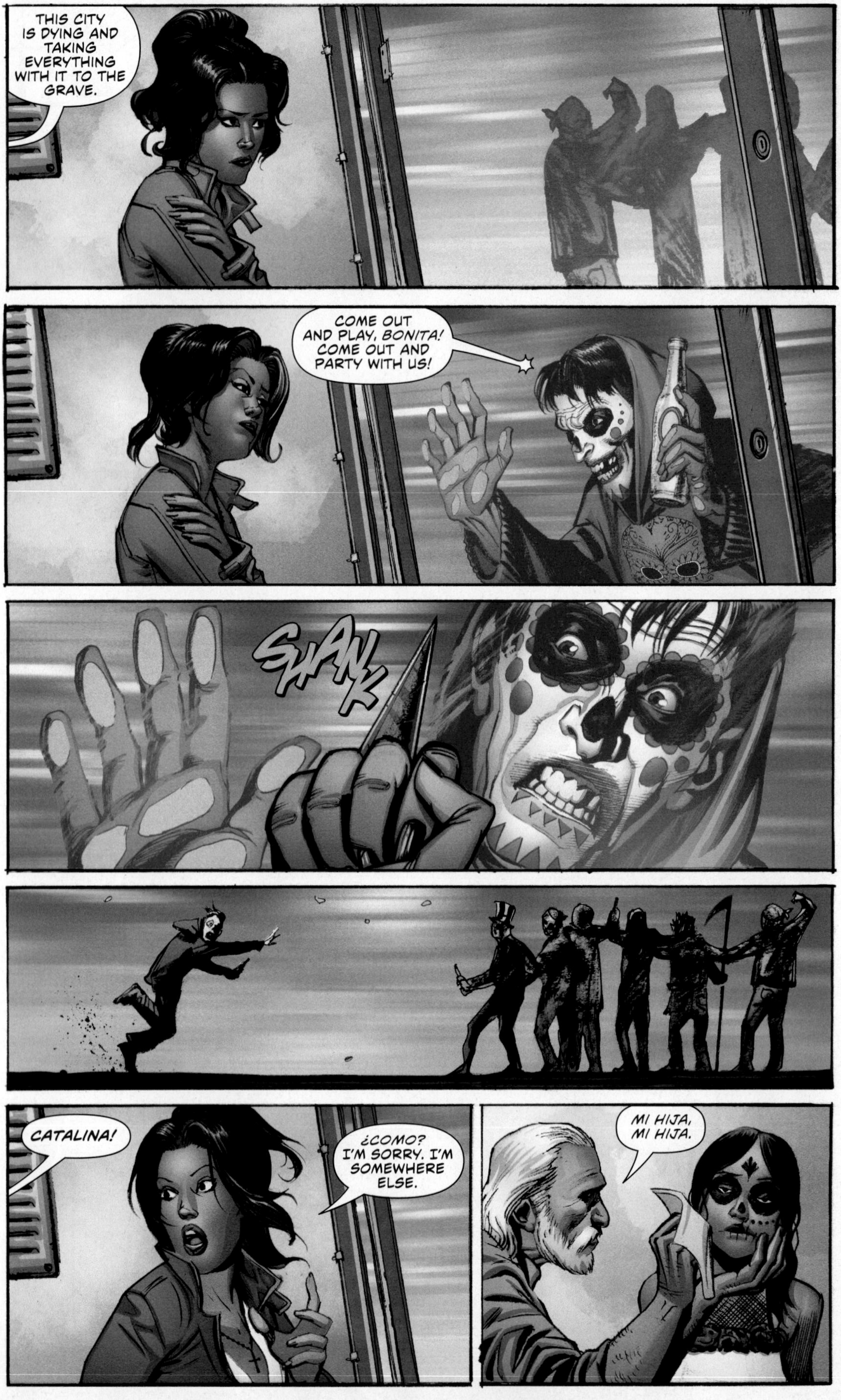
THIS CITY IS DYING AND TAKING EVERYTHING WITH IT TO THE GRAVE.
COME OUT AND PLAY, BONITA! COME OUT AND PARTY WITH US!
SHANK
CATALINA!
¿COMO? I'M SORRY. I'M SOMEWHERE ELSE.
MI HIJA, MI HIJA.

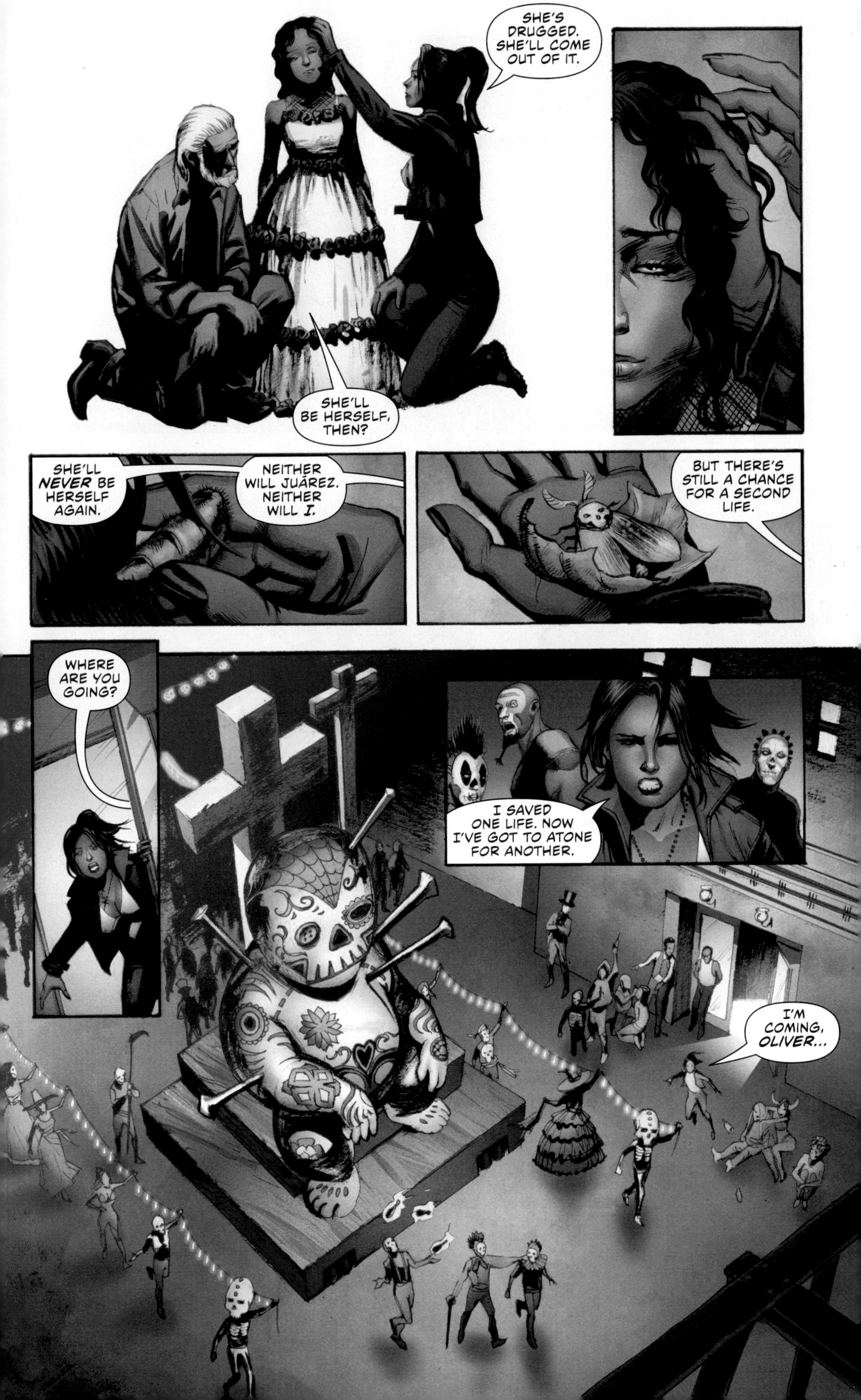
SHE'S DRUGGED. SHE'LL COME OUT OF IT.
SHE'LL BE HERSELF, THEN?
SHE'LL NEVER BE HERSELF AGAIN.
NEITHER WILL JUÁREZ. NEITHER WILL I.
BUT THERE'S STILL A CHANCE FOR A SECOND LIFE.
WHERE ARE YOU GOING?
I SAVED ONE LIFE. NOW I'VE GOT TO ATONE FOR ANOTHER.
I'M COMING, OLIVER...

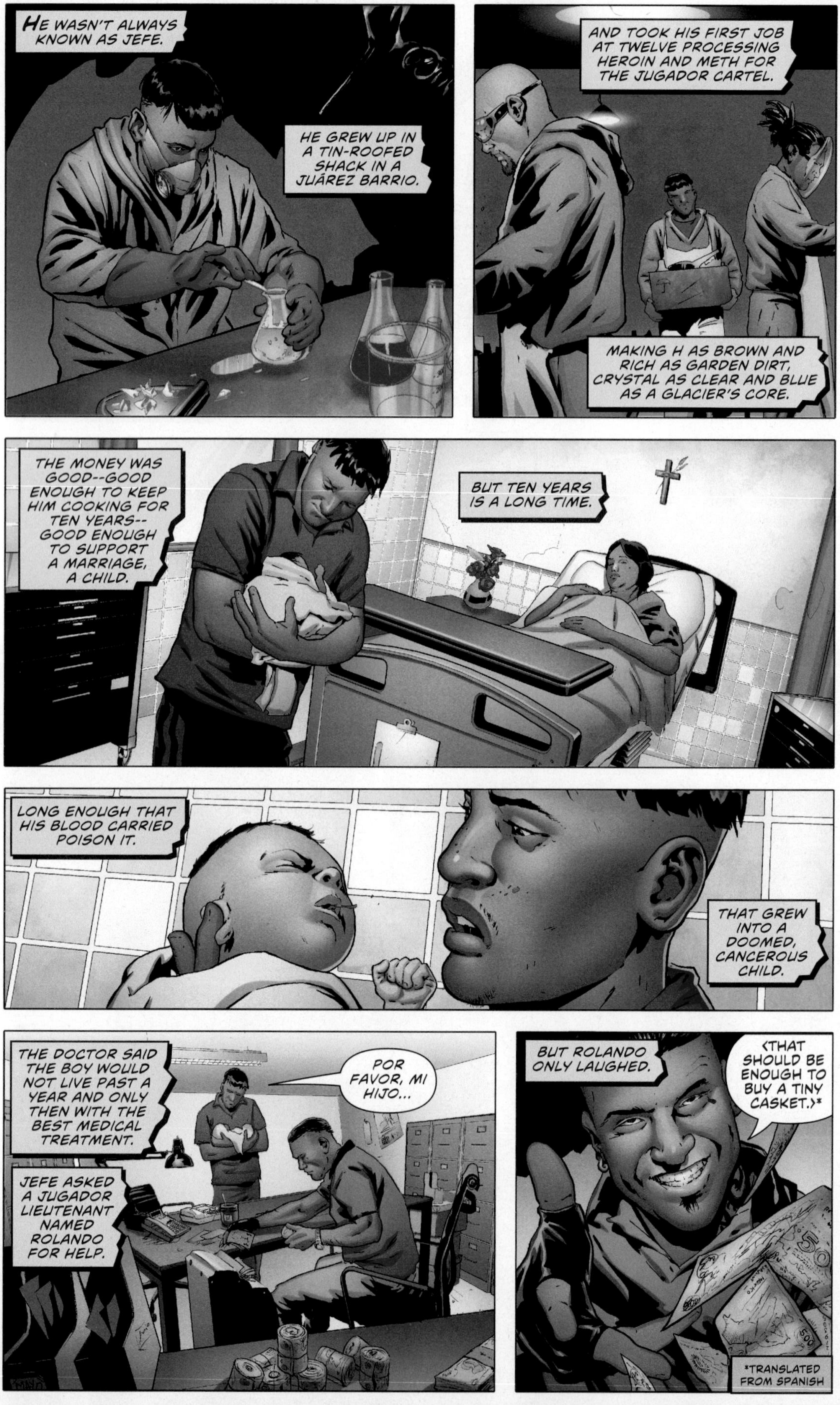
HE WASN'T ALWAYS KNOWN AS JEFE.
HE GREW UP IN A TIN-ROOFED SHACK IN A JUÁREZ BARRIO.
AND TOOK HIS FIRST JOB AT TWELVE PROCESSING HEROIN AND METH FOR THE JUGADOR CARTEL.
MAKING H AS BROWN AND RICH AS GARDEN DIRT, CRYSTAL AS CLEAR AND BLUE AS A GLACIER'S CORE.
THE MONEY WAS GOOD--GOOD ENOUGH TO KEEP HIM COOKING FOR TEN YEARS--GOOD ENOUGH TO SUPPORT A MARRIAGE, A CHILD.
BUT TEN YEARS IS A LONG TIME.
LONG ENOUGH THAT HIS BLOOD CARRIED POISON IT.
THAT GREW INTO A DOOMED, CANCEROUS CHILD.
THE DOCTOR SAID THE BOY WOULD NOT LIVE PAST A YEAR AND ONLY THEN WITH THE BEST MEDICAL TREATMENT.
JEFE ASKED A JUGADOR LIEUTENANT NAMED ROLANDO FOR HELP.
POR FAVOR, MI HIJO...
BUT ROLANDO ONLY LAUGHED.
<THAT SHOULD BE ENOUGH TO BUY A TINY CASKET.>*
*TRANSLATED FROM SPANISH

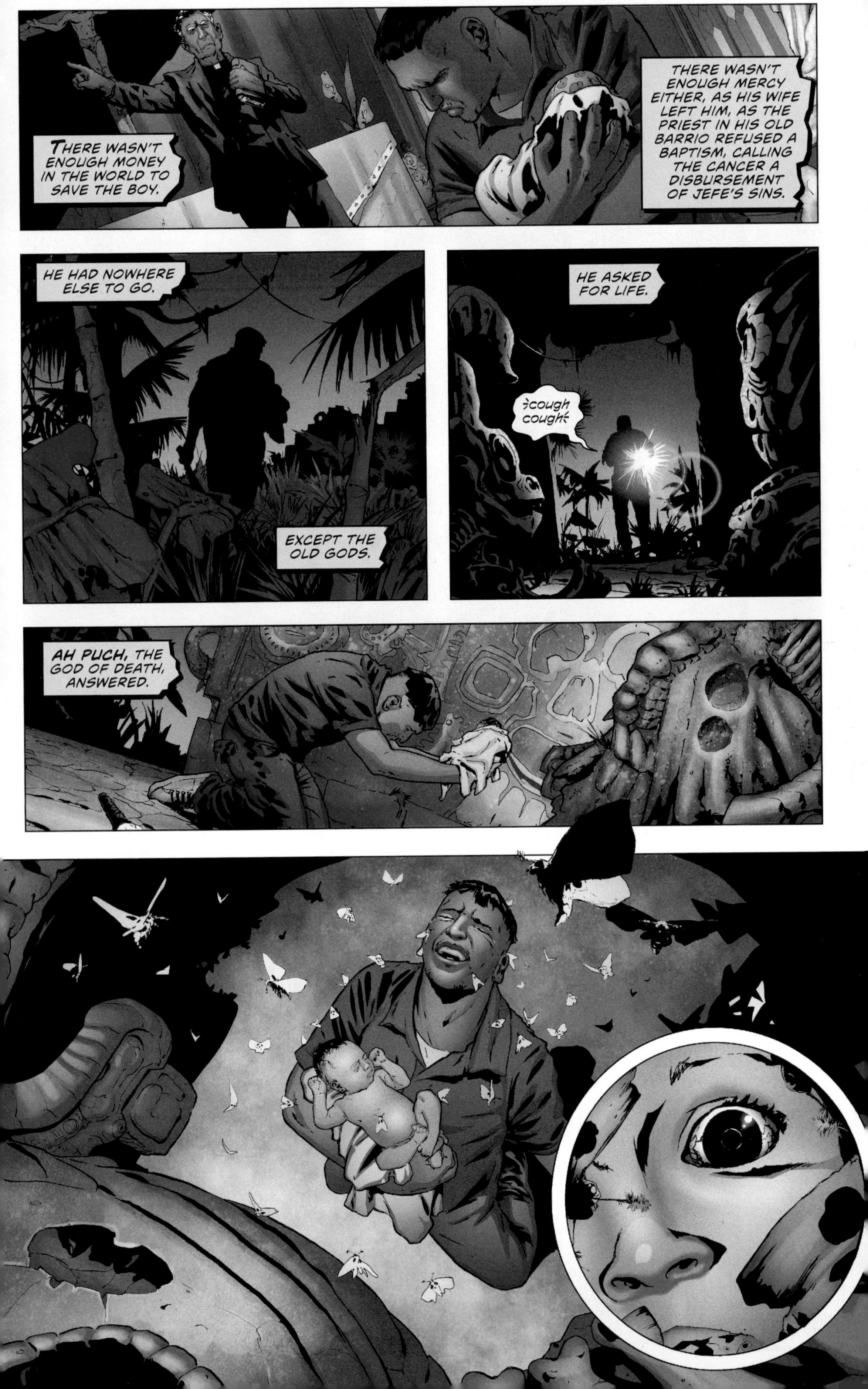
THERE WASN'T ENOUGH MONEY IN THE WORLD TO SAVE THE BOY.
THERE WASN'T ENOUGH MERCY EITHER, AS HIS WIFE LEFT HIM, AS THE PRIEST IN HIS OLD BARRIO REFUSED A BAPTISM, CALLING THE CANCER A DISBURSEMENT OF JEFE'S SINS.
HE HAD NOWHERE ELSE TO GO.
EXCEPT THE OLD GODS.
HE ASKED FOR LIFE.
cough cough
AH PUCH, THE GOD OF DEATH, ANSWERED.

THE MAYANS WOULD PLAY A GAME-- CALLED *PITZ*--WITH SEVERED HEADS IN THE PLACE OF BALLS.

ROLANDO'S WAS THE FIRST OF MANY HARVESTED.

AH PUCH TAUGHT HIM THERE WAS POWER IN BONES. POWER THAT COULD BE HARVESTED. THE DISTILLATION OF A LIFE.

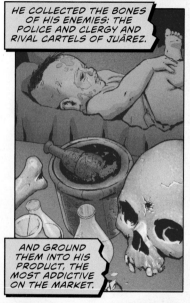

HE COLLECTED THE BONES OF HIS ENEMIES: THE POLICE AND CLERGY AND RIVAL CARTELS OF JUÁREZ.

AND GROUND THEM INTO HIS PRODUCT, THE MOST ADDICTIVE ON THE MARKET.

suckle

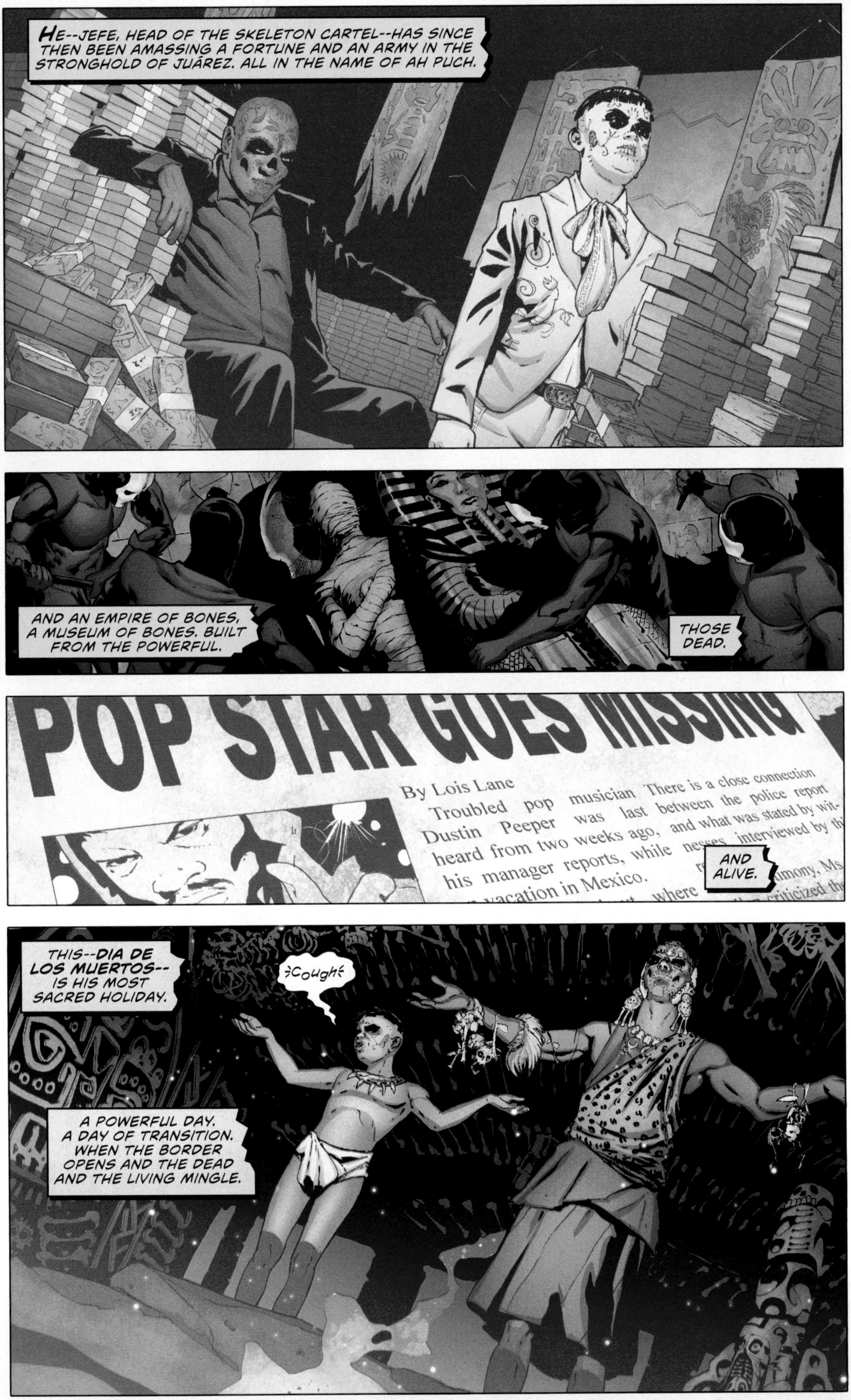
HE--JEFE, HEAD OF THE SKELETON CARTEL--HAS SINCE THEN BEEN AMASSING A FORTUNE AND AN ARMY IN THE STRONGHOLD OF JUÁREZ. ALL IN THE NAME OF AH PUCH.
AND AN EMPIRE OF BONES, A MUSEUM OF BONES. BUILT FROM THE POWERFUL.
THOSE DEAD.
POP STAR GOES MISSING
By Lois Lane
Troubled pop musician Dustin Peeper was last heard from two weeks ago, his manager reports, while on vacation in Mexico.
There is a close connection between the police report and what was stated by witnesses interviewed by th
AND ALIVE.
THIS--DIA DE LOS MUERTOS--IS HIS MOST SACRED HOLIDAY.
COUGH
A POWERFUL DAY. A DAY OF TRANSITION. WHEN THE BORDER OPENS AND THE DEAD AND THE LIVING MINGLE.

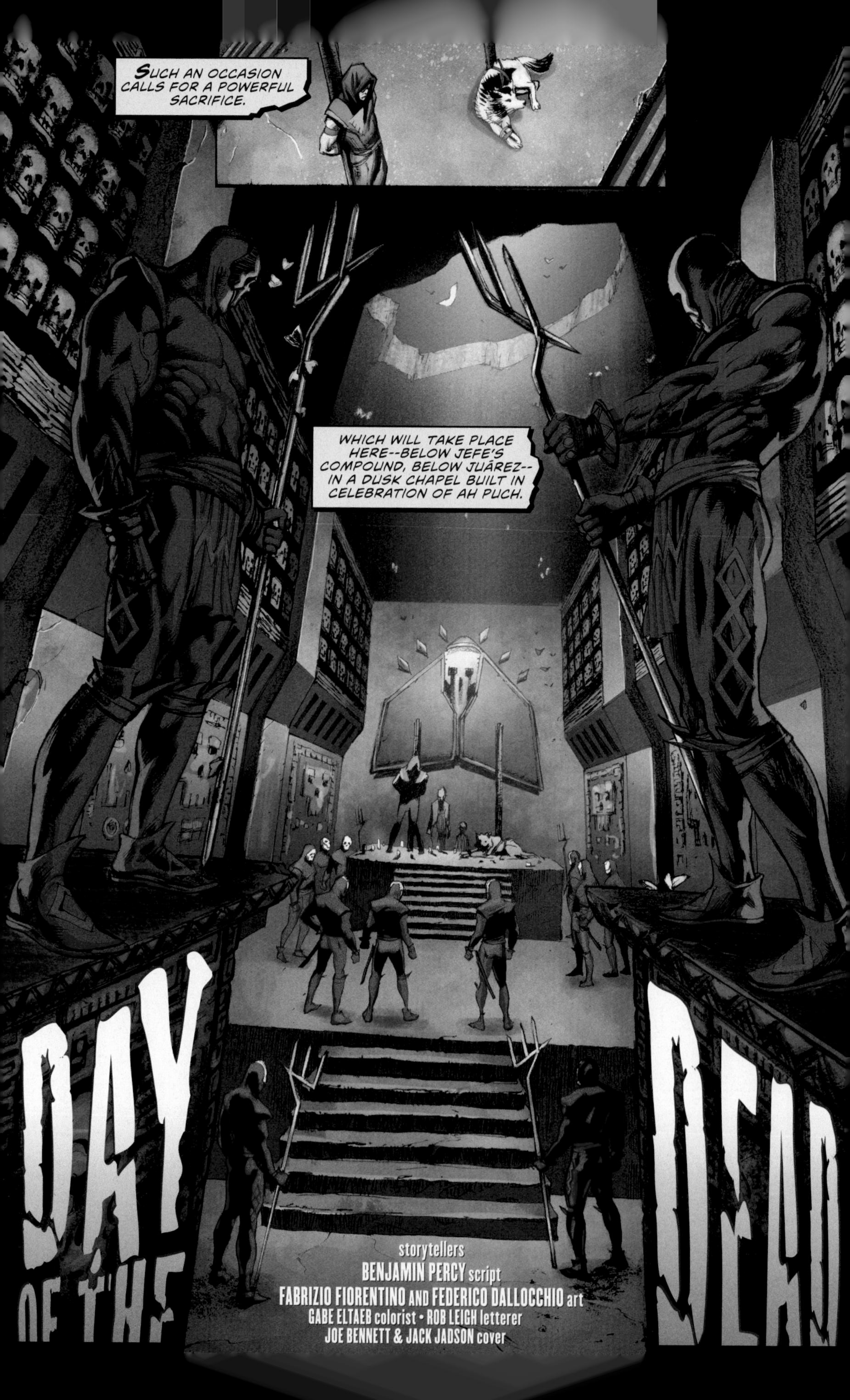

SUCH AN OCCASION CALLS FOR A POWERFUL SACRIFICE.
WHICH WILL TAKE PLACE HERE--BELOW JEFE'S COMPOUND, BELOW JUÁREZ--IN A DUSK CHAPEL BUILT IN CELEBRATION OF AH PUCH.
DAY OF THE DEAD
storytellers
BENJAMIN PERCY script
FABRIZIO FIORENTINO AND FEDERICO DALLOCCHIO art
GABE ELTAEB colorist • ROB LEIGH letterer
JOE BENNETT & JACK JADSON cover

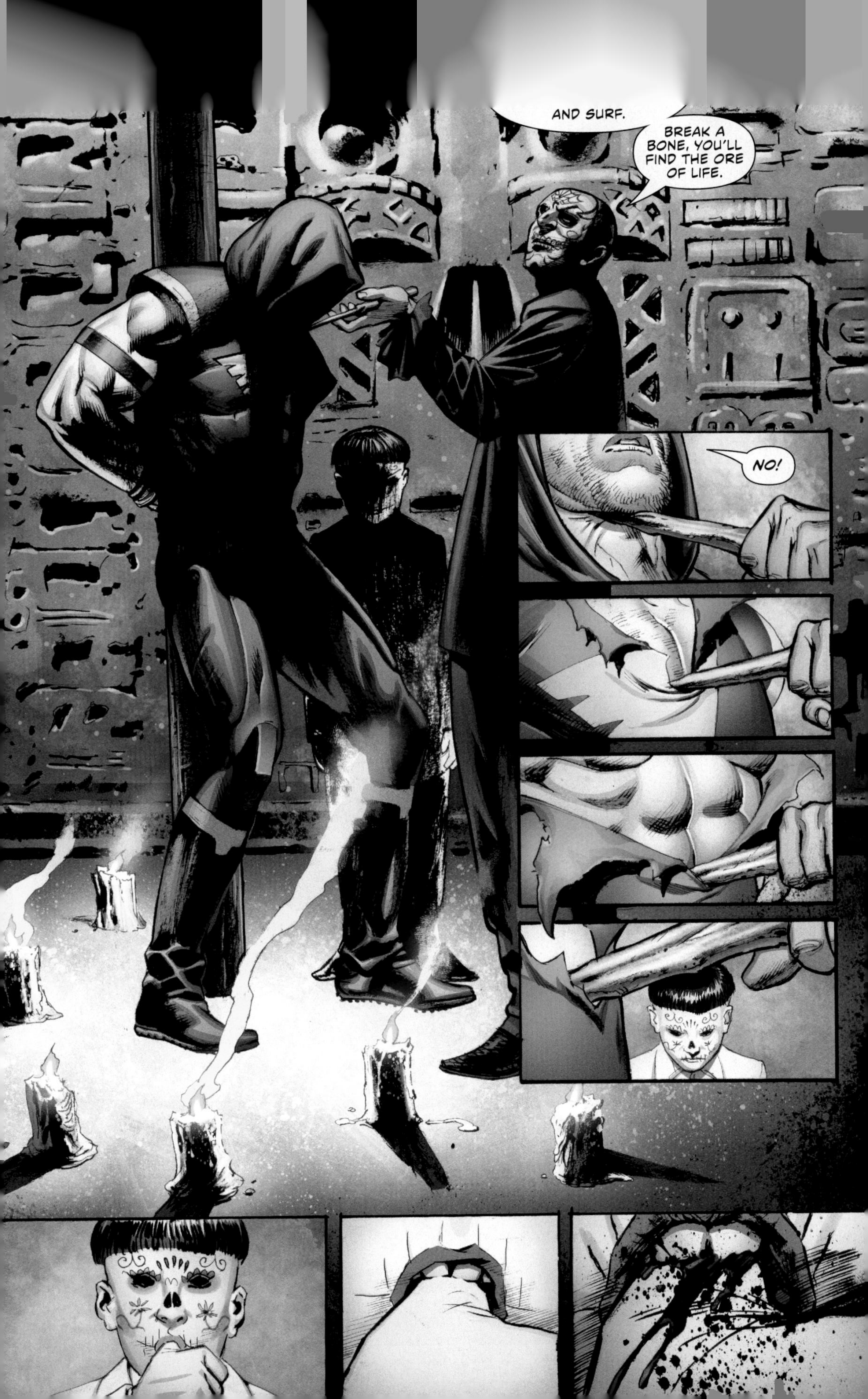
AND SURF.
BREAK A BONE, YOU'LL FIND THE ORE OF LIFE.
NO!

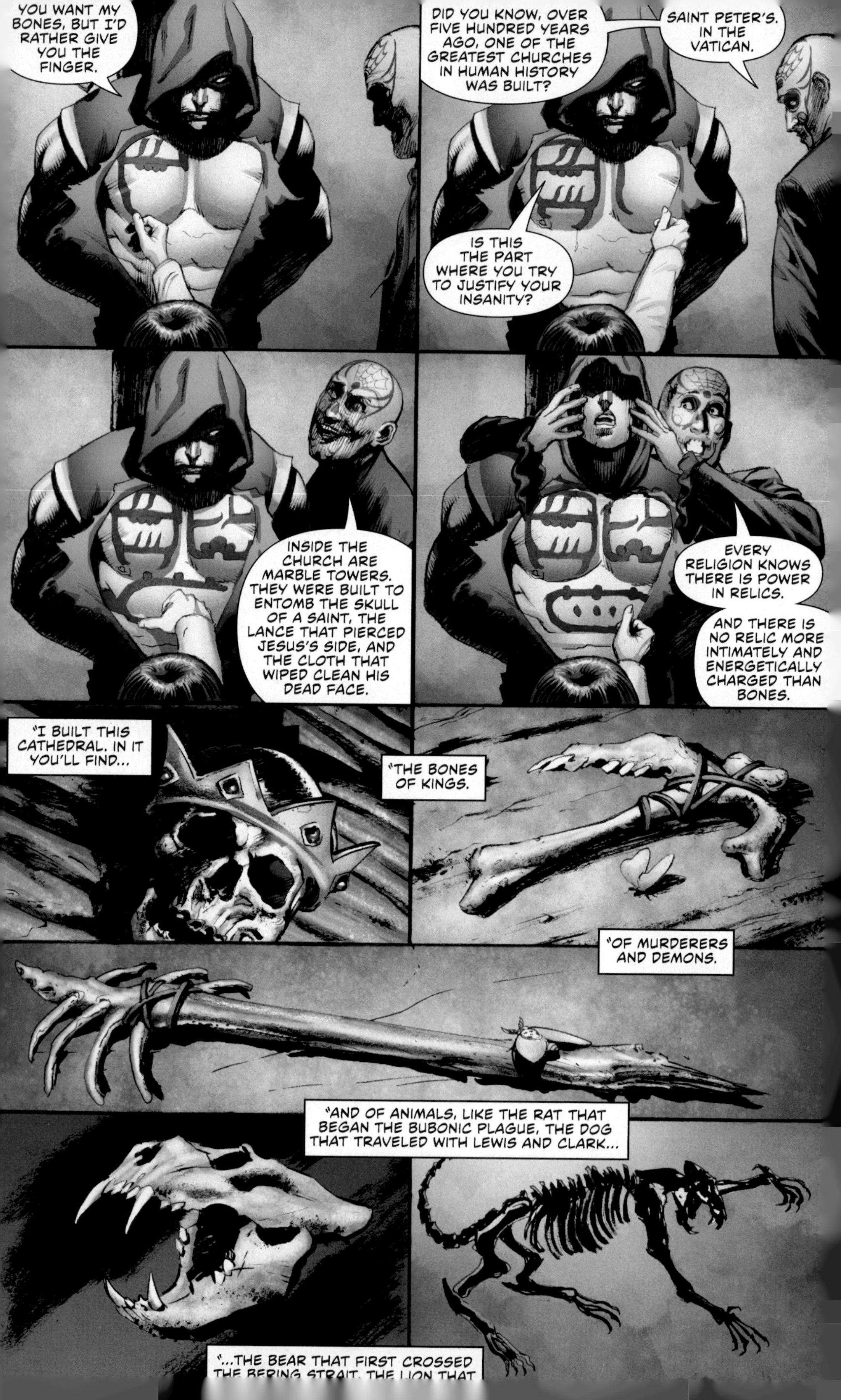
YOU WANT MY BONES, BUT I'D RATHER GIVE YOU THE FINGER.
DID YOU KNOW, OVER FIVE HUNDRED YEARS AGO, ONE OF THE GREATEST CHURCHES IN HUMAN HISTORY WAS BUILT?
SAINT PETER'S. IN THE VATICAN.
IS THIS THE PART WHERE YOU TRY TO JUSTIFY YOUR INSANITY?
INSIDE THE CHURCH ARE MARBLE TOWERS. THEY WERE BUILT TO ENTOMB THE SKULL OF A SAINT, THE LANCE THAT PIERCED JESUS'S SIDE, AND THE CLOTH THAT WIPED CLEAN HIS DEAD FACE.
EVERY RELIGION KNOWS THERE IS POWER IN RELICS.
AND THERE IS NO RELIC MORE INTIMATELY AND ENERGETICALLY CHARGED THAN BONES.
"I BUILT THIS CATHEDRAL. IN IT YOU'LL FIND...
"THE BONES OF KINGS.
"OF MURDERERS AND DEMONS.
"AND OF ANIMALS, LIKE THE RAT THAT BEGAN THE BUBONIC PLAGUE, THE DOG THAT TRAVELED WITH LEWIS AND CLARK...
"...THE BEAR THAT FIRST CROSSED

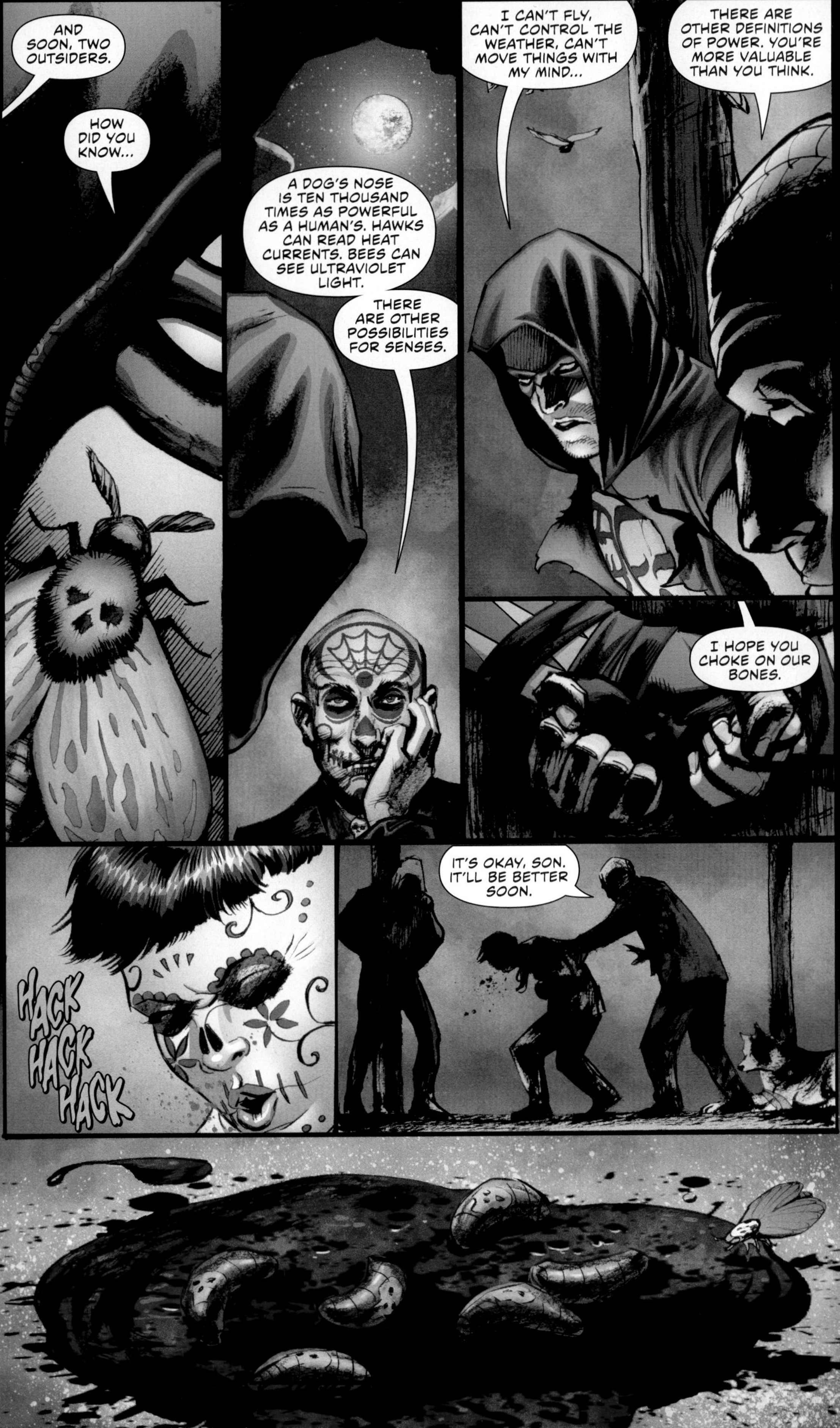
AND SOON, TWO OUTSIDERS.
HOW DID YOU KNOW...
A DOG'S NOSE IS TEN THOUSAND TIMES AS POWERFUL AS A HUMAN'S. HAWKS CAN READ HEAT CURRENTS. BEES CAN SEE ULTRAVIOLET LIGHT.
THERE ARE OTHER POSSIBILITIES FOR SENSES.
I CAN'T FLY, CAN'T CONTROL THE WEATHER, CAN'T MOVE THINGS WITH MY MIND...
THERE ARE OTHER DEFINITIONS OF POWER. YOU'RE MORE VALUABLE THAN YOU THINK.
I HOPE YOU CHOKE ON OUR BONES.
HACK HACK HACK
IT'S OKAY, SON. IT'LL BE BETTER SOON.

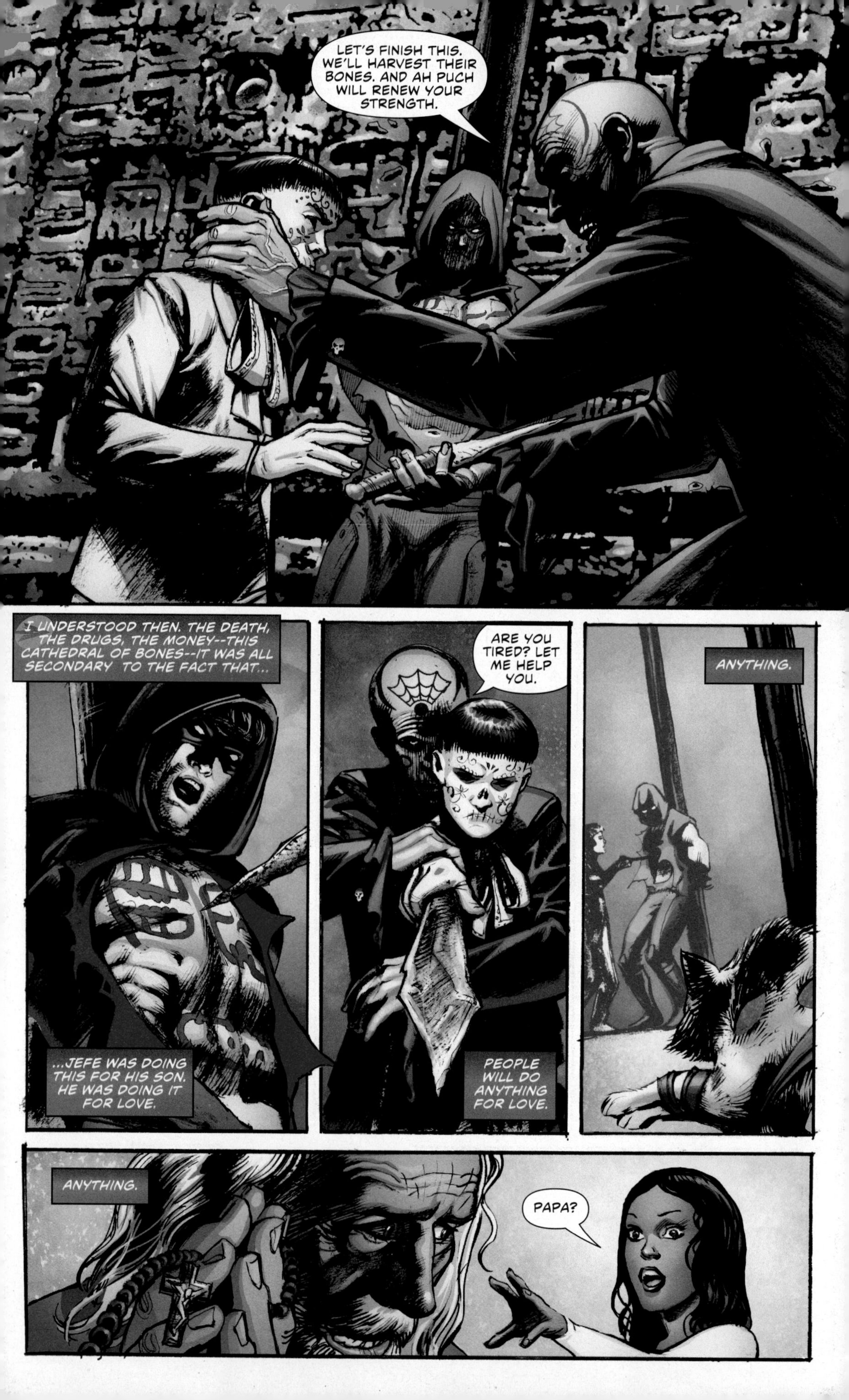
LET'S FINISH THIS. WE'LL HARVEST THEIR BONES. AND AH PUCH WILL RENEW YOUR STRENGTH.
I UNDERSTOOD THEN. THE DEATH, THE DRUGS, THE MONEY--THIS CATHEDRAL OF BONES--IT WAS ALL SECONDARY TO THE FACT THAT...
...JEFE WAS DOING THIS FOR HIS SON. HE WAS DOING IT FOR LOVE.
ARE YOU TIRED? LET ME HELP YOU.
PEOPLE WILL DO ANYTHING FOR LOVE.
ANYTHING.
ANYTHING.
PAPA?

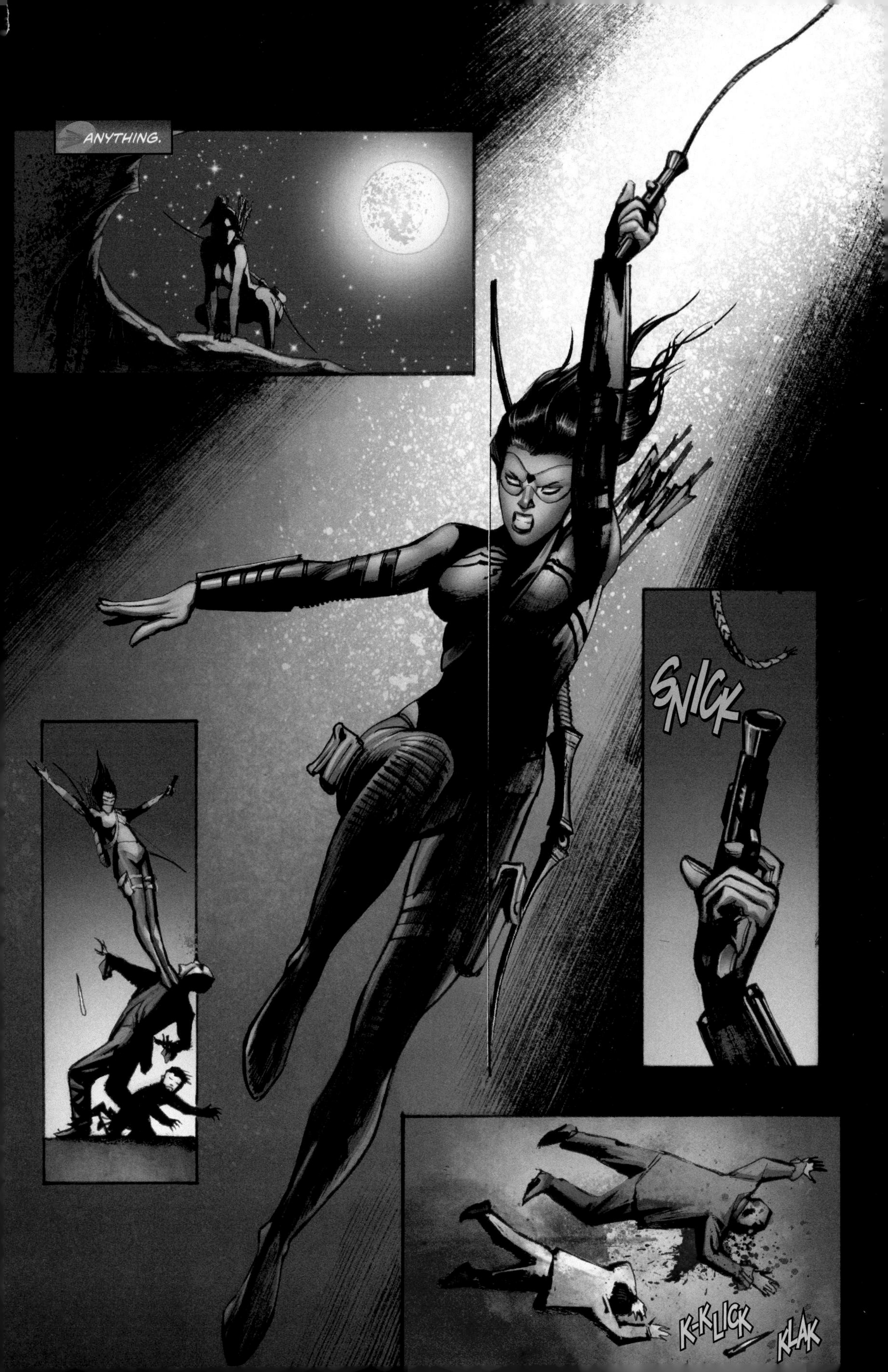
ANYTHING.
SNICK
K-KLICK
KLAK

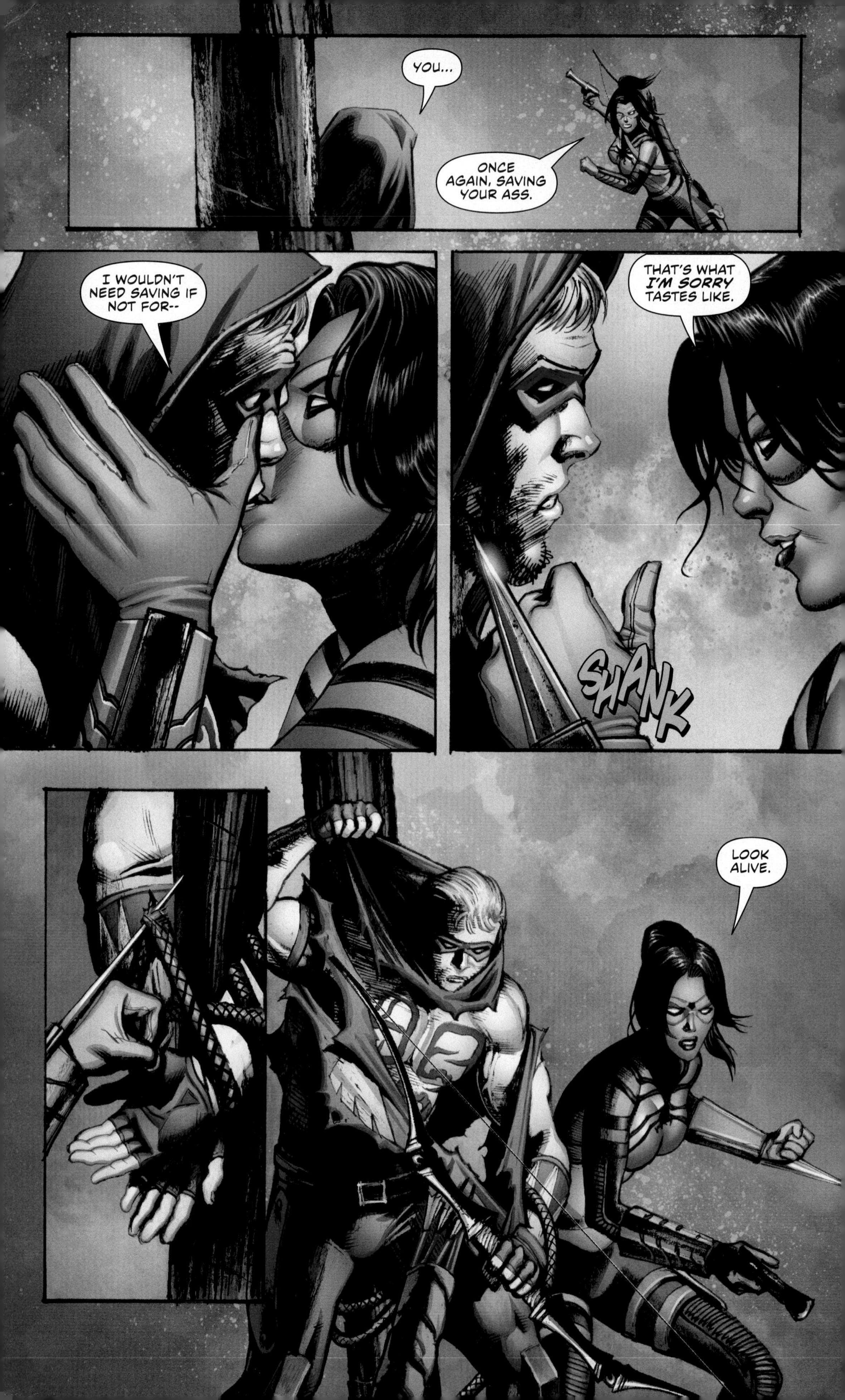
YOU...
ONCE AGAIN, SAVING YOUR ASS.
I WOULDN'T NEED SAVING IF NOT FOR--
THAT'S WHAT *I'M SORRY* TASTES LIKE.
SHANK
LOOK ALIVE.

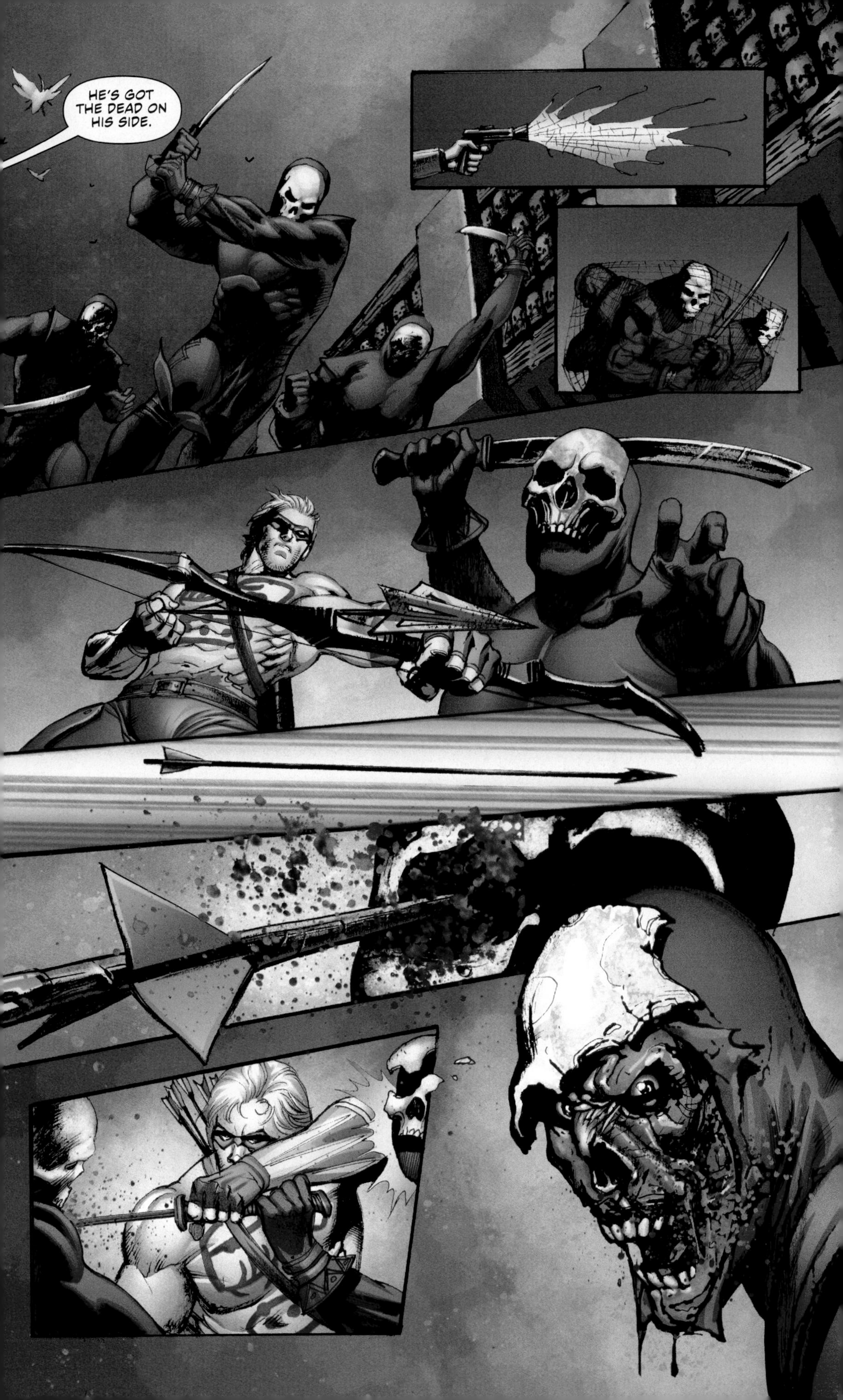
HE'S GOT THE DEAD ON HIS SIDE.

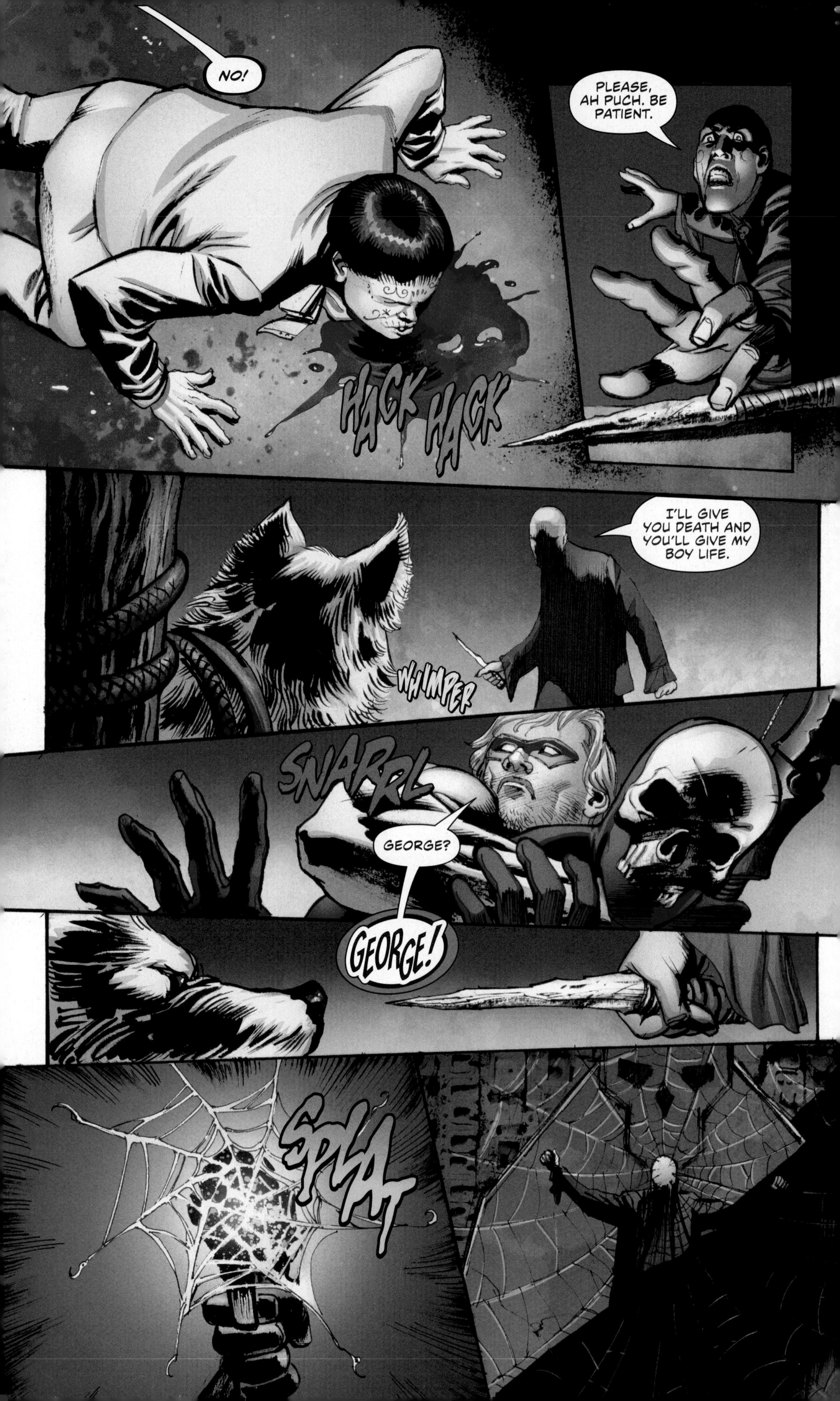
NO!
PLEASE, AH PUCH. BE PATIENT.
HACK HACK
I'LL GIVE YOU DEATH AND YOU'LL GIVE MY BOY LIFE.
WHIMPER
SNARRL
GEORGE?
GEORGE!
SPLAT

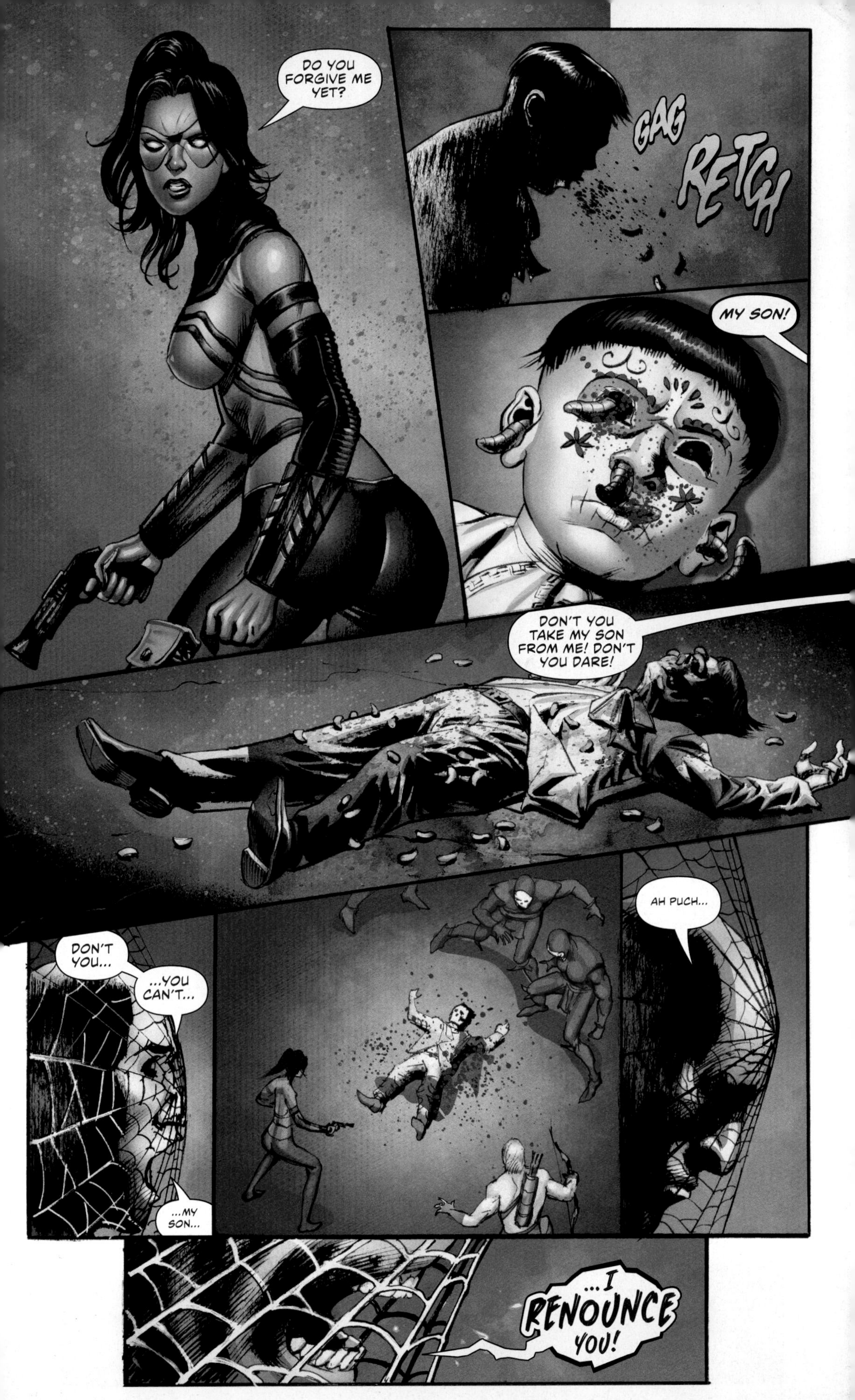
DO YOU FORGIVE ME YET?
GAG
RETCH
MY SON!
DON'T YOU TAKE MY SON FROM ME! DON'T YOU DARE!
DON'T YOU...
...YOU CAN'T...
...MY SON...
AH PUCH...
...I RENOUNCE YOU!

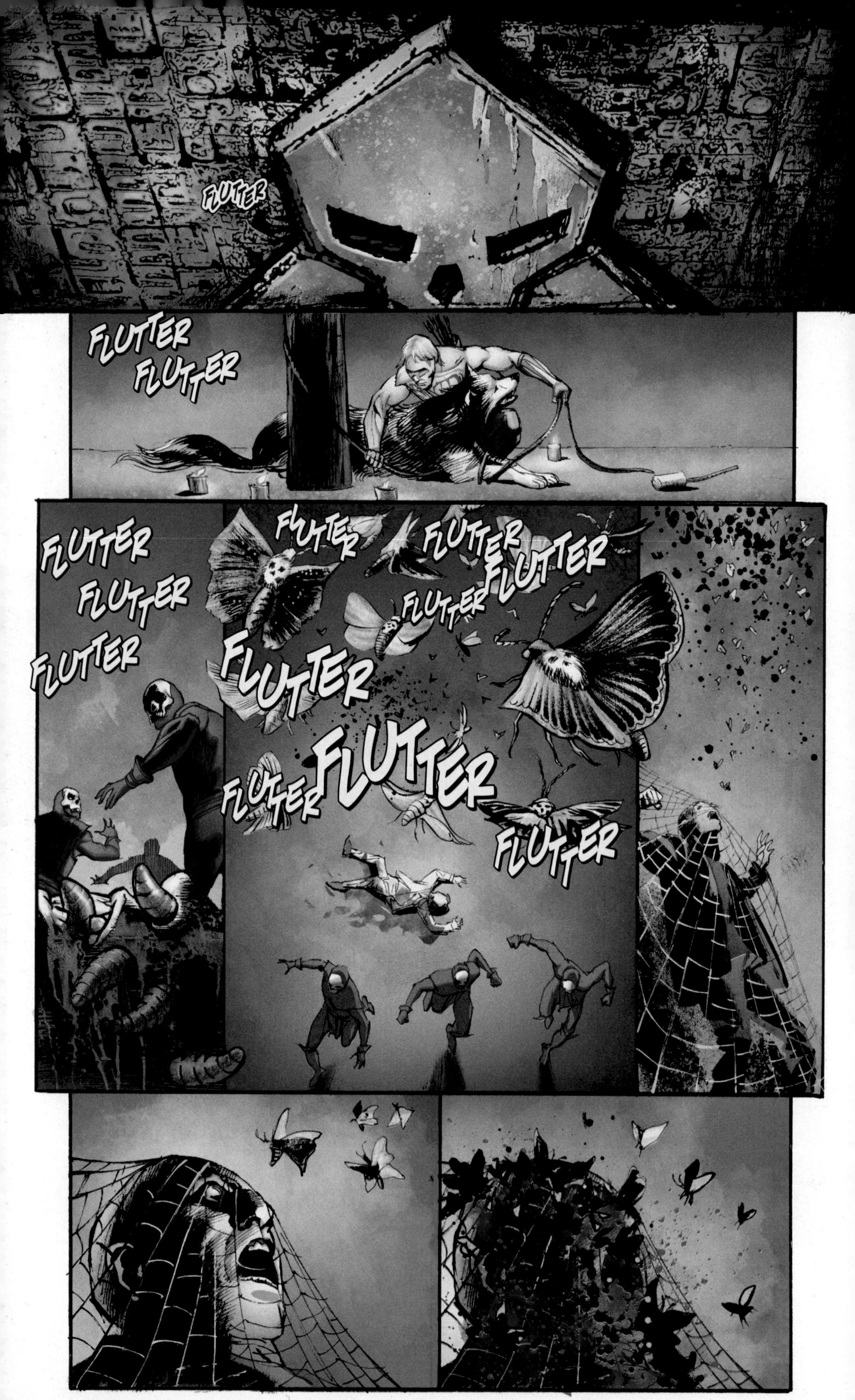
FLUTTER
FLUTTER
FLUTTER
FLUTTER
FLUTTER
FLUTTER
FLUTTER
FLUTTER
FLUTTER
FLUTTER
FLUTTER
FLUTTER
FLUTTER
FLUTTER

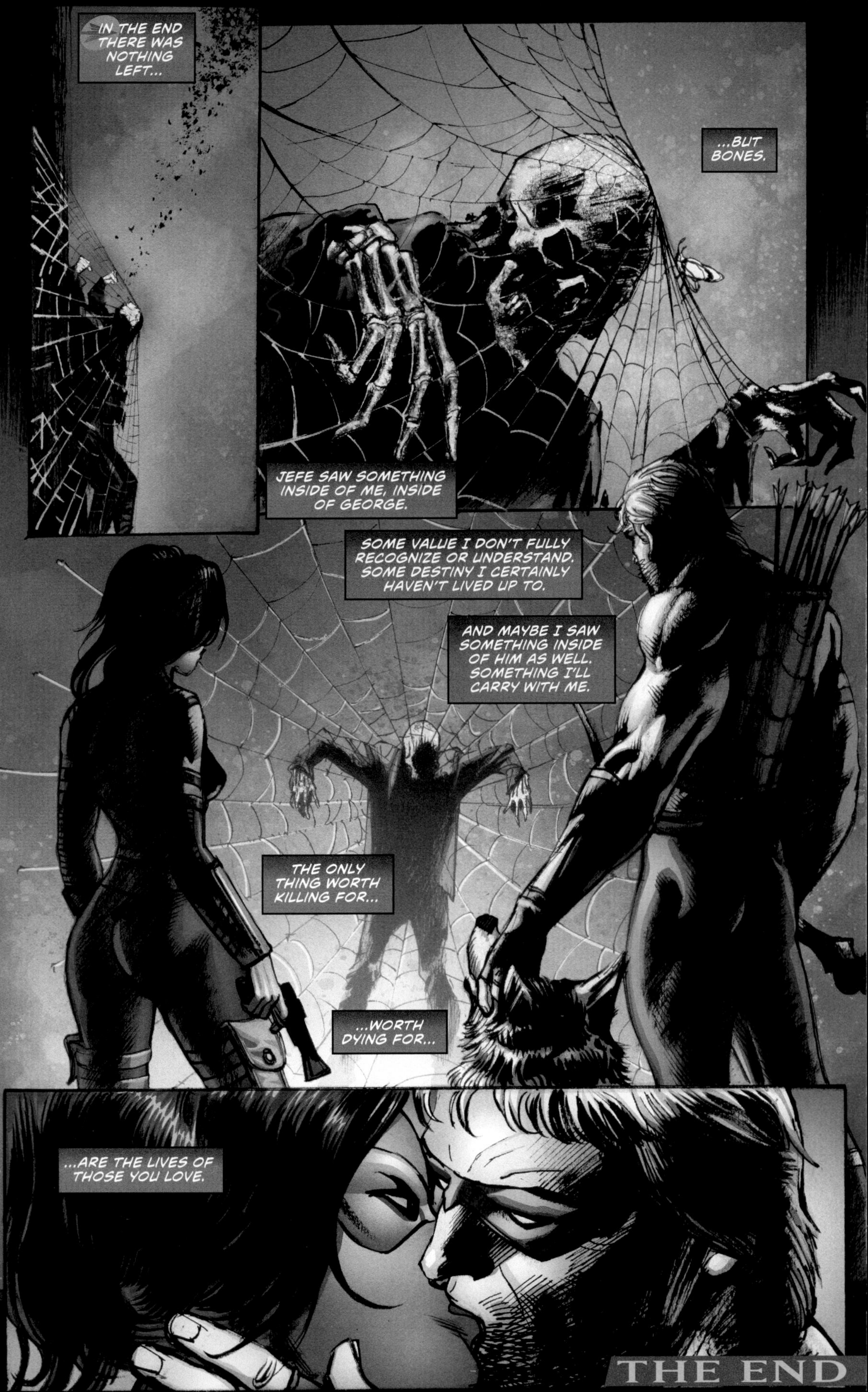
IN THE END THERE WAS NOTHING LEFT...
...BUT BONES.
JEFE SAW SOMETHING INSIDE OF ME, INSIDE OF GEORGE.
SOME VALUE I DON'T FULLY RECOGNIZE OR UNDERSTAND. SOME DESTINY I CERTAINLY HAVEN'T LIVED UP TO.
AND MAYBE I SAW SOMETHING INSIDE OF HIM AS WELL. SOMETHING I'LL CARRY WITH ME.
THE ONLY THING WORTH KILLING FOR...
...WORTH DYING FOR...
...ARE THE LIVES OF THOSE YOU LOVE.
THE END

GREEN ARROW 41

Joker 75th Anniversary variant cover by Bill Sienkiewicz

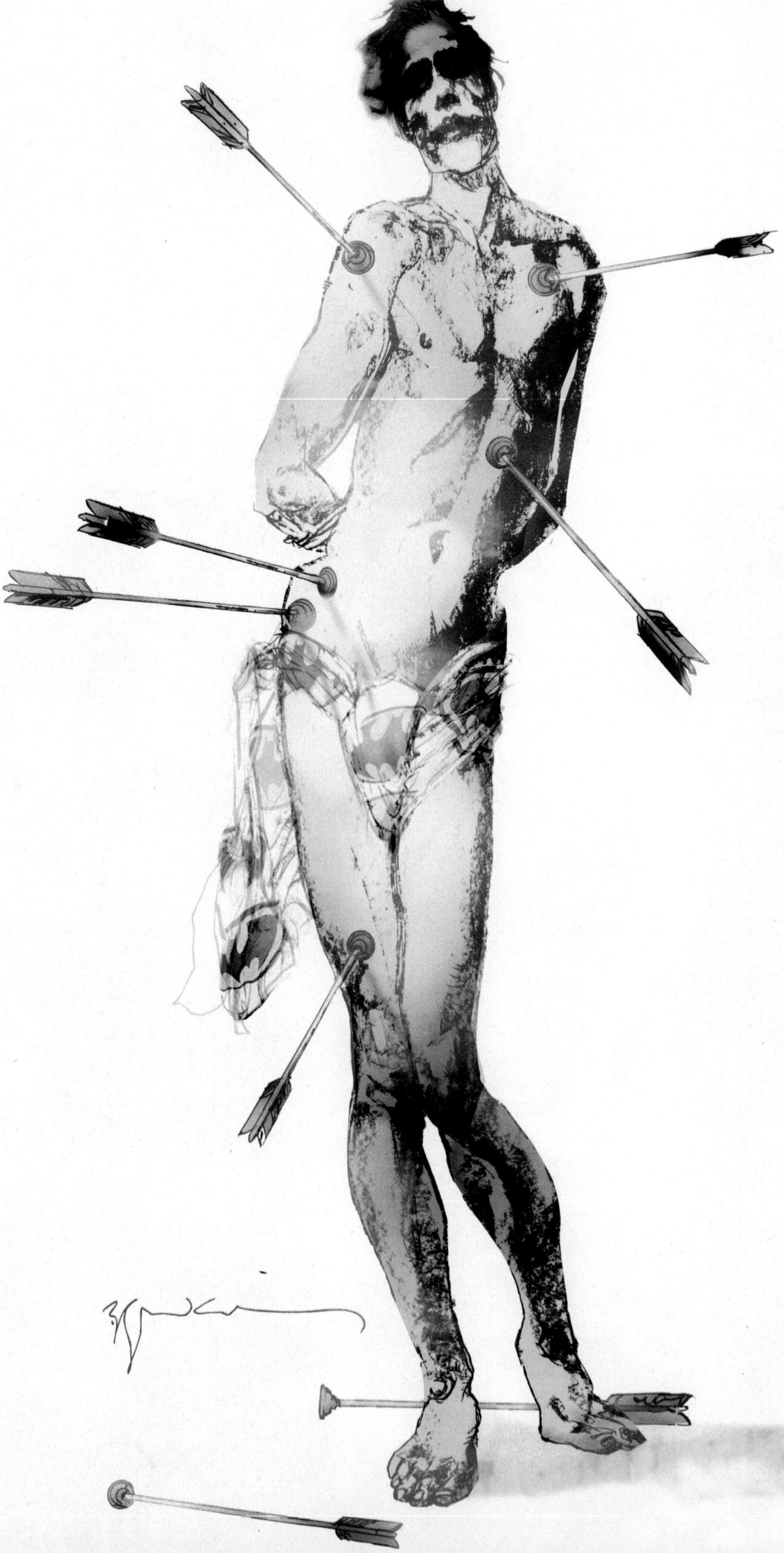

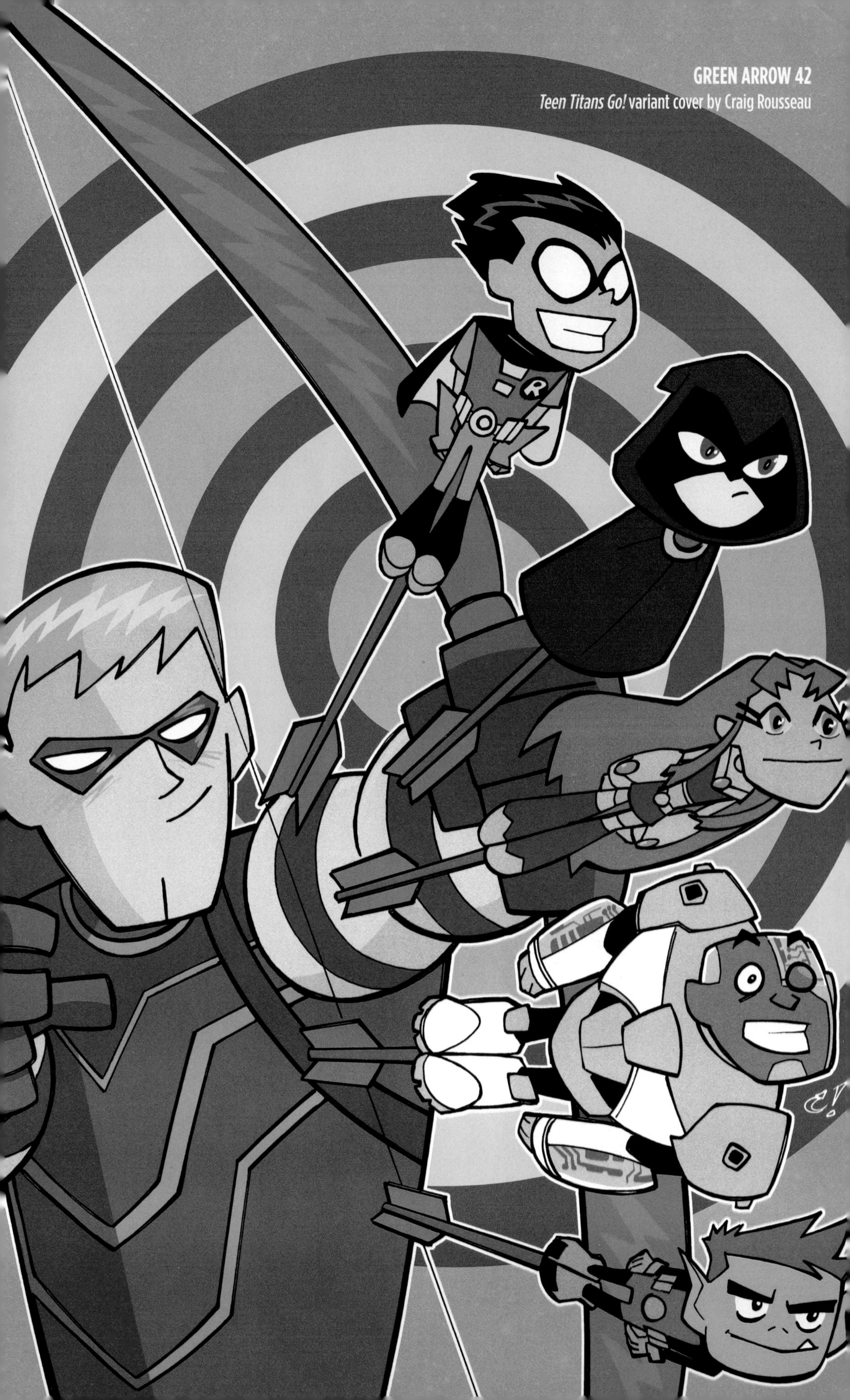

GREEN ARROW 42
Teen Titans Go! variant cover by Craig Rousseau

GREEN ARROW 43
Bombshells variant cover by Ant Lucia

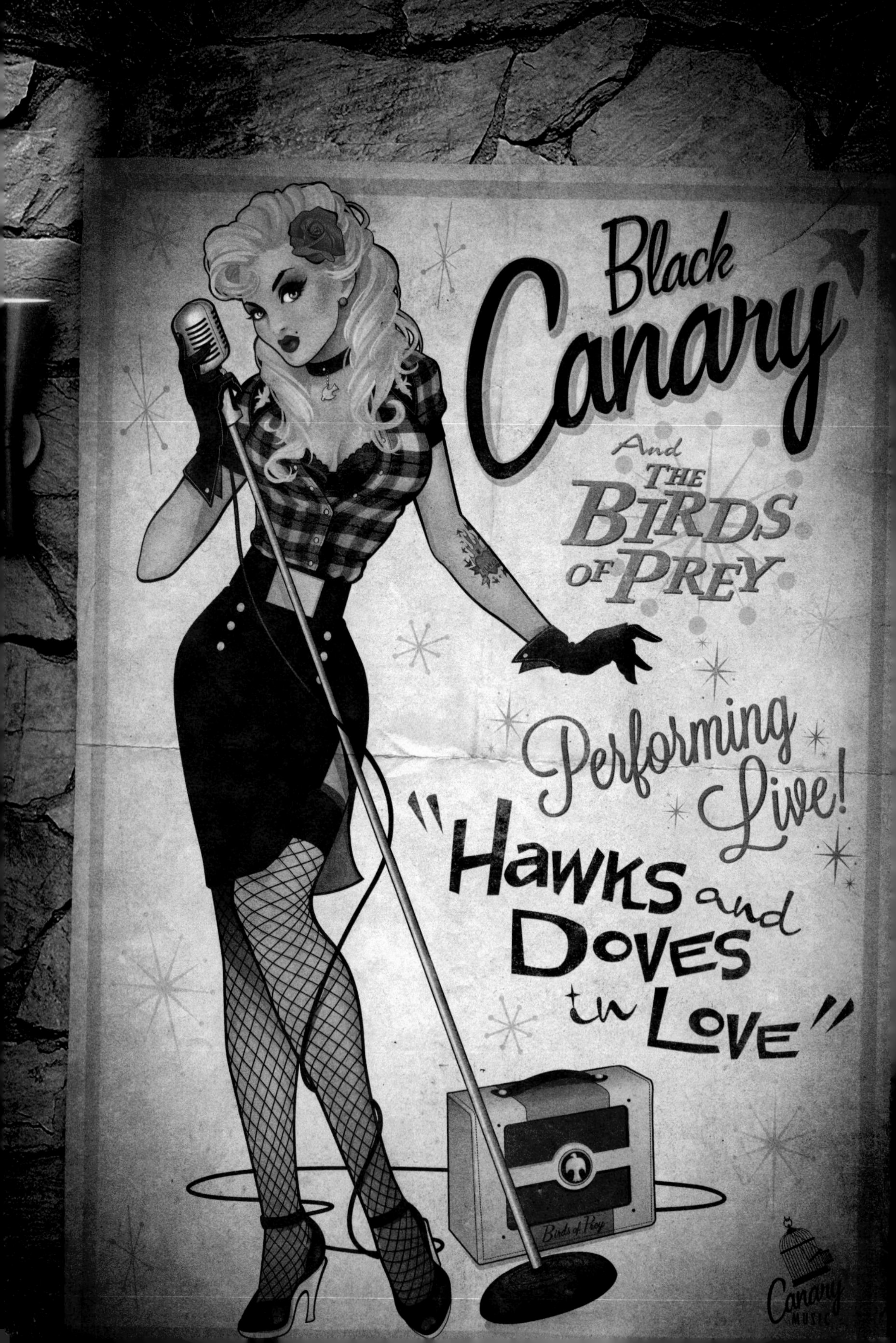
Black Canary
And THE BIRDS OF PREY
Performing Live!
"Hawks and Doves in Love"
Birds of Prey
Canary MUSIC

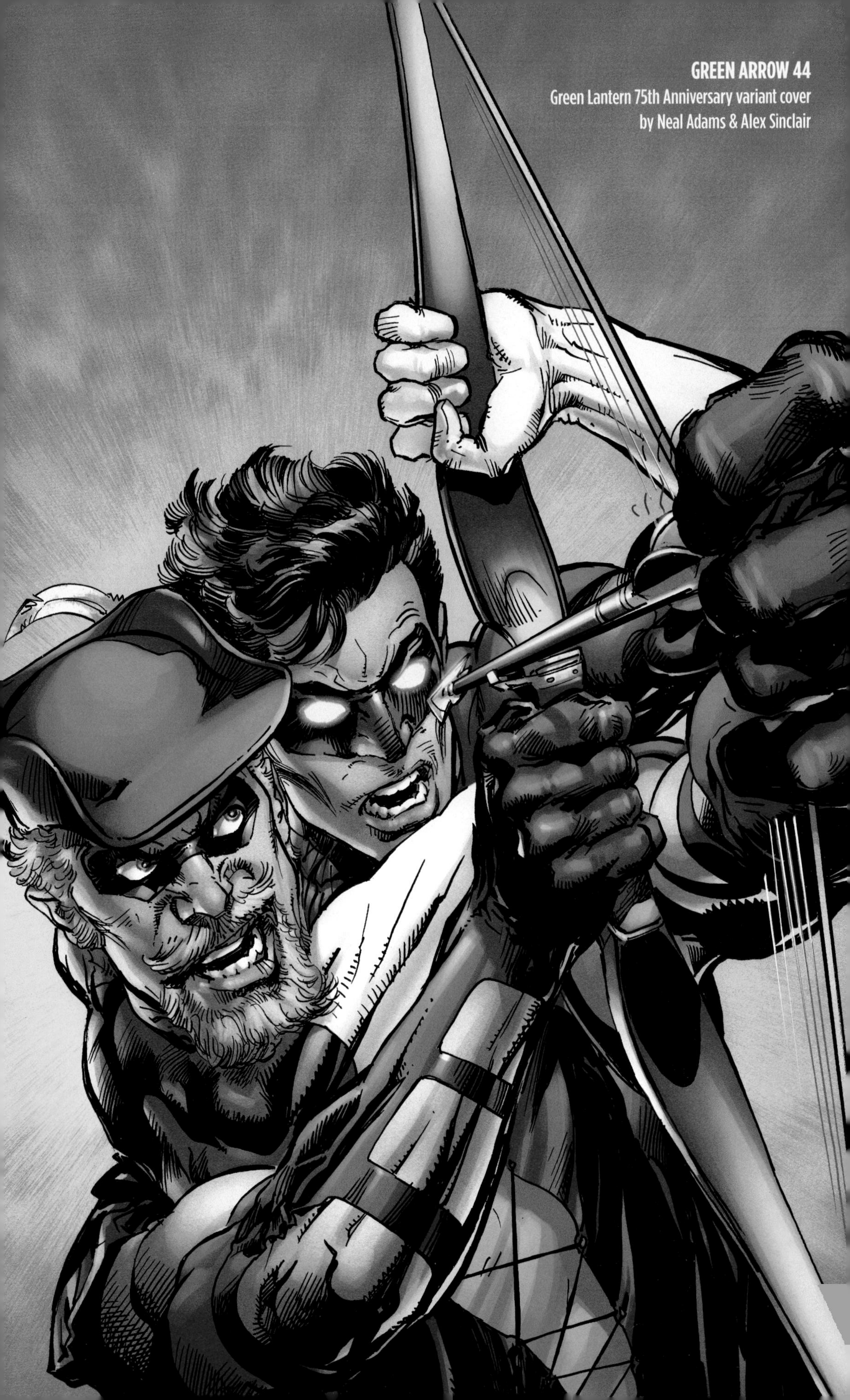

GREEN ARROW 44

Green Lantern 75th Anniversary variant cover
by Neal Adams & Alex Sinclair

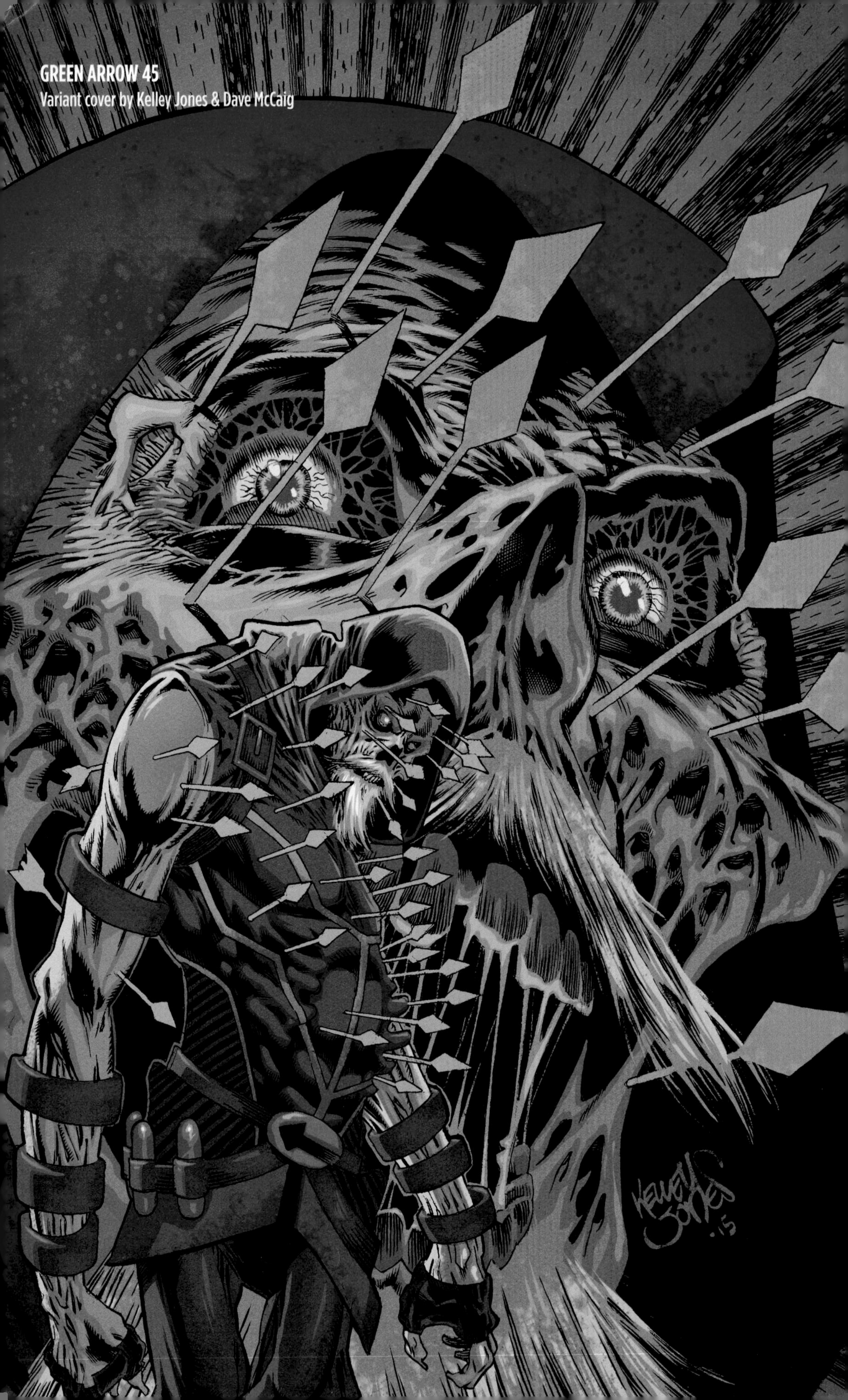

GREEN ARROW 45
Variant cover by Kelley Jones & Dave McCaig

GREEN ARROW 46

Looney Tunes variant cover by Kevin Nowlan and Spike Brandt

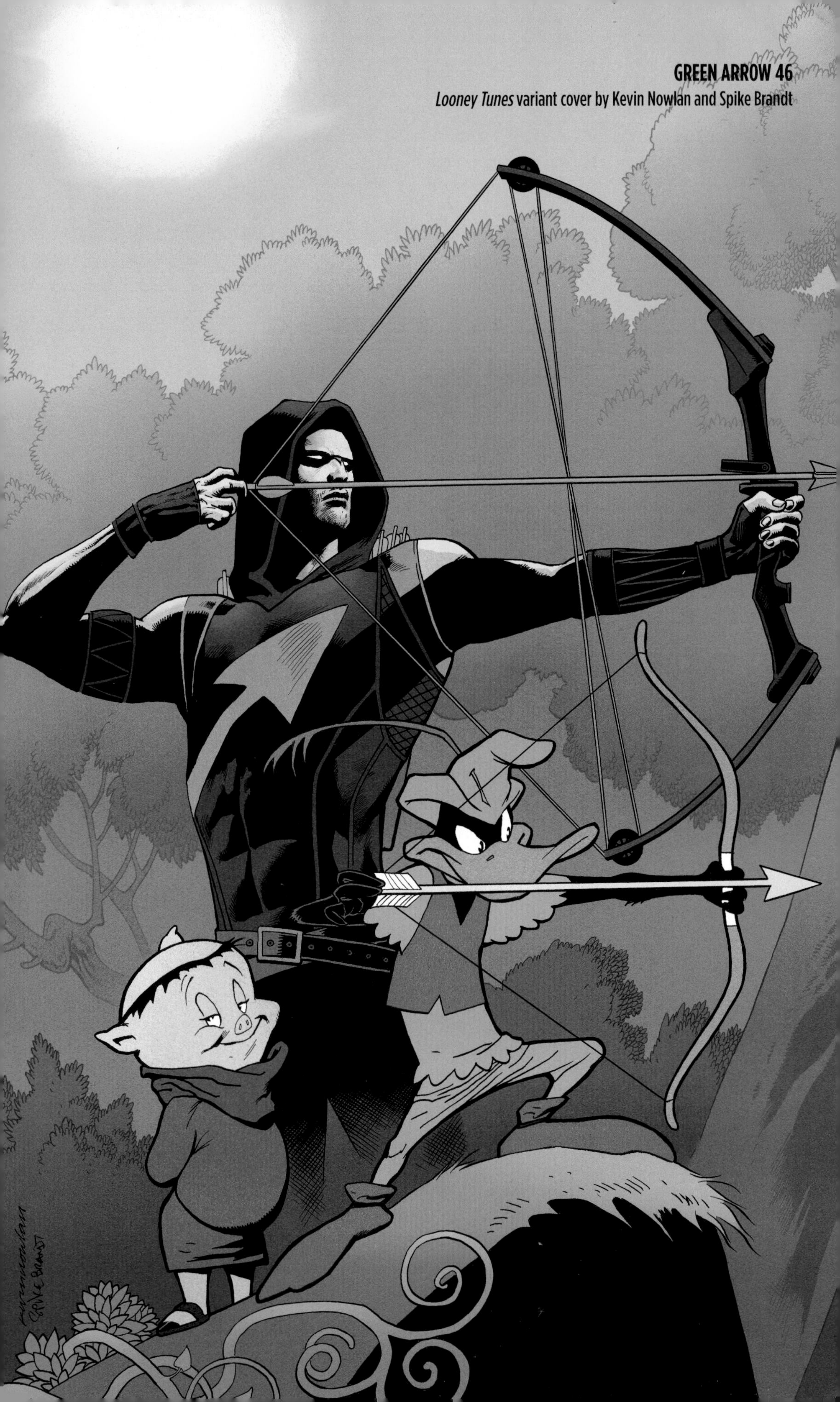

GREEN ARROW 47
HARLEY'S LITTLE BLACK BOOK variant cover by
Tim Sale & Brennan Wagner

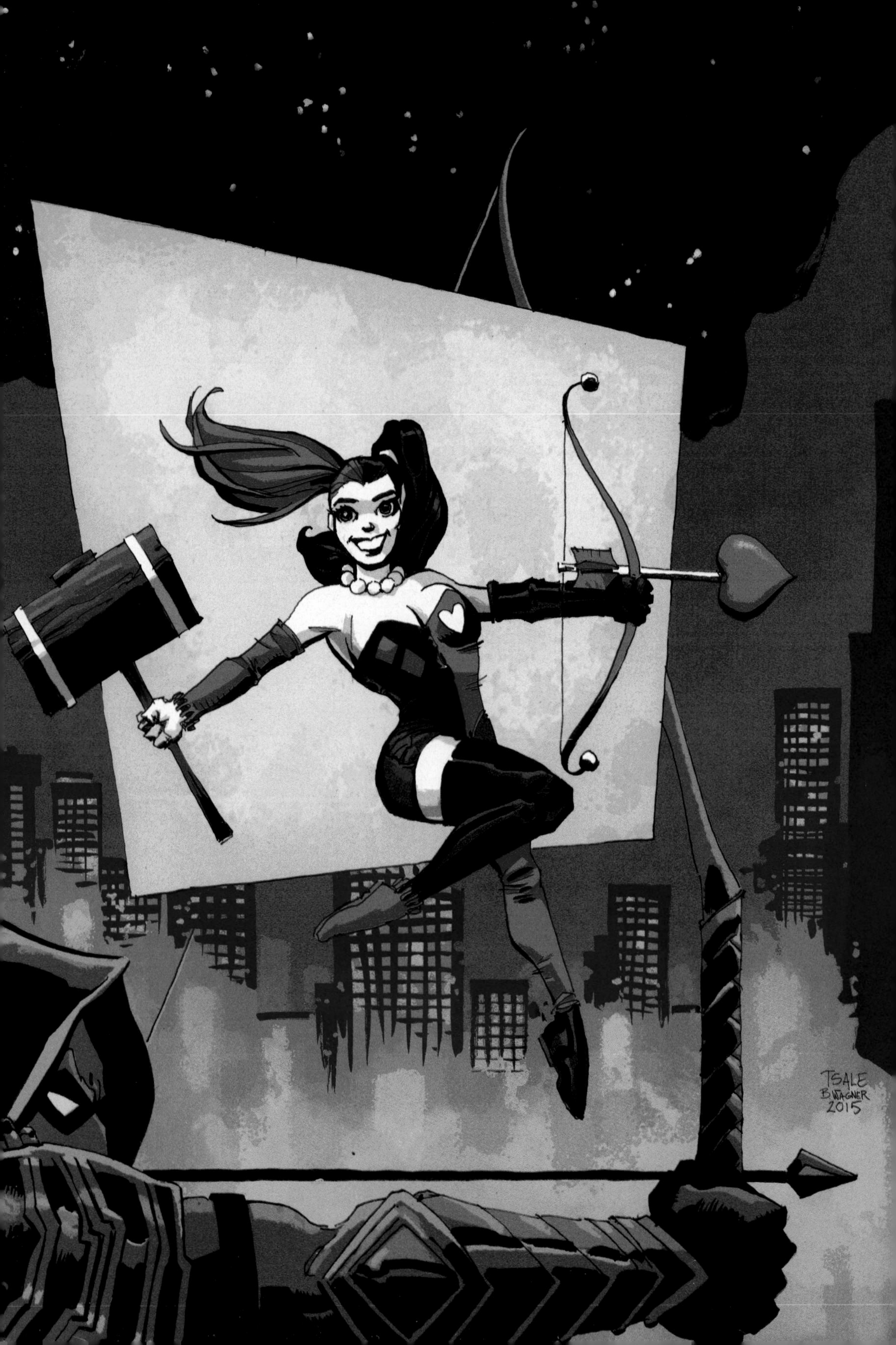
TSALE
BWAGNER
2015

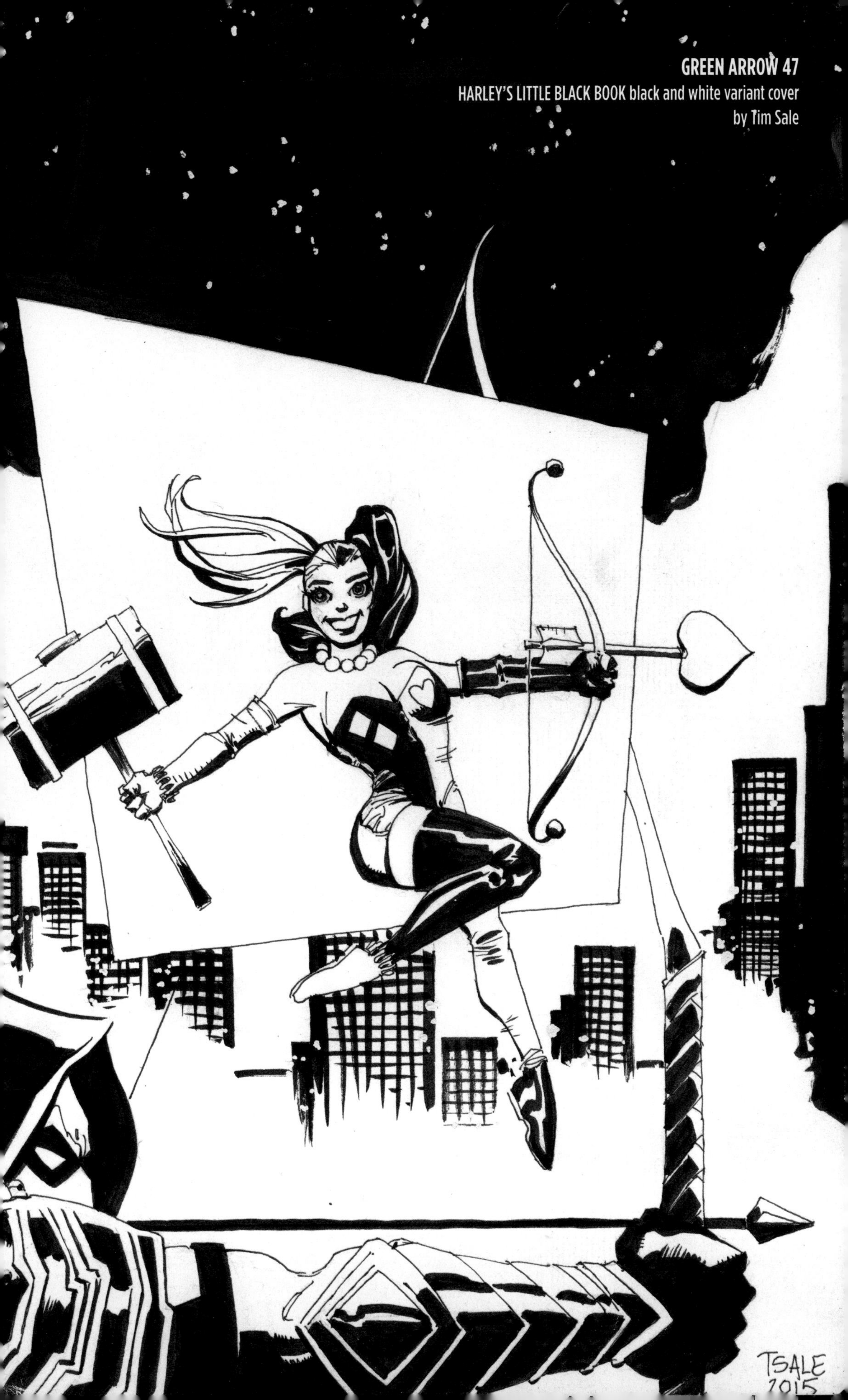
TSALE
2015

GREEN ARROW 47
HARLEY'S LITTLE BLACK BOOK black and white variant cover
by Tim Sale

GREEN ARROW 47
HARLEY'S LITTLE BLACK BOOK sketch variant cover
by Tim Sale

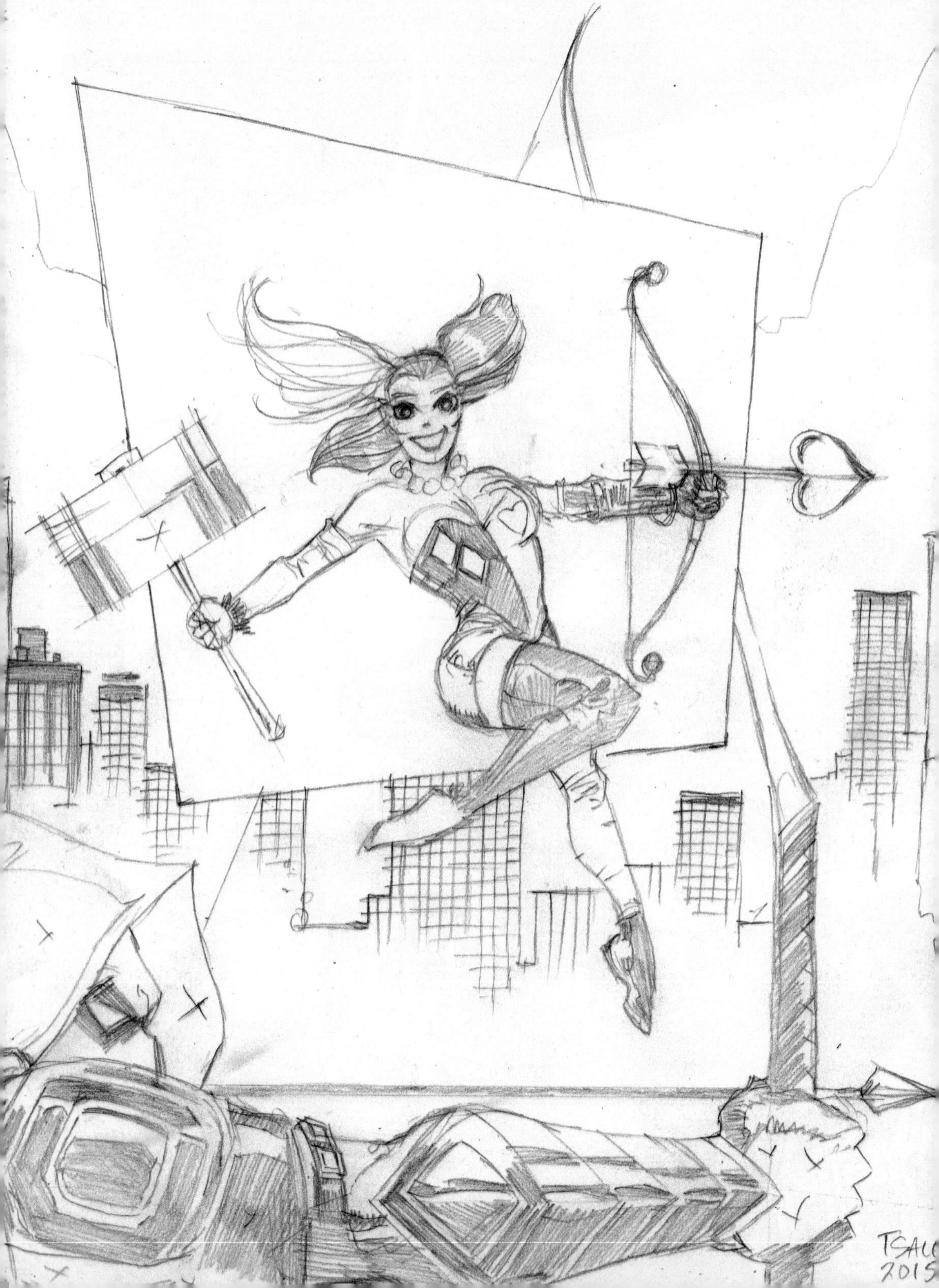